COLLECTED STUDIES SERIES

Tradition and Authority
in the Reformation

FOR SELINDE AND GILES

Scott H. Hendrix

Tradition and Authority
in the Reformation

VARIORUM
1996

This edition copyright © 1996 by Scott H. Hendrix.

Published by VARIORUM
Ashgate Publishing Limited
Gower House, Croft Road,
Aldershot, Hampshire GU11 3HR
Great Britain

BR
305.2
.H43
1996

Ashgate Publishing Company
Old Post Road,
Brookfield, Vermont 05036
USA

ISBN 0–86078–590-4

British Library CIP Data

Hendrix, Scott H.
Tradition and Authority in the Reformation.
(Variorum Collected Studies Series; CS535).
1. Reformation. 2. Protestantism–History.
I. Title.
270. 6

US Library of Congress CIP Data

Hendrix, Scott H.
Tradition and Authority in the Reformation / Scott H. Hendrix.
p. cm. – (Collected Studies Series; CS535)
Includes Index. (cloth: alk paper).
1. Reformation–Germany. 2. Tradition (Theology)–History of
doctrines–16th century. 3. Authority–Religious aspects–Christianity–
History of doctrines–16th century. 4. Germany–Church history–
16th century. I. Title. II. Series: Collected Studies; CS535.
BR305. 2H43   1996   96–12097
270. 6–dc20   CIP

The paper used in this publication meets the minimum requirements of the
American National Standard for Information Sciences – Permanance of Paper
for Printed Library Materials, ANSI Z39.48–1984. ∞ TM

Printed by Galliard (Printers) Ltd, Great Yarmouth, Norfolk, Great Britain

COLLECTED STUDIES SERIES C535

CONTENTS

CHURCH

SOCIETY

LUTHER'S AUTHORITY

vii

This volume contains xii+330 pages

PUBLISHER'S NOTE

The articles in this volume, as in all others in the Collected Studies Series, have not been given a new, continuous pagination. In order to avoid confusion, and to facilitate their use where these same studies have been referred to elsewhere, the original pagination has been maintained wherever possible.

Each article has been given a Roman number in order of appearance, as listed in the Contents. This number is repeated in each page and is quoted in the index entries.

PREFACE

This book assembles in one volume seventeen of my articles that appeared in the course of a twenty-year period from 1974 to 1993. It reflects both the continuity and the change that marked my study of the Reformation over that period. The continuity is evident in the setting and the subject matter of most of the articles. I have written mainly about the Protestant Reformation in Germany; consequently, the essays contain a modest amount of material about the Catholic reformation or about Protestantism elsewhere in Europe.

I have focused on two figures in the German Reformation: Martin Luther, who needs no introduction, and Urbanus Rhegius, who does. Unlike Luther, Rhegius never held an academic chair and served both as a urban reformer in south Germany and as a country bishop in the north. Since he was such a prolific author, his writings and his career offer a frontline perspective of the Reformation which the academic setting in Wittenberg does not readily provide. Although both Rhegius and Luther certainly became Lutheran, I have not concentrated on their confessional similarities but on their different evolution as Protestant leaders and on their contributions to the Reformation as a whole.

Several of the essays contain my early advocacy of the importance of ecclesiology for understanding the Reformation. I still believe the doctrine and structure of the church are important, especially for appreciating the impact of the Reformation on church history. Although recent studies of the Reformation question its lasting effects on personal piety and on society, there can be no question that the Reformation restructured Western Christianity into a diverse global religion for the modern world. The ecclesiology of the reformers legitimated that historic change, and some of its roots are explored here.

A major shift has occurred, however, in the method and focus of my research and that shift is mirrored here as well. Beginning in 1990 I began to apply to the Reformation concepts derived from an intergenerational behavioral theory known as contextual therapy or relational ethics. My study and practice convinced me that this way of understanding human behavior and social systems could illustrate and explain aspects of the Reformation which had interested me the most: why people made the radical changes necessary to become Protestant and how they reworked their personal and religious legacies into their new lives.

I have experimented with this approach in four of the articles contained here. Essays XIII and XIV contain my initial attempts to understand Luther's development in these terms and the consequences of this development for the shape of Protestantism. In articles V and VIII I use the concepts of deparentification and multilateralism not to explain historical process but to clarify content and to adjust the historical lens so that I can take a fresh look at the material. In none of these cases am I practicing what some scholars call psychohistory and I have no intention, in my past or future work, to reduce the complexity of historical explanation to what occurs in the human mind.

Regardless of that shift in focus, all of the essays treat the theme of this volume. Whether they address an intellectual, social, or personal transition, they explore how new elements of the medieval tradition were transformed into new claims of authority by the Reformation. As a whole, the essays try to discover what motivated people to choose Protestantism and how they justified that choice for themselves and for others whom they attempted to persuade.

More than a monograph, a collection like this makes me mindful of the people in many settings who have encouraged my work and contributed to it over these years. Finally, I dedicate this book to my children, Selinde and Giles, who grew and matured even as these pieces did and who deserved more attention from me than my work sometimes seemed to allow. They have given me immense pleasure and satisfaction, much more than the paper children in this book, and I thank them for it.

Blue Bell, Pennsylvania   SCOTT H. HENDRIX
January, 1996

ACKNOWLEDGEMENTS

Grateful acknowledgement is made to the following persons, editors, institutions and publishers for their kind permission to reprint the articles included in this volume: Kathleen DuVall, Managing Editor of *Interpretation. A Journal of Bible and Theology* (for article I); the Institute for Luther Studies, Gettysburg (II); Duke University Press, Durham, N.C. (III); Ferdinand Schöningh, Paderborn (IV); Philipp von Zabern, Mainz (V); the University of California Press, Berkeley, Calif. (IV); Gerd Mohn, Gütersloh (VII, XI, XIV); E.J. Brill, Leiden (VIII, XIII); the editors of *Concilium* (IX); the Sixteenth Century Journal Publishers, Inc., Kirksville, Mo. (X, XII, XVII); Associated University Presses, Cranbury, N.J. (XV); Helmar Junghans, editor of *Lutherjahrbuch* (XVI).

I

Luther Against the Background of the History of Biblical Interpretation

Luther's interpretation is marked not so much by ideas that can be applied to any age as by his desire to speak the liberating word for his "today."

IT WOULD BE MUCH EASIER to find Luther's place in the history of biblical interpretation if medieval and Reformation exegesis could be sharply distinguished from each other. The Reformation did not, however, mark with clarity a new era in the history of exegesis. The Bible did exercise enormous influence on the course of the Reformation through vernacular translations and through the debates over biblical sanction for reforms that were undertaken. The sixteenth century interpreters of Scripture nevertheless used a variety of hermeneutical methods which they learned from their ancient and me-
* dieval predecessors. |One cannot, therefore, argue that exegetes during the Reformation were medieval exegetes or that Protestant exegetes like Luther found Christ in more passages of Scripture than did his predecessors.| The dividing line between medieval and Reformation interpretation of Scripture is blurred.

The interpretation of the Song of Songs, a book beloved in the early and medieval church, is a good example of this ambiguity. Most frequently, medieval exegetes interpreted the relationship between bride and bridegroom allegorically as the relationship between Christ and the soul or between Christ and the church. Occasionally, the Song was understood in the tradition of Jewish

* The sentence beginning 'One cannot,...' *should read*: One cannot, therefore argue that exegetes during the Reformation were more interested in the literal or historical sense of Scripture than were medieval exegetes or that Protestant exegetes like Luther found Christ in more passages of Scripture than did his predecessors.

I

exegesis as a paradigm of God's relationship to his people Israel.[1] During the Reformation the Song received less attention than it did in the Middle Ages, but the treatment was still diverse. On one side, Calvin's successor in Geneva Theodore Beza followed the traditional allegorical line of interpretation which made the Song celebrate the love that existed between Christ and the church.[2] On the other side, in the preface to his commentary, Martin Luther inveighed against the unedifying allegories of the medieval exegetes. Instead of extracting the literal meaning from the Song as a love poem, however, Luther found its meaning in a metaphorical interpretation: Solomon was praising God for the blessings of peace and for the gift of his Word, which were the greatest treasures any earthly realm could enjoy.[3] Although the hermeneutical perspectives of Beza and Luther were different, neither line of interpretation severed them from the medieval exegesis of the Song.

Despite the absence of a sharp demarcation between medieval and Reformation exegesis, the former is subject to one generalization which reveals the contrast between Luther and his predecessors. The fourfold level of interpretation—literal, tropological, allegorical, anagogical—was used much more frequently as a hermeneutical method by medieval exegetes than by Luther. Already in his first lecture course on the Psalms (1513-1515), Luther practically ignored the future-directed or anagogical meaning and concentrated on the application of the text to the individual Christian and to the church, the so-called tropological and allegorical senses of Scripture.[4] In his lectures on Galatians in 1519, Luther argued that the fourfold method was useful only as ornamentation to the "main, legitimate sense" of a text. It could be used, as Paul himself used the allegory of Sara and Hagar in Galatians 4:22-31, to help simple folk understand the text, but it would never be strong enough to support a doctrinal point in controversy.[5]

---

1. A thorough overview of the medieval commentaries is given by Helmut Riedlinger, *Die Makellosigkeit der Kirche in den lateinischen Hoheliedkommentaren des Mittelalters* (Münster, Westfl. Aschendorff, 1958).

2. Beza published 31 sermons on the Song in 1586. One commentator on Beza's work believes his exegesis did manifest a "new epoch" (Tadataka Maruyama, *The Ecclesiology of Theodore Beza: The Reform of the True Church* [Geneva, Libraire Droz, 1978], p. 151).

3. *D. Martin Luthers Werke. Kritische Gesamtausgabe* (Weimar, Bohlau, 1883 [hereinafter cited WA]), 31/II, 588-92. Trans. *Luther's Works* (American ed., Philadelphia, Fortress Press, 1961; hereinafter cited LW) 15, 194-95, 196.

4. Discussed by Gerhard Ebeling, "Luthers Psalterdruck vom Jahre 1513," *Lutherstudien*, Vol. 1 (Tübingen, J.C.B. Mohr [Paul Siebeck], 1971), 127-30. For a detailed treatment of the medieval background, including a discussion of the fourfold sense, see Wilfrid Werbeck, *Jacobus Perez von Valencia: Untersuchungen zu seinem Psalmenkommentar* (Tübingen, J.C.B. Mohr [Paul Siebeck], 1959), pp. 102-37. On Luther against this background, see J. Samuel Preus, *From Shadow to Promise: Old Testament Interpretation from Augustine to the Young Luther* (Cambridge, Harvard Univ. Press, 1969), esp. pp. 142-49.

5. WA 2, 550.29-35. See the discussion of allegory in the new ed., *Operationes in psalmos*, Part II, *Archiv zur Weimarer Ausgabe* . . . (Cologne, Böhlau, 1981 [hereinafter cited AWA]), 2, 74-75, n.14.

Luther Against the Background of the History of Biblical Interpretation

Although Luther never gave up the use of allegory, he sharply restricted its application after 1519 and carefully defined its meaning.[6] Allegory should properly be understood as metaphorical language in the text itself and not as a spiritual or figurative meaning imposed on the text from outside. In the Genesis lectures of his later years, Luther argued that any allegorical interpretation had to be based on the historical and literal meaning of the text. From the moment that he embraced the historical sense, recalled Luther not quite accurately, he shied away from allegories unless they were in the text or unless the meaning of the allegory could be found elsewhere in Scripture (WA 42,173.26-29; 173.41-42; 174.37-40. LW 1,232-33,234).

To the extent that Luther departed from the fourfold sense of Scripture and restricted the use of allegory, he did indeed simplify the complex hermeneutical methods of the Middle Ages.[7] In the Genesis lectures, Luther claimed that he had explained simply the first three chapters according to the historical sense, "which is genuine and true." Exegetes ought to follow this method, he continued, in order to discover some "certain and simple meaning," especially in the face of so many different interpreters, Latin, Greek, and Hebrew, who have not bothered about the historical meaning or, worse, undermined it with illsuited allegories (WA 42,172.40-173.3. LW 1,231). Luther overestimated his own consistency, but it is true nonetheless that by 1519 he was troubled by the arbitrariness of interpretation to which uncontrolled allegorizing or spiritualizing of the text could lead. In his second lecture course on the Psalms (1519-1521), Luther said he was not good at allegorizing, "especially since I seek that legitimate, proper and germane sense, which will do battle in controversy and support the cultivation of faith" (AWA 2,119.9-11).

Luther's concern for the "legitimate" meaning of a text points to a second contrast between his exegesis and the medieval tradition, but this contrast has to be carefully drawn. The contrast is not between Luther's concentration on the historical sense and a medieval preference for figurative or spiritual meanings, as if, for example, Luther always interpreted the Old Testament as the story of Israel while medieval exegetes interpreted the Old Testament as the story of Christ and the church. Some medieval exegetes whom Luther knew very well, like Nicholas of Lyra, paid careful attention to Old Testament history; and Luther frequently made the Old Testament refer to Christ as its fulfillment. The contrast is rather a difference in balance and development.

---

6. Ebeling, *Evangelische Evangelienauslegung* (Darmstadt, Wissenschaftliche Buchgesellschaft, 1969²), p. 87.
7. Hans W. Frei, *The Eclipse of Biblical Narrative* (New Haven/London, Yale Univ. Press, 1974), p. 19. Contrasted with the exegesis of Johannes von Staupitz, Luther's interpretation was both simpler and unique (see David Steinmetz, *Luther and Staupitz* [Durham, Duke Univ. Press, 1980], pp. 35-67).

I

From the time of Augustine, medieval exegesis was interested both in the literal sense of the text and in a figurative or spiritual meaning. The use of the fourfold level placed emphasis on the spiritual meaning, but a strong reaction during the high Middle Ages redoubled efforts to recover in the tradition of Augustine an edifying literal sense. Moving in one direction under the influence of Jewish exegesis in northern France, the school of St. Victor concentrated on the letter of the Old Testament text and its historical setting.[8] Nicholas of Lyra, while making use of Jewish exegesis in explaining the historical sense, moved in a different direction. As Thomas Aquinas had done, Lyra posited a double literal sense: one intended by the human author and the other, often referred to as the true literal sense, intended by the divine author, the Holy Spirit. For the Old Testament, this theory meant that a christological interpretation, intended by the Spirit, was as much or more so a literal meaning as that which the text had in its original setting. Concentration on this true literal sense of the Old Testament led late medieval exegetes whom Luther consulted, such as Jacob Perez of Valencia and Jacques Lefèvre, to an intensive christological interpretation of books like the Psalms.[9]

In his earliest Psalms lectures Luther joined this christological chorus but he gradually altered his orientation. By the time of his second Psalms course (1519-1521), Luther departed from the traditional emphasis on the christological meaning and made independent exegetical decisions based on the Hebrew text. Luther called this procedure "theological philology."[10] As his exegesis of Psalm 1 illustrates, he explored the significance of each Hebrew word in the first verse ("Blessed is the one who walks not in the counsel of the ungodly"). In the meaning of "ungodly" Luther found a basic theological guideline for his interpretation: godliness and ungodliness concern attitudes and only secondarily are they behavioral. Therefore, the godly or pious individual lives by faith in God even though that person's conduct may not appear as pleasing as the behavior of the ungodly (AWA 2,31.15-32.9. LW 14,288-89). After this grammatical and theological analysis, Luther concluded that,

8. See Brevard S. Childs, "The *Sensus Literalis* of Scripture: An Ancient and Modern Problem," in Herbert Donner et al., eds., *Beiträge zur alttestamentlichen Theologie. Festschrift für Walther Zimmerli zum 70. Geburtstag* (Göttingen, Vandenhoeck und Ruprecht, 1977), pp. 80-93, esp. 83-86. Childs summarizes the fundamental contribution of Beryl Smalley, *The Study of the Bible in the Middle Ages* (Notre Dame, Univ. of Notre Dame Press, 1964²), esp. pp. 83-195.

9. Childs, pp. 85-86. Karlfried Froehlich, " 'Always to Keep the Literal Sense in Holy Scripture Means to Kill One's Soul': The State of Biblical Hermeneutics at the Beginning of the Fifteenth Century," in Earl Miller, ed., *Literary Uses of Typology from the Late Middle Ages to the Present* (Princeton, Princeton Univ. Press, 1977), pp. 20-48, esp. 35-48. Werbeck, *Jacobus Perez von Valencia*, 118-37. Preus, *From Shadow to Promise*, 137-42.

10. AWA 2, 38.19. "Theological philology" is the trans. suggested by Siegfried Raeder in *Grammatica Theologia: Studien zu Luthers Operationes in Psalmos* (Tübingen, J.C.B. Mohr [Paul Siebeck], 1977), p. 36. LW (14,294) reads "a grammatical and theological exposition."

I

Luther Against the Background of the History of Biblical Interpretation

because the Word of God is eternal, it should apply to people of all times. Since attitudes of godliness and ungodliness remain the same throughout all ages, Luther argued that Psalm 1 could be applied to his contemporaries (AWA 2,34.9–35.11. LW 14,290–91).

The discovery of a theologically edifying meaning apart from a christological interpretation of an Old Testament text stands in striking contrast to the tendency of late medieval exegesis. However, Luther did not approach the text devoid of all theological prejudice. He extracted the meaning of godly and ungodly while bringing to the text a previously acquired understanding of faith and its priority over works. This grammatical and theological approach did not rule out a christological interpretation, however, if that would best express the meaning of the psalm. For example, in the same Psalms lecture, Luther interpreted Psalm 3 christologically—partly because he was convinced by Augustine's argument that verse 5 ("I wake again, for the Lord sustains me") could refer only to Christ and partly because he believed that the Hebrew word for "wake again" more aptly described resurrection than awaking from sleep (AWA 2,120.8–121.14).

Whether or not the legitimate sense of the text required an explicit reference to Christ, it was to be understood spiritually, that is, as the meaning imparted by the Spirit which must be received in faith.[11] Luther agreed with the late medieval exegetes that the proper (or "true literal") sense of Scripture is that which the Spirit intends, but he did not always demand a reference to Christ. The legitimate sense could also involve the experience of the Old Testament faithful. By contrast, Perez once said that if David had wanted to talk about his own experience in the psalms, he would not have needed the Holy Spirit.[12]

The combination of literal, historical, and christological elements is especially noticeable in Luther's treatment of the prophets. In the preface to the expanded second edition of his Isaiah lectures published in 1534, Luther extolled the value of history for understanding the prophet's message and for teaching faith and charity. Such knowledge of history also required knowledge of Hebrew grammar and linguistic idioms. At the same time, Luther affirmed the principal message of all the prophets as preparing people for the coming of Christ. The "manifest prophecies" of Christ confirmed the faith which had already been instructed by the letter and the historical circumstances of the text.[13] Such manifest prophecies, however, could arise out of the historical cir-

---

11. AWA 2, 233.14–15 and n. 4. See Raeder, *Grammatica Theologia*, pp. 29–30.
12. Werbeck, *Jacobus Perez von Valencia*, p. 127.
13. WA 25, 87.36–88.42. For the importance of history, cf. the pref. to Isa. in the new study ed. of Luther's works (Hans-Ulrich Delius, ed., *Martin Luther: Studienausgabe*, Vol. I [Berlin, Evangelische Verlagsanstalt, 1979], pp. 413–16, esp. 413.26–31). For the message of the prophets, see e.g., WA 23,501.17–502.2.

233

cumstances in a manner which can only be called allegorizing, even for Luther. In 1527, for example, he applied Zechariah 9:8 ("I will arm my house with soldiers . . . so that . . . no oppressor overruns them any longer; for now I have seen it with my own eyes" [author's trans.]) to the time in which the Philistines became Christian and the temple was destroyed. Hence, the house was Christendom and the soldiers were the apostles and holy teachers who would resist the oppressors, that is, teachers of works righteousness. Christ the bishop, Luther explained, oversees and rules the people through his own presence instead of through the alien eyes of Moses and the prophets (WA 23,613.9-31. LW 20,287).

Luther's exegesis, therefore, differed from the medieval tradition not in the absence of allegory or of christological interpretation of the Old Testament but rather in his aversion to excessive allegorizing and in his willingness to find the legitimate meaning in the grammatical and historical analysis of the text. For Luther it was not a matter of choosing one level of meaning (i.e., literal or spiritual) over another but of choosing the meaning of the text which best fit the significance of the words, the historical circumstances, and his own theological perspective.

This hermeneutical stance explains Luther's openness to the interpretations of other exegetes, an openness present in his writings from the earliest period. In the dedication of his second Psalms commentary to Elector Frederick in 1519, Luther confessed that he was not sure whether his understanding of the Psalms conformed to the prescribed or intended meaning of the text. Nevertheless, he did not doubt that his interpretation was true, just as the interpretations of others were also true, even though they were sometimes far removed from the literal sense (AWA 2,13.11-15. LW 14,285).

Already in the first Psalms lectures Luther had warned against presuming that one ever understood all the truth which a text contained. The words of Scripture were testimonies (Ps. 119:24), promises to be fulfilled in the future and witnesses to that fulfillment. Therefore, every text had an infinite potential of meaning; and one should not repudiate the interpretation of others, for they might see what another cannot yet see. "One always has to progress in the understanding of Scripture" (WA 4,318.35-319.4). Luther's last recorded observation indicates that the same view prevailed at the end of his life. Nobody could presume to have tasted the Scriptures sufficiently, he cautioned, unless one had ruled over the church with the prophets for a hundred years. In our approach to Scripture "we are beggars; that is true" (WATR 5,317.16-318.3. LW 54,476).

The inexhaustibility of Scripture gave Luther the exegete tremendous freedom in the interpretation of a text, so much freedom in fact that it seems Luther could easily have fallen prey to the arbitrariness of medieval allegorizers which he so strongly condemned. If no single meaning of the text was true for all time, then how was Luther to decide which meaning was the legitimate sense at the moment of his interpretation? Luther tried to answer this question in two ways, both of which set him apart from much of the preceding and subsequent exegetical tradition. In the first place, Luther drew on the hearer or reader as an exegetical resource. Second, Luther's contemporary application of the text was never far from his mind as he searched for that legitimate sense.

Luther described the involvement of the addressee in several ways. One way was to speak of tuning oneself to the text. In his comments on Psalm 1, for example, Luther stressed that the feelings (*affectus*) of the reader had to be adjusted to the attitudes expressed in the psalm in order for it to be understood rightly. When reading about the person who does not walk in the counsel of the ungodly, one should detest the counsel of the ungodly both for one's own life and for the whole church. Such an appropriation of every verse would lead to a fruitful praying of the psalm that would discover "the most abundant treasure of insights and feelings."[14] The right approach to the Psalter was not to analyze it as a textbook about the proper relationship to God but to see it as a laboratory in which to practice that relationship while praying the text. Luther called it a training room for the feelings.[15]

Not only the Psalter was subject to illumination from experience. Luther's procedure for studying all of Scripture stressed the tuning of the interpreter to the text. One should pray for the illumination of the Spirit, meditate verbatim on the text, and relate the text to the trials (*tentationes; Anfechtungen*) of one's own life. Only in this way could one learn "not only to know and understand, but also to experience how right, how true, how sweet, how lovely, how mighty, how comforting God's Word is, wisdom beyond all wisdom" (WA 50,659.1–660.4. LW 34, 285–87). This was the lesson learned by David, as expressed in Psalm 119, and the lesson which Luther said he learned through constant attention to the Word in the midst of attack and persecution. "For as soon as God's Word takes root and grows in you, the devil will harry you and make a real doctor of you, and by his assaults will teach you to seek and to love God's Word."[16] In his *Table Talk* Luther asserted that reading the Bible would not have taught him anything if events and his adversaries had not prompted him to learn (WATR 3,618.15–17 [No. 3793].

---

14. AWA 2, 62.6–63.17, LW 14,310. Cf. AWA 2,14.21–15.6. LW 14,286. This adjustment of the reader was not unprecedented in the medieval tradition. Luther refers to both Augustine and Athanasius as calling for such an adjustment.

15. "*Palaestra et exercitium*": AWA 2,62.9. LW 14,310.

16. WA 50,660.8–10. LW 34,287. The involvement of the experience of the reader was seen by Karl Holl as the uniqueness of Luther's exegesis, his "personal accomplishment," over against the tradition. See his 1920 essay, "Luthers Bedeutung für den Fortschritt der

I

The danger of utilizing the experience of the reader was a rampant subjectivism which imposed an extraneous meaning on Scripture. Luther admitted the danger, but claimed from his earliest days at the lectern that the power of Scripture was such that it was not changed into the one who studied it but instead transformed its admirer into itself and into its own powers (WA 3,397.9–11). Scripture could indeed be called its own interpreter. According to Psalm 119:130 ("The unfolding of your words gives light; it imparts understanding to the simple"), illumination and understanding were given through the words of God alone. They were the source which must be zealously studied and through which the Spirit would come of its own accord to expel our spirit so that a proper theological understanding could emerge without peril.[17] Could one be sure that the transformation took place in the right direction and that the Holy Spirit and not one's own spirit did the directing? Luther assumed one could; but he also believed the content of the text was uncovered through linguistic, historical, and theological analysis. That content would reveal an individual's experience for what it truly was and change it into the relationship which Scripture depicted as faith.

One could, therefore, identify an objective content of the text through analysis, but there was for Luther a sense in which Scripture was not fully interpreted until it encountered and illumined the life of the addressee. This dimension of interpretation was what Luther sought to describe with his redefinition of the hermeneutical categories "spirit" and "letter." "Letter" was no longer the literal or metaphorical text itself but the operation of the text on the hearer or reader at any level as law without grace. And "spirit" no longer meant the spiritual levels of interpretation which even unbelievers could devise but the operation of the text as grace alone which led to a spiritual understanding that was, properly understood, "life itself and the law experienced as written in the soul through grace by the finger of God."[18] For this redefinition Luther was helped substantially by Augustine's understanding of II Corinthians 3:6 "for the written code kills, but the Spirit gives life." Letter and spirit were really two sermons or preaching offices, wrote Luther in 1521: a preaching of the Old Testament and a preaching of the New, a preaching of the law and a preaching of the gospel (WA 7,653.14–17; 653.29–655.2 39, 182–83). One had to hear the law first in order to appreciate the gospel be-

Auslegungskunst," *Gesammelte Aufsätze zur Kirchengeschichte*, Vol. I, *Luther* (Tübingen, J.C.B. Mohr [Paul Siebeck], 1948⁷), 544–82, esp. 549, 555–56. Holl highlights a passage from the second Psalms commentary: AWA 2,379.5–8, *"Intellectum et sensum non dat nisi ipse affectus et experientia . . ."*
17. WA 7,97.20–35. The meaning of this passage from the *Assertio omnium articulorum* (1520) is brilliantly analyzed by Walter Mostert, "Scriptura sacra sui ipsius interpres. Bemerkungen zum Verständnis der Heiligen Schrift durch Luther," *Lutherjahrbuch* 46 (1979), 60–96.
18. From the Galatians commentary of 1519. WA 2, 551.28–34. LW 27,311.

cause grace was given only to those who thirsted for it (WA 7,656.27-31. LW 39,185). The tragedy of his time, commented Luther was just the opposite. The "murderous sophists" in their summas and confessional manuals had tortured people by demanding satisfaction for sin in good works, with the result that Christ was unknown, the gospel lay hidden, and the office of the New Testament was silenced (WA 7,657.27-35 LW 99, 186-87;).

The remedy for that condition was not, in Luther's mind, a hermeneutical shift to a different level of spiritual interpretation, or even a return to the literal sense. In fact, Luther began his discussion of II Corinthians 3:6 by refuting Emser's traditional definition of the senses of Scripture and by rejecting the fourfold method of interpretation (WA 7,652.13-22. LW 39,180-81). Such methods might have been employed for good reasons by such theologians as Origen and Jerome against the Jews and heretics of their time. The methods which were appropriate in their day, however, were not appropriate in his, argued Luther. The remedy for his day was the Augustinian understanding of letter and spirit, which, applied to Scripture, would allow the Spirit to address tortured consciences out of the spoken Word, giving strength and courage to the heart (WA 7,654.6-7. LW 39,182). The hearers were to be confronted with the futility of their striving and their hearts were to be changed. Therefore, it was a huge mistake to label allegory and tropology as "spirit," since they both were confined to the letter, which was powerless to make alive. In contrast, grace (the Spirit and the gospel) had no other receptacle than the heart.[19]

Due to this concern for the operation of the text on the reader and hearer, Luther moved frequently and explicitly to an application of the text to his day. The word "today" (*hodie*) became a refrain in his exegesis after his struggles with medieval theology and the papacy began. The Psalms lectures of 1519-1521 were laced with criticism of the contemporary church in addition to the new grammatical exegesis and theological redefinition. For example, Psalm 5:12 ("Let all who hope in you rejoice") led Luther to ponder the nature of hope and the wobbly basis it had assumed in his time. Hope could not be based on satisfactions, indulgences, and pilgrimages, as taught by the deceitful instructors of his day. Today (*hodie*), exclaimed Luther, there was no end to such teachers (AWA 2,282.8-20)! He launched a long attack on the substance of medieval theology and the practice of the late medieval church (AWA 2,283-321). After his grammatical exposition of Psalm 1:1, described

---

19. WA 7, 655.27-30. LW 39, 184. Luther's reply to Emser forms much of the basis for the argument of Friedrich Beisser that the true meaning of the text for Luther lies in the Word as it is spoken and works in the hearer, i.e., when it works as Spirit. For Beisser this distinguishes Luther from both medieval and modern exegesis (*Claritas Scripturae bei Martin Luther* [Göttingen, Vandenhoeck und Ruprecht, 1966], pp. 9-74, esp. 25-33,51-54,72-73).

I

above, Luther made a similar application to "his own times." Those occupied the "seat of the scornful" who "fill the church of Christ with the opinions of the philosophers, human traditions, and the counsel of their own minds, and oppress poor souls. They neglect the Word of God, through which alone the soul is fed, lives and is sustained" (AWA 2,38.6–9. LW 14,293).

Where does this understanding of Scripture finally leave Luther in the history of biblical interpretation? The best answer is that he is in a category by himself. At the outset of his career he was heavily dependent on the medieval exegetical tradition and arrived at his own interpretation after consulting and weighing the exegesis of his predecessors. As the years went by he often followed a different course, even while allowing that their exegesis was true in their own time or way. He did not, however, apologize for his exegetical decisions, convinced as he was that his handling of the Word was the crucial remedy for his own time. To the medieval tradition he owed his concern for both an edifying literal meaning and for the unity of Scripture manifested in the promises of Christ found in the Old Testament. The way in which Luther allowed that edification to occur was nevertheless his own. He was conscious early of that independence: "I will follow my own spirit and indulge in my own opinion without prejudice to anyone" (AWA 2,163.3–4).

His own way was, however, not a hermeneutical method in the sense of much modern biblical criticism.[20] A procedure, yes, for reader and teacher to encounter Scripture, as outlined in the preface to the Wittenberg edition of his German works. While grammatical and historical study formed the basis of an edifying interpretation of the text, Luther was unwilling to make the sharp distinction encouraged by modern criticism between what the text meant and what it means. He did not ignore this distinction and could leave the meaning of a text at the level of historical or theological analysis. At the same time, he often utilized personal experience and his diagnosis of the contemporary church to make the text speak immediately to his own day and thus to reveal its meaning. Exegetes from seventeenth century Orthodoxy, who held to a strict literal sense, as well as Pietists, who were more sympathetic to spiritual and edifying levels of meaning, might claim Luther as an ancestor.[21] For Luther himself, however, the appropriate interpretation of a text lay neither in the recovery of the unique literal sense nor in the unfolding of multilevel meanings, but in the discovery of the legitimate meaning, based on grammatical and historical analysis, informed by theological reflection, and applied to one's own life and the church of the present.

The predominance of theological reflection and of application to the pres-

---

20. Beisser, *Claritus Scripturae*, pp. 51–54 (see n. 19).
21. See the discussion by Frei, *The Eclipse of Biblical Narrative*, pp. 37–40.

Luther Against the Background of the History of Biblical Interpretation

ent makes Luther's exegesis attractive while also revealing its limitations. In contrast to his frequently time-bound applications, both medieval and modern commentaries seem timeless and indeed are intended to be so, subject to the revisions of scholarship. Even the commentaries of another sixteenth century exegete like John Calvin appear more critically objective and usable to modern readers, although Calvin's appeal to the internal testimony of the Spirit echoes Luther's stress on the involvement of the addressee.[22] Luther's exegesis is not always time-bound; even when it is, it can carry the power which only the Word spoken in a specific situation can bring. But just for that reason his exegesis often reads more like a sermon than a commentary. It does not always serve well as a repository of ideas about the text which can be applied in any age. Instead, like sermons, his commentaries function (as he said about the Psalter) as models of the Word at work. But then, Luther intended it that way. He did not expect his interpretation to exhaust the possibilities of Scripture for all time but to speak the crucial, liberating Word for his "today."

---

22. The similarity between the two exegetes is stressed by Frei, who is mainly analyzing Calvin's biblical interpretation with the help of an article by Hans-Joachim Kraus (*ibid.*, pp. 19-20). Kraus's delineation of Calvin's exegetical principles, however, makes him appear much more of a critical, methodical interpreter than Luther. Kraus's article appears in Eng. as "Calvin's Exegetical Principles," Interp. 31:8-18 (Jan. 1977).

II

The Authority of Scripture at Work: Luther's Exegesis of the Psalms

Hermeneutical Guidelines

By January of 1518 Martin Luther had been lecturing on the Bible for five years. After he succeeded Johannes von Staupitz in the chair of Biblical Studies at Wittenberg, Luther launched his teaching career by offering a lecture course on the Psalms which took him two years to complete. In rapid succession thereafter, he exegeted for his students the New Testament epistles to the Romans and to the Galatians; and in January of 1519 he was in the middle of a lecture course on Hebrews when he was asked by George Spalatin to explain the best way of studying Scripture. After pleading the limitation of his learning and gifts, Luther replied to Spalatin by revealing his own method:

> "It is absolutely certain that one cannot enter into the meaning of Scripture by study or innate intelligence. Therefore, your first task is to begin with prayer. You must ask that the Lord in his great mercy grant you a true understanding of his words, should it please him to accomplish anything through you for his glory and not for your own glory or that of any other man. For there is no one who can teach the divine words except he who is their author, as he says: 'They shall all be taught by God' (John 6:45). You must therefore completely despair of your own diligence and intelligence and rely solely on the infusion of the Spirit. Believe me, for I have had experience in this matter. . . . Having achieved this despairing humility, read the Bible in order from beginning to end, so that you first get the simple

story in mind." Luther admits that the letters and commentaries of Jerome can be of great help in this, as Erasmus had insisted. But, he says, "for an understanding of Christ and the grace of God (for a more hidden understanding which is given by the Spirit), Augustine and Ambrose seem to me to be far better guides."[1]

This brief description of his hermeneutical method reveals that for Luther the interpretation of Scripture was more than an academic exercise, even though his job was to interpret Scripture in an academic setting. Study of the text and familiarity with it are necessary, of course, as his admonition to read the entire Bible and his own astounding knowledge of the text indicate. That knowledge and study are only starting points, however. To interpret the text in such a way as to absorb the message that Scripture imparts to us requires more. It requires the interpreter to be humble enough to ask for help: help from the author of Scripture who sends his Spirit to be the true teacher; help from other interpreters who have struggled with the texts themselves; and, finally, help from the experience of one's own struggle to find the appropriate meaning of Scripture.

These guidelines do not differ markedly from what Luther said about the interpretation of Scripture near the end of his thirty-four year career as a teacher of the Bible. Twenty-one years later, when his collected German writings were published against his wishes, Luther wrote a preface for the collection in which he recommended guidelines similar to those which he had outlined for Spalatin in 1518. Using the 119th Psalm as his model, Luther set down three rules for the correct study of theology, which for Luther meant the proper interpretation of Scripture. The three rules are: *oratio, meditatio, tentatio*—prayer, meditation, and the experience of opposition.

First, says Luther, "kneel down in your little room and pray to God with real humility and earnestness that he through his dear Son may give you his Holy Spirit, who will enlighten you, lead you and give you understanding. . . .

"Secondly, you should meditate, that is, not only in your heart, but also externally, by repeating the words out loud and comparing oral speech with the written words, reading and rereading them with diligent attention and reflection so that you may see what the Holy Spirit means by them. . . .

"Thirdly, there is *tentatio, Anfechtung*. This is the touchstone which teaches you not only to know and understand, but also to experience how right, how true, how sweet, how lovely, how mighty, how comforting God's Word is, wisdom beyond all wisdom." On the last point, Luther notes how often David in Psalm 119 complains about all kinds of enemies, arrogant princes or tyrants, false spirits and factions. "As soon as God's Word takes root and grows in you," Luther concludes, "the devil will harry you, and will make a real doctor of you, and by his assaults will teach you to seek and to love God's Word." Luther then speaks of his own experience under attack: "I myself (if you will permit me, mere mouse-dirt to be mingled with pepper) am deeply indebted by my papists that

II

through the devil's raging they have beaten, oppressed and distressed me so much. That is to say, they have made a fairly good theologian of me, which I would not have become otherwise."[2]

Luther promises his readers that if they follow David's example and study hard according to these rules, they can sing and boast with David in Psalm 119 (:72): "The law of thy mouth is better to me than thousands of gold and silver pieces" and "Thy commandment makes me wiser than my enemies, for it is ever with me. I have more understanding than all my teachers, for thy testimonies are my meditation. I understand more than the aged, for I keep thy precepts" (Ps. 119:98-100). "Then the books of the fathers will taste stale and putrid to you by comparison. You will not only despise the books written by your opponents but will become less and less pleased with your own. And when you have reached this point, you may finally dare to hope that you have become a real theologian."[3]

The rules established by Luther in this 1539 preface not only confirm his lifelong approach to the study of Scripture, they also give us an important clue to his understanding of the authority of Scripture. Verses 98-100 of Psalm 119, which he cites as the proper boast of the interpreter who has followed David's rules, are used by Luther in his Psalms lectures of 1513-1515 to verify the authority of Scripture for the diligent exegete who meditates spiritually on the law of Christ. This spiritual meditation makes the interpreter wiser than his enemies and gives him more understanding than his teachers and all the aged because "the spiritual man judges all things and is judged by no one" according to I Corinthians 2:15.[4] During the Middle Ages, this same verse was frequently applied to the pope in order to establish his authority as the superior spiritual man in the church. Luther now applies this verse to any interpreter of Scripture according to the rules of David. Luther's own struggle to understand the Scriptures led therefore to a new understanding of the authority of Scripture, which was confirmed for him, as he says in 1539, by his conflict with the papists. That conflict became the *tentatio*, the assault, which convinced him that the Spirit had led him, in his own persistent encounter with Scripture, to an understanding which was sounder than that of his enemies.

Both Luther's exegetical guidelines and Luther's career tell us, therefore, that the authority of Scripture was a conviction which emerged for Luther in his lifelong encounter with the Word and with his opponents. Of course, Scripture possessed authority for him even before he took up the task of exegeting the text as his occupation in the church. But, then, Scripture possessed authority for every doctor of the church who was sworn to teach pure doctrine. The key for Luther is that Scripture assumed a new kind of authority as he struggled with the text and its message for the church in the face of severe opposition. It is that kind of authority which the churches of the Reformation have attempted to capture in the motto *sola scriptura*.

My contention is that this motto should be understood according to Luther not as a principle to be proven once and for all, but as a claim which has to be

II

validated again and again in the life of every reader of Scripture and in the life of the church which appeals to it. In order to explain this, I would like to use an imperfect illustration. The authority of Scripture for Luther was not like a mathematical theorem which can be proven true for all time by the use of self-evident axioms and logically irrefutable arguments. Luther did not argue that Scripture was authoritative by combining a series of propositions such as, "Scripture is the Word of God; God is truth, what God says must be true; therefore, Scripture possesses infallible authority."

Rather, I would suggest that Luther approached Scripture as we would approach a great work of art. We recognize that the work of art possesses authority and as such has a claim on our life. However, if we cannot perceive what that claim is and how it speaks authoritatively to our situation, then its authority remains only a formal claim. That formal claim may secure for the work of art a place in a picture book of the great masters, but the book will remain unopened on our shelves and never become the source of authority for our lives. Only as we struggle to understand the work of art, and bring to it the tools necessary to interpret it aright, and receive some of the same inspiration which the artist himself enjoyed in creating it, will the external claim of that work to be authoritative validate itself in our life.

At the risk of squeezing more out of this illustration than permissible, I would like to combine it with examples from Luther's exegesis of the Psalms to show how Scripture validated its claim to authority for him as he struggled to understand what the Psalter was saying. Luther himself set down only three rules; but I would like to expand these three rules to seven— seven rules which indicate how Luther allowed Scripture to work authoritatively, much as a work of art.

Seven Rules

1. *Learn to copy the model*

From his use of Psalm 119 to establish the three rules, you can already see that the Psalter was a very important book for Luther. It was the most interpreted book of the Middle Ages and Luther did not surprise anyone when he began his teaching career by lecturing on this book. As he began his second lecture course on the Psalms in 1518 after only a three-year interlude, he could rightly say that there was no book of the Bible to which he had devoted as much labor as to the Psalter.[5] The Psalter was not more authoritative for him than the rest of Scripture, but he did prize the entire Psalter, and especially some individual Psalms, as particularly helpful in the time of trial. While waiting in suspense at the Coburg in 1530, Luther exegeted his favorite Psalm 118 as a gift for Frederick Pistorius in Nuremberg, saying that "although the entire Psalter and all of Holy Scripture are dear to me as my only comfort and source of life, I fell in love with this Psalm especially. Therefore, I call it my own. When emperors and kings, the wise and the learned, and even saints could not aid me, this Psalm proved a friend and helped me out of many

II

148

great troubles."[6] Psalm 118(:17) is also the source of his personal motto: "I shall not die, but I shall live and recount the deeds of the Lord."

Now, in his exposition of the Psalms, Luther does not call the Psalter a work of art, although he does refer to individual verses as "masterpieces." He does say, however, that the Psalms teach the art of being Christian; and this has prompted me to suggest that Scripture, and the Psalter in particular, function like a model work of art in establishing a claim to authority over his life. A good example is the way in which Luther deals with verses 17-18 of Psalm 118: "I shall not die, but I shall live and recount the deeds of the Lord. The Lord has chastened me sorely, but he has not given me over to death."

> Luther describes these verses as the joyful song of believers who put their trust in God and not in man. Verse 17 describes the trouble out of which God's hand delivers believers. This trouble is death. Nothing is more effective for the believer as he faces death than to sing this little song of victory. To sing it aright, however, he must forget himself and put all his trust in the strength of God. But, says Luther, it is an art to forget self. We must keep learning this lesson as long as we live, even as all the saints before us, with us, and after us must do.
> Therefore, we must recognize this verse as a masterpiece, just like the one which follows it. It declares: "The Lord has chastened me sorely, but he has not given me over to death." The believer recognizes that the threat of death is only the chastisement of God, who is acting like a dear father chastening his child. It may hurt a little, and it is not sugar; it is a rod. However, it does not actually kill, but helps me live, i.e. helps me enjoy the consolation of eternal life.
> "This is surely a good interpretation and an effective confutation," says Luther, "to make a benevolent rod out of the word 'death.' Only the Holy Spirit and the right hand of God can teach this art. It hurts beyond measure when to suffering there are added blasphemy, mockery, wagging of the head and hostility, as the Jews did to Christ on the Cross. Flesh and blood would do the opposite and turn a benevolent rod into death and hell, for it is ready to give up and despair if it lacks as much as a loaf of bread. This is a poor interpretation. It is a much greater art to be able to sing this verse when the devil, as he did to Job and many other saints, becomes so hostile that death appears."[7]

The art which these verses teach, then, is the art of faith, the art of forgetting oneself and all human resources and trusting in the strength of the Lord, which alone turns death into life. This art is taught only by the Holy Spirit and the right hand of God, but it is taught by them through the masterpieces of Scripture. The Psalter serves as a model which perfectly embodies the art which it is designed to teach to those who copy it. As the would-be artist learns basic techniques by copying the works of the masters, so should the Christian learn the art of faith by practicing on the text of the Psalms.

In the preface to his second lectures on the Psalms (1519), Luther sums up this model character of the Psalms. In this respect it is different from other books of the Bible. In other books we are taught by both precept and example what we ought to do. The Psalter not only teaches, but also gives the means and the method by which we may keep the precept and follow the example. "As a teacher will compose letters or little speeches for his pupils to write to their parents, so by this book [God] prepares both the language and the mood in which we should address the Heavenly Father and pray for that which the other books have taught us to do and to imitate."[8] One example of this language and mood is the joyful song of believers in Psalm 118, a model song of faith, which requires artistic mastery to sing in the face of death.

2. Diligently inspect the text

Remember that for Luther the mastery of this art is not accomplished with ease. Just as the understanding of a work of art requires detailed inspection of the work, so too does the text of Scripture require close examination and familiarity with it. Luther drives home this point in his exposition of Psalm 117, the shortest of the psalms, which he also wrote at the Coburg in 1530.

"This is a short, easy Psalm," Luther says, "doubtless made this way so that everyone might pay more attention to it and remember what is said. No one can complain about the length or content, much less about the sharpness, difficulty or profundity of the words. Here we find only short, precise, clear and ordinary words, which everyone can understand if he will only pay attention and think about them. All God's words demand this. We must not skim over them and imagine that we have thoroughly understood them, like the frivolous, smug and bored souls, who, when they hear some Word of God once, consider it old hat and cast about for something new. They think they have thoroughly mastered all they have heard. This is a dangerous disease, a clever and malicious trick of the devil. Thus he makes people bold, smug, forward, and ready for every kind or error and schism."[9]
Luther is relentless in his sarcasm when describing such careless handling of God's Word. "The meanest bungler who hears a sermon or reads a chapter in German immediately makes himself a doctor of theology, crowning his own asininity, and convincing himself most marvelously that he can now do everything better than all his teachers." The superiority of the interpreter of Scripture over his teachers is therefore not a boast that any careless reader of Scripture can make. One should name such presumptuous fellows "Master Smart Alecks" (Meister Klügel), " who can bridle a steed in its hind end." This presumption and foolishness is the "result of reading and listening to God's Word carelessly instead of concentrating on it with fear, humility and diligence."[10]
Luther frankly admits that he himself had to fight against such carelessness and presumption, an admission that is quite believable in the case of a person who knew the Scripture so well and had to handle it every day. "I confess this freely as an example to anyone; for here am I, an old doctor of theology and a preacher, and certainly as competent in Scripture as such smart alecks. At least I ought to

II

be. Yet even I must become a child; and early each day I recite aloud
to myself the Lord's Prayer, the Ten Commandments, the Creed,
and whatever lovely Psalms and verses I may choose, just as we
teach and train children to do. I dare not say in my heart: 'The Lord's
Prayer is worn out; you know the Ten Commandments; you can
recite the Creed.' I study them daily and remain a pupil of the
Catechism. I feel, too, that this helps me a lot, and I am convinced
by experience that God's Word can never be entirely mastered, but
that Psalm 147:5 speaks truly: 'His understanding is beyond measure.' "[11]

Luther reaffirms his own rule of *meditatio* in this text. His diligent attention
to the text is attested not only by such personal confessions, but also by the
length of his exegetical works. How could one lecture for two years on the
Psalter and reach only Psalm 22, or risk losing students over ten years with
lengthy verse by verse expositions of Genesis? Verbosity, perhaps, and re-
dundancy are part of the answer, as Luther has often been accused. Theological digression and belabored polemics are also responsible. But careful
exegesis and the patience to struggle with the text also account for Luther's
lengthy expositions. Explanations of great works of art are often longer than
the works themselves. Luther examines every verse, and frequently every
word of every verse, in the conviction that the most applicable meaning of that
text, no matter how difficult, can best be discovered by paying the most
careful attention to every word.

In Psalm 117 Luther spends over eight pages (in the Weimar
Edition) exegeting the forthright statement of verse 2: "For great is
his steadfast love towards us" (GOTTES GUETE WALTE ÜBER
UNS). Luther says that these are unusually fine words and we
should not skim over them coldly or without feeling. People babble
these words with their mouth but they interpret them wrongly.
"These are deep words," he says, "and a profound understanding is
required to grasp that God's grace and truth, or his love and faithful-
ness, rule over us and prevail."[12]

3. *Apply the tools of interpretation*
Detailed inspection requires knowing and applying the tools of interpretation—the techniques of craftsmanship. In the case of a great work of art, this
means knowing something about brush strokes, colors, paints and the
techniques of drawing. Applied to Scripture, this means knowing the language of the text, the meaning of words and the technique of writing.
Luther knew Greek and Hebrew, but his appreciation of biblical languages
is best illustrated by his use of Hebrew in the interpretation of the Psalms. We
know more about Luther's use of Hebrew, too, since Siegfried Raeder has
devoted most of his scholarly life and three books to tracing Luther's use of the
language in his exegesis of the Psalter.[13] Luther knew some Hebrew when he
began his first Psalms lectures in 1513, but he used it primarily to help him
understand better the Latin text of the Vulgate. Between 1515 and 1518,

while lecturing on New Testament books, Luther studied Hebrew on the side in preparation for his second try at the Psalter. In these second lectures he was able to base his exposition on the Hebrew text, and to call that exposition *grammatica theologica*, "theological philology."[14] By this Luther meant that the Hebrew language itself had theological quality and should serve as the basis for the theological exposition. As he scrutinizes the Psalter for the second time, therefore, he pays unusually close attention to the Hebrew text. At the end of the twentieth psalm, he pauses to reflect on the work he has done, commenting on the fact that he is still learning both the language and the spirit. Although he notes that the spirit is more important than language, he affirms that both are necessary for the interpreter of Scripture.[15]

Luther pays even higher tribute to the importance of languages in 1524 in his admonition *To All Councilmen of All Cities in Germany That They Establish and Maintain Christian Schools*. There Luther distinguishes between a simple preacher and a person who expounds Scripture.

"A simple preacher (it is true) has so many clear passages and texts available through translations that he can know and teach Christ, lead a holy life, and preach to others. But when it comes to interpreting Scripture, and working with it on your own, and disputing with those who cite it incorrectly, he is unequal to the task; that cannot be done without languages. Now there must always be such prophets in the Christian Church who can dig into Scripture, expound it, and carry on disputations. A saintly life and right doctrine are not enough. Hence, languages are absolutely and altogether necessary in the Christian Church."[16] Although Luther admits, therefore, "that faith and the gospel may indeed be proclaimed by simple preachers without a knowledge of languages," he believes that "such preaching is flat and tame; people finally become weary and bored with it, and it falls to the ground. But where the preacher is versed in the languages, there is a freshness and vigor in his preaching, Scripture is treated in its entirety, and faith finds itself constantly renewed by a continual variety of works and illustrations."[17]

To close his case, Luther refers, as he often does, to his own career. While acknowledging the necessity of the Spirit, as he did in his Psalms commentary, he highlights the crucial role which languages played: "I know full well that while it is the Spirit alone who accomplishes everything, I would surely have never succeeded if the languages had not helped me and given me a sure and certain knowledge of Scripture. I too could have lived uprightly and preached the truth in seclusion; but then I should have left undisturbed the pope, the sophists, and the whole kingdom of the Antichrist. The devil does not respect my spirit as highly as he does my speech and pen when they deal with Scripture. For my spirit takes from him nothing but myself alone; but Holy Scripture and the languages leave him little room on earth, and wreak havoc in his kingdom."[18]

While it is tempting to apply these remarks to seminary curricula, our purpose is to point out the importance which Luther attributed to linguistic ability for the interpreter of Scripture. The art of interpreting Scripture is in part dependent on the skill at using the tools of interpretation. And note that this is especially true when the authority of Scripture is at stake in controversy. Knowledge of Greek and Hebrew can enliven preaching—this is also an art—but beyond that, they are absolutely necessary when the correct interpretation of Scripture must be defended against the claims of adversaries.

The notion, therefore, that every person is his or her own interpreter of Scripture must be qualified by emphasizing that the diligent inspection of the text and the application of linguistic tools are necessary in order to discern which interpretation has a valid claim to authority in the church at large. Through his translation work, it is true, Luther tried to make Scripture accessible to everyone and did not deny to anyone the ability to follow the rules of David and find meaning in the text. He did not intend, however, to make the diligent, and even learned, study of Scripture superfluous; nor did he mean to imply that any meaning of a text was as good as any other meaning, subject to the individual's own cursory reading of the Bible. "By Scripture alone" would not have meant for Luther, therefore, "by my own interpretation alone," i.e., a careless relativizing of the authority of Scripture.

4. *Relate the text to experience*

The art of interpreting Scripture does not lie only in the diligent inspection and analysis of the text. This alone does not establish the authority of the text in one's life. The interpreter must, in addition, be able to hear in the text a word spoken to his own experience. The text which is inspected and opened up by the tools of interpretation becomes a living text, a living work of art, that speaks to the interpreter's own life and to the life of the church.

Luther implies this in most of his exegesis, but he states it explicitly in his interpretation of v. 23 of Psalm 118: "This is the Lord's doing; it is marvelous in our eyes." The reference is to the stone which the builders rejected but which God made the cornerstone.

Luther interprets the cornerstone as Christ and says that although dear saints and Christians take no offense at this, it is still amazing to their hearts and difficult to believe; they must study it all their life to believe it. "My little books show and testify how well and thoroughly I know this. But when I enter the battle and must come to grips with the devil, sin, death, trouble, and the world; when there is no help, counsel, and consolation except this cornerstone, then I understand how little I can do and what an art it is to believe in Christ. Then I understand well what David means when he says: 'It is marvelous in our eyes. . . .' Even though all Scripture says that God is marvelous in all his works, and calls him a worker of miracles, the world does not believe this until it experiences it personally."[19]

Luther is referring, of course, to his third rule, *tentatio*, the necessity of experiencing opposition and undergoing attack before one can truly understand Scripture and master the art of believing its message. Only as Scripture touches the sore points of our experience does it prove its claim to have authority for our life.

It would be possible, of course, to twist Luther's emphasis on experience into an arbitrary and subjective— we might say experimental or existential— handling of Scripture, in which the text is made to conform to our experience. In this case our own experience would become authoritative and not Scripture. "By Scripture alone" would then become "by our own experience alone." Luther was well aware of this danger. He knew that some people ascribe to Scripture the flexibility of a waxen nose and say it is like a bending reed. They reach the point where the Word of God fits everything and therefore is fit for nothing.[20]

In contrast, says Luther, the Word of God is called by Scripture a rod of iron or a scepter (Psalm 2:9), because of its inflexible and invincible straightness.[21] Therefore, we cannot adjust the Scripture to our feelings and experience. Precisely the contrary is required. We should adjust and adapt our mind and feelings so that they are in accord with the sense of the Psalms. The Psalter is a kind of school and exercise for the disposition of the heart. Here Luther uses the word *palestra*, a wrestling school or arena. The interpreter must wrestle his own feelings into conformity with those of the psalmist. For example, says Luther, "when you read Psalm 1:1: 'Blessed is the man who does not walk in the counsel of the ungodly,' it should at the same time move you to detest and despise the counsel of the ungodly, not only for yourself but, in general, for the whole church."[22]

Just as the viewer of a work of art, therefore, attempts to penetrate the experience of the artist which is expressed in the work itself, so must the reader of Scripture identify with the experience out of which the text arises. When that happens, the reader of Scripture discovers that the text illuminates areas of his own experience which may have been ignored or repressed by him. Scripture, like a work of art, gives new insight into one's life and challenges the interpreter to face his life and experience for what it really is, rather than what he may have construed it to be. In this way, the text becomes authoritative for our life rather than vice versa.

> Accordingly, Luther notes that what we read in Scripture may initially contradict our own feelings and experience. Discussing "God's steadfast love and faithfulness" in Psalm 117:2, Luther says that outwardly God's grace "seems to be nothing but wrath, so deeply is it buried under two thick hides or pelts. Our opponents and the world condemn and avoid it like the plague . . . , and our own feelings about it are not different." But, says Luther, remember II Peter (1:19): "The Word is like a lamp shining in a dark place." "Most certainly it is a dark place! God's faithfulness and truth must always become a great lie before it becomes truth. The world calls

II

this truth heresy. And we, too, are constantly tempted to believe that God would abandon us and not keep his Word; and in our hearts he begins to become a liar. In short, God cannot become God unless he first becomes a devil. We cannot go to heaven unless we first go to hell."[23]

When the Word confronts you, therefore, the proper response is not to turn it into a mirror of your own feelings or charge against it with great force, as Luther accuses heretics, Turks and sects of doing. But "beware and yield. Give ground and obey in good time; for it must conquer whether you bow gracefully or ungracefully, for we read (I Peter 1:25): 'The Word of the Lord abides forever.' "[24]

The Word of God establishes its authority over our lives not because we make it relevant to our own experience, but because it conquers our misconception of our experience and opens our eyes to what our experience really is and to what God is really doing. You may see a glimmer of Luther's theology of the Cross in these words, and rightly so. God works under contrary experiences not only in the events which Scripture reports, but also in the very work which he does when his Word overpowers us.

5. *Pray for the inspiration of the Spirit*

The proper preparation for encountering Scripture therefore includes prayer. The interpreter must implore the aid of the Spirit to discern what attitude and emotion are required in order to understand the text. Just as the viewer of a work of art seeks the same inspiration which the artist enjoyed in the creation of the work, so too does the reader of Scripture seek the inspiration of the Spirit, the author of Scripture, to interpret it aright. The fifth verse of Psalm 118 was a good opportunity for Luther to stress this point: "Out of my distress I called upon the Lord; the Lord answered me and set me free."

"You must learn to call," Luther says. "Do not sit by yourself or lie on a couch, hanging and shaking your head. Do not destroy yourself with your own thoughts by worrying. . . . Say to yourself: 'Come on, you lazy bum; down on your knees and lift your eyes and hands toward heaven.' Read a psalm or the Our Father, call on God and tearfully lay your troubles before him. Mourn and pray as this verse teaches. . . . Hear you learn that praying, reciting your troubles and lifting up your hands are sacrifices most pleasing to God. . . . He wants you to be too weak to bear and overcome such troubles; he wants you to grow strong in him. By his strength he is glorified in you. Out of such experiences men become real Christians. Otherwise, men are mere babblers, who prate about faith and spirit but are ignorant of what it is all about or of what they themselves are saying."[25]

To call upon God in the time of trouble is the "great art and wisdom of faith" which the Scripture teaches. Faith rises above all tribulation and need and sees "God's fatherly heart behind his unfriendly exterior." That is "skill above all skills" and it is the work of the Holy Spirit alone which is known only by pious and true Christians.[26] This attitude of faith is taught by the Spirit as he leads us through the text to despair of ourselves and trust in God. There is not room, therefore, for a neutral, uninvolved recognition of the truth of Scripture in the sense of what orthodox theologians would call a "theology of the unregenerate." For Luther, the claim of Scripture to be true and authoritative is validated by the Spirit only in those whom he leads to faith. The Spirit does not work apart from the Word, but through the Word to open eyes and hearts to accept the claims made by the Word. "By Scripture alone," therefore, means always for Luther "by Scripture alone through faith and Spirit."

6. *Seek out the central core*

The art of faith required for understanding Scripture implies that the object of that faith be consistently and reliably present in Scripture itself. The Spirit does not teach faith in Scripture, but faith in the Word of God revealed in Scripture. For Luther that Word of God has definable and reliable content. That is the Gospel of God about his Son, Jesus Christ. By identifying a consistent message in Scripture as the definitive content of the Bible, Luther provides additional security against subjective and arbitrary interpretations of Scripture which could appeal to experience alone or to personal illumination of the Spirit apart from Scripture. There is objective content in Scripture, albeit a content which cannot become truly authoritative for us unless the Spirit leads us to believe it.

At the end of his exegesis of Psalm 117, Luther establishes a hermeneutical rule which supplements the rules we have already met. That principle is "to search out and deal with the core of Christian doctrine, wherever it may be found throughout the Bible. And the core is: that without any merit, as a gift of God's pure grace in Christ, we attain righteousness, life and salvation, and that there is no other path, no other means or effort, that can help us attain it." Luther's insistence on pursuing this core is conditioned, unsurprisingly, by his own experience: "Every day I experience only too well how insistently the devil assails this core in an effort to wipe it out. And although tired saints consider it unnecessary to keep at this matter—they imagine they know it inside out and have learned all there is to know—still I know how wrong they are. . . ."[27] Scripture can in fact be misleading and dangerous if this central core is not kept in mind. A few times, Luther says, when he did not keep it in mind, "the devil caught up with me and plagued me with Scripture passages until heaven and earth became too small for me."[28] On a broader scale, says Luther, "Wherever sects arise, you may be sure that they have certainly fallen away from this principal teaching, regardless of the fact that they do a great deal of mouthing about Christ and put on much polish and finery." "If this one teaching stands in its purity," however, "then Christendom will also remain pure and good, undivided and unseparated; for this alone, and nothing else, makes and maintains Christendom."[29] Scripture alone without the Gospel is a snare for the interpreter, rather than a sure guide to the Word of God.

II

It is tempting to accuse Luther of reducing the Scripture to the Gospel and of discovering the Gospel in every nook and cranny of the Bible. This criticism was made of Luther in his own lifetime and two things should be said in response to it. First, Luther was aware that more was given to God's people in Scripture than a monotonous repetition of the words: "God saves us by grace in Christ." In his exegesis of Psalm 147:19, he notes that the psalmist uses three names for God's Word: his "Word," which means God's promise; his "statutes," which mean the order and manner of divine worship; and his "ordinances," which mean the law under which God commanded the people of Israel how to conduct themselves toward others and practice works of love. These three, Luther says, must exist in every people that wants to be a people of God, just as we Christians also have the promise of the Gospel, the sacraments, the office of preaching ministry and the doctrine of good works.[30]

Luther, however, goes to great lengths to argue that the ordinances and statutes of Scripture, as he calls them, can never claim authority apart from the central core of Scripture, which is the promise of God embodied in Christ. It was precisely the thrust of his reforming work to prevent this from happening—on the left or on the right. Positively expressed, this means that the worship of the church and the conduct of the Christian life, while also dealt with in Scripture, must be judged by the way in which they support or detract from this central core.

Secondly, there were personal reasons for Luther's insistence on the Gospel as the central theme which must always be preserved. Luther anticipates the question which contemporaries and we ourselves may have put to him:

> "Now," says Luther, "someone might say to me: 'Can't you ever do anything but speak only about the righteousness, wisdom and strength of God rather than of man, always expounding Scripture from the standpoint of God's righteousness and grace, always harping on the same string and singing the same old song?' To this I answer: Let each one look to himself. As for me I confess: Whenever I found less in the Scriptures than Christ, I was never satisfied; but whenever I found more than Christ, I never became poorer. Therefore, it seems to me to be true that God the Holy Spirit does not know and does not want to know anything besides Jesus Christ."[31]

Twenty years of wrestling in the *palestra* of Scripture lie behind these words, years of personal struggle to discern the Word of God for him and for the church, and years of struggle with opponents on both sides who would wrest from him the authority of that Gospel which had validated its claim on his life and on the lives of his people. To perceive and pursue this core was an art which he had learned at great personal cost, and one which he could not easily forget and certainly not give up.

7. Acknowledge the inexhaustibility of Scripture

From his many warnings to the contrary, we should not imagine that once Luther found and insisted upon this core, he then assumed he had milked

Scripture for all it could give or gloried in a job well-done and completed. The pursuit of this central core does not make the interpretation of Scripture easier. In fact, it becomes more difficult. It is an art, he says, that cannot be completely learned or of which anyone could boast that he were the master. It is an art that will always have us as pupils while it remains the master. Only when he perceived what the central message of Scripture was, and learned how difficult was the art of holding onto it in faith, did Luther recognize fully the inexhaustible quality of Scripture. Luther's experience was like that of a person, who, looking into a deep well, can only see how deep it really is by focusing on a gleaming coin at the bottom. Or, if we come back to our illustration of a work of art: once we identify a recurring motif in the works of an artist, then we see how limitless are the ramifications of this motif which can be discerned in any one picture.

Luther constantly stresses that the understanding we are given of any one part of Scripture, even of one psalm, is partial; we can never exhaust the meaning or the power of Scripture. As Luther published the first fascicles of his second Psalms commentary in 1519, he wrote: "I do not want anyone to suppose that I shall accomplish what none of the most holy and learned theologians have ever accomplished before, namely, to understand and teach the correct meaning of the Psalms in all particulars. It is enough to understand some of the Psalms, and those only in part. The Spirit reserves much for himself, so that we may always remain his pupils."[32]

That was in 1519. Luther did not change his mind on this subject after he gained more practice. In 1530 when he sets out to expound the two verses of Psalm 117 at the Coburg, he believes that no one truly knows everything the Holy Spirit says in this one psalm. "I have taken it upon myself to interpret this psalm, so that one may see how clear God's Word is, how simple, and yet how altogether inexhaustible. And even though everything were reasonable, which is not the case, still it is inexhaustible in power and virtue. It renews and refreshes the heart, restoring, relieving, comforting and strengthening us constantly."[33]

Clear, and yet inexhaustible. The clarity of Scripture, especially the clarity of its central core, does not imply that the meaning of Scripture can be exhausted. I believe that Luther is also speaking here of the kind of authority which Scripture exercises over our lives. Of course, he believed that the Gospel was clearly expressed in Scripture and authoritative in itself. We do not give it authority. But if that Gospel is to function with authority in our lives, then it has to be claimed again and again in our encounter with the Scripture which expresses it. And we can only claim it by entering into the *palestra* of Scripture texts like the Psalter, diligently inspecting them and applying our tools, wrestling with the text out of our own experience, imploring the Spirit to illuminate our experience and conform it to the experience that produced the text itself. Luther advises: "Practice on one psalm, even one little verse of the psalm. You will progress enough if you learn to make only one verse a day, or even one a week, live and breathe in your heart. After this beginning is made, everything else will follow, and you will have a rich treasury of understanding and affection."[34]

Progress, Not Mastery

Progress is possible, but not complete mastery of the art of interpretation. Even after one has discovered the central motif of an artist's work and built up a body of interpretation from which to approach each individual work, new insights are always possible as one encounters old works anew. And even the old works must reestablish their claim on our lives and the lives of succeeding generations as they are viewed out of new and changing life experiences. They are never exhausted, and the art of interpreting them never mastered, and their authority can never be taken for granted.

So it is with Scripture and so it was with Luther's interpretation of it. He made progress, but even psalms which he had interpreted early in his life were examined again and again for new insights and brighter light which they could shed on the life of faith. In 1525 Luther brought out a new edition of his first published work—a commentary on the Penitential Psalms dating from 1517. Although he did not find anything wrong with the first edition, yet, he says, he often missed the meaning of the text. "Now, however, since the Gospel has reached high noon and is shining brightly, and I also have made some progress in the meantime, I considered it good to publish this work again, but improved and based more accurately on the right text."[35]

Luther was not much further along in mastering his beloved art on the day before he died. It is only appropriate that his last recorded words confess his inadequacy for the task which had been his chief occupation for thirty-four years, the task of interpreting Scripture. Those thirty-four years were not enough for him to exhaust the meaning of Scripture.

> "Nobody can understand Vergil in his *Bucolics* and *Georgics* unless he has first been a shepherd or a farmer for five years. Nobody understands Cicero in his letters unless he has been engaged in public affairs of some consequence for twenty years. Let nobody suppose that he has tasted the Holy Scripture sufficiently unless he has ruled over the churches with the prophets for a hundred years. . . . We are beggars. That is true."[36]

Luther had been seized by the authority of Scripture all his working life. He claimed it for himself and for the church he sought to bring under its sway. Yet he was never able to master the art of interpretation, but died as he lived, praying and meditating and struggling, never a master, but still a pupil of the Word.

NOTES

[1]*WABr(=Weimarer Ausgabe, Briefe)* 1.133,31-134,44 (Nr. 57:18 January 1518). *LW (=Luther's Works, American Edition)* 48.53-54.
[2]*WA* 50.659,3-4; 659,10-12; 659,22-25; 660,1-14. *LW* 34.285-287.

[3]WA 50.660,17-27. *LW* 34.287.
[4]WA 4.353,5-17. *LW* 11.481.
[5]WA 5.22,38-23,1. *LW* 14.285.
[6]WA 31/I.66,17-22. *LW* 14.45.
[7]WA 31/I.140,27; 146,30-32; 149,28-30; 151,21-23; 158,25-159,22. *LW* 14.80, 83, 85, 88-89.
[8]WA 5.23,20-23; 23,29-32. *LW* 14.286.
[9]WA 31/I.223,6-225,3. *LW* 14.7.
[10]WA 31/I.227,4-10. *LW* 14.7.
[11]WA 31/I.227,13-25. *LW* 14.8.
[12]WA 31/I.242-250. *LW* 14.24-32.
[13]Siegfried Raeder, *Das Hebräische bei Luther, untersucht bis zum Ende der ersten Psalmenvorlesung* (Tübingen 1961); *Die Benutzung des masoretischen Textes bei Luther in der Zeit zwischen der ersten und zweiten Psalmenvorlesung* (Tübingen 1967); *Grammatica Theologica: Studien zu Luthers Operationes in Psalmos* (Tübingen 1977).
[14]WA 5.27,8; 5.32,19. *LW* 14.287 and 294. See Raeder, *Grammatica Theologica,* 34ff.
[15]WA 5.597,23-31.
[16]WA 15.40,16-24. *LW* 45.363.
[17]WA 15.42,6-11. *LW* 45.365.
[18]WA 15.42,22-43,6. *LW* 45.366.
[19]WA 31/I.174,23-26;174,34-175,3; 175,10-12. *LW* 14.98-99.
[20]WA 5.66,6-9. *LW* 14.338.
[21]WA 5.65,38 - 66,1. *LW* 14.338.
[22]WA 5.46,15-20. *LW* 14.310.
[23]WA 31/I.249,16-27. *LW* 14.31.
[24]WA 31/I.230,38 - 231,3. *LW* 14.11.
[25]WA 31/I.95,36 - 97,18. *LW* 14.60-61.
[26]WA 31/I.93,30 - 94,25. *LW* 14.59.
[27]WA 31/I.254,28 - 255,5. *LW* 14.36-37.
[28]WA 31/I.255,34 - 256,3. *LW* 14.37.
[29]WA 31/I.255,13-16; 255,5-8. *LW* 14.37.
[30]WA 31/I.453,11-23. *LW* 14.131-132.
[31]WA 18.529,1-9 *LW* 14.204.
[32]WA 5.22,26-29. *LW* 14.284.
[33]WA 31/I.228,6-11. *LW* 14.8.
[34]WA 5.46,34 - 47,4 *LW* 14.310.
[35]WA 18.479,10-13. *LW* 14.140.
[36]WATR 5.317,12-17 (Nr. 5677). *LW* 54.476.

III

The Use of Scripture
in Establishing Protestantism:
The Case of Urbanus Rhegius

Urbanus Rhegius's career as a Reformer falls naturally into two parts: the time he spent in south Germany as a Protestant preacher in Augsburg from 1524 to 1530, and his time in north Germany as superintendent of the church in the Duchy of Lüneburg from 1530 until his death in 1541.[1] Rhegius was lured to Lüneburg by Duke Ernest the "Confessor," who intended for him to organize the newly reformed church in his territory according to Protestant teaching and practice. Although he had seen controversy enough in Augsburg, which was a maelstrom of religious currents during the 1520s,[2] Rhegius scarcely anticipated the difficulties that awaited him in Lower Saxony. His skill in the interpretation of Scripture would prove to be a trusted resource in the rocky vineyard of north Germany. This same skill would also illustrate the extent to which Scripture became a tool in the hands of Reformers like Rhegius who were charged with establishing Protestantism.

Rhegius's exegetical skills were acquired and honed during his south German years. His most important acquisition was training in biblical languages, a skill he had in common with other scholars influenced by humanism. Rhegius may have learned Greek at the University of Freiburg (1508–12) or subsequently at Ingolstadt (1512–18); his earliest works demonstrate familiarity with the language. The origin of his enthusiasm for Hebrew is uncertain. Maximilian Liebmann speculates that John Eck may have sparked Rhegius's interest in both languages. Liebmann points out that the earliest manuscripts of Rhegius that we possess—two course announcements from the year

1512—contain the name of Rhegius (at that time Rieger) written with Hebrew letters.[3] Rhegius could have been exposed to the language in Freiburg, where Eck studied Hebrew with the Carthusian prior Gregor Reisch (d. 1525), or in Ingolstadt, where Reuchlin lectured on the grammar of Kimchi and named Eck as one of his students.[4] Rhegius might also have learned Hebrew from Matthäus Adrianus (fl. 1501–21), who taught the language in Heidelberg from 1513 to 1516 and had Johannes Oecolampadius and Wolfgang Capito as his students.[5] Wherever he learned it, Rhegius demonstrated special fondness for Hebrew[6] and referred to medieval Jewish grammarians like Abraham Ibn Ezra and David Kimchi along with Christian scholars like Sebastian Münster.

In later years Rhegius frequently used Hebrew in his explanations of Old Testament passages,[7] and he preached what he practiced. Advising a young pastor near Hannover in 1540 how to study Scripture, Rhegius first stressed that biblical languages should be learned with diligence. Without knowledge of Hebrew, exegetes were forced to look at the Old Testament with "foreign eyes." How perilous that could be for the prospective theologian had now become obvious, especially to those who had trusted the translations of Jerome for so many years but now did not always follow his rendering, even though they still commended his effort.[8] Rhegius recommended that the pastor not only read daily a chapter or two of the Old Testament in Hebrew, but that he also compare the Hebrew text with the Greek version. This comparison, claimed Rhegius, would help him in a marvelous way to learn the true sense of Scripture and to attain the gift of the Holy Spirit.[9]

The same disciplined pattern of study in both the Old and the New Testaments very likely accounts for Rhegius's impressive familiarity with Scripture. He could quote passages from all parts of the Bible as freely and easily as Luther could, and he did not have the ritual of monastic worship or an academic chair in exegesis to imprint the verses on his mind. In Ingolstadt Rhegius did lecture on Lefèvre's introduction to the *Politics* of Aristotle, but his academic training gives no evidence of an unusual concentration on Scripture. Besides the acquaintance he made through the study of Greek and Hebrew, Rhegius acquired his ready knowledge of the Bible on the job, as cathedral preacher in Augsburg and as chaplain at Hall in Tirol. After

Urbanus Rhegius

his conversion to Protestantism Rhegius supplemented his preaching in Augsburg with weekday exegetical lectures on Paul's Epistles.[10] His intensive study of Paul also generated two popular writings, first published in 1523, that exhibit his knowledge of Scripture and his readiness to use it. *A Brief Explanation of Some Common Points of Scripture* was an exposition of forty-eight theological loci found in Scripture, and *The Twelve Articles of Our Christian Faith* was an interpretation of the Apostles' Creed which showed how a proper understanding of the creed was based on Scripture.[11]

The regular study and exposition of Scripture remained part of Rhegius's schedule after he assumed his duties in north Germany. We can safely make such an assertion without adopting the effusive flattery of his translator and admirer, Johannes Freder (Irenaeus), who declared him worthy to be called bishop not just of Lüneburg but of all Germany.[12] As a close reader and translator of his works, Freder expressed general admiration for Rhegius's devotion and learning, but he singled out for special praise Rhegius's knowledge of languages (Latin, Greek, Hebrew) and his most popular exegetical work, the massive collection and interpretation of messianic passages from the Old Testament, the *Dialogus von der schönen predigt*.[13]

In north Germany Rhegius was challenged by three major tasks: (1) to break Catholic resistance to the Reformation in the territory of Lüneburg and in cities like Lüneburg and Hannover; (2) to protect Protestants from the threat of Anabaptist influence and the taint of Anabaptist excesses at Münster; and (3) to educate pastors for the new Protestant parishes in Lower Saxony. The nature of these tasks determined the kind of works that Rhegius produced during the 1530s and directly affected the way he used Scripture in these writings.

The first two tasks—the assertion of Protestant principles against Catholic and Anabaptist views—elicited a number of polemical works from his pen. Typical of these is his refutation of "a monstrous, astounding formula of absolution" allegedly written by nuns in the cloisters of Lüneburg and then used by two seventy-year-old confessors who could neither recite it nor understand it.[14] Rhegius decided to publish the absolution in order to warn simple people against the blasphemy of Christ that was still rampant under the papacy.[15] His method of refutation was straightforward. He dealt with the absolution one phrase at a time and refuted each phrase by listing passages of

Scripture which proved the phrase false. For example, against the attribution of forgiveness to the merit of Mary, Rhegius listed seven passages of Scripture, discussed one (Romans 3) in detail, and concluded that if the nuns thought that the merit of Mary added power to the merit of Christ, then all the passages cited would be false.[16] Rhegius also used Scripture to expose the social forces at work behind the resistance of cloistered women to the Reformation. Citing 1 Corinthians 1:26 ("not many were wise.... not many were powerful, not many were of noble birth"), Rhegius made fun of their status as noblewomen and ridiculed their claim to have died to the world. After visiting some of the cloisters, Rhegius quipped that the nuns lived as much apart from the world as kidneys lived apart from the body.[17]

The third task, training Protestant clergy and educating the laity who suddenly found themselves Protestant, consumed Rhegius's remaining energy.[18] There was no theological faculty in Lower Saxony until the University of Helmstedt was founded in 1576. Those Protestant preachers who did not study at Wittenberg learned the new theology from writings of the Reformers or heard it from their superintendents and colleagues in the church. Besides his advice to pastors to study Scripture on their own, Rhegius went about his pedagogical task in two ways.

First, he published works that were specifically designed to ensure the proper education and certification of Protestant pastors. The most popular of these was a homiletical handbook entitled *How to Preach on the Chief Points of Christian Doctrine Carefully and without Giving Offense*.[19] It was addressed to younger ministers of the Word in Lüneburg and was prompted by the poor sermons Rhegius himself had heard from misguided and brash young Protestant pulpiteers. In order to help dispel the laity's confusion over sensitive issues such as repentance, good works, predestination, and illumination by the Spirit, Rhegius cited key passages of Scripture that could serve the preachers as guidelines for a correct and balanced proclamation. Rhegius also wanted to make sure that new preachers would be much better prepared to use Scripture. Soon after the *Formulae caute,* Rhegius outlined an examination to be given to all candidates for ordination in the Duchy.[20] The structure of the exam was based on carefully selected passages, beginning with the familiar exhortations about church leaders in 1 and 2 Timothy and moving to a biblical argument for dividing all of Scripture into the categories of law and gospel.[21] This distinction was not sufficient, however. Ordinands had to be prepared to recite copiously passages from Scripture that correctly explained temporal and external punishments, the divinity of Christ, and all the articles of the Apostles' Creed. Furthermore, candidates were expected to show exactly which parts of Scripture were law and which were gospel and where in Scripture Christ was promised and where he was explicitly shown to be the Messiah.[22] When candidates appeared for the examination, they had to be loaded with Scripture.

As a second method of educating clergy, Rhegius himself demonstrated what he required. In Celle Rhegius revived his custom of exegeting Scripture on weekdays, showing a marked preference for the Old Testament, at least according to the sermons and lectures that he selected for publication. When he assisted with the Reformation in the cities of Lüneburg and Hannover, he instructed his fellow preachers in the exegesis of Scripture by modeling the discipline for them. In Lüneburg Rhegius lectured on Romans and then formulated theses based on the lectures to be defended by the preachers in debates with one another.[23] In Hannover in 1535 Rhegius lectured on the prophet Obadiah in order to show evangelical preachers how to understand and expound the prophets.[24] Although he did not hold a university chair in exegesis, his teaching activity resembled a modern extension or continuing education program, in which Rhegius became the professor of theology and exegesis for students who were already in the field.

Owing to his strong interest in the education of clergy and laity, Rhegius's reforming work has been described as predominantly pastoral and his use of Scripture judged typical of the edifying nature of much Reformation exegesis.[25] Certainly his love of proof texts and the copious citations in his polemical works make his use of Scripture appear unremarkable. Nevertheless, Rhegius developed a concept of interpretation which he applied consistently and quite visibly in his exegetical works. This concept was based on two principles: one can be labeled "apostolic," and the other "catechetical." These principles were stated and explained in the form of advice to preachers and fit, therefore, into the polemical and pedagogical purposes of his work.[26]

The apostolic principle of interpretation requires the preacher to use the Old Testament as the apostles did in order to find support for

III

the gospel in the law and the·prophets. This apostolic custom, according to Rhegius, is demonstrated in the Epistles of the New Testament and in the Book of Acts. These parts of the New Testament show us the right interpretation and use of the Old Testament, since the New is the light of and key to the Old.[27] If, however, the light seems dim and the Old Testament remains obscure, preachers should use the following syllogism in order to remind them of the method: (1) all the prophets were seeking the salvation and reconciliation of humanity with its creator; (2) no righteousness or salvation was promised apart from Jesus Christ; (3) ergo, all the prophets foretold the coming of Christ.[28] The syllogism itself was based on selected New Testament passages, especially 1 Peter 1:10–12, which identifies the prophets as foretellers of grace and predictors of the sufferings and glory of Christ.

A christological interpretation of the Old Testament is hardly distinctive, but Rhegius gave it an unusual twist. He did not stress the use of the New Testament to interpret the Old, but the use of the Old to confirm the New. The main reason for reading the Old Testament as the apostles did was not to understand it better but to strengthen faith.[29]

Rhegius went about the task of confirming the New Testament and strengthening faith with astounding energy. The most amazing product of this energy is the enormous collection of Old Testament passages which Rhegius identified as prophecies of Christ. The *Dialogus,* as he called it, was allegedly based on conversations between Rhegius and his wife Anna and first was written as a dialogue between them in 1532. Feeling sad one Easter Day, Anna said she wished she could hear the comforting sermon which Jesus must have preached to the two disciples on the road to Emmaus, when, "beginning with Moses and all the prophets, he interpreted to them in all the Scriptures the things concerning himself" (Luke 24:27).[30] Anna wanted to hear that sermon so that she could be joyful in the Lord and have her faith strengthened.

That desire was only too welcome to Urbanus Rhegius, who confirmed her feeling that people did not know Christ as they ought, even though they heard many sermons about him.[31] Therefore one should hear the best sermon of all, the sermon that Christ preached about himself. Urbanus warned his wife that the sermon would be long because Luke says that Christ used "all the Scriptures." But Anna offered no protest, and Urbanus rolled off six hundred pages of Old

42

III

Testament prophecies of Christ, beginning with the first promise of
grace in Genesis 3. At the end, sounding skeptical and exhausted,
Anna objected that the road from Jerusalem to Emmaus was surely
not long enough for Christ to have preached all that; but Rhegius
reminded her, the length notwithstanding, how marvelously the sermon strengthened faith. The prophets were the oldest teachers on
earth, he said, and the gospel was the oldest teaching.[32]

Rhegius apparently believed that the more Scripture that was cited,
the stronger faith would become. In his view there was no difference
between the message of the prophets and the message of the evange-
lists. The sum of the prophets' teaching was repentance and faith in
Christ, exactly as it is stated in Acts 20:21. The prophets preached
repentance by scolding those who broke the law, and they preached
faith by announcing the promise of grace.[33] Since Moses and David
were also prophets, a large portion of the Old Testament was included
under gospel. The difference that mattered was not the gap between
the Old and New Testaments but the difference between the two ways
in which Christ was proclaimed: through dark promises and figures as
if seen from a distance, and through clear promises expressed in
unambiguous language.[34]

Rhegius's *Dialogus* was designed to save readers of the Old Testament the work of making this distinction for themselves. It exposed
the teaching about Christ in every possible Old Testament passage and
formed a repository of texts stripped of their ambiguity and ready to
use. This repository would also equip the preacher to engage more
effectively in controversy. Rhegius argued that many preachers knew
the gospel but did not read the law and the prophets. Only that
preacher who was equipped with the apostolic principle of interpretation and thus had his arsenal filled with Old Testament ammunition
was qualified to preside over the church.[35]

Rhegius illustrated the use of this principle in the lectures on
Obadiah that he delivered in Hannover in 1535. The prophet provided
him with ammunition to use against both "papists" and Anabaptists.
In his lectures Rhegius does not ignore the historical sense, but he does
identify the enemies of Israel—the Edomites—with contemporary
persecutors of the gospel, and the Israelite kingdom with the Catholic
church.[36] Two phrases in verse 17 allow him to elaborate. The holiness
of Mount Zion, which is a figure of the true church, leads him to

43

distinguish the evangelical understanding of the church's holiness from the perfectionism of Anabaptists and monasticism.[37] Furthermore, the possession of the house of Jacob, mentioned in the same verse, means that the church will possess people from all nations, an insight that refutes the blindness of the Jews and chiliastic interpretations. His twenty-year-old battle with the chiliasts, says Rhegius, has forced him to study this passage closely along with other prophecies, and he invokes his knowledge of Hebrew as an aid. If one can understand the idiosyncrasy of the Hebrew language, one can see that a spiritual possession, and not an earthly kingdom, was intended by Obadiah and by the Holy Spirit who spoke through him.[38] Obviously Rhegius's long polemical career enhanced his knowledge of Scripture and led him to rely on the apostolic principle of interpretation that he now recommends so highly to his evangelical coworkers.

Rhegius's second hermeneutical principle was the catechetical principle, which called for the preacher to use a doctrine from the catechism in order to explain the text of the sermon.[39] But the principle encompassed a larger understanding of catechism than documents produced for the instruction of the faithful. Rhegius maintained that Scripture should always be interpreted in accord with the received dogma of the church universal, and that preachers should be ready to cite opinions of the church fathers in support of their points.[40] Not just any opinion of a church father could be used, but only those which agreed with the consensus of the church that was required by the principle of catholicity. Rhegius described this use of dogma as the interpretation of Scripture in the "ecclesiastical sense" and argued that a proper understanding of Scripture was not to be found outside the *ecclesia catholica*.[41] Rhegius's Lutheran biographer, Gerhard Uhlhorn, was so nonplussed by this statement that he hastened to assure the reader that Rhegius did not abide by his own principle.[42] In fact, Rhegius abided by it very well, insofar as he understood both the early church and Scripture to support an evangelical interpretation of the faith. And the principle served him very well in the work he had to accomplish.

In the first place, he wanted to ensure that a consistent message was presented from Protestant pulpits. Rhegius recommended that all the pastors in one city study the Gospel text for the coming Sunday under the guidance of the superintendent, so that the "dogmas of our faith" would be explained in concert. If a difficult or controversial text had to be expounded, then testimonies from the church fathers should be used.[43] An example is the sermon on good and bad angels that Rhegius preached on the Day of Saint Michael and All Angels, September 29, 1535. In the sermon he cites Basil the Great in support of his assertion that the church has always believed in guardian angels. We should not, however, put our trust in them or invoke them, because Scripture teaches that we should hope in Christ alone. Since Rhegius, by his own admission, is afraid this prohibition will irritate people, he cites a long passage from Augustine on its behalf. Although he argues that the church has not rejected Augustine's words because they are grounded in Scripture,[44] he implies that Scripture alone is not enough to convince the people.

The second reason for interpreting biblical texts with the help of basic doctrines and the church fathers was to draw a practical lesson from the texts that people could apply easily to their lives. Rhegius suggested that the words of Jesus against killing in Matthew 5:21–26 be related to the Fifth Commandment, and that the stories of Jesus raising the dead be referred directly to the credal belief in the Resurrection.[45] Daily application of this catechetical principle would reveal many specific relationships between Scripture and articles of faith. Most important, preachers should inculcate the catechism in people, "for I have experienced over now these many years how greatly this labor profits the churches."[46]

Again, Rhegius practiced what he advised. According to his interpretation of Obadiah, verse 17, Edom's betrayal by its allies illustrates the First Commandment because in time of trouble Edom looked to human aid instead of to God, who alone is trustworthy.[47] Rhegius's exposition of Psalm 14 emphasizes the same idea. The fool who says in his heart "there is no God" speaks for all of us. Because of the corruption of original sin, we cannot believe that God cares about us and deserves our trust. And if we cannot keep the First Commandment, we will fail to observe the others as well.[48] In this commentary on Psalm 14 Rhegius recounts one situation in which catechetical interpretation had not had the desired effect. He once confronted a notorious drinker with the scriptural declaration that drunkards could not enter the kingdom of heaven. The man replied that Rhegius should go to church if he wanted to preach. Rhegius's comment on the incident is that the man misunderstood the meaning of "church"; he thought of the building instead of the people.[49]

The church order that Rhegius wrote for the city of Hannover reveals a third and more familiar purpose of the catechetical principle. Evangelical preachers should refer to the early church in order to refute the accusation that Protestants were teaching a new and different doctrine.[50] For example, when Rhegius rejected the merits of the saints as a basis for absolution (as we saw in the formula of the nuns), he argued unabashedly that this teaching not only stood in opposition to Holy Scripture but contradicted the Christian faith and the "ancient teachers" as well.[51] All Protestants tried to trace their roots to the early church; Rhegius was no exception. His extensive knowledge of the church fathers and his promptness to supplement texts of Scripture with evidence from the early church distinguish him, however, as a leader among Protestants who were eager to show they were truly catholic. This strong interest in the roots of Protestantism was for Uhlhorn the only mitigating aspect of Rhegius's adherence to the ecclesiastical sense of Scripture.[52] Uhlhorn should also have been comforted by Rhegius's appeals to the early church to support key Lutheran or Protestant teachings. Following one's own private understanding of Scripture instead of the church's interpretation had led, according to Rhegius, to the denial of the real presence of Christ in the Lord's Supper and to the application of the rock in Matthew 16:18 to Peter instead of to Christ.[53]

The apostolic and catechetical principles recommended by Rhegius suggest several conclusions about his own use of Scripture that can be applied to an appraisal of sixteenth-century exegesis.

First, in regard to Protestant exegesis of the Old Testament, the apostolic principle suggests that the central issue was not whether to interpret the Old Testament literally or figuratively, but how christological a legitimate interpretation of the Old Testament could be. By recommending that Protestant preachers follow the model of the apostles and, according to Luke 24, even of Christ himself, Rhegius stated and practiced an extreme form of christological exegesis of the Old Testament. Rhegius was more apostolic than the apostles; not even Luke dared to reconstruct the sermon of Christ on the road to Emmaus! Although Rhegius used the original language and the historical sense as the basis of a text's true meaning, he was not interested mainly in the literal sense but in the meaning it contained about the person and work of Christ. Were Protestants distinctive because they attended to the literal or historical sense of the Old Testament more than exegetes before them, or did they use the Old Testament to confirm their own reading of the New Testament as did generations of their predecessors?

Second, the catechetical principle enunciated by Rhegius indicates that he did not adhere to the principle of *sola scriptura*. Stated more precisely, Rhegius realized that such a principle did not exist and that Scripture was being distorted by people who thought it did. Uhlhorn's amazement notwithstanding, Rhegius argued that no true understanding of Scripture could exist apart from the fundamental articles of the faith as these were forged during the earliest centuries of the church. He certainly believed that no teaching or practice which stood in manifest contradiction to Scripture could be condoned, but he also argued that no group could stand on its private interpretation of a text. Rhegius was facing a twofold challenge. On the one side, his non-Protestant opponents were also appealing to Scripture, while on the other side, some of his followers were claiming that they did not need to know Scripture at all but could be enlightened immediately by the Spirit.

Therefore, says Rhegius in the *Formulae caute,* he has to explain verse 13 from Isaiah 54, which was cited in John 6:45 and became one of Luther's favorite proof texts for the priesthood of believers: "And they shall all be taught by God."[54] According to Rhegius, Christ intended for these words to refer to the "common teaching of the gospel" by which every one of the predestined is enlightened and saved. Beyond this illumination, however, the gift of prophecy (1 Corinthians 14:3) is given only to the teachers of the church, whose task it is to interpret Holy Scripture for the benefit of the faithful.[55]

These teachers were, of course, the pastors of Protestant parishes, and we have seen how their interpretation should conform to the catholic consensus of the early church. Rhegius was concerned both about the catholicity of the emerging Protestant churches and about the disorder which could result from lay access to Scripture and the concept of a common priesthood. In effect, Rhegius was designing a Protestant magisterium: pastors trained to exegete Scripture in accord with the credal doctrines of the early church. This principle may have widened the gap between Protestant clergy and laity, but Rhegius was less concerned about this gap than he was about replacing Roman priests with pastors who could give proper evangelical instruction to the people.[56]

Third, Rhegius's principles of interpretation illustrate how the task of establishing Protestantism shaped both its exegesis and its teaching. In this regard Rhegius's model was Philip Melanchthon, whose influence was not mediated through exegetical principles or personal impact, although Rhegius supported Melanchthon in the negotiations at Augsburg.[57] Instead, Melanchthon's influence was mediated through his *Unterricht der Visitatoren,* which Rhegius knew and used in Lüneburg.[58] As we know from his *Dialogus,* Rhegius was generally fascinated by the twenty-fourth chapter of Luke's Gospel, especially the story of Jesus' appearance on the road to Emmaus. But he was also specifically taken with a verse that Melanchthon had used to support the necessity of teaching repentance as the way to faith. According to Luke 24:47, "repentance *and* forgiveness of sins should be preached in his name to all nations."[59] This verse, supplemented by passages like Acts 20:21, became the foundation of Rhegius's own call for the preaching of both repentance and faith.[60] It also supported the division of doctrine into law and gospel in his outline for an ordination exam: According to Luke 24:47, the teaching of the gospel is twofold, repentance and the forgiveness of sins, and all of Scripture is subsumed under these two headings.[61]

Much more is involved here than Rhegius's support of Melanchthon against Agricola in the first antinomian controversy.[62] Melanchthon's work was a model for the clarification of Protestant teaching and practice, which Rhegius also had to provide for his preachers and parishes in Lüneburg. Thorny issues such as the place of repentance and the law in the Christian life had to be faced. In his own "instruction," the *Formulae caute,* Rhegius discusses elaborately such controversial issues as predestination and good works (the stress on good works is especially noticeable). The directions for examining ordinands seriously admonish pastors to preach faith and good works in such a way that neither is impugned. The preaching of good works, says Rhegius, should season the sermon with a little theological salt.[63] The concentration on these issues and the use of Scripture passages like Luke 24 to explicate them were determined by the situation

Rhegius faced in educating the first generation of Protestant clergy and laity.

For the shape of Lutheranism, however, there was a further implication. The basis and scope of Lutheran teaching was broadened beyond Luther to include the practical concerns and theological perspective of superintendents like Rhegius. Rhegius by no means rejected Luther; on the contrary, among Protestant leaders there was no more ardent admirer of Luther.[64] Even he was aware, however, that Protestant claims had to avoid too much dependence on Luther in order to establish their validity. In practical ways Rhegius demonstrated that Luther was not the only true exegete. Part of his advice to younger preachers was to study Melanchthon's commentaries on Romans and Colossians and Bucer's commentary on Romans in addition to Luther on Galatians.[65] Also, Rhegius knew and used Luther's translations of Old Testament books, but he sometimes preferred to rely on his own knowledge of Hebrew and deviate from Luther's interpretations.

This independence befit Rhegius's own apostolic and catechetical principles, according to which the interpretation of any one exegete had to be placed in the broader context of the faith of the church. The rule also applied to Luther, and Rhegius's willingness to learn from the early church and from other reformers may have contributed to the critical stance against Luther which later marked the University of Helmstedt.[66] Be that as it may, at the end of the Hannover church order Rhegius argued that Protestant doctrine did not depend on the exegesis or preaching of any individual teacher such as Luther. Instead he appealed to a passage which undergirded both his principles and, as far as he could see, did not need to be put into context. Protestants believed their doctrine, he asserted, regardless of who taught it, for the sake of him who said in the first place: "Repent and believe in the gospel" (Mark 1:15).[67]

III

Notes

The Use of Scripture in Establishing Protestantism

1. The only complete biography of Rhegius is still the older work by Gerhard Uhlhorn, *Urbanus Rhegius: Leben und ausgewählte Schriften* (Elberfeld: Friderichs, 1861). For an updated treatment of many aspects of Rhegius's early career

and a summary of the literary treatment of this Reformer, consult Maximilian Liebmann, *Urbanus Rhegius und die Anfänge der Reformation* (Münster: Aschendorff, 1980). The second part of his career has been studied in several works by Richard Gerecke: "Studien zu Urbanus Rhegius' kirchenregimentlicher Tätigkeit in Norddeutschland," *Jahrbuch der Gesellschaft für niedersächsische Kirchengeschichte* 74 (1976): 131–77 (hereinafter *JGNKG*); "Die Neuordnung des Kirchenwesens in Lüneburg," *JGNKG* 77 (1979): 25–95; "Urbanus Rhegius als Superintendent in Lüneburg (1532–1533)," in *Reformation vor 450 Jahren: Eine Lüneburgische Gedenkschrift* (Lüneburg: Museumsverein für das Fürstentum Lüneburg, 1980), 71–93. Liebmann's book contains the best bibliography of Rhegius's works in both manuscripts and printed editions.

2. For the role of Rhegius in the Reformation in Augsburg see, in addition to Liebmann, Friedrich Roth, *Augsburgs Reformationsgeschichte 1517–1530*, 4 vols., 2d ed. (Munich: Ackermann, 1901–).

3. Liebmann, *Urbanus Rhegius*, 102, n. 239, and 341, Mss 1 and 2.

4. On Reisch, see *Correspondence of Erasmus* (Toronto: University of Toronto Press, 1976), 3:37. Reisch also taught Capito; see Beate Stierle, *Capito als Humanist*, Quellen und Forschungen zur Reformationsgeschichte 42 (Gütersloh: Gerd Mohn, 1974), 30 (hereinafter QFRG). On Reuchlin, see Ludwig Geiger, *Das Studium der Hebräischen Sprache in Deutschland vom Ende des XV. bis zur Mitte des XVI. Jahrhunderts* (Breslau: Schletter'sche Buchhandlung, 1870), 30. Reuchlin, however, did not live in Ingolstadt until late 1519, after Rhegius had left the city; Geiger, *Johann Reuchlin: sein Leben und seine Werke* (Leipzig: Duncker and Humblot, 1871), 461–62.

5. Geiger, *Das Studium*, 41–48, 109. See James Kittelson, *Wolfgang Capito: From Humanist to Reformer*, Studies in Medieval and Reformation Thought 17 (Leiden: Brill, 1975), 21–22 (hereinafter SMRT); see also Stierle, *Capito*, 34–35. On Adrianus, see *Correspondence of Erasmus*, 4:301, 40n; 5:191, 11n.

6. Uhlhorn, *Rhegius: Leben*, 219.

7. A typical case is his discussion of the meaning of "fool" (נָבָל) in Psalm 14:1. For Rhegius the word connotes not a simpleton but a person whose heart is perverted and who has bad intentions. This interpretation includes the sinner in all people according to Paul in Romans 3. *Der XIIII. Psalm inn eil ausgelegt / durch D. Urbanum Regium / an einen guten freund* (Magdeburg: Michael Lotther, 1536), Aiiii verso–B verso.

8. *Perbrevis ratio fructuose studendi in sacris literis . . .* , in *Opera Urbani Regii latine edita* (Nuremberg: Johannes Montanus and Ulrich Neuber, 1562), pt. 3, XIV verso.

9. Ibid., XV recto: "In Testamento veteri placet, ut legas quotidie caput unum vel duo. Et idiotismos hebręos, quos Monsterus, vel alii eius linguae periti ostendunt, diligenter observabis, et cum septuaginta interpretum versione, vel

communi, quae graeca est, conferes, quae quidem collatio mirum in modum iuvabit te, ut verum scripturae sensum eruas, et dono spiritus sancti consequaris."
10. Liebmann, *Urbanus Rhegius,* 192–93.

11. *Ain kurtze erklärung etlicher leüſſiger puncten aim yeden Christen nutz und not zů rechtē verstand der hailigē geschrifft zů dienst; Die zwòlff artickel unsers Christlichē glaubens mit anzaigūg d hailigen geschrifft....* Both of these works were first published in Augsburg in 1523. See Liebmann, *Urbanus Rhegius,* 372–73 (D 41 and D 42).

12. Johannes Freder, *Epistola dedicatoria,* in Rhegius, *Prophetiae veteris testamenti de Christo collectae et explicatae* (Frankfurt: Peter Brubach, 1542), ii verso.

13. Ibid. Rhegius's work: *Dialogus von der schönen predigt die Christus Luc. 24. von Jerusalem bis gen Emaus den zweien júngern am Ostertag aus Mose und allen Propheten gethan hat* (Wittenberg: Josef Klug, 1537). See Liebmann, *Urbanus Rhegius,* 396 (D 115).

14. *Eine ungehewre wunderbarliche Absolution der Closterfrawen jm Fürstenthumb Lüneburg...* (Wittenberg: Georg Rhau, 1532), Aii verso.

15. Ibid., Aiii recto.

16. Ibid., B–Bii verso.

17. Ibid., Dii verso.

18. Uhlhorn, *Rhegius: Leben,* 217–18, calls it the chief goal of Rhegius, especially the education of clergy.

19. *Wie man fürsichtiglich und ohne Ärgerniss reden soll von den fürnemesten Artikeln christlicher Lehre (Formulae quaedam caute et citra scandalum loquendi),* ed. Alfred Uckeley (Leipzig: Deichert [Böhme], 1908). The Latin version was printed first by Hans Lufft in Wittenberg in 1535. See Liebmann, *Urbanus Rhegius,* 390 (D 101).

20. *Examen episcopi in Ducatu Luneburgensi* (Erfurt: Sturmer, 1538). For a discussion of the date of the *Examen* and its content, see Ferdinand Cohrs, "Urbanus Rhegius' 'Examen episcopi in ducatu Luneburgensi,' 1536 (?). Ein Beitrag zur Geschichte des Prüfungswesens in der evangelischen Kirche," in *Studien zur Reformationsgeschichte und zur praktischen Theologie. Gustav Kawerau an seinem 70. Geburtstage dargebracht* (Leipzig: M. Heinsius Nachfolger, 1917), 57–69. Cohrs suspected but did not know of the existence of the 1538 Erfurt edition. It was reprinted in Frankfurt in 1545.

21. *Examen,* A2 verso.

22. Ibid., A4 recto, A5 recto.

23. Gerecke, in *Reformation vor 450 Jahren,* 83.

24. *Abdias propheta explanatus commentariolo....* (Magdeburg: Lotther, 1537), A2 verso. See Waldemar Bahrdt, *Geschichte der Reformation der Stadt Hannover* (Hannover: Hahn'sche Buchhandlung, 1891), 101–2.

III

Notes to Pages 41–44

25. See Hermann Beck, *Die Erbauungsliteratur der evangelischen Kirche Deutschlands. Erster Teil von Dr. M. Luther bis Martin Moller* (Erlangen: Deichert, 1883), 40–41; Bahrdt, *Geschichte*, 106.

26. In *Perbrevis ratio* (see above, n. 5), and in *Alia ratio tractandi scripturas sacras quibusdam verbi ministris praescripta*, in Rhegius, *Opera*, 3:XV verso–XVI verso.

27. *Alia ratio*, XV verso–XVI recto. *Perbrevis ratio*, XIV verso: "Et cum novum testamentum sit expositio veteris et velut clavis." See *Abdias*, D8v: "At novum Testamentum, quod est lux veteris, abunde docet, qualis sit Rex noster Messias in Prophetis promissus."

28. *Perbrevis ratio*, XV recto.

29. *Alia ratio*, XV verso–XVI recto.

30. *Dialogus*, 3v. Citations are from the 1539 edition published in Wittenberg by Josef Klug.

31. Ibid., 1 verso.

32. Ibid., 295 recto–96 recto.

33. *Abdias*, A3 verso: "Diversitas est in tempore, caeterum in doctrina, quantum ad mysteria Christi attinet, nulla est, nisi quod Prophetae cecinere futurum Christum, Nos exhibitum et praesentem docemus. . . . Eadem est docendi ratio, quantum ad doctrinae summam attinet, in Prophetis et Evangelistis. Summa Apostolicae doctrinae haec est, ut Acto. 20. legimus, poenitentia et fides in Christum."

34. *Dialogus*, 9 recto: "Denn Christus wird auff zweierley weis inn der Schrifft verkündiget / Einmal durch tunckele Verheissung / und figuren von ferns her. Zum andern / durch klare Verheissung / und helle ausgedruckte wort."

35. *Alia ratio*, XVI recto. Although the stated purpose of the *Dialogus* was to confirm the truth of the New Testament through the Old, it is likely that Rhegius also had another purpose in mind. The accumulation of messianic passages could be an answer to the anthology of Jewish anti-Christian apologetic called the *Nizzahon*, which was a medieval rebuttal of the messianic interpretation of the Old Testament that Rhegius knew well. For a detailed discussion of this possibility, see my forthcoming article: "Toleration of the Jews in the German Reformation: Urbanus Rhegius and Braunschweig (1535–1540)," *Archiv für Reformationsgeschichte* 81 (1990).

36. *Abdias*, C5 verso: "Caveant igitur et nostri Edomitae Evangelii persecutores, qui palam nunc Edomiticum in nos animum declarant, et dicere non verentur, se male contra nos bella gerere, quam contra Turcas."

37. *Abdias*, D4 verso: "Haec verbosius tractavi propter nostros Anabaptistas Καθα ρῶς et Novatianos, qui reliquiis peccatorum etiamnum in nobis grassantibus ita offenduntur, ut putent nullam esse Ecclesiam nisi plane perfecta adsit sanctitas, in qua porro nihil queat desiderari." Ibid., D5 verso–D6 recto: "Hinc

III

etiam confunditur pestifera vanitas Pharisaeorum nostrorum id est Monachorum
et monacharum, vocant enim ordines suos sanctos formaliter et effective, quasi
sancti sint et alios sanctificent."

38. Ibid., D7 recto: "Iam vide Acta et Epistolas Apostolorum, et invenies
possessionem illam praeclaram, cuius Abdias meminit. . . . Sicque nationes quae
antea iuxta carnem possederunt Iudaeos, tandem a Iudaeis Apostolis et eorum
successoribus, factae sunt possessiones domus Iacob, id est, per Evangelii prae-
dicationem in Ecclesiam Christi congregatae sunt. Et hic est verus Prophetae
sensus." Ibid., D7 verso–D8 recto: "Et quod horrendum est auditu, etiam hodie
velamen cordibus Iudaeorum et Iudaisantium quorundam impositum est, ut
legem et Prophetas de Christi regno vaticinantes nequeant intelligere, somniant
enim talem Messiam in lege et Prophetis promissum, quo Chanaan occupet et
omnes gentes suo subdat imperio. . . . Fuit mihi cum Recutitis acre certamen
annis plus minus viginti de Messia et regno eius, qui semper hos et similes locos
carnali sensu tractatos mihi obiecerunt." Ibid., D8 verso: "Verum ubi idiotismos
Hebraicae linguae et circumstantias omnes exacte animadvertimus, haud difficile
fuerit intelligere, Christi servos Prophetas, de rebus longe maioribus nempe
spiritualibus et aeternis, non ex ratione humana, sed instinctu spiritus sancti
vaticinatos, quam sint omnia huius visibilis mundi regna cum omni potentia,
honore, splendore, opulentia et apparatu seculari, quod ut rudioribus planum
fiat, recensebo aliquot circumstantias vaticiniorum de regno Christi, ex quibus
facile intelligemus, Prophetas de regno spirituali et aeterno non corporali
locutos."

39. *Alia ratio,* XVI verso: "Proderit et hoc plurimum in docendo populum, si
omnia Evangelia, quae per anni circulum se offerunt enarranda, ita excutiamus,
ut semper ad aliquem Catechismi articulum ea referamus. Sic enim non solum
Catechismus memoriis hominum firmius insculpetur, sed etiam Evangelia intel-
ligentur clarius, et velut ad usum transferentur, atque in omnes vitae casus,
semper velut remedium facilius depromentur."

40. For a detailed discussion of Rhegius's use of the church fathers, see Scott H.
Hendrix, "Validating the Reformation: The Use of the Church Fathers by
Urbanus Rhegius," in *Ecclesia Militans. Studien zur Konzilien- und Reformationsgeschichte,* ed. Walter Brandmüller, Herbert Immenkötter, and Erwin Iserloh, 2 vols. (Paderborn: Schöningh, 1988), 2:281–305.

41. *Alia ratio,* XVI recto: "Non igitur adferas vel sensum sine scripturis, ut
Anabaptistae, vel scripturas in sensu, qui fidei non est analogus, sed adfer
scripturas in sensu Ecclesiastico, hoc est, in eo sensu, qui semper a temporibus
Apostolorum fuit in Ecclesia orientali et occidentali. Neque enim scripturae
intellectus extra Ecclesiam Catholicam invenitur, et spiritus sanctus Ecclesiam, ut
suum templum, et suam domum inhabitat, haereticorum Synagogas execratur."

42. Uhlhorn, *Rhegius: Leben,* 220.

43. *Alia ratio,* XV verso.

44. *Ein Sermon von den guten und bösen Engeln/zu Hannover geprediget durch D. Urbanum Rhegium* (Wittenberg: Josef Klug, 1538), E recto: "Derhalben der Christlichen Kirchen glaube allzeit aus der Schrifft gewesen ist / das ein jeglicher seinen eigen Engel habe / Wie Basilius magnus / de spiritu sancto schreibet / als einen Zuchtmeister und hirten / der im sen leben richte." Ibid., Eii verso–F recto: "Die Schrifft leret uns / man sol vertrawen und hoffnung inn niemands setzen / denn inn den einigen / waren Gott / und sollen auch inn der not allein den selbigen / als den waren nothelffer anrüffen / wie wir im ersten und andern gebot lernen / und die Schrifft spricht. . . . Höret aber / was man vor tausend jaren inn der Christenheit von der Engel anbeten gehalten habe / damit ir nicht argwonig seiet / ich lere hierinn etwas newes / Augustinus uber den xcvi. Psalm spricht also."

45. *Alia ratio,* XVI verso.

46. Ibid.

47. *Abdias,* B8 verso–C recto: "Et haec omnia pertinent ad primum praeceptum de fide et spe. In solum enim Deum in omni tribulatione sperandum est, solus enim ex vult et potest nos ex malis omnibus eripere, sicut apud Isaiam ait cap. 43. Ego sum, Ego sum Dominus, et non est absque me salvator, et non est qui de manu mea eruat [Is. 43:11, 13].

48. *Der XIIII. Psalm,* Aii verso: "Ein jeglicher tregt im busen diesen Nabal / das ist / ein solchen Gottlosen thoren. . . . Drück den Nabal mit dem ersten und andern gepott / und frag / ob er trew an seinem trewen Gott gehalten hab / so wirt er bekennen müssen / Es fehle im allenthalb inn Gottes gepoten / und sonderlich inn der ersten tafel Mosi. Denn wiewol er list inn der schrifft / an der predig hört / und inn teglichen gutthaten leibs und der seel von Gott gegeben / erfert und greifft / das ein Gott ist / und das er warhafftig / trew und barmhertzig ist." Ibid., B recto: "Wenn man nu das erst gepot nicht helt / so ists unmöglich / das man die andern halte nach Gottes befehl / denn wer inn seinem hertzen Gott nicht recht kent / nichts nach im fragt / der ist Gottlos odder glaublos / wie kan denn der mund im andern gepott / Gottes namen preisen."

49. Ibid., Ciiii verso.

50. *Kirchenordnung der statt Hannofer durch D. Urbanum Regium,* in *Die evangelischen Kirchenordnungen des XVI. Jahrhunderts,* ed. Emil Sehling (Tübingen: Mohr [Siebeck], 1957), pt. 6/1, vol. 2, p. 1004: "Und dieweil unser widerpart saget, wir predigen neue lere, müssen sich auch unsere prediger befleissen, alle artikel christlicher lere daran unser heil ligt, mit zeugnis der alten kirchen zu befestigen, auf das die einfeltigen klar sehen, wie unser lere nicht neu, sondern die rechte, alte christliche lere ist, wie sie in der christlichen kirchen in der ganzen welt vor tausent jaren gehalten und gepredigt worden ist."

51. *Absolution,* C verso.

52. Uhlhorn, *Rhegius: Leben,* 220.

53. *Alia ratio,* XVI recto.

54. Uckeley (ed.), 63: "Diesen spruch zihe ich nicht vergeblich an, denn er von vielen Ungelehrten gerhümet wird, als werden darin gelobt die, so keine schrifft lernen noch wissen, und meinen, sie haben allhie für sich Gottes wort, dadurch alle löbliche künste, da zu die Heilige Schrifft, verworffen werden."

55. Ibid., 64: "Hie redet Christus von der gemeinen lere des Evangelii, so jederman zur seligkeit von nöten ist, dadurch wir Christum lernen erkennen, das er sey umb unser willen mensch worden, und an in als unsern einigen Heiland gleuben. Durch diese lere werden gewislich alle ausserwelten erleucht, und wer die selbige nicht hat, der mus verloren werden. Aber uber diese gemeine lere und erkenntnis ist ein ander kunst und sonderlicher verstand inn der Christenheit, welchs heisst die gabe der Weissagung, damit nicht on unterscheid alle Christen begnadet werden, sondern ettliche so der Christenheit furstehen sollen inn der lere, das sie die heilige Schrifft auslegen, zur besserung, zur vermanung, zu trostung."

56. *Kirchenordnung,* pt. 6/1, vol. 2, p. 1000: "Erstlich, dieweil Paulus, 1. Corin. 14 (28:26), ordnet, das der in der kirchen schweigen sol, der die schrift nicht kan auslegen, und das alle ding in der gemeine sollen zur besserung geschehen, so hat uns dis gebot gedrungen, die bepstischen priester, die auf ihrem irthum harren abzustellen; denn sie können die schrift in der kirchen nicht auslegen nach der schnur des apostolischen verstands."

57. Liebmann, *Urbanus Rhegius,* 265–67, 279–85.

58. Rhegius mentions the *Unterricht* in his discussion of schools in the Hannover church order; see *Kirchenordnung,* pt. 6/1, vol. 2, p. 1011.

59. Melanchthon, *Unterricht der Visitatoren,* in *Melanchthons Werke in Auswahl,* ed. Robert Stupperich, 7 vols. (Gütersloh: Bertelsmann/Gerd Mohn, 1951), 1:221.8–222.27, 244.1–3.

60. *Wie man fürsichtiglich,* 31.

61. *Examen,* A2 verso: "Evangelium duo tradit, Lucae ult. 1. Poenitentiam. 2. Remissionem peccatorum. In iss duabus partibus universa scriptura comprehenditur." Cf. *Abdias,* D verso: "Dein et per Apostolos lex vitae et verbum Evangelii exivit de Zion in totum orbem, quae lex est doctrina de poenitentia et remissione peccatorum sub nomine Christi in omnes gentes sparsa initio facto, ut Lucas ait, ab Ierosolymis."

62. That controversy led Melanchthon in the *Unterricht* to stress the necessity of preaching repentance. Melanchthon says that his experience in the Saxon visitation first led him to define contrition as the beginning of repentance. See *Melanchthons Briefwechsel,* vol. 1, *Regesten 1–1109 (1514–1530),* ed. Heinz Scheible (Stuttgart–Bad Cannstatt: Frommann-Holzboog, 1977), no. 604, pp. 270–71. One

can follow the beginning of the controversy in the summaries of Melanchthon's correspondence beginning with this letter to Caspar Aquila written in October 1527.

63. *Wie man fürsichtiglich*, 45–49, 58–61. *Examen*, A5 verso–A6 recto: "Quomodo de bonis operibus loquendum, ut sermo Episcopi sit conditus sale theologico. . . . Hic serio monendus Epicopus, ut sic praedicet opera, ne qua fiat contumelia gratiae CHRISTI. Rursus sic vehat magnificam CHRISTI gratiam, ne qua fiat contumelia operibus bonis, hoc est, ne contemnantur vel negligantur."

64. On his way from Augsburg to Lüneburg in 1530 Rhegius stopped at Coburg to meet Luther personally for the first time and to plead the case for concord between Bucer and the Wittenbergers. Later, Rhegius recalled the day spent with Luther as the happiest day of his life and praised Luther as a theologian without equal in any age. These comments were excerpted from letters addressed by Rhegius from Lüneburg to friends in south Germany in 1534; the excerpts were published independently in 1545 under the title *Iudicium D. Urbani Rhegii de D. Martino Luthero*. The *Iudicum* was printed at the end of a collection of patristic and theological sources used by Rhegius and published posthumously by Johannes Freder as *Loci theologici* (Frankfurt: Peter Braubach, 1545), 251 verso–252 recto.

65. *Perbrevis ratio*, XV verso.

66. This stance critical of Luther and its history at the university is discussed in detail by Inge Mager, "Reformatorische Theologie und Reformationsverständnis an der Universität Helmstedt im 16. und 17. Jahrhundert," *JGNKG* 74 (1976): 11–33.

67. *Kirchenordnung*, pt. 6/1, vol. 2, pp. 1014–15: "Ob aber unser gegenpart sagte, es werde das evangelium niemands verboten, sonders des Luthers lere, die wir angenomen haben, dazu antworten wir, das wir keins menschen lere, er habe namen, wie er wölle, angenomen haben, sondern das ware, reine evangelium Jhesu Christi, welchs durch den heiligen Geist vom himel herab gesand ist, und verstehen dasselbige evangelium in allen artikeln unsers heiligen glaubens, wie es die apostel gelert und die christliche kirche allzeit verstanden und gehalten hat. Dieweil aber D. M. Lutherus aus sonderlicher gnade Gottes dasselbige evangelium dem deudschen land rein, apostolisch, one menschenlere und verfelschung in sensu ecclesiastico, wie es sich in einem christlichen generalconcilio in der warheit erfinden wird, wider herfurgebracht und geprediget hat, so nennen unsere widerwertigen solch evangelium des Luthers lere, auf das sie der unschuldigen lere ihr glaubwirdigkeit hinnemen und ihr menschenlere wider vertedingen mögen. . . . Darumb sagen wir also: es predige das evangelium Luther oder andere, so söllen wirs gleuben, nicht umb Luthers willen, sonder umb des willen, der gar ernstlich gebeut, Mar. 1 [15]: Bessert euch und gleubet dem evangelio."

IV

Validating the Reformation:
The Use of the Church Fathers
by Urbanus Rhegius

By the Leipzig Disputation (1519) at the latest, it became obvious that the controversy between Luther and the Roman Church would focus on the question whether Luther's teaching was old or new. For Luther's opponents, among them Cajetan and Eck, the Wittenberg theologians were teaching something new about the sacrament of penance and ecclesiastical authority.[1] Like John Hus, with whom Eck identified Luther and whom Luther notoriously defended,[2] the Wit-

---

[1] In the account of his meeting with Cajetan at Augsburg, Luther began the defense of his seventh thesis with this comment about his opponents (WA 2,13.10): *Hanc theologiam n o v a m videri putant et erroneam.* Cajetan had already written that Luther's position amounted to "building a new church". For a fuller discussion, see S. HENDRIX, Luther and the Papacy: Stages in a Reformation Conflict, Philadelphia 1981, 61 f., 173 (n. 74); O.H. PESCH, "Das heisst eine neue Kirche bauen"; Luther und Cajetan in Augsburg, in: Begegnung. Beitr. zu einer Hermeneutik des theol. Gesprächs, ed. M. SECKLER et al., Graz 1972, 645-661. The charge of novelty continued to be levelled at reformers by Catholic theologians. One of them, Johannes Dietenberger (✝ 1537), defined in his "Phimostomus scripturariorum" (1532) what constituted the "nova dogmata" of the reformers and whether they should be accepted if they could not be disproved with specific texts of Scripture. See U. HORST, O.P., Das Verhältnis von Heiliger Schrift und Kirche nach Johannes Dietenberger, in: ThPh 46 (1971) 223-247, here 226.

[2] See S. HENDRIX, "We Are All Hussites"? Hus and Luther Revisited, in: ARG 65 (1974) 134-161, here 138-141.

282

tenbergers were to be regarded as heretics who not only questioned papal authority but also departed from the theological consensus of the early church. The Wittenbergers responded to the charge of novelty by arguing that their appeal to Scripture was an appeal to the oldest and so far the only divinely-given authority for the church.[3] Their teaching was not a novelty but a recovery and reassertion of the gospel which, in their view, had been suppressed in the late medieval church.

In this clash of claims about what was old and new, the church fathers were caught in the middle. At the Leipzig Debate, they were accepted as authorities by both sides, but that authority possessed a different value for Eck than it did for Luther. For Eck, the authority of the fathers provided a positive safeguard against the misguided individual interpretation of Scripture that could result in heresy.[4] In fact, Luther's criticism of his appeal to the fathers[5] led Eck to make precisely this charge against Luther by mocking his lack of monastic humility and by associating Luther with Hus.[6] For the Roman hierarchy,

---

[3] Luther's response to Cajetan's charge of novelty and error was to list numerous passages from Scripture and one reference each to Augustine and Bernard which were in turn supported by passages from Scripture (WA 2,13.12-16.5). This appeal to Scripture backed by the fathers as the oldest norm of truth was articulated formally and forcefully for the first time by Luther at the Leipzig Debate (WA 59,466.1059-1066): *Nec est in potestate Romani pontificis aut inquisitoris haereticae pravitatis, novos condere articulos fidei, sed secundum conditos iudicare. Nec potest fidelis Christianus cogi ultra sacram scripturam, quae est proprie ius divinum, nisi accesserit nova et probata revelatio. Immo ex iure divino prohibemur credere, nisi quod sit probatum, vel per scripturam divinam vel per manifestam revelationem, ut Gerson etiam etsi recentior in multis locis asserit, et divus Augustinus antiquior pro singulari canone observat, . . .*

[4] See Eck's remark in defense of his interpretation of Matthew 17:27 (WA 59,523.2803-2807): *At ego non meo capite sed sanctorum patrum verba sacrae scripturae accipio. Nam ex hoc beatus Ambrosius voluit denotatum Petrum reliquis superiorem futurum, quod et Augustinus in Quaestionibus evangeliorum testatur expressissime. Quare nostro sensui non innitamur sed sanctis patribus.*

[5] WA 59,464.989-992. *Dominus doctor Eccius voluit iure divino probare, et mox sui oblitus incidit in auctoritates patrum, quas pro maiore parte iam tractavimus, et vidimus eos in diversis locis diversa aliquando sensisse, et multo plures et saepius pro me quam pro domino doctore Eccio.*

[6] WA 59,470.1174-1181: *Sed quam modeste et humiliter reverendus pater Augustinianus responderit, aliorum sit iudicium, cum unus se promiserit tot sanctis patribus se oppositurum. Hoc est verum Bohemicum, plus velle intelligere sacram*

an attack upon the fathers was tantamount to asserting that the Holy Spirit had deserted the church and deceived the faithful.[7] The fathers were a critical link in the tradition of teaching that included conciliar and papal decrees along with Scripture itself. If the church's official and oft-canonized teachers had falsely interpreted Scripture, the church's credibility was severely undermined. The papal bull "Exsurge Domino" demonstrated how untenable such an admission would have been for the Roman Church.[8]

At Leipzig Luther debated with vigor those passages from the fathers which Eck cited against him. He also valued the authority of the fathers and had claimed their authority alongside canon law and Scripture in the defense of his "Ninety-five Theses".[9] The debate with

---

scripturam, quam summi pontifices, concilia, doctores et universitates in magno vigore existentes, cum tamen spiritus sanctus ecclesian suam non deseruerit. Et mirum esset, si illam veritatem deus tot sanctis et martyribus occultasset usque ad adventum reverendi patris.

[7] This danger was articulated in popular form by Johann Rubius in the poem which he published about the debate in order to defend Eck: "Ein neues Büchlein von der löblichen Disputation in Leipzig" (1519). Rubius not only criticized the possibility that the church had been in error and that the fathers had not understood Scripture, but he also admonished his readers to remain true to the old faith of their ancestors: A. LAUBE, S. LOOSS, A. SCHNEIDER (ed.), Flugschriften der frühen Reformationsbewegung (1518-1524), II, Vaduz 1983, 1274.26-27,30-35: *Sol die christliche kirche gestanden seyn yn yrthum bisz hie her,/ ich hoff wir wollen gar balt horen neue mer./ .../Ir solt genczlich gleuben und nit dar an czweyffel,/ das die vier lerer und ander lerer yczund yn dem hymel/ solden nit verstande haben von den heyligen geyst die schrifft,/ das wer warlich allen christen menschen ein grosse gyfft./ Lat uns gleuben was unser forfarn glauben,/ so wirt uns Got auch den hymel mit tylen.*

[8] In: C. MIRBT - K. ALAND (ed.), Quellen zur Geschichte des Papsttums und des römischen Katholizismus I, Tübingen [6]1967, 508: *Nam ex eisdem erroribus, vel eorum aliquo, vel aliquibus, palam sequitur, eamdem Ecclesiam, quae Spiritu Sancto regitur, errare, et semper errasse. Quod est utique contra illud, quod Christus discipulis suis in Ascensione sua (ut in sancto Evangelio Matthaei legitur) promisit dicens, "Ego vobiscum sum usque ad consummationem saeculi"; Necnon contra sanctorum Patrum determinationes, Conciliorum quoque, et Summorum Pontificum expressas ordinationes, seu canones, quibus non obtemperasse, omnium haeresum, et schismatum, teste Cypriano, fomes, et causa semper fuit.*

[9] Resolutiones disputationum de indulgentiarum virtute 1518 (WA 1,529.33-530.1): *Primum protestor, me prorsus nihil dicere aut tenere velle, nisi quod in et ex sacris literis primo, deinde Ecclesiasticis patribus, ab Ecclesia Romana receptis, hu-*

284

Eck, however, disabused Luther of the notion that he could claim the authority of church fathers and councils uncritically for himself. The result was not a complete rejection of other authorities besides Scripture, but rather a nuanced hierarchy of authorities in which Scripture exercised the normative critical function.[10] For example, in response to Eck's citation of Bernard against him, Luther asserted that he respected Bernard, but in debate only that genuine and proper sense of Scripture ought to be accepted which was able to stand up in battle.[11] Church fathers and councils would henceforth play an important but secondary and selective role in the defense of Protestant teaching.

The reformers believed that their teaching was both old and new: old, in the sense that it was a recovery of the gospel; and new, in the sense that it was a rediscovery and reassertion of a truth that had been distorted and buried during the preceding centuries. Accordingly, the purpose of citing the church fathers by Luther's followers was twofold: to refute the claims of their opponents that Protestant teaching was new in the sense of novel and heretical; and, where they could claim precedent for their teaching in the fathers, to demonstrate that their doctrine stood in the orthodox catholic consensus forged by the early church.

These purposes led to a critical and sometimes ambivalent stance toward the fathers by Protestant theologians. They cited the fathers frequently and sometimes with enthusiasm, but their writings also betray curious lapses in attention to the fathers and a wariness about conceding too much authority to them. This ambivalence toward the fathers abated, however, as its mainline spokesmen began to view the Reformation in historical perspective. Gradually, Protestant theologians called upon the church fathers to give their new teaching the validity that Scripture alone was not able to impart.

---

cusque servatis, et ex Canonibus ac decretalibus Pontificiis habetur et haberi potest. See HENDRIX, Luther and the Papacy 40-41.

[10] Ebd. 88-89.

[11] WA 59,445.411-415: *Respondeo. Divum Bernardum veneror et eius sententiam non contemno, sed in contentione accipiendus est sensus genuinus et proprius scripturae, qui stare in acie possit; a quo sancti patres nonnunquam locupletandae orationis gratia digrediuntur et sine culpa.*

Nowhere is this critical stance toward the fathers clearer than in the writings of the Augsburg preacher and Lüneburg reformer Urbanus Rhegius (1489-1541). Like Zwingli, Melanchthon and Calvin, whose appreciation of patristic literature has been well documented,[12] Rhegius was trained as a humanist scholar before he became a Protestant theologian. Among the authors of antiquity whom he read as a student, patristic writers were certainly represented. His most influential theological mentor prior to reading Luther was John Eck, whom he followed to Ingolstadt in 1512 and praised extravagantly in several poems.[13] The steady production of theological works that Rhegius initiated in 1518 with a treatise on the priesthood and ended in 1541 with an exposition of the fifty-second psalm could have been peppered throughout with citations from the writings of Christian antiquity.

According to his nineteenth-century biographer, Gerhard Uhlhorn, Rhegius knew the church fathers better than most of his contemporaries and never failed to cite abundant prooftexts from them for his teaching.[14] Indeed, selections from the corpus of Rhegius testify that he knew the fathers well. The most obvious example is the copious collection of citations from the fathers and from more recent theologians which were edited and published by Johannes Freder four years after Rhegius' death. This collection, to which Rhegius had

---

[12] For Zwingli: A. SCHINDLER, Zwingli und die Kirchenväter, Zürich 1984; for Melanchthon: P. FRAENKEL, Testimonia patrum: the Function of the Patristic Argument in the Theology of Philipp Melanchthon, Geneva 1961, and E.P. MEIJERING, Melanchthon and Patristic Thought, Leiden 1983; for Calvin: F. WENDEL, Calvin: the Origin and Development of his Religious Thought, trans. P. MAIRET, London 1963, 123-126. Cf. the notes to Calvin's dedicatory address to Francis I in the 1536 "Institutes", in: Calvin: Institutes of the Christian Religion I (LCC 20), ed. J.T. McNEIL and trans. F.L. BATTLES, Philadelphia 1960, 18-23; cf. Calvini Opera Selecta I, Munich 1926, 27-30. See also P. POLMAN, L'élément historique dans la controverse religieuse du XVIe siècle, Gembloux 1932, 5-94.

[13] M. LIEBMANN, Urbanus Rhegius und die Anfänge der Reformation (RGST 117), Münster 1980, 93-96.

[14] G. UHLHORN, Urbanus Rhegius. Leben und ausgewählte Schriften, Elberfeld 1861, 219: "Die Kirchenväter kannte Rhegius selbst wie wenige seiner Zeitgenossen. Jede seiner Schriften gibt davon Zeugnis; niemals versäumt er, für seine Lehre auch Beweisstellen aus den Vätern in großer Anzahl beizubringen."

IV

286

given the title "Loci Theologici,"[15] was offered to Freder by his widow. In their published form, the "Loci" contain 502 pages of citations from a variety of authors on fifty-nine theological topics. According to Freder, Rhegius did not intend for these citations to be published; rather, he collected them as he studied in order to have them as a ready reference when he was writing.[16] Although it is uncertain when he started this collection, for most of his career Rhegius was probably armed with a growing arsenal of quotes from his predecessors. This allusion to combat was made by Freder, in whose eyes the adversaries of the Protestants had distorted the fathers. Hence, evangelical theologians like Rhegius had to equip themselves with the fathers correctly cited and interpreted as they marched into literary battle.[17]

Besides the bulk of evidence provided by the "Loci", several other works demonstrate that Rhegius dealt explicitly with patristic material. Freder quoted from the "iudicium" of Cyprian's treatise on almsgiving[18] that Rhegius had written in response to a friend's query but which was not published until after his death.[19] In 1521, while he was still the cathedral preacher in Augsburg, Rhegius published a German translation of Cyprian's exposition of the Lord's Prayer, an exposition that Rhegius called "very beautiful and useful".[20] In the same

[15] Loci Theologici e patribus et scholasticis neotericisque collecti per D. Urbanum Rhegium, Frankfurt 1545 = LIEBMANN D140 (= the modern critical bibliography of Rhegius' works in LIEBMANN 319-416). Sixteenth-century collections of his Latin and German works were promoted by Rhegius' son, Ernst, and printed in 1562 in Nürnberg: Opera Urbani Regii latine edita, and: Urbani Regii weylandt Superintendenten im Fürstenthumb Lüneburg Deutsche Bücher und Schrifften, Nürnberg 1562.

[16] For the practice of excerpting see W. BRÜCKNER (ed.), Volkserzählung und Reformation. Ein Handbuch zur Tradierung und Funktion von Erzählstoffen und Erzählliteratur im Protestantismus, Berlin 1974, 63-75.

[17] See Freder's dedication of the published Loci to George of Anhalt, in: Loci Theologici 4-5ᵛ.

[18] De opere et eleemosynis, in: CSEL III/1, 373-394.

[19] Iudicium Urbani Rhegii de Cypriani libello, quem de Eleemosyna inscripsit, secundum canonem Scripturae Sanctae, & Orthodoxos, Frankfurt 1545 = LIEBMANN D141, in: Opera latine edita II, XLIIIᵛ-XLVᵛ.

[20] Ain uberschöne und nützliche erklärung über das Vater unser des hailigen Cecilij Cypriani durch Urbanum Regium der hayligen geschrift Doctor verteutscht, Augsburg 1521 = LIEBMANN D30, in: Deutsche Bücher und Schrifften I, LXXXIXᵛ-XCVIII.

year he translated a sermon by John Chrysostom which, as Rhegius noted in the title, argued that the dead benefitted from the good works of the living.[21] Sometime during the five years preceding the Diet of Augsburg (1530), Rhegius published his last translation of a patristic work, a summary of the main doctrines of the faith attributed to Athanasius.[22]

The topic that finally took Rhegius beyond translation into a detailed discussion of the church fathers was the mass. While still in Augsburg, Rhegius prepared for his colleague Johann Frosch a collection of material from Scripture and from the early church which could be used to study the mass.[23] Their discussion of this topic was generated in part by the publication in 1526 of John Eck's three books on the sacrifice of the mass.[24] In Book Two, Eck assembled passages from church fathers, early popes, and councils to support his contention that the mass was itself a sacrifice and not, as he accused the reformers (including Rhegius) of having maintained, just a memorial of the sacrifice on the cross.[25]

According to letters exchanged between Eck and Rhegius in 1527 or 1528,[26] their disagreement over this question led to a final, bitter

---

[21] Ain schöne Predig des hailgen Bischoffs Joannis Chrisostomi. Das man die sünder lebendig und tod klagen und bewainen sol. Das auch der lebendigen guten werck den todten nützlich seyen, Augsburg 1521 = LIEBMANN D29, in: Deutsche Bücher und Schrifften I, CCXL^V-CCXLIIII^V.

[22] Die rechten haupt puncten unsers heyligen Christlichen glaubens durch Athanasium zusamen gezogen, Augsburg 1525-1530 = LIEBMANN D79. The work by Athanasius could be the "Expositio fidei" or the "Sermo maior de fide", both attributed either to Eustathius of Antioch or to Marcellus of Ancyra. See J. QUASTEN, Patrology III, Westminster, MD 1983 (1960) 30-31.

[23] Materia cogitandi de toto missae negocio partim ex scripturis, partim è priscae Ecclesiae ruinis eruta, Augsburg 1528 = LIEBMANN D72, in: Opera latine edita I, LVII-LXXV^V. The main issue to be studied was formulated by Rhegius as follows (ebd. LVII^V): *Illud potius perquirendum, cur & quomodo e coena domini facta sit Missa, hoc est, repraesentatio illa caerimoniosa in vestitu, rituque gestuoso, quae hactenus aliquot seculis habita est pro sacrificio iugi in Ecclesia, pro vivis & mortuis.*

[24] J. Eck, De sacrificio missae libri tres, Augsburg 1526, in: CCath 36, ed. E. ISERLOH, V. PFNÜR, P. FABISCH, Münster 1982.

[25] Ebd. III.8.1 (CCath 36, 167 f.).

[26] The correspondence involves three letters, one by Eck dated 1527 and two by Rhegius dated 1527 and 1528, that are printed in Rhegius' Opera latine edita

288

rupture of their friendship. Eck was told that Rhegius had put together a book that "vomited many blasphemies against the holiest sacrifice of the mass." Up to this point, said Eck, he had supported Rhegius and wished the best for him, but now that malice had entered his heart, he had given up hope of Rhegius' salvation and would have to avoid him, as Paul commanded, like a heretic.[27] To justify himself, Rhegius recalled that Eck had advised him to read his books and had promised publicly to respond to any questions which Rhegius might raise. Accordingly, said Rhegius, he reread carefully the books on the mass and, having found them weak, decided to respond, not harshly, but with a few brief arguments that were drawn not from human commentaries, but from canonical Scripture and from prophecies that agreed with the faith – the only source from which Christians should present arms for battle.[28]

These "few brief arguments" circulated in manuscript for two years before they were printed in 1529. By then at the latest, the brief arguments had grown to a book of 264 pages.[29] Perhaps the size of his response persuaded Rhegius to omit a rebuttal to the second book of Eck's work which contained prooftexts from the fathers. Originally, Rhegius intended to respond to that section of Eck's work as well.[30] When the "Responsio" appeared, however, the title identified it as an answer directed specifically to the first and third books of Eck's work.

II, VI[v] and XLII-XLIII. The correct sequence and dating is not yet clear. A case for changing the date of Eck's letter was made by E. ISERLOH, Die Eucharistie in der Darstellung des Johannes Eck (RGST 73/74), Münster 1950, 58-59 n. 11. ISERLOH's arguments are cogent, but he took into account only two of the letters.

[27] Opera latine edita II, XLII.

[28] Ebd. II, VI[v]: *Te itaque sic volente & iubente, libros tuos Missalis sacrificii patronos denuo perlegi, quae infirma videbantur passim annotans, non ut conviciis responderem, sed ut paucis brevibusque argumentis citra virulentiam tecum agerem, idque non ex commentariis hominum, sed scripturis Canonicis, & Prophetiis fidei convenientibus, è quibus solis ad pugnam Christiani sua arma proferunt.*

[29] Responsio Urbani Rhegii ad duos libros primum et tertium de Missa Ioannis Eccij, Augsburg 1529 = LIEBMANN D73, in: Opera latine edita, II, VI[v]-XLI[v].

[30] This conclusion can be drawn from his letter to Eck (supra n.28) where Rhegius said he would respond with Scripture and with "prophecies that agreed with the faith". Elsewhere in this letter to Eck and in at least one other place Rhegius used the term "prophetiae" to refer to statements of the fathers. Cf. Opera latine edita II, XLI; III, LXXIX.

In defending his omission of the fathers, Rhegius did not use the length of his response as an excuse. Instead he argued that the fathers were at best secondary authorities. While he did not despise their "prophecies", he judged what they said according to the criterion of the Apostle Paul (Rom. 12:6) that the gift of prophecy should be exercised according to the measure of faith. Some of Eck's citations from the fathers, if they were correctly examined, would turn out not to oppose Rhegius' position; and in the case of others, because they were further removed from the simplicity of Scripture, it was not worth the effort to search for a congenial interpretation. Finally, asserted Rhegius, even if certain writings of the fathers seemed to support Eck's view of the mass as sacrifice, the evangelical position was adequately protected by Scripture.[31]

Several years later, however, Rhegius did not so lightly dismiss evidence from the church fathers cited by Catholic theologians. In 1532 two evangelical pastors from Braunschweig sent Rhegius a list of twenty citations from the fathers, with which their "haughty opponents" were defending the canon of the mass and other "ungodly teachings". The patristic passages troubled them especially because they seemed to define the mass not just as thanksgiving but as the offering of a sacrifice for the dead. From this teaching, the pastors said, they recoiled in horror as if they had stepped barefoot on a viper.[32]

In reply Rhegius expressed pleasure that the pastors had been reading the fathers "since they were learned and holy bishops of the church whose prophecies should not be spurned." Moreover, in the current storms of controversy, "our faith is not a little confirmed by the statements of the orthodox [fathers] because we see that our teaching agrees with the doctrine of such great men." Rhegius promptly

---

[31] Opera latine edita II, XLI: *Patrum dictis quae tu libro secundo copiose adduxisti, & ego iam vix summis digitis attigi, inter diluendum obiecta, alias respondero. Non enim aspernor Prophetias, sed illud Pauli prae oculis habeo: εἴτε προφητείαν, κατὰ τὴν ἀναλογίαν τῆς πίστεως. Nam quaedam sunt eiusmodi, ut nostram adsertionem, si recte expendantur, non impugnent: nonnulla a scripturae simplicitate alieniora, quam ut in his commode interpretandis multum operae expediat collocare. Denique si maxime quaedam Patrum scripta sic sonent, ut subscribere sententiae tuae videantur, scriptura tamen sancta nostram sententiam confirmante, satis tuti erimus.*

[32] Ebd. III, LXVIII. The list of citations sent by the pastors differs widely from those offered by Eck in his treatise of 1526.

issued a caveat, however. Although the fathers were called orthodox because they held sound and correct doctrine, some of their interpretations of Scripture should be read with discretion since the fathers openly admitted their inability to understand everything.[33]

After that warning, Rhegius argued at length that, despite the language of sacrifice, the fathers never meant that the mass itself was a propitiatory sacrifice which forgave sin. Instead, the mass only recalled the sacrifice of Christ on the cross and presented it to the Father through a faithful remembrance that strengthened faith and gave thanks for the redemption already accomplished.[34] According to Rhegius, the notion that the sacrifice of the mass forgave sin was a papistic corruption of the fathers' teaching. As proof of this accusation, Rhegius cited a passage from the "Sentences" commentary of Thomas Aquinas, which Rhegius knew from Gabriel Biel's exposition of the canon of the mass.[35] Indeed, Biel not only cited Thomas to the

---

[33] Orthodoxorum Patrum Sententiae aliquot de Missali Sacrificio, Wittenberg 1533 = LIEBMANN D97, in: Opera edita latine III, LXXIX: *Primo omnium placet, quod Patrum sententias legitis: Cum enim viri docti & sancti Episcopi Ecclesiae fuerint, non aspernandae sunt eorum Prophetiae. 2. Thessa. 5 [1 Thess. 5.20 f.]. Et fides nostra in his praesertim procellis, Orthodoxorum sententiis non parum confirmatur, quia cernimus nostram Doctrinam tantorum hominum Doctrinae consentire. Vocantur enim orthodoxi, quod in articulis fidei & doctrinae Christianae summam, rectamque doctrinam retinuerunt sanam, etsi in nonnullis scripturae expositionibus cum iudicio sint legendi. Nam & ipsi ingenue fatentur, se non omnia intellexisse.*

[34] Ebd. III, LXXX: *Sic in coena, praesens dicimus missam esse sacrificium, ab eo quod fuit, non ab eo, quod est. Iam enim Christus non offertur, quia amplius non moritur. Christiani tantum fideli commemoratione mortis dominicae obtrudunt illud Christi sacrificium Deo patri... Ubi non expiamus nostra peccata nova oblatione, quae sit opus nostrum, sed veterem illam oblationem Christi revocamus in memoriam, eaque fidem nostram excitamus, alimus, conformamusque, & gratias agimus pro redemptione iam facta.*

[35] Ebd.: *Certum est Augustinum & patres firmiter credidisse, & confessos esse libris editis: Quod sola Christi mors peccata nostra deleverit, nos Deo reconciliaverit, plena satisfactio pro peccatis nostris fuerit, quo concesso non est dubium, eos non habuisse illam erroneam opinionem in Missa, quam Papistae habent, qui non erubescunt sic docere: Eucharistia est sacrificium Deo oblatum, virtute operis operati tollens peccatum veniale, & mortale, & sumentium & omnium eorum pro quibus offertur, quantum ad reatum poenae & culpae. Certe non sic sentit Augustinus, nec alii patres. Est figmentum scholasticorum, ut apud Thomam in 4. Sentent: distinc. 12.q.5. art. 2.* Rhegius paraphrased Gabriel Biel's summary of Thomas' position;

effect that the sacrifice of the mass would remove sin even from those who were not already in a state of grace; Biel also argued that a statement from Augustine could not be used against this assertion of Thomas.[36] After this indirect rebuke of Biel for dismissing Augustine in favor of Thomas, Rhegius examined the patristic statements that were brought to his attention by the Braunschweig pastors. His strategy remained the same in every case: to show that the mere terms "sacrifice" or "offer" did not mean that Augustine or other fathers viewed the mass as a propitiatory sacrifice.

Why did Rhegius spend time refuting his opponents' use of the fathers in 1532-33 when he disdained the task in 1527? The answer hinges mainly on his new responsibility in 1532. At the Diet of Augsburg Rhegius accepted the invitation of Duke Ernest of Lüneburg to leave that city and take charge of the reformation in his North German territory. In time Rhegius became superintendent of the clergy and a theological resource for North German Lutheranism. When, therefore, he was besought by evangelical pastors to help them resist a serious threat to their work, he felt obligated to respond even though the city of Braunschweig was not under his jurisdiction. In Augsburg, Rhegius had felt no need to enter directly into a literary debate with Eck over, as it were, secondary authorities. In principle, Rhegius did not concede any more authority to the fathers in 1533 than in 1527. In practice, however, he felt compelled to reassure other Protestant clergy that the fathers posed no threat to evangelical teaching.

Rhegius was apparently guided by a similar collegial concern when he wrote a formal opinion of various church fathers in 1532. This memorandum was contained in a letter which Rhegius sent to John Timann [of Amsterdam], an evangelical preacher in Bremen, and it appeared in Timann's own printed collection of passages from the fathers and from Scripture.[37] The letter, or an abstract of its content, was probably preserved in Rhegius' collected Latin works under the

---

cf. *Canonis misse expositio* IV, ed. H.A. Oberman and W.J. Courtenay, Wiesbaden 1967, 105 (Lect. 85 L).

[36] Ebd. 105: *Nec contra illud est, quod Augustinus Ad RENATOS dicit: "Quis offerat corpus christi, nisi pro his qui sunt membra christi?" Intelligitur enim pro membris christi offeri, quando offertur pro aliquibus, ut sint membra christi.*

[37] Liebmann D91.

title "De legendis veteribus Orthodoxis, iudicium Urbani Regii."[38] Receiving Timann's own collection was an occasion for Rhegius to assert his position that the fathers should be read judiciously. His comments reveal that some of the old orthodox theologians were for Rhegius more orthodox than others. For example, even though the name of Augustine was, as expected, the first to appear on Rhegius' list, he did not recommend everything written by the Bishop of Hippo. In addition to "De trinitate" and "De civitate Dei", Rhegius favored the anti-Donatist and anti-Pelagian works. Echoing Luther and Melanchthon, Rhegius commented that among the ancients no one treated Paul better than Augustine; "Pelagius put him to the test so that he would learn the grace of Christ."[39] At the same time, Rhegius said that some of Augustine's sermons on the Psalms were outstanding while in others the Bishop of Hippo was "frigidior".[40]

Rhegius' comments on other fathers ranged from laudatory to outright critical. The works of Athanasius ought to be devoured since he was completely pure.[41] Among the Greek fathers Cyril was the purest and handled the Incarnation best of all.[42] Jerome's exegesis of the Psalms could help the novice in theology and even Chrysostom, though he was ever the rhetorician and philosopher, explained Scripture with erudition. Basil the Great could also be read because of his learning but no one should spend too much time on him. Origen should be entirely ignored because of impure teachings; even though he was learned, reading him was not worth the time.[43] Eusebius

---

[38] LIEBMANN D142 (1), in: Opera latine edita III, LXX-LXX^V. The letter to Timann (8 Febr. 1532; LIEBMANN D91) and the "Iudicium" (LIEBMANN D142[l]) are very likely the same document. UHLHORN (219) quoted a statement from Rhegius' letter that is almost identical with language in the "Iudicium".

[39] Ebd. III, LXX. On Melanchthon, see W. MAURER, Der Einfluß Augustins auf Melanchthons theologische Entwicklung, in: KuD 5 (1959) 165-199. On Luther, see H. JÜRGENS, Die Funktion der Kirchenväterzitate in der Heidelberger Disputation Luthers (1518), in: ARG 66 (1975) 71-78; JÜRGENS confirms the judgment about Luther's use of Augustine rendered by L. GRANE, Divus Paulus et S. Augustinus, interpes eius fidelissimus: über Luthers Verhältnis zu Augustin, in: Festschrift für Ernst Fuchs, ed. G. EBELING, E. JÜNGEL, G. SCHUNACK, Tübingen 1973, 133-146.

[40] Opera latine edita III, LXX.

[41] Ebd.: *Athanasii opera, quae haberi possunt devorentur, nam totus purus est.*

[42] Ebd.

[43] Ebd. III, LXX^V.

should be read in order to learn about the faith of the early church
and the victories of the orthodox fathers. Not to know this history
would cause one to remain a child in the church of God.[44] In conclusion Rhegius recommended his own procedure for study. A set of
commonplaces should be made out of the most striking passages so
that one could readily cite testimonies from the ancient church.[45]

Rhegius' "Iudicium" demonstrates that he had read widely in the
fathers and knew them well. Uhlhorn was nonetheless wrong when he
maintained that this knowledge could be seen in everything that Rhegius wrote. Given the size of the arsenal which stood at the ready in
his "Loci", Rhegius referred to the fathers less than one might expect
and certainly less than Uhlhorn imagined. Uhlhorn's hyperbole was
based, in all likelihood, on a desire to show that his hero knew the fathers as well as his more famous contemporaries like Melanchthon. If
Rhegius had cited the church fathers as often as Uhlhorn imagined,
his use of them would be less interesting that his occasional restraint
suggests. Therefore, the pattern of his references to the fathers merits
closer scrutiny.

During the 1520s, the first decade of his career that Rhegius spent
mostly in Augsburg, his writings reveal a striking paucity of references
to patristic authors. His translations of several patristic works into
German can leave the impression that Rhegius referred to the fathers
more often than he actually did.[46] One searches in vain for extensive
reference to the fathers during these years. A good example is the
pamphlet that Rhegius wrote in defense of Luther's teaching in 1521
and published under the pseudonym Henricus Phoeniceus von
Roschach.[47] Although the pamphlet begins with a quote from Chry-

---

[44] Ebd.

[45] Ebd.: *Legantur illi sic, ut quae apud eos sunt insignia in quosdam locos
communes redigantur, ut semper in promptu sint, quoties veteris Ecclesiae, vel dog-
matibus vel sensibus victis, proferenda testimonia sunt.*

[46] Cf. the comment on the Augsburg pamphleteer Haug Marschalck's anti-
Roman sentiment and view of history by P.A. Russell, Lay Theology in the Reformation: Popular Pamphleteers in Southwest Germany 1521-1525, Cambridge
1986, 137: "Marschalck himself had very little knowledge of the church fathers.
He may have heard about them from Rhegius, who often cited Augustine, Cyprian, and John Chrysostom in his sermons."

[47] Anzaygung dass die Romisch Bull mercklichen schaden in gewissin manicher menschen gebracht hab und nit Doctor Luthers leer, Augsburg 1521 =

sostom and enlists a number of fathers in support of Luther's early statements about purgatory,[48] very few other references are made to them.[49] In the popular apologetic treatise that Rhegius entitled "Nova Doctrina" (1526),[50] he seldom called on the fathers to support his contention that, contrary to the charge of his opponents, he and other evangelical preachers were not innovators but proclaimers of the old and heavenly doctrine of the spirit (i.e., the gospel).[51] Rhegius claimed that a good part of what his opponents defended as the genuine old teaching had been unknown to the fathers; besides, everything that the fathers wrote did not breathe the sincerity of the apostolic spirit.[52] In light of this comment, it is not surprising that Rhegius preferred to demonstrate the antiquity of evangelical teaching with quotations from Scripture instead of from the fathers.

Other works from the 1520s show a similar disinclination to invoke the fathers. Rhegius' most popular work of this decade, his manual of comfort entitled "Seelenärtzney",[53] contains no reference at all to a

---

LIEBMANN D27. LIEBMANN (148) refers to this work as Rhegius' early "summa theologica Lutherana."

[48] Ebd. Cii. The fathers listed are Augustine, Ambrose, John Damascene, Gregory Nazianzus, John Chrysostom, Gregory of Nyssa, Athanasius, and Basil the Great. This list might be of Rhegius' own making, but one reference to Augustine is taken directly from Luther's explanation of Thesis 15; cf. WA 1,555.36-40.

[49] Arguing in support of Luther that marriage was not a sacrament, Rhegius did note (Anzaygung Biii^v): *die hailgen vetter habens nie ain sacrament genempt.*

[50] Nova Doctrina per Urbanum Regium, Augsburg 1526 = LIEBMANN D63.

[51] Ebd. a2^v.

[52] Ebd. a2: *Nam bona pars eorum, quae nostri damnatores docent, priscis etiam patribus ignorantur; tantum abest, ut pro veteribus & Apostolicis doctrinis haberi debeant. Ad haec quae Patres scripserunt, non omnia Apostolici spiritus synceritatem resipiunt.*

[53] Seelenärtzney für die gesunden und kranken zu disen gefärlichen zeyten durch Urbanum Rhegium, Augsburg 1529 = LIEBMANN D76, in: G. FRANZ, Huberinus-Rhegius-Holbein. Bibliographische und Druckgeschichtliche Untersuchung der verbreitetsten Trost- und Erbauungsschriften des 16. Jahrhunderts (Bibliotheca Humanistica & Reformatorica 7), Nieuwkoop 1973, 241-260. As noted above (n. 31), Rhegius did not think it worthwhile to discuss the patristic prooftexts marshalled by Eck in support of the sacrifice of the mass. But Rhegius did discuss some texts from the fathers in the material on the mass that he assembled for his colleague Frosch (supra n. 23).

IV

theologian of the ancient church. Responding to a long letter from Theobald Billican in 1525, Rhegius did cite several patristic passages in support of the real presence. But he assured Billican that he did not mean to leave Scripture behind and to take refuge in human opinions; rather, he was making bold to show that some of the most famous fathers did not agree with the "other [Karlstadtian] side."[54] Rhegius did not enlist the early church theologians in a cause that would lend itself to citing patristic authorities – his major refutation of Anabaptist teaching published in 1527.[55] Although he played an active role in the caucuses of evangelical theologians who in 1530 used patristic sources in constructing the "Confessio Augustana", in his own theological work in Augsburg Rhegius mentioned the fathers with notable infrequency.

Rhegius paid more attention to the fathers in the 1530s after he moved north to Lüneburg. Why was this? Partly, as we have seen, it was because he received specific requests from clergy to respond to patristic authorities cited against evangelical positions. Apparently one of these requests grew out of Rhegius' participation in the reformation of the city of Lüneburg. His evaluation of Cyprian's "little treatise"[56] was written from Lüneburg and discussed the relationship of faith to works in reference to Romans 3, a text from which Rhegius prepared theses to be debated by the city's evangelical preachers.[57]

Mainly, however, Rhegius quoted the fathers more extensively during the 1530s because Protestants felt compelled to assert the validity of their churches in the face of efforts by Emperor Charles V to reunite them with Catholics. The multiple roles which the fathers played in this assertion of Protestant legitimacy can be seen in the

---

[54] Letter to Billican, 18 Dec. 1525, in: Opera latine edita II, V^v: *Quae omnia non in hoc produco, ut in rebus fidei, relicta scripturarum lucerna, ad hominum glossemata confugiam, sed ut ostendam, quam non temere sim cunctatus, qui videbam veteres quoque primarii nominis, parti adversariae plena, quod aiunt, caera nunquam subscripsisse.*

[55] Wider den newen Taufforden; Notwendige Warnung an alle Christgleubigen, Augsburg 1527 = LIEBMANN D67.

[56] Supra n.19.

[57] LIEBMANN D142(m), in: Opera latine edita III, LXXI-LXXIII^v. See R. GERECKE, Urbanus Rhegius als Superintendent in Lüneburg (1532-1533), in: Reformation vor 450 Jahren. Eine Lüneburgische Gedenkschrift, Lüneburg 1980, 83.

preface to the church order that Rhegius wrote in 1536 for the city of Hannover. First, the fathers served as models of the fight against heresy, which had always been necessary in the church.[58] The Protestant reformers who were resisting the errors fostered by popes, bishops and monks ignorant of Scripture[59] followed in the steps of these "outstanding, learned men". Second, the fathers served as models for the orthodox, apostolic understanding of Scripture. The humanists of France and Germany, to whom Rhegius gave credit for initiating the Reformation, stimulated the theologians to read both the Bible and the "old, orthodox" fathers who dealt with Scripture far differently from the way it had been treated "under the papacy".[60] Third, the fathers either asserted or demonstrated the necessity of resisting bishops who made demands contrary to the gospel.[61] Rhegius summarized this point elsewhere: "If to dissent from the bishops is to be cut off from the church, then Irenaeus, Jerome, Augustine, Cyprian, Cyril and many other "pii Doctores" would have been outside the church."[62] In all the above ways, the church fathers supported the

---

[58] Kirchenordnung der statt Hannofer durch D. Urbanum Regium, Magdeburg 1536 = LIEBMANN D107, in: Die evangelischen Kirchenordnungen des XVI. Jahrhunderts VI/1/2, ed. E. SEHLING, Tübingen 1957, 980-981: *Denn Christus erweckt allzeit dagegen auch treffliche, gelerte leut, die mit dem schwert des heiligen Geistes alle ketzerey zerschmetterten. Also erwecket er wider die Arrianer das concilium zu Nicea, auch Alexandrum, Athanasium, Hilarium, Ambrosium etc. Wider den Novatum erwecket er den heiligen Cyprianum, wider die Donatisten, Manicheer und Pelagianer Augustinum. Wider den Jovinianum, Helvidium, Vigilantium, Pelagium und chiliasten den heiligen Hieronymum. Wider den Nestorium und Julianum erweckt er Cyrillum und Nazianzenum.*

[59] Ebd. 990 f., 1000.

[60] Ebd. 994: *Sie sahen und funden, das die bibel an vielen orten ubel gefelscht und viciert war und sich des jamers niemand wolt annemen. Also huben sie an mit aller bescheidenheit, solche irthum und unordentlich wesen der welt anzuzeigen, straffen und zu einer reformation ermanen. Und sonderlich erweckten sie die gelerten, zu lesen die alten orthodoxen, Augustinum, Hieronymum, Ambrosium und andere, die gar anders die schrift tractieren, denn unterm bapstum geschehen ist.*

[61] Ebd. 997 f.

[62] Disputatio de schismate huius saeculi, & de Ecclesia = LIEBMANN D142(c), in: Opera latine edita III, IIII^v: 20. *Si dissentire alicubi ab Episcopis pro divinis humana docentibus, & idololatricos cultus contra veritatem defendentibus, est proscindi ab Ecclesia, Irenaeus, Hieronymus, Augustinus, Cyprianus, Cirillus, & alii multi pii Doctores separati fuissent ab Ecclesia, quod absit.*

claim of Protestants to be the true church, i. e., the genuine heirs of apostolic and orthodox Christianity.

Also during the 1530s Rhegius cited the fathers more readily on specific issues. In defending the necessity of private confession to the city council of Rostock in 1531, Rhegius argued that private confession was not peculiarly papist (in spite of what the common people thought), but could be found long before the papacy in the church fathers.[63] In the "Sermon on Good and Bad Angels" preached in Hannover (1536) Rhegius appealed to Basil the Great for evidence that the church had always taught that believers had personal angels.[64] At the same time, Rhegius appealed to Augustine to support his argument (resisted, we may assume, by some of the faithful in Hannover) that these same angels should not be the objects of prayer.[65] Although Rhegius failed to make significant use of the fathers in earlier writings against the Anabaptists, he followed a different strategy in 1535 when attacking the radicals in Münster. The title of his refutation of Rothmann reveals how Rhegius identified the Münster Anabaptists with the Valentinian and Donatist heresies of the early church.[66] Casting the radicals in the role of heretics enabled Rhegius to portray their Protestant opponents as orthodox and to summon the early fathers as witnesses to that orthodoxy. Indeed, in this treatise, Rhegius wanted to cite the fathers more extensively than he did,

---

[63] Sabine PETTKE, Das Gutachten des Urbanus Rhegius für den Rostocker Rat vom 8. November 1531, in: JGNKG 84 (1986) 93-103, here 97: *Desglichen finden wir von solcher Rhatsfragender Beicht, die trost der gwisnj in dem wort Gots sucht bei predigeren, jn dem Alten lerer Tertulliano, Der gelert hat in der Christenhait vor 1300 jaren, solchs ist auch lichtlich zu bewären us Origene, Cypriano, Hilario, Basilio, Hieronymo, Augustino, Ambrosio und Paulino, Dise alten prediger haben ie Bäbstischer Tyrannej kein schuld, man hat zu ieren zitten nit uff pabstisch gebeichet, und hat doch beichtet, wie wir ietz leren, one bezwang pabsticher tradition.*

[64] Ein Sermon Von den guten und bösen Engeln zu Hannover geprediget durch D. Urbanum Rhegium, Wittenberg 1538 (= LIEBMANN D125), E: *Derhalben der Christlichen Kirchen glaube allzeit aus der Schrifft gewesen ist/ das ein jeglicher seinen eigen Engel habe/ Wie Basilius magnus/ de spiritu sancto schreibet/ als einen Zuchtmeister und hirten/ der jm sein leben richte.*

[65] Ebd. F-Fii.

[66] Widderlegung der Münsterischen newen Valentinianer und Donatisten bekentnus, Wittenberg 1535 = LIEBMANN D106, in: Schriften von evangelischer Seite gegen die Täufer (Veröff. d. hist. Kommission f. Westfalen 32), ed. R. STUPPERICH, Münster 1983.

because they wrote about the true incarnation of God "aus klarem grund der schrifft".[67]

This last statement demonstrates how, despite more frequent reference to them in the 1530s, the fathers remained for Rhegius secondary authorities. They provided important and persuasive support to the Protestant movement because they testified to the evangelical teaching of Scripture. But Rhegius also realized that the fathers could prove fickle in providing evidence for some evangelical teachings. Over against Eck, Rhegius had admitted that some statements from the fathers about the mass as sacrifice could be harmonized with the evangelical position, but he also admitted that some could not. Even where harmonization was possible, it could require considerable effort. Rhegius demonstrated that fact in 1532 as he struggled to reconcile two passages from Augustine's sermons with each other and with his own view that the mass could not be a propitiatory sacrifice.

Augustine could not have believed the mass to be such a sacrifice, argued Rhegius, when he taught in all his writings that the sacrifice of Christ provided sufficient expiation for all sins. The Bishop of Hippo would not have preached differently from what he had written.[68] What then should be done with the sermon in which Augustine said that prayers and sacrifice and alms could be offered on behalf of the dead? There, countered Rhegius, Augustine said nothing explicit about the sacrament as a means of forgiving the sins of the departed.[69] In another sermon, Augustine had said that the bread and the cup were "offered". This time Rhegius pointed to the word "significetur" in the text to show that the offering of the sacrament only signified the remission of sins. "This one text", concluded Rhegius triumphantly, "testifies that Augustine was not guilty of the papist error, unless one would not be ashamed to say that Augustine was so ab-

---

[67] Ebd. 99: *Ich hette wol lust, lieben freund, das ich ewerm glauben zu trost und sterckung anzeigte, wie herrlich ding und mit was freuden von der waren menschwerdung Gottes die fromen alten Christen Ignatius, Ireneus, Athanasius, Ciprianus, Cyrillus, Nazianzenus, Augustinus, Ambrosius und andere aus klarem grund der schrifft geschrieben haben. Es würde zu lang.*

[68] Orthodoxorum patrum Sententiae (supra n. 33), in: Opera latine edita III, LXXX^v.

[69] Ebd. The reference is to Augustine's Sermo de verbis apostoli 32 = Sermo 172,2, in: PL 38, 936 f.

sent-minded that he forgot one day what he preached the day before."[70]

It turns out that Rhegius was both right and wrong about Augustine's memory. On the one hand, the second sermon attributed to Augustine was actually taken from the works of Ambrose,[71] but Rhegius can hardly be faulted for that mistake. On the other hand, if one examines the context of the statements from these sermons, the correctness of Rhegius' judgments is at least arguable. The first excerpt presented to Rhegius was part of Augustine's response to the question of what happened when the sacrament was offered for the dead. Augustine's answer was twofold: 1) the sacrament only benefitted those who had lived in such a way as to deserve its benefits; 2) it did not produce new merits for the dead, but only reaped the consequence of what they did while they were alive. Therefore, Rhegius was probably correct in protesting that Augustine did not regard the sacrament, when offered for the dead, as an expiatory sacrifice.[72]

---

[70] Opera latine edita III, LXXX^v: *Cum [Augustinus] subiungit, Quotiescunque offertur sacrificium, mox se exponit, & dicit mortem, elevationem Domini, & remissionem peccatorum significari. Ecce, aperte ostendit, quale sit sacrificium missae, scilicet significatorium: non impetrat remissionem peccatorum, aut fit pro peccatis remittendis, sed significat remissionum [sic] peccatorum. Hic unus locus satis testatur Augustinum in errore papistarum non fuisse, nisi quis dicere non erubescat, Augustinum fuisse obliviosissimum, qui in sermone hodierno oblitus sit, quod in hesterno docuerit.* Rhegius was referring to Augustine's Sermo de verbis Domini 28 = Sermo 84 (Appendix), in: PL 39, 1907-1909.

[71] De sacramentis V 4, in: CSEL 73, 65-72.

[72] Cf. Augustine, Sermo 172.2, in: PL 38, 936 f.: *Hoc enim a patribus traditum, universa observat Ecclesia, ut pro eis qui in corporis et sanguinis Christi communione defuncti sunt, cum ad ipsum sacrificium loco suo commemorantur, oretur, ac pro illis quoque id offerri commemoretur. Cum vero eorum commendandorum causa opera misericordiae celebrantur, quis eis dubitet suffragari, pro quibus orationes Deo non inaniter allegantur? Non omnino ambigendum est, ista prodesse defunctis; sed talibus qui ita vixerint ante mortem, ut possint eis haec utilia esse post mortem. Nam qui sine fide quae per dilectionem operatur [Gal. 5:6], eiusque Sacramentis, de corporibus exierunt, frustra illis a suis huiusmodi pietatis impenduntur officia, cuius, dum hic essent, pignore caruerunt, vel non suscipientes, vel in vacuum suscipientes Dei gratiam, et sibi non misericordiam thesaurizantes, sed iram. Non ergo mortuis nova merita comparantur, cum pro eis boni aliquid operantur sui, sed eorum praecedentibus consequentia ista redduntur. Non enim actum est, nisi cum hic viverent, ut eos haec aliquid adjuvarent, cum hic vivere destitissent. Et*

IV

300

Rhegius' interpretation of the text incorrectly attributed to Augustine is less convincing. Ambrose was reproaching his congregation for not taking the sacrament daily although they knew that the death, resurrection, elevation of Christ, and the remission of sins were signified every time the sacrament was offered. Rhegius based his argument against the propitiatory nature of the offering on Ambrose's use of "significetur"; but the parallel that Ambrose drew between the sacrament and Job's sacrifice to cover the possible sins of his sons (Job 1:5) indicates that the sacrament possessed some expiatory function for Ambrose.[73] It remains uncertain whether or not Ambrose meant that sin was removed directly by the daily offering of the sacrifice, and equally uncertain whether or not Rhegius' argument was valid.

For our purpose the correctness of his interpretation is less significant than the effort which Rhegius expended on claiming the support of Augustine. He analyzed closely the text as presented to him because the support of Augustine was important; but apparently he did not examine the context of the statements in the collected works of the church father. Rhegius cared enough about the support of Augustine to argue that specific statements from his works could not be used against the evangelical view of the mass. Since, however, even Augustine's opinion remained secondary to that of Scripture, he did not undertake an intensive historical analysis of the texts. This neglect of the sources brought Rhegius sharp criticism from his biographer Uhlhorn. He claimed that Rhegius showed no historical appreciation for the church fathers and selected only those texts from the fathers that agreed with Protestant positions.[74]

---

ideo istam finiens quisque vitam, nisi quod meruit in ipsa, non poterit habere post ipsam.

[73] De sacr. V 4 25, in: CSEL 73, 69.64-70.76: Si cottidianus est panis, cur post annum illum sumas, quemadmodum Graeci in oriente facere consuerunt? Accipe cottidie, quod cottidie tibi prosit! Sic vive, ut cottidie merearis accipere! Qui non meretur cottidie accipere, non meretur post annum accipere. Quo modo Iob sanctus pro filiis suis sacrificium offerebat cottidie, ne forte aliquid vel in corde vel in sermone peccassent [Job 1.5]. Ergo tu audis, quod, quotienscumque offertur sacrificium, mors domini, resurrectio domini, elevatio domini significetur et remissio peccatorum, et panem istum vitae non cottidianus non adsumis? Qui vulnus habet, medicinam requirit. Vulnus est, quia sub peccato sumus, medicina est caeleste et venerabile sacramentum.

[74] UHLHORN 220.

This criticism is, however, anachronistic and misses the point of Rhegius' use of the fathers. He was not a patristics scholar interested in the fathers for their own sake. Consequently, he judged their works with a criterion that set some fathers on a higher level than others and recommended some works of the same theologian as more useful to read than the rest.[75] By making such judgments and by choosing texts (from Scripture as well as from the fathers) that supported his theology, he placed himself in good sixteenth-century company.[76] His discriminatory reading of the fathers was similar to that recommended by Philipp Melanchthon in late 1520 and early 1521. Melanchthon commented that none of the more recent or older theologians helped "our theology" besides Augustine and a few Greeks. It was better to go to the sources, i. e., to Scripture itself.[77] Although Rhegius' 1532 list of worthwhile fathers was longer than Melanchthon's list of 1520 and 1521, the principle of discrimination governed both. Among the old theologians, concluded Melanchthon, only a few understood properly the distinction between law and grace and in their theology followed Paul.[78]

---

[75] In: De legendis veteribus Orthodoxis (supra nn. 40-44).

[76] Rhegius himself criticized Eck for proving his case for the mass as sacrifice by amassing Scripture passages in a chain of prooftexts (Opera latine edita II, XXᵛ): *Utinam certiora ex scripturis adferremus. Nam fidem catholicam hostibus deridendam propinamus, quoties tam incertis nitimur. Cogita Ecci, quam arduum conscientiae negocium hic agatur. Quare non dubiis enarrationibus scripturae, sed certissimo & plano Dei verbo obfirmanda est conscientia in fidei articulis, ut in tentationum tempestate consistere queat adversus portas inferorum, atque etiam iudicium tentantis Dei.* But ISERLOH (Die Eucharistie 80) pointed out that Eck was drawing from a pool of traditional prooftexts. POLMAN (L'élément historique 5-44, here 31, 44) noted with criticism Luther's "opportunistic" attitude toward the fathers while preferring what appeared to him to be – wrongly – greater objectivity on the part of the humanist Melanchthon.

[77] Melanchthon to Georg Ebner in Leinburg bei Nürnberg, 12 Feb. 1521 (cf. Melanchthons Briefwechsel I, ed. H. SCHEIBLE, Stuttgart-Bad Cannstatt 1977, 87 f. [Nr. 124]), in: CR 20, 704 f.: *Nostram Theologiam videntur adiuvare nulli neque neotericorum, neque veterum scriptorum, praeter Augustinum, et pauculos Graecos. Origenes nimium philosophatur. Hieronymus ne in dialogis quidem, aut Pauli commentariis adsequutus est Pauli sententiam. Quare nullum feceris magis operae pretium, quam ubi te ad ipsos fontes, ad ipsam scripturam contuleris.*

[78] Idem Philippus Melanthon [sic], quonam iudicio legendi Autores, in: CR 20, 705: *Veterum ac novorum (mihi crede) pauci fuere, qui Legis et Gratiae discrimen proprie intellexerint, et iuxta Pauli sententiam tractarint.* According to Me-

IV

302

The failure to undertake an historical-critical approach to the fathers is not a sign of their unimportance for Rhegius and other reformers. On the contrary, their selection of passages from patristic writings after the same fashion as they used Scripture testifies to the significance of patristic support. The fathers were to be sure secondary authorities, but they formed an essential second line of witnesses to the truth of the evangelical message. While Scripture was always regarded by them as the principal and reliable criterion for defining that truth, the authority of the fathers became increasingly important, especially as opponents confronted them with patristic passages that conflicted with their teaching. Accordingly, after 1530, Rhegius took more initiative to claim the authority of the "old, orthodox" fathers for evangelical practice and for the validity of new Protestant churches. And, though begrudgingly at first, he also admitted that contrary evidence cited from the fathers had to be taken seriously.

In his later works Rhegius' expanded interest in patristic support resulted in two qualifications to the principle of "sola scriptura", one of which horrified his biographer Uhlhorn. Late in his career Rhegius produced a memorandum which advised evangelical preachers how they should interpret Scripture. They should reject all the interpretations of their opponents (papists, Anabaptists, and sacramentarians) which were not in accord with the rule of faith (Rom. 12:6). Rhegius admonished the preachers to consult the opinion of the early church because citing Scripture by itself was not sufficient. They should cite Scripture in the "ecclesiastical sense"; for, according to the later Rhegius, there was no proper understanding of Scripture outside the

lanchton (ebd.), Hilary and Cyprian were more solid than Origen, Jerome and Ambrose, but even Cyprian frequently distorted Scripture. After also listing the books of Augustine in which he thought the anti-Pelagian teaching on grace was most clearly enunciated, Melanchthon warned (ebd.): *Reliqua cum iudicio lege.* Melanchthon's critical view of the fathers has been noted and discussed in depth. His attitude toward Augustine was explained by W. MAURER (Der Einfluß Augustins 165-199, here 186) as a tactic whereby Melanchthon was criticizing Augustine internally within the Wittenberg theology and according to its norm, while he was defending Augustine externally against Wittenberg's opponents. According to P. FRAENKEL (Testimonia Patrum 283-306, esp. 299-302), Melanchthon could criticize the fathers while claiming their support because he was pursuing a "repurgatio doctrinae", i.e., he was attempting to find in the fathers the "one, unimpaired faith of the Church", which he believed they taught and which the Reformation could now extract from their errors.

church catholic.[79] Uhlhorn was so taken aback by this apparent adulteration of "sola scriptura" that he hastened to assure readers that Rhegius did not practice what he preached.[80] Rhegius at least thought he practiced it, but if explicit reference to the fathers is an indication of citing Scripture in the ecclesiastical sense, then he applied this principle selectively, and more frequently later in his career as it became necessary to defend the catholicity of Lutheranism against its opponents.

The second challenge to "sola scriptura" appeared in the broadening of the category of church father itself. On the one hand, "church father" still connoted for Rhegius the bishops and theologians of the early church and he appealed to them as individuals and as a distinct group. On the other hand, in his "Loci" the patristic writers are represented indiscriminately with sixteenth-century reformers and even some medieval theologians. The most frequently quoted theologian in Rhegius' "Loci" is Martin Luther, whom he nicknamed "Theophoretus",[81] and Melanchthon is often cited as well. Their theology was

---

[79] Alia ratio tractandi scripturas sacras quibusdam verbi ministris praescripta, in: Opera latine edita III, XVI: *Non igitur adferas vel sensum sine scripturis, ut Anabaptistae, vel scripturas in sensu, qui fidei non est analogus, sed adfer scripturas in sensu Ecclesiastico, hoc est, in eo sensu, qui semper a temporibus Apostolorum fuit in Ecclesia orientali et occidentali. Neque enim scripturae intellectus extra Ecclesiam Catholicam invenitur, et spiritus sanctus Ecclesiam, ut suum templum, et suam domum inhabitat, haereticorum Synagogas execratur.* Rhegius gave two examples of private or unecclesiastical interpretation (ebd.): 1) in the words of institution to understand "est" as "significat" was to contradict Theophylact's treatment of Matthew 26; 2) in Matthew 16 to interpret "petra" as Peter and not as Christ was to go against Chrysostom and Augustine. Rhegius' concern to utilize the early church as protection against the private interpretation of Scripture is strikingly similar to Eck's argument at Leipzig (supra n.4).

[80] UHLHORN 220.

[81] The significance of this nickname was devoutly supplied by Freder in his dedicatory preface (Loci 2ᵛ): *Obiter autem annotavit* [Rhegius] *libros etiam & capita cuiusque loci, e sanctissimis lucubrationibus reverendi in Christo Patris D. Doctoris Martini Lutheri, quem Theophoreti nomine designat, quod verus Dei homo & fidelis mysteriorum divinorum oeconomus sit, & quod verum Deum doceat ipsumque Dei spiritum in pectore gestet, quodque Deus hoc organo in repurganda sua doctrina his novissimis temporibus usus, veram solidamque sui ac filii sui cognitionem, per aliquot secula pene amissam, per virum hunc ter maximum nobis restituere sit dignatus.*

IV

the norm by which all other authors were judged – medieval as well as patristic.

For example, in discussing the presence of sin after baptism, Rhegius noted how the fathers had disagreed about Paul's intention in the seventh chapter of Romans. In good medieval fashion, Rhegius proposed a distinction to show how those fathers who denied that sin remained in the righteous could be reconciled with the evangelical exegesis of Paul.[82] Rhegius certainly desired the support of the early fathers for his interpretation of Scripture, but he also felt free to reject them when their testimony did not support the evangelical position. He both demonstrated and defended this freedom by invoking a late medieval authority in the person of Jean Gerson: not everything that had been approved by the popes and the church had to be believed; otherwise the works of the doctors like Saints Augustine and Jerome would demand acceptance.[83]

Rhegius' belated interest in the church fathers was enhanced by the desire to build a case for the theological validity of the Protestant Reformation. That concern persisted throughout the sixteenth century and remained pronounced even in later defenses of the Reformation by Lutheran apologists. In the early eighteenth century Johann Georg Walch launched his extensive history of religious controversies with the assertion that the Lutherans were the old, true church and not a novel movement as the "papists" had charged.[84] Whereas

---

[82] The distinction itself was Lutheran: sin could be treated according to law or according to gospel (Loci 8): *Manet tamen sub utroque vere et naturaliter peccatum, ideo Patrum authoritates, si qui negant peccatum esse in iusto, omnes intelligendae sunt secundum gratiam, qua Deus credenti non vult imputare, qui secundum iustum iudicium posset damnare, sed non intelligatur secundum naturam peccati vel legem, Christus enim nos liberavit, ut iam non simus sub lege, sed sub gratia. Ioan. 1.*

[83] Loci 28: *Addit Gerson. Non omnia per Pontifices summos, imo per Ecclesiam approbata de fide esse censentur, alioqui obligarent ad sui credulitatem opera Doctorum sanctorum Augustini, Hieronymi, quod dici nequit.* In reference to the division of the fathers over Romans 7, Rhegius had already stated (ebd. 7ᵛ): *Non igitur in arenam humanorum sensorum, sed in petram verbi Dei aedificet, qui contra tempestates errorum vult muniri.*

[84] J.G. WALCH, Historische und Theologische Einleitung in die Religions-Streitigkeiten der Evangelisch-Lutherischen Kirchen I, Jena ²1733 (Stuttgart-Bad Cannstatt 1972), 2: *Es ist unsere Kirche die wahre Kirche, und kan deswegen nicht vor neu ausgegeben werden, wie uns die Papisten vorwerffen, als wenn*

IV

The Use of the Church Fathers by Urbanus Rhegius   305

Luther had defended himself against the charge of novelty by recourse mainly to Scripture, his successors like Rhegius turned more frequently, albeit discriminately, to the fathers for additional arms in their fight for the validity of the Reformation. In so doing, they revealed that the evangelical movement never relied on Scripture alone as the exclusive source of authority. Rather, its ancient credentials also included what the reformers regarded as the best of the patristic heritage.

die Lehre der Lutheraner neu wäre, und mit Luthers erst aufgekommen; ihre aber alt und von den Zeiten der Apostel beständig in der Kirche erhalten worden, Denn wir lehren in unsrer Kirche nichts anders, als was die reine, alte Apostolische und Christliche Kirche gelehret.

V

DEPARENTIFYING THE FATHERS:
THE REFORMERS AND PATRISTIC AUTHORITY

1. The Problem

For some time historians have noted how prominent Protestant reformers made selective use of the church fathers. Evaluators of that selectivity have subjected it, however, to very different judgments. For example, in his careful study of Zwingli's use of the fathers, Alfred Schindler described the Swiss reformer's attitude toward them as »consciously ambivalent *(bewusst ambivalent)*«.[1] In Schindler's view, Zwingli was guided by his own self-interest when he appealed to patristic authority, and this self-interest manifested itself in ambivalence. Zwingli was quite willing to concede authority to the fathers as long as they agreed with Scripture; but when they disagreed among themselves, Zwingli only noted the discrepancy when he could exploit it in his favor. This ambivalent appeal to the fathers in one's self-interest was, Schindler believed, to some degree common to all the reformers.[2] According to Anthony N. S. Lane, it was certainly true of John Calvin. Responding to the question of how fair Calvin was in his use of the fathers, Lane wrote: »Calvin's use of the fathers is open not so much to the charge of inaccuracy as to the charge of selectivity. He was not seeking to give a balanced detached assessment of the fathers. He was appealing to them for support. This means that he was, not unreasonably, selective in his use of them.«[3]

Other scholars have not reacted to the motive of self-interest with the same objectivity. For example, Jean Boisset denied outright that John Calvin borrowed ideas from the church fathers just because they agreed with Calvin's own views. First, claimed Boisset, Calvin searched Scripture for the genuine Word of God and then selected texts from the fathers which supported that divine Word.[4] In the admiring eyes of Boisset, Calvin's appeals to the fathers served the Word of God with genuine disinterest. In stark contrast to such admiration stands the

---

[1] *Alfred Schindler*, Zwingli und die Kirchenväter (147. Neujahrsblatt zum Besten des Waisenhauses Zürich), Zürich 1984, 46.

[2] *Alfred Schindler*, Zwingli und die Kirchenväter, in: Charisma und Institution, ed. *Trutz Rendtorff*, Gütersloh 1985, 393-404: 395. Cf. *Jean V. Pollet*, Huldrych Zwingli et le Zwinglianisme. Essai de synthèse historique et théologique mis à jour d'après les recherches récentes, Paris 1988, 336-337.

[3] *Anthony N. S. Lane*, Calvin's Use of the Fathers and the Medievals, CTJ 16 (1981), 149-205: 189.

[4] *Jean Boisset*, La reforme et les Peres de l'Eglise, in: Migne et le renouveau des études patristiques. Actes du colloque de Saint-Flour, 7-8 juillet 1975, ed. *André Mandouze* and *Joël Fouilheron*, Paris 1985, 39-51: 49.

V

56

harsh criticism of Urbanus Rhegius by his nineteenth-century biographer, Gerhard Uhlhorn. He claimed that Rhegius showed no historical appreciation for the church fathers and selected only those patristic texts that agreed with Protestant positions.[5] Writing more than sixty years ago, Pontien Polman called Luther's attitude toward patristic authority »opportunistic«,[6] and he illustrated that opportunism with two texts. In an open letter to Duke Albrecht of Prussia in 1532, Luther acknowledged that, unlike himself, the fathers had often applied the sixth chapter of John to the Lord's Supper. Nevertheless, he said he would not condemn the ancient doctors for that mistake because their underlying conviction was the same as his own, namely, that true flesh and blood of Christ were present in the sacrament.[7]

Polman was not satisfied with this method of claiming patristic support, and he contrasted that claim with Luther's disavowal of the fathers in the debate at Marburg with Oecolampadius and Zwingli. When they held up to him passages from the fathers that suggested how Christ could be in only one place at the time (i.e., in heaven), Luther responded that even if all the fathers were on Zwingli's side, why should he abandon the Word of God and cling to the fathers?[8] Then Luther continued: »We want to honor the fathers insofar as we interpret as best we can the writings through which they have served us, so that they remain in agreement with Holy Scripture. Where, however, their writings do not agree with God's Word, it is better for us to admit that they erred than for their sake to abandon God's Word.«[9]

To dismiss the opinions of the fathers if they disagreed with Scripture and then, three years later, to assert the importance of agreeing with the fathers on

5 *Gerhard Uhlhorn*, Urbanus Rhegius. Leben und ausgewählte Schriften, Elberfeld 1861, 219. Cf. *Scott Hendrix*, Validating the Reformation. The Use of the Church Fathers by Urbanus Rhegius, in: Ecclesia Militans. Studien zur Konzilien- und Reformationsgeschichte, ed. *Walter Brandmüller, Herbert Immenkötter, Erwin Iserloh*, Paderborn 1988, 2, 281-305: 300.

6 *Pontien Polman*, L'Elément historique dans la controverse religieuse du XVIe siècle, Gembloux 1932, 31.

7 WA 30/III, 548,28-32: »Doch hie mit wir nicht verdammen die Veter und Ierer, so Johannis am sechsten Capittel zum Abendmal gebraucht und gefüret haben, wie sie wol mehr spruche offtmals uneben füren, Denn jre meinung ist doch ja recht und gut, das sie da mit bezeugen, Es sey warhafftig fleisch und blut Christi im Abendmal.« Cf. WA 30/III, 552,3-8.

8 Andreas Osiander [Report of the Marburg Colloquy], in *Andreas Osiander d. Ä*, Gesamtausgabe, vol. 3: Schriften und Briefe 1528 bis April 1530, ed. *Gerhard Müller* and *Gottfried Seebass*, Gütersloh 1979, 424-442: 435,6-8: »Und wann gleich die väter all auff euer maynung weren, wie kömen wir darzu, das wir umb der väter willen Gottes wort solten faren lassen und inen anhangen?«

9 Ibid., 435,11-16: »So wöllen wir nun den lieben vättern die eer gern thun, das wir ir schryfft, damit sy uns gedient haben, auffs pesst wöllen ausslegen, wie wir können, damit sy mit der heyligen schryfft ainhellig pleyben. Wo aber ir schryfft mit Gottes wort nit überainkommen, ist vyl pesser, wir sprechen: 'Sy haben geirrt', dann das wir umb irenwillen solten Gottes wort faren lassen.« Cf. Luther's remark in Tischrede Nr. 584, WA TR 1, 272,1-4: »Patres quanqaum saepe errant, tamen sunt reverendi propter testimonium fidei. Sic Hieronymum et Gregorium et alios veneror, das man dennoch fulen kan, das sie geglaubt haben wie wir, quod ecclesia ab initio crediderit, sicut nos credimus.«

V

the same eucharistic issue was for Polman a blatant inconsistency. Luther's self-interest, therefore, had to be self-serving.

2. A New Model

Were the reformers guilty of opportunism, however, when they invoked the fathers only in support of their arguments or to demonstrate that the fathers disagreed among themselves? Not at all, especially if »opportunistic« means taking advantage of a situation without regard to principle. I would say instead that most Protestant reformers adopted an intentionally balanced stance toward the fathers of the church. This attitude, while it did serve their self-interest, was not self-serving. In fact, I want to argue that the selective use of the fathers by certain reformers resulted mainly from their theological freedom. This freedom enabled them to adopt a balanced stance toward the fathers which acknowledged both their limitations and their contributions without granting to the fathers undeserved authority.

To describe that stance, I am using a term from the field of family therapy: *deparentification*.[10] I use this term not as a psychological explanation of historical process but as a way of positively portraying the stance of the reformers. In relationships deparentification is a way in which people rework their attitudes toward figures of authority. To parentify a person is to award authority and responsibility to that person which he or she has neither earned nor deserved. By the same token, to deparentify a person is to refuse any longer to attribute inappropriate authority to that person and to assume more responsibility for oneself. I can give an example from the academic field: as graduate students mature into scholars, they often become less willing to accept uncritically the authority of their mentors; instead, they become more selective and appropriate some of the ideas and methods which they received while rejecting others. In this way students gradually deparentify their teachers.

The model of deparentification suggests itself all the more readily for our topic because the authorities of the ancient church were called fathers.[11] That is, however, only a coincidence. A more compelling reason for choosing this model is the correspondence of deparentification to the balanced stance toward the fathers that emerges from so many Protestant texts. Take, for example, the words of Luther at the Marburg Colloquy quoted above. Luther's main point was to emphasize the superior authority of Scripture, and he preferred to say that the fathers erred before he would abandon God's Word. On that basis, Luther could have

10 For discussion of both parentification and deparentification, see *Ivan Boszormenyi-Nagy* and *Geraldine Spark*, Invisible Loyalties. Reciprocity in Intergenerational Family Therapy, New York ²1984, 151-166; and *Ivan Boszormenyi-Nagy* and *Barbara Krasner*, Between Give and Take. A Clinical Guide to Contextual Therapy, New York 1986, 327-329.
11 For the origin and use of the term father for bishops and theologians in the early church. see *Berthold Altaner* and *Alfred Stuiber*, Patrologie. Leben, Schriften und Lehre der Kirchenväter, Freiburg ⁷1966, 1-4.

discounted the fathers, but instead he made a point of acknowledging their contributions and stood willing to integrate them into his own theology insofar as they agreed with Scripture: »So wöllen wir nun den lieben vättern die eer gern thun, das wir ir schryfft, *damit sy uns gedient haben* [emphasis mine], auffs pesst wöllen ausslegen, wie wir können, damit sy mit der heyligen schryfft ainhellig pleyben.«[12]

While it may not surprise us that Protestant reformers were willing to accept a limited authority of the fathers beneath Scripture, no historical necessity compelled them to adopt that stance. They could have rebelled against the fathers and rejected them completely or they could have submissively sought their support. In either case they would not have used the fathers freely as a resource, but would have felt bound to reject them or obligated to agree with them. What can look like a self-serving or ambivalent attitude toward the fathers can therefore also be read in a more positive way. The reformers selected support from the fathers not only because it served their apologetic interest to do so,[13] but also because they were secure enough in the biblical grounding of their own theology to choose patristic support if they wished. They were free to acknowledge both the contributions and the limitations of the fathers and to use them as resources accordingly.

3. Luther and Calvin

Before I cite examples of this balanced stance in the writings of other reformers, I want to examine some statements of the older Luther. His words reveal another dimension of a deparentified approach to the fathers: to treat them not just as dead authorities but also as human beings and living believers.

In the 1540s Luther was the moving force behind the appearance of two patristic sourcebooks. Georg Major published in 1544 a purged edition of the lives of the fathers which also contained the *verba seniorum* and a preface by Luther.[14] And in 1543 Georg Spalatin published a collection of comforting sayings and examples from the fathers for which Luther also wrote a preface.[15] Both Major and Spalatin said that they assumed these tasks because Luther wanted them done. Luther's prefaces made clear, however, that he did not promote these editions for the formal authority which they might lend to evangelical theology. Instead, the fathers appealed to the later Luther because he was convinced that contemporary believers could identify with their spiritual struggles. The fathers were worthy of emulation because they were not perfect. The fathers who taught rightly

---

12 See note 9 above.

13 This was a main conclusion of my study, Validating the Reformation (n. 5 above), 302, 304.

14 *Georg Major*, Vitae patrum, in usum ministrorum verbi, quoad eius fieri potuit repurgatae. Per D. Georgium Maiorem, cum praefatione D. Doctoris Mart. Luth., Wittenberg: Veit Creutzer 1562 [1st ed.: Peter Seitz, 1544]. For Luther's preface see WA 54, 109-111.

15 *Georg Spalatin*, Magnifice consolatoria exempla et sententiae ex vitis et passionibus sanctorum collectae, Wittenberg: Nikolaus Schirlentz, 1544. For Luther's preface see WA 54, 113-115.

(*Orthodoxi*) kept their balance and walked a *via media*: they neither indulged in sins nor boasted of perfection, but they considered grace and salvation to be for sinners who repented and believed.[16] As imperfect sinners, the fathers could therefore strengthen »our consciences« by proposing many old examples and witnesses »who felt, said, did, and suffered the same as we do«.[17] Even if our faith were sufficient for withstanding the gates of hell, it was no light matter, continued Luther, to be surrounded by those witnesses, as »we have learned from Scripture and as we experience daily in ourselves«.[18]

These words demonstrate that the authority of the fathers was not just a formal, intellectual problem for Luther but an experiential question which his personal history and his theology helped him to resolve.[19] Likewise, by acknowledging both the contributions and the limitations of the fathers of the church, Luther was able to accept them where they supported evangelical faith and life even though he refused to place the fathers on the same level with biblical authors. The calling of the fathers was not equal to the calling of the apostles and prophets, he wrote. They were saints, but they were also human and though their spirit was willing, it encountered a flesh not just weak but resistant.[20] Even if their life were judged to be irreprehensible *coram hominibus*, still *coram Deo* the fathers relied only on God's mercy and goodness; and, most importantly, they knew how to make that distinction. Accordingly, affirmed Luther, they had strong contributions to make to live under the gospel. When the spirit was ruling what they said and did, then their words and deeds were to be gathered up like fragments of the gospel (*fragmenta Evangelica*), i.e., as words and deeds which Christ himself produced in them. Where, however, that old adversary the flesh influenced their thoughts and actions, they were not to be condemned, but on the contrary excused and tolerated. For, concluded Luther, their limitations con-

---

16 WA 54, 111,29-31: »Contra Orthodoxi media et recte via incedentes nec peccatis indulgent nec perfectiones sibi arrogant, sed peccatoribus, poenitentibus et credentibus remissionem peccatorum, gratiam, vitam et salutem tribuunt.«

17 WA 54, 113,8-14: »Pertinent enim haec ipsa non solum ad obstruendum os loquentium iniqua contra nos ... Verum etiam ad confirmandas nostras conscientias tot testimoniorum & exemplorum Veterum nube eruditas, qui eadem nobiscum senserunt, dixerunt, fecerunt & tulerunt.«

18 WA 54, 114,1-6: »Nam etsi unicuique sufficere debet sua fides in verbum DEI, ... Tamen, ut est iuxta spiritum promptum caro infirma, non levi aut parvo momento movetur pius animus, si viderit tot secula, tot exempla, tot excellentes homines ante & circa se similes sibi fuisse & similia semper facta esse per illos, qualia nos ex Scripturis didicimus & experientia quotidiana cognoscimus in nobis.«

19 Luther had been liberated from his own striving for perfection by giving credit to his father for his good intention in questioning Luther's call to the monastic life. See the dedicatory letter of his treatise on monastic vows (De votis monasticis iudicium 1521): WA 8, 573-576. I have traced this process and its effects in: Luther's Loyalties and the Augustinian Order, in: Augustine, the Harvest, and Theology (1300-1600). Essays Dedicated to Heiko Augustinus Oberman in Honor of his 60th Birthday, ed. *Kenneth Hagen*, Leiden 1990, 236-258.

20 WA 54, 115,1-4: »Non fuit eorum vocatio aequalis Apostolorum & Prophetarum vocationi. Sancti fuerunt, sed homines & quorum spiritus promptus patiebatur carnem non modo infirmam, sed et repugnantem.«

V

tribute to »our most certain consolation, [when] we see the saints of God to be similar to us weak [sinners] and to carry around their own weakness in this flesh of sin [Rom 8,3]«.[21]

This one passage illustrates how Luther freely measured the fathers against his own evangelical criterion and simultaneously integrated their contributions into the Christian struggle with sin. In other Reformation documents, this deparentification of the fathers was encoded in a principle which, at the Marburg Colloquy, Caspar Hedio imprecisely named the *regula Lutheri*: »When the fathers speak, receive them according to the canon of Scripture; if they appear to contradict that canon, either help them out with glosses or reject them.«[22] Luther's criterion was better paraphrased by Georg Major in his preface to the fathers' lives: »Let those who read this history first arm themselves with knowledge of the gospel and then bring [to their reading] a wholesome opinion about all aspects of the Christian life so that they can tell which details are appropriate to faith and which are merely superstitions.«[23] The contributions of the fathers were to be measured against the daily life of faith with all its struggles and not merely against Scripture as a formal criterion.

The *regula Lutheri* did appear more formally, however, in Reformation documents which stressed the superiority of Scripture. The *Florilegium Patristicum*, undertaken by Martin Bucer and completed by Matthew Parker, asserted twice that the authority of Scripture should receive preference over councils and the holy fathers. Canon law was cited to prove that even St. Augustine was subject to this rule, and well-known excerpts from his writings were used as additional proof.[24] The *Epitome* of the *Formula of Concord* prohibited the writings of the fathers from being placed on a par with Scripture and allowed them to be used only as testimony that the teaching of the apostles and the prophets had been faithfully preserved.[25] At the same time, the catalogue of witnesses affixed to the *Book*

---

[21] WA 54, 115,5-11: »Ubi ergo spiritu dominante loquuntur et operantur, sunt eorum verba & opera colligenda ceu fragmenta Evangelica, ut quae Dominus Christus in eis operatus sit, et vere sint Christi ipsius opera. Ubi vero carne adversante loquuntur et operantur, damnandi sane non sunt, sed excusandi vel tolerandi pro nostra certissima consolatione, qui videmus Sanctos Dei nobis infirmis similes fuisse et suam unumquenque in carne ista peccati circumtulisse infirmitatem.«

[22] In Martin Bucers Deutsche Schriften (hereafter cited DS), vol. 4, ed. *Robert Stupperich*, Gütersloh 1975, 348,17-19: »Regula Lutheri: Quando patres loquuntur, accipiantur juxta canonem scripturae. Quod si videntur contra scribere, adjuventur glossa, vel rejiciantur.«

[23] *Georg Major*, Vitae patrum (1562), B5v: »Qui igitur hanc historiam legent, sint antea praemuniti Evangelii cognitione, et adferant rectum et pium iudicium de omnibus partibus vitae Christianae, videant quae sint analoga fidei, quae econtra sint superstitiosa.«

[24] Martini Buceri Opera Latina, vol. 3: Martin Bucer et Matthew Parker, Florilegium Patristicum. Edition critique, ed. *Pierre Fraenkel*, Leiden 1988, 121-122, 151-152. The familiar text, cited from Augustine's anti-Donatist work De baptismo, claims that the writings of canonical Scripture take precedence over letters of bishops; see De baptismo contra Donatistas 2.3.4 in MPL 43, 128-129.

[25] Die Bekenntnisschriften der evangelisch-lutherischen Kirche (hereafter cited: BSLK), Göttingen ⁶1967), 767,25 - 768,7: »Andere Schriften aber der alten oder neuen Lehrer, wie sie Namen haben, sollen der heiligen Schrift nicht gleich gehalten, sondern alle zumal miteinander derselben unterworfen und anders oder weiter nicht angenommen werden, dann als Zeugen, welchergestalt

of Concord insisted, in the face of criticism, that Lutheran theologians had written about the two natures of Christ in the same terms which had been used by the fathers and by the early churches.[26] Such statements, which could be multiplied, echo little of the living connection between the struggles of reformers like Luther and the writings of the fathers.

These statements, however, were the distillation of a process of deparentification, the elements of which appear in the writings of other reformers. Take, for example, John Calvin. In his reply to Sadoleto, Calvin enunciated a balanced approach to the authority of Scripture and the fathers. Responding to Sadoleto's accusations that Protestants considered no one in the entire church worthy of trust, Calvin affirmed: »Even though we consider the Word of God alone to be beyond all judgment, we do wish to give to councils and to the fathers a certain degree of authority as long as they hold to the Word as a norm; and thus we grant to councils and to the fathers such honor and stature as they rightfully deserve under Christ.«[27] The formality of that statement is complemented in the *Institutes* by the appreciation which Calvin showed for the contributions and for the limitations of the fathers. In the prefatory address to King Francis I, Calvin claimed that if the outcome of the contest with the Roman Church were to be determined by patristic authority, then the tide of victory, to put it modestly, would turn to »our side.« And Calvin continued: »Now these fathers have written many wise and excellent things. Still, what commonly happens to men has befallen them, too. ... But we do not despise them; in fact, if it were to our present purpose, I could with no trouble at all prove that the greater part of what we are saying today meets their approval.«[28]

nach der Apostel Zeit und an welchen Orten solche Lehre der Propheten und Apostel erhalten worden.«
    26 Ibid., 1103,2-30: »Nachdem besonders im Artikel von der Person Christi etliche mit Ungrund vorgeben, dass im Buch der Concordien von den phrasibus und modis loquendi, das ist, von Weise und Art zu reden, der alten reinen Kirchen und Väter abgewichen, ... Sind dem christlichen Leser zum wahrhaftigen und gründlichen Bericht dieselbigen [Zeugnüssen der alten Kirchen und Väter] zum Ende dieses Buches in guter Anzahl auf unterschiedlichen Punkten beigedrucket worden, ...«
    27 *Calvin*, Responsio ad Sadoleti epistolam, in: Joannis Calvini Opera Selecta (hereafter OS), ed. *Peter Barth* 1, Munich 1926, 457-489: 488: »Calumnias illas, quia ad finem propero, praeterire cogor: quod nostro innitentes capiti, neminem reperimus in tota ecclesia, quem putemus fide aliqua dignum; calumnias tamen esse, iam iam satis demonstravi. Tametsi enim solum Dei verbum extra omnem iudicii aleam constituimus, concilia vero et patribus ita certam demum autoritatem constare voluimus, si ad eius normam respondeant: eo tamen honore locoque concilia et patres dignamur, quem obtinere sub Christo par est.«
    28 *Calvin*, Institutes of the Christian Religion, ed. *John T. McNeill* and trans. *Ford Lewis Battles*, Philadelphia 1960, 1, 18-19 (»Prefatory Address to King Francis I of France«). Cf. OS, vol. 3, ed. *Peter Barth* and *Wilhelm Niesel*, Munich ³1967, 17,16-30: »Praeterea calumniose nobis Patres opponunt (antiquos et melioris adhuc seculi scriptores intelligo) acsi eos haberent suae impietatis suffragatores; quorum authoritate si dirimendum certamen esset, melior victoriae pars (ut modestissime etiam loquar) ad nos inclinaret. Verum quum multa praeclare ac sapienter ab illis Patribus scripta sint, in quibusdam vero iis acciderit quod hominibus solet: ... Tum improbis clamoribus nos obruunt, ceu Patrum contemptores et adversarios. Nos vero adeo illos contemnimus, ut

Although Calvin claimed that he could appeal to the fathers, he resisted the temptation to invest excessive authority in them by basing the truth of his arguments on their opinions. Instead, using biblical phrases, he recalled that believers in Christ were not beholden to the fathers but that the reverse was true, namely, that the fathers were to serve believers by promoting obedience to Christ: »We use their writings in such a way as to remember always that all things are ours [I Cor. 3:21-22], to serve us, not to lord it over us [Luke 22:24-25], and that we all belong to the one Christ [I Cor. 3:23], whom we must obey in all things without exception [cf. Col. 3:20]. Whoever does not observe this distinction will have nothing established as certain in religion, inasmuch as these holy men were ignorant of many things, often disagreed among themselves, and sometimes even contradicted themselves.«[29]

According to this passage obedience to Christ alone gave Calvin the theological leverage to make selective use of the fathers. He was activating a free, deparentified approach when he asked how the fathers could serve believers instead of binding the faithful to their opinions.[30]

Calvin applied this balanced judgment toward the fathers when he commented on what they said about the Lord's Supper. There he both noted their limits and gave them credit at the same time: »I observe that the ancient writers also misinterpreted this memorial ... because their Supper displayed some appearance of repeated or at least renewed sacrifice. ... Certainly, since I see that they have kept a devout and orthodox sense of this whole mystery, and I do not find that they intended even in the slightest degree to detract from the Lord's unique sacrifice, *I cannot bring myself to condemn them for any impiety* [emphasis mine]; still, I think they cannot be excused for having sinned somewhat in acting as they did.«[31]

In effect, Calvin was saying that in regard to the Eucharist the fathers had good intentions despite the corruption of their ideas and that consequently he could not condemn them even if he was unwilling to excuse them. This tolerant stance toward the fathers allowed Calvin to utilize patristic writers, such as Chrysostom, to enrich his exegesis with resources from the catholic tradition.[32]

si id praesentis instituti esset, nullo negotio mihi liceat meliorem eorum partem quae hodie a nobis dicuntur, ipsorum suffragiis comprobare.«

[29] *Calvin*, Institutes, 1,18-19; cf. OS 3, 17,30 - 18,6: »Sic tamen in eorum scriptis versamur, ut semper meminerimus, omnia nostra esse, quae nobis serviant, non dominentur: nos autem unius Christi, cui per omnia, sine exceptione, parendum sit ... Hunc delectum qui non tenet, nihil in religione constitutum habebit; quando multa ignorarunt sancti viri illi: saepe inter se conflictantur, interdum etiam secum ipsi pugnant.« For the way in which Calvin treated one church father on different levels as it suited his needs, see *Irena Backus*, Calvin's Judgment of Eusebius of Caesarea. An Analysis, SCJ 22 (1991), 419-437. Backus describes Calvin's selectivity as combining »cavalier judgments with some very sensitive historical insights« (437).

[30] Calvin's qualified respect for the fathers has been pointed out by *Lane*, Calvin's Use of the Fathers and the Medievals, 167, 169. My point is to show how this qualified respect fits into a broader, coherent stance of the reformers toward the fathers.

[31] Institutio IV.18.11, in *Calvin*, Institutes, 2,1439-1440; cf. OS 5, 427,14-25.

[32] Calvin's appreciation for the universal church and its tradition is attributed in part to his use of the fathers by *Alexandre Ganoczy* and *Klaus Müller*, Calvins handschriftliche Annotationen

V

4. Melanchthon, Bugenhagen, Rhegius, Bucer

In the writings of other reformers we also find statements about the fathers which are characteristic of deparentification. These statements do one or more of the following: 1) they admit that the fathers made mistakes; 2) they acknowledge the limitations under which the fathers lived and wrote; and 3) they recognize the potential contributions which the fathers made to evangelical faith and life. The assertion of patristic error is the basis of Protestant refusals to attribute absolute authority to the fathers. Their mistakes, however, are often attributed to the fact that the fathers worked under limitations or that the problems of the sixteenth century were more difficult than those of the patristic era. For example, in the *Apology of the Augsburg Confession*, Philipp Melanchthon argued that although the ancients spoke of prayer for the dead, they did not support the efficacy of the Lord's Supper for the dead *ex opere operato*. There was great disagreement among the fathers, said Melanchthon; they were human and could be deceived. If they came back to life now and saw how their statements were being twisted to support the transfer of sacramental benefits to the dead, then, imagined Melanchthon, the fathers would express themselves very differently.[33] In his pamphlet on adultery and desertion, Johann Bugenhagen claimed that Augustine and other fathers extended the statement of Jesus about divorce beyond what Jesus intended. If, however, Augustine or Jerome had had so much trouble with marital issues as we, then without doubt, said Bugenhagen, the suffering of the people would have forced them to apply Scripture and the words of Christ differently. Besides, thought Bugenhagen, in what they wrote they were following their own understanding, and they did not intend to bind anyone to their opinion if that person could arrive at better insight into God's Word.[34]

Both Melanchthon and Bugenhagen probably overestimated the church fathers, but at least they were thinking of the fathers as human and not just of their statements. In his defense against Eck, written after the Leipzig Disputation, Melanchthon discussed the humanity of the fathers at some length. Although he

zu Chrysostomus. Ein Beitrag zur Hermeneutik Calvins, Wiesbaden 1981,33-34. Cf. *Lane*, Calvin's Use of the Fathers and the Medievals, 172-173.

[33] Apology XXIV,94-95, in BSLK, 375,44-52: »Quod vero allegant adversarii patres de oblatione pro mortuis, scimus veteres loqui de oratione pro mortuis, quam nos non prohibemus, sed applicationem coenae Domini pro mortuis ex opere operato improbamus. ... Et patrum magna dissimilitudo est. Homines erant et labi ac decipi poterant. Quamquam si nunc reviviscerent, ac viderent sua dicta praetexi luculentis illis mendaciis, quae docent adversarii de opere operato, longe aliter se ipsi interpretarentur.«

[34] *Bugenhagen*, Vom Ehebruch und weglauffen D. Johan Bugenhagen Pomer / an Königliche Maiestat zu Denemarcken etc., Wittenberg: Klug, 1540, Pivᵛ: »Etliche wörter Christi vom Scheidebrieff / hat Augustinus und andere auch / auff andere sachen gedeutet / da Christus nicht von redet / Dem haben die Babstrechte nach geleiret. Hette aber Augustinus oder Hieronymus mit den Ehesachen so viel zu schaffen gehabt als wir / sonder zweiffel weren sie / umb der Leute not willen gedrungen/ die Schrifft und wörter Christi und Pauli anders anzusehen/ Denn sie waren dazu gelert und from genug ... Wenn sie aber als die verstendigen / und Christlichen Lerer gefraget würden / so antworten sie und schreiben nach jrem verstand / und wolten gar nicht jemand anbinden an jren verstand / so ers besser aus Gottes wort küntde verstehen.«

clearly enunciated the principle that various opinions of the fathers ought to be judged by Scripture and not *vice versa*,[35] he took pains to explain why the exegetical opinions of the fathers differed from one another. As human beings, supposed Melanchthon, when they interpreted Scripture they were moved by various feelings and attitudes just as we are, and sometimes these feelings led them to misuse Scripture. Melanchthon did not condemn the fathers for that all too human error, but he did caution that, in disputes over the meaning of Scripture, it prevented the fathers from being used as reliable judges.[36]

Later in his career, when Protestant unity and survival were at stake, Melanchthon found patristic opinion to be more coherent and reliable as a theological guide. In the much disputed question of the real presence of Christ in the sacrament, Melanchthon believed that a patristic consensus existed and that it was unnecessary for him to go beyond that consensus in order to explain how Christ was present. In a letter to Veit Dietrich in 1538, Melanchthon reported that he upheld a presence of Christ in the sacrament during its administration (*in usu*) so that he would not stray too far from the opinion of the ancient theologians. In this way, continued Melanchthon, I speak piously and with respect for the creeds and stay near to the view of the fathers.[37] Melanchthon confirmed this stance in 1541 at the Regensburg Colloquy. We reject those, he said, who do not confess the true presence of the body and blood of Christ, and we hold what the Gospel teaches and what the holy fathers confess. Furthermore, Melanchthon claimed, our confession testifies that we retain the true opinion of the catholic church handed down in the gospel and in the ancient fathers.[38] For Melanchthon the patristic consensus on the presence of Christ was a contribution not just to evangelical theology but also to the church catholic.

Despite the criticism of his biographer Uhlhorn, Urbanus Rhegius admired the fathers at least as much as Melanchthon. When I first reviewed Rhegius' use of patristic sources,[39] I was surprised to discover very few instances in which Rhegius criticized the fathers. His tendency was rather to protect them, as he did for

---

[35] Defensio Phil. Melanchthonis contra Joh. Eckium (1519), in: Melanchthons Werke in Auswahl, ed. *Robert Stupperich* 1, Gütersloh 1951, 12-22: 19,34-36: »Patribus enim credo, quia scripturae credo, cui vim fieri non licet propter varias illorum sententias.« Cf. ibid., 17,36 - 18,6.

[36] Ibid., 18,7-33, esp. 18,22-26: »In eum modum sancti patres et affectu quodam rapti in sensum non malum quidem, sed impertinentem saepenumero scriptura sunt abusi. Quod ut non damno, sic tamen recipio, ut in controversia parum valere arbitrer.«

[37] *Melanchthon*, letter to Veit Dietrich, 23. April 1538, in CR, ed. *Carolus Gottlieb Bretschneider*, 3, Halle 1836, 514 (no. 1667): »Egoque ne longissime recederem a veteribus, posui in usu Sacramentalem praesentiam, et dixi, datis his rebus, Christum vere adesse, et efficacem esse.« Ibid., 515: »Ego hoc modo et religiose, [kai euagos], et verecunde de symbolis me loqui existimo, et proxime ad veterum sententiam accedere.«

[38] Scriptum Philippi [Melanchthonis] septima Maii adversariis oblatum, in: Die Vorbereitung der Religionsgespräche von Worms und Regensburg 1540/1541, ed. *Wilhelm H. Neuser*, Neukirchen 1974, 214: »Improbamus igitur eos, qui non confitentur veram praesentiam corporis et sanguinis Christi, et tenemus, quod docet evangelium et quod confitentur s[ancti] patres. Ut Hilarius inquit: ... Et Chrysostomus: ... Haec nostra confessio satis testatur nos retinere veram et catholicae ecclesiae sententiam, traditam in evangelio et antiquis patribus.«

[39] See *Hendrix*, Validating the Reformation (note 5 above).

example in 1532 when he struggled to reconcile two conflicting passages from Augustine's sermons with each other and with his own view that the mass could not be a propitiatory sacrifice.[40] He also expressed collective appreciation for the fathers in the preface to the church order which he wrote for the city of Hannover. In this historical defense of the evangelical movement, Rhegius declared that the fathers served as models of the fight against heresy which had always been, and still was, necessary in the church. Second, the fathers served as models for the orthodox, apostolic understanding of Scripture. Finally, the fathers either asserted or demonstrated the necessity of resisting bishops who made demands contrary to the gospel.[41] Although he admired them, Rhegius did not attribute excessive authority to the fathers; his statements rank them below the authority of Scripture. Nevertheless, he mentioned their limitations less frequently than the other reformers examined here.

Strong appreciation also set the tone for Martin Bucer's views of the church fathers. With special zeal Bucer cited the fathers in support of incorporating a system of discipline into the life of a reformed church. In his work on pastoral care, Bucer argued that Tertullian, Cyprian, Ambrose, and other fathers testified to the earnest practice of public confession and penance in the early church and that such discipline deserved a place in the church of his day.[42] To one recent student of Bucer it seemed that, in this argument for public penance, he gave the early church almost as much weight as Scripture.[43] Granting so much authority to the fathers was consistent with a statement in Bucer's preface to his 1536 commentary on the gospels: »I judge that those most holy ancient fathers should be regarded with the highest esteem, and singular reverence paid to the doctrines they taught and the customs they observed, because Christ lived, taught, and wrote in them.«[44] To that ringing endorsement of the fathers, however, Bucer added the typical evangelical caveat: »... even though they [the fathers] were also human and revealed it repeatedly by failings which must not be glossed over.«[45]

40 See *Hendrix*, Validating the Reformation, 298-299.

41 Kirchenordnung der statt Hannofer durch D. Urbanum Regium (Magdeburg, 1536), in: Die evangelischen Kirchenordnungen des XVI. Jahrhunderts VI/1/2, ed. *Emil Sehling*, Tübingen 1957, 980-981, 994, 997-998. See *Hendrix*, Validating the Reformation, 296.

42 *Bucer*, Von der waren Seelsorge (1538), DS 7, ed. *Robert Stupperich*, Gütersloh 1964, 67-246: 162,11 -19: »Daher ist die offentlich beicht und buss entstanden, von deren wir lesen bei dem Tertulliano, Cypriano, Ambrosio und allen alten heiligen Vättern. Wo jemant von den Christen etwan in schwere und offentliche sünd gefallen ware, durch die auch andere verergeret wurden, die hat man zur gemeinschafft des Tischs Christi nit gelassen, biss sie der Kirchen von irer Rewe und besserung dapffere und satte anzeige gegeben und genug getohn haben, das ist, sich bewisen, als denen ir sünd warlich leidt waren, und sich von hertzen zur besserung begeben hatten.« Cf. ibid., 163,18-20: »Ob diser zucht und buss der sünden haben die alten h. Vätter gar ernstlich gehalten, wie man das bei inen allen liset.«

43 *Amy Nelson Burnett*, The Yoke of Christ. Penance and Church Discipline in the Thought of Martin Bucer, Ph.D. diss. University of Wisconsin 1989, 199; cf. ibid.,407-408.

44 In sacra quatuor Evangelia (1536), ii; cited and quoted by *Donald W. Tyler Carr*, The Influence of Patristic Writings on the Ecclesiology of Martin Bucer, Ann Arbor, University Microfilms International 1982, 51. Cf. *Burnett*, The Yoke of Christ,175-176.

45 *Carr*, The Influence, 51.

That caveat notwithstanding, Bucer used the fathers with regularity in his exegesis and he invoked the fathers as a precedent on issues other than penance. In
1530, for example, he cited the fathers on behalf of his view that images should
not be allowed in the churches. The argument for appealing to the fathers on this
issue was similar to Luther's general rationale for consulting the fathers: confir-
mation of one's faith by ancient witnesses brings comfort and strength. After af-
firming that the Word of God was sufficient for true Christians as soon as they
understood it, Bucer added: »Still they rejoice and find comfort in the fact that
other saints have also followed it [God's Word]. Accordingly, we will now show
that the apostles, the martyrs and all the holy, learned fathers have agreed with
the truth which we have demonstrated about images, until, that is, the Goths and
Vandals delivered a heavy blow to our faith and to our correct understanding of
the truth.«[46]

The views of the fathers were definitely important for Bucer as precedents and
authorities, but just as valuable was the impact of their consensus on the morale
of sixteenth-century believers.

Despite this appreciation for the fathers, Bucer was still no slave to their views.
He refused to parentify them absolutely, holding his ground when he obviously
disagreed with them. Thus, in the same treatise on pastoral care in which he had
argued so strongly for public penance, he disagreed vigorously with the tendency
of the fathers to reject the marriage of clergy. The words in which St. Paul extolled celibacy had been taken by the fathers too far, Bucer thought, so far, in
fact, that they shunned marriage as if it hindered holiness. That could not be
true, said Bucer, since marriage was a work and blessing of God which was
instituted in paradise and which in its essence no sin could stain. Nevertheless, he
said, the »dear old fathers« got it into their head that marriage was too fleshly to
be compatible with the ministry or with any serious form of Christian life. For
that reason, the fathers praised virginity and widowhood so highly and
disapproved so strongly of second marriages.[47]

---

[46] *Bucer*, Das einigerlei Bild (1530), in DS 4, 174-177: 174,18-25: »Wiewol ein warer Christ in
alln dingen sich am wort Gottes, sobald er das versteht, gentzlich benügen lesset, noch frewet
und tröstet in, wenn er erkennet, das solichem auch andere heiligen gefolget haben. Derhalb
wölln wir nun anzeygen, das mit uns anzeygte warheit von bildern, glaubt und ghalten haben die
Apostel, martyrer und alle heil[igen], glerten väter, biss durch die Gothen und Wandalen unser
glaub und alle rechte erkantnus der warheit einen schweren stoss gnommen.«

[47] *Bucer*, Von der waren Seelsorge, DS 7, 126,31 - 127,10: »Es haben die lieben Vätter die wort
Pauli, damit er die keuscheit ausser der Ehe so hoch preiset, gar zeitlich zu weit verstanden und
ab der Ehe an ir selb etwas gescheuhet, gleich als ob sie an ir selb die heiligkeit verhinderte, das
solch nit sein mage; Dann sie ein werck und segen Gottes ist, im Paradis eingesetzet, welche die
sünd auch nit hat könden an ir selb veronreinen. Dises aber haben die lieben alten Vätter nit ge-
nugsam bedacht und sich imer duncken lassen, es sei in der Ehe zufil fleischlicheit [sic], darumb
sie sich mit dem Kirchendienst, ja mit allem recht eiferigem Christlichem leben ubel vertrage.
Derhalben sie dann die Jungfrawen und Witwenstende so hoch geprisen und ab der anderen ehe
so fil urtrutz gehebt haben.« Other reformers cited church fathers in support the marriage of
clergy. For example, see *Andreas Althamer*, Ain Sermon von dem eelichen stand/ dz er auch den
priestern frey sey/ gethon zu Schwebischen Gemünd ... im Jar 1525 (n.p. 1525), Bii: »Es bezeugen

It appears, therefore, that Bucer could deparentify the fathers as well as the next reformer. He used their writings as precedents and valued their support, but he also acknowledged their humanity, their limitations, and their errors. Unlike a recent student of Bucer and the fathers,[48] I therefore see little difference between the stance of Bucer and that of other magisterial reformers. Even if it were true that Bucer established a consensus of the fathers as a model for Christian society, it might not differ markedly from Zwingli's model of a reformed church, which, in the view of Alfred Schindler, was not a reconstruction of biblical conditions but of the patristic synthesis of the fourth century.[49] And although Bucer and Melanchthon might not have appealed to the fathers in identical terms, they were nevertheless able to agree on the limits of a patristic model for a reformation of the church. At their meeting in Leipzig in 1539, Georg Witzel and Georg von Karlowitz proposed to Bucer and Melanchthon the use of the first eight centuries as such a model.[50] Bucer and Melanchthon objected, however, that the fathers had taken too many contradictory and unacceptable positions on issues in dispute between Protestants and Catholics, especially if one went so far as to include the reign of Gregory the Great. Both Bucer and Melanchthon were adamant in rejecting private masses for the dead, mandatory clerical celibacy, and monastic vows, all of which, in their opinion, had been approved in some form during those centuries but still contradicted the gospel as the reformers taught it.[51]

auch jre aygne Doctores/ als Ignatius/ Tertulianus Ambrosius/ Hieronymus/ unnd ander mee/ das die hayligen Apostel haben Eeweyber gehabt/ ...«

[48] Carr claims that Bucer used the fathers as more of an authority than Melanchthon did, with the following qualification (The Influence, 54): »However, Bucer used the most significant patristic writers and did not question their doctrinal or ecclesiastical purity. His goal of unity affected his approach. On almost every topic he established the consensus of the fathers as the authoritative statement each time with the vision of a pure Christian society and church in mind.«

[49] *Schindler*, Zwingli und die Kirchenväter, 77. Cf. *Pollet*, Huldrych Zwingli et le Zwinglianisme, 337.

[50] For a summary of what happened at the colloquy, see *Günther Wartenberg*, Die Leipziger Religionsgespräche von 1534 und 1539. Ihre Bedeutung für die sächsische-albertinische Innenpolitik und für das Wirken Georgs von Karlowitz, in: Die Religionsgespräche der Reformationszeit ed. *Gerhard Müller*, Gütersloh 1980, 35-41: 38-39. See also *Heinz Scheible*, Melanchthons Auseinandersetzung mit dem Reformkatholizismus, in: Vermittlungsversuche auf dem Augsburger Reichstag 1530, ed. *Rolf Decot*, Stuttgart 1989, 68-90: 73.

[51] See the report on the colloquy by Chancellor Gregor von Brück to Elector John Frederick of Saxony, January 3, 1539, CR 3, 626: »So hat Magister Philippus und Butzer hier neben Erklärung gethan, wie es um die Patres und ihr Schreiben gelegen wäre, wie unbeständig und widerwärtig (widersprechend) Ding sie je zuweilen der jetzt streitigen Puncte halben vorgegeben. Denn wiewohl die ersten Väter bis auf Gregorium von der Winkelmesse keine Meldung thäten, sondern allein von der Communion und offenbaren (öffentlichen) Messe: so hätte doch derselbe Gregorius solche Messen durch närrische Träume eingeführt, und dieselben ein Opfer genennt für Lebendige und Todte, das bei der Alten keinem gefunden wäre. Denn obwohl etliche derselben bei der messe der Verstorbenen gedacht hätten, so hätten sie doch aus der Messe kein Opfer für die Todten gemacht. Haben darnach weiter geredt und Bericht gethan, wie die Möncherei aufkommen wäre; item wie widerwärtig die Väter der Priesterweiber halben Satzungen gemacht etc., und dasselbe dahin angezeigt, wie Karlowitz Vorgeben, dass man auf ein solch Richtscheit schwierig zur Vergleichung sollte kommen mögen.« See also the later response (January 7, 1540) to the proposal of Witzel by the Wittenberg theologians, in WABR 9, 8-11: 9,26-31: »Es ist durch

68

5. Conclusion

The appeal of Protestant reformers to the fathers was not, as we have seen, uniform; on specific issues such as the presence of Christ they certainly disagreed. In general, however, the reformers approached the fathers from a balanced stance which acknowledged both their limitations and their contributions without granting them undeserved authority. This deparentified, evangelical stance also remembered that the fathers were human beings as well as theological authorities. In an article written forty years ago, Wilhelm Schneemelcher proposed, in specific reference to Athanasius, that a similar attitude toward the fathers was appropriate for evangelical historians and theologians. The task of the patristic historian was not to condemn Athanasius as a politician or to glorify him as a saint, but to present him as a theologian, i.e. as a human being, who with all his deficits and mistakes struggled with perennial theological issues and who, with the means at his disposal, tried to realize the claim of God in his life.[52] That attitude, it seems to me, was already anticipated by Protestant reformers in the sixteenth century.

Gottes Gnad die Lehr auf unserm theil also licht und hell, und mit solchem Fleiss gefasst, dass sie keiner Glossen bedarf, und dass alle Gottfurchtigen in allen Landen bekennen mussen, es sey die rechte, reine christliche Lehr. Dergleichen ists von aller nöthigen äusserlichen Stucken, als von Abthuung aller Privatmessen, aller Anrufung der heiligen, Möncherei, von Ehestand und Brauch des Sacraments.«

[52] *Wilhelm Schneemelcher*, Wesen und Aufgabe der Patristik innerhalb der evangelischen Theologie, EvTh 10 (1950/1951), 207-222: 221 in reference to Athanasius: »Der Patristiker, d.h., der, der sine ira et studio sich der theologiegeschichtlichen Stellung des Athanasius zuwendet, wird ihn weder als Politiker zu verurteilen noch als Heiligen zu verherrlichen versuchen, sondern wird ihn als Theologen, d.h. als Menschen, der mit all seinen Mängeln und Fehlern im Rahmen der Theologiegeschichte steht und um die Fragen, die zu allen Zeiten die Theologie bewegten, gerungen hat, der als solcher Mensch unter dem Wort Gottes gestanden hat und auf seine Art und mit den ihm verfügbaren Mitteln um die Verwirklichung des Anspruches Gottes in seinem Leben sich bemüht hat, zeigen können.«

VI

IN QUEST OF THE *VERA ECCLESIA*: THE CRISES OF LATE MEDIEVAL ECCLESIOLOGY

The quest for the true church is almost as old as the church itself. Prior to the year 1300 this search manifested itself most frequently in the call for personal and communal reform and renewal. The predominant model for this reform was the *ecclesia primitiva*, an idealized picture of the earliest Christian community. This picture was a composite of the simple life and teachings of Jesus and his disciples, the allegedly unadulterated gospel of the apostles and, finally, the unselfish communal life shared by the earliest Christians as portrayed in such New Testament passages as Acts 4:32ff.[1] The last-named element served as the most important basis for the exemplary form of the quest, monasticism, which in the West became the vehicle for the Christian idea of reform.[2] The monastic renewal movement of the tenth and eleventh centuries, spearheaded by such monasteries as Cluny and Hirsau, resulted in the stringent clerical reform of Gregory VII and in the proliferation of stricter orders such as the Cistercians of the twelfth century.

Reform on the model of the apostolic ideal was also the mother of dissent in the

---

[1] The literature on the *ecclesia primitiva* as a model of reform has grown steadily since the groundbreaking work of Gerhart B. Ladner, *The Idea of Reform: Its Impact on Christian Thought and Action in the Age of the Fathers* (Cambridge, Mass. 1959); see also his article "Erneuerung" in *Reallexicon für Antike und Christentum* 6 (Stuttgart 1966) 240-275 (esp. 266-269) with extensive bibliography (269-275); and more recently, "Gregory the Great and Gregory VII: A Comparison of their Concepts of Renewal," *Viator* 4 (1973) 1-31 (with a note on the computer methods used by David Packard [27-31]). Other recent studies include Glenn Olsen, "The Idea of the *Ecclesia primitiva* in the Writings of the Twelfth-Century Canonists," *Traditio* 25 (1969) 61-86; J. S. Preus, "Theological Legitimation for Innovation in the Middle Ages," *Viator* 3 (1972) 1-26; Peter Stockmeier, "Causa reformationis und Alte Kirche: Zum Geschichtsverständnis der Reformbewegungen," in *Von Konstanz nach Trient: Beiträge zur Geschichte der Kirche von den Reformkonzilien bis zum Tridentinum. Festgabe für August Franzen,* ed. R. Bäumer (Munich 1972) 1-13. According to Stockmeier (1 n. 1) the church father Origen measures the church of his time against the ideal of the "first love"; *Homilia in Jes.* 4.2 (Griechische christliche Schriftsteller 33.259). This reference would antedate the writings of John Cassian (ca. 365-435) which, according to Olsen (66-67), seem to contain the earliest references to the idea of the primitive church. See also Louis B. Pascoe, S.J., "Jean Gerson: The 'Ecclesia primitiva' and Reform," *Traditio* 30 (1974) 379-409. Additional bibliography is cited by Olsen (61 n.1), Stockmeier (1 n.1) and Pascoe (379 n.1).

[2] Ladner, *Idea of Reform* 317ff.

© 1976 by the Regents of the University of California. Reprinted from *Viator* 7, pp. 347-378, by permission.

early Middle Ages.[3] This dissent was sparked by the failure of the Roman Church to live up to the standards of simplicity and poverty set by the ideal picture of the primitive church. As the Roman hierarchy became more and more unwilling and unable to fulfill the demands for reform imposed by dissenters such as the Humiliati and the Waldensians, it excluded them from the church, labeled them heretical, and sought to repress them by means of the Inquisition.[4]

Beginning with the fourteenth century, however, the quest for the true church assumed a multifaceted form which resulted in a much more complex ecclesiological landscape than had hitherto existed. The ideal of the primitive church was not discarded, but it was supplemented by a variety of ecclesiological theories which went beyond the simple call for a return to the apostolic ideal. These theories were embodied in treatises which were devoted primarily to ecclesiological questions. Whereas prior to 1300 ecclesiological issues seldom received exclusive attention except in the writings of the canonists, the next two centuries were punctuated by the appearance of tracts *De ecclesia* which sought to define the locus of the true church and to spell out the foundation of its authority. These screeds were written by papalists, conciliarists and advocates of views which can be classified as neither of the above. Studies of the church and its authority were composed by orthodox and heterodox alike, from the Augustinian James of Viterbo at the turn of the fourteenth century[5] to the ex-Augustinian Martin Luther at the end of the Middle Ages.[6]

---

[3] Jeffrey B. Russell, *Dissent and Reform in the Early Middle Ages* (Berkeley 1965) 5ff. The key role played by the apostolic way of life in religious movements of dissent was stressed most emphatically by Herbert Grundmann, *Religiöse Bewegungen im Mittelalter,* ed. 3 (Darmstadt 1970) esp. 13-69. Grundmann wrote already in the first edition of his work (Berlin 1935) 21: "Der Gedanke der christlichen Armut und des apostolischen Lebens als Wanderprediger ist der wesentliche Gehalt der Ketzerei sowohl in Köln als in Südfrankreich, und dieser Gedanke ist tatsächlich das Hauptmotiv der Ketzerei bis in den Anfang des 13. Jahrhunderts, bei den Katharen wie bei den Waldensern, immer geblieben." This theme has been pursued in detail for the later Middle Ages by Gordon Leff, *Heresy in the Later Middle Ages,* 2 vols. (Manchester 1967); idem, "The Apostolic Ideal in Later Medieval Ecclesiology," *Journal of Theological Studies* 18 (1967) 58-82; idem, "The Making of the Myth of a True Church in the Later Middle Ages," *Journal of Medieval and Renaissance Studies* 1 (1971) 1-15. See also Preus 12-19.

[4] On these developments and especially the role of Innocent III see Grundmann 70-156; Leff, *Heresy* 1.1-47; Hans Wolter, S.J., in *Handbuch der Kirchengeschichte,* ed. H. Jedin, 3.2 (Freiburg 1968) 197-213 (with extensive bibliography).

[5] The treatise of James of Viterbo (*De regimine christiano* 1302) was only part of the large volume of publicist literature produced by the curialists in defense of Boniface VIII against Philip IV of France. Similar works, such as *De ecclesiastica sive de summi pontificis potestate* (1301-1302) of Giles of Rome and *De potestate papae* (1301) of Heinrich of Cremona, dealt primarily with the relationship between papal and temporal power. For a detailed survey, see Richard Scholz, *Die Publizistik zur Zeit Philipps des Schönen und Bonifaz' VIII* (Stuttgart 1903; repr. Amsterdam 1969). H.-X. Arquillière called the work of James of Viterbo the "oldest treatise on the church"; *Le plus ancien traité de l'Eglise. Jacques de Viterbe: De regimine christiano (1301-1302). Etude des sources et édition critique* (Paris 1926). W. Kölmel judiciously qualifies this statement by pointing out that James's intention was not to write a doctrine of the church *per se,* since the primary focus of all these works was the relationship between the two powers; *Regimen christianum: Weg und Ergebnisse des Gewaltenverhältnisses und des Gewalten-*

The variety and sophistication of these ecclesiological works transposed the late medieval quest for the true church into a higher key. The new intensity which marked this quest was sparked by a crisis of confidence in the papal hierarchy which began in the thirteenth century with the challenge of the Waldensians and the Franciscan Spirituals. It received added fuel in the conflict between the papacy and the French and imperial rulers and burned brightest during the conflict between pope and pope, and pope and council, during the Great Schism (1378-1417). In the aftermath of the schism the quest appeared to die down, only to flame up again, at first a mere flicker, in the reluctant resistance of Martin Luther which finally ignited the Protestant Reformation. In all stages of the crisis, critics of the established church and especially of the papal hierarchy proposed ecclesiological alternatives which substantially limited (and occasionally eliminated) the authority of the papacy in their views of the church. Dissident groups and thinkers constructed models of the church which in many cases were far removed from the existing ecclesial reality.

The new quest for the church thus resulted in a broad spectrum of ecclesiological options being made available to late medieval men. Consequently, to a number of historians who have taken note of the complexity of late medieval ecclesiology, the late Middle Ages have appeared to be a period of ecclesiological confusion and uncertainty.[7] A few have even used this disagreement on the nature and authority of

---

verständnisses (8. bis 14. Jahrhundert) (Berlin 1970) 361. Kölmel discusses the curialist position, which he labels the "hierarchical theory" and the "ecclesiarchal doctrine" in considerable detail, 263-454, 591-608. These curialist treatises point up the way in which the crisis of papal authority demanded a more detailed and sophisticated treatment of the church's nature than had previously been necessary. However, such treatment was not unprecedented in the thirteenth century. In his treatise against the Cathars and the Waldensians, Moneta of Cremona († ca. 1260) devoted one of his chapters to the topic: "De ecclesia catholica quae sit?" *Summa adversus Catharos et Valdenses* 5.1, ed. T. Ricchini (Rome 1743) 389-408. A guide to the varieties of late medieval ecclesiology including curialist thought is provided by Friedrich Merzbacher, "Wandlungen des Kirchenbegriffs im Spätmittelalter," *Zeitschrift der Savigny-Stiftung für Rechtsgeschichte* 70, kan. Abt. 39 (1953) 264-361. Merzbacher's emphasis on the development of ecclesiological thinking away from spiritual-mystical categories to legal ones (281, 355) is counteracted by the more balanced survey of Yves Congar, *Die Lehre von der Kirche von Augustinus bis zum Abendländischen Schisma,* Handbuch der Dogmengeschichte 3.3c (Freiburg 1971) and *Die Lehre von der Kirche vom Abendländischen Schisma bis zur Gegenwart, ibid.* 3.3d (Freiburg 1971).
    [6] It is ironical that the protest of Martin Luther against papal sovereignty was made by a member of the same order which had spawned the most ardent defenders of this sovereignty in the early fourteenth century (James of Viterbo, Giles of Rome, Augustinus Triumphus of Ancona). On the place of these theologians within the Augustinian Order, see A. Zumkeller, "Die Augustinerschule des Mittelalters: Vertreter und Philosophisch-theologische Lehre," *Analecta Augustiniana* 27 (1964) 176-186, 192-193, 196-199, 201-203. The ecclesiological variety within the Augustinian Order itself (see below on Augustinus Favaroni) is a good example of the range of ecclesiological positions which were represented in the later Middle Ages.
    [7] See Brian Tierney, *Origins of Papal Infallibility 1150-1350,* Studies in the History of Christian Thought 6 (Leiden 1972) 170: "At the beginning of the fourteenth century the whole field of Catholic ecclesiology was in a state of considerable disarray." Congar (n. 5 above) 3.3d. 1-2 uses the term "crisis": "Mit dem 14. Jahrhundert tritt man in die Zeit der Krise, ja der Auflösung der überkommenen Ordnung: ... In dem Bewusstsein, das man von der Kirche hat,

VI

350

the church to discredit the later Middle Ages in contrast to the preceding centuries and to explain how the Reformers of the sixteenth century were able so easily to captivate late medieval people.[8] Just as crisis does not equal decline, however, neither is variety equivalent, to confusion and decadence. Crisis periods do, to be sure, tear down old securities and ideals. However, they also produce new solutions and new certainties. Instead of disparaging the diversified late medieval quest for the true church as a sign of theological and ecclesiastical degeneration, it is historically more productive to look for its provenance and significance in the context of its times.

The heightened sense of urgency which characterized the quest both distinguishes it from its early medieval manifestations and identifies it as part and parcel of the crisis atmosphere of the late Middle Ages in general. This crisis went deeper than a crisis of confidence in the papacy. It presented many faces — social, political, economic, and ecclesiastical[9] — and historians are by no means agreed on which factors ought to be weighed most heavily in assessing the crisis.[10] Recently, however, F. Graus has offered a tentative explanation for the ecclesiological crisis of the later Middle Ages which deserves attention for its ability to interrelate economic, social,

---

treten eine offizielle, hierarchische Seite und eine christliche Seite ... auseinander." See E. Iserloh in *Handbuch der Kirchengeschichte* 4 (Freiburg 1967) 9: "Die Unsicherheit war besonders gross hinsichtlich des Kirchenbegriffs"; H. Jedin, "Ekklesiologie um Luther," *Fuldaer Hefte,* ed. G. Klapper, 18 (Berlin 1968) 10: "Seit dem Ende des 13. Jahrhunderts, etwa seit Johannes von Paris, wird die Kirche, ihre Reform und im Zusammenhang damit ihr Begriff zum Problem. Das ganze Spätmittelalter ... ist erfüllt von Auseinandersetzungen um den Kirchenbegriff."

[8] For example, J. Lortz's pessimistic view of the late Middle Ages and his negative assessment of the Reformation appear to have mutually influenced each other. Particularly detrimental, in his opinion, was the "theological confusion" of the late medieval period: "Die theologische Unklarheit innerhalb der katholischen Theologie war eine der besonders wichtigen Voraussetzungen für die Entstehung einer kirchlichen Revolution. Sie ist einer der Schlüssel, die das Rätsel des gewaltigen Abfalls einigermassen lösen"; *Die Reformation in Deutschland,* ed. 4, 2 vols. (Freiburg 1962) 1.137. See the summary of Lortz's views by Steven Ozment, *The Reformation in Medieval Perspective* (Chicago 1971) 3-11. See Jedin (n. 7 above) 28: "Auch Luther will das Christentum als Kirche. Er findet keine geschlossene Ekklesiologie vor, er stösst sich aber begreiflicherweise an der Gestalt der Kirche, die ihn umgibt."

[9] For a comprehensive survey of the literature, see F. Graus, "Das Spätmittelalter als Krisenzeit: Ein Literaturbericht als Zwischenbilanz," *Mediaevalia Bohemica* supp. 1 (1969).

[10] Graus 26 notes that most historians have come to acknowledge the central role played by the agrarian crisis of the fourteenth century. The explanations offered for this crisis are mostly demographic and link population shifts with the effects of the Black Death (*ibid.* 46-47). However, Graus believes that population statistics for the fourteenth century are too unreliable to support unequivocally a demographic explanation and generally concludes that the discussion of causes of the crisis is still too much in flux to draw any final conclusions (*ibid.* 55). J. Engel has insisted that intellectual and political decisions must be taken into account when considering the causes of the economic vagaries of medieval society. Engel graphically illustrates his point: the responsible agent in the rapid, and often agriculturally devastating, proliferation of sheepherding was not the sheep, but the shifting attitude of those men who decided that taking up the crook was more profitable than pushing the plow; *Handbuch der europäischen Geschichte,* ed. T. Schieder, 3 (Stuttgart 1971) 432.

political and religious factors.[11] According to Graus, the description of a crisis includes all the phenomena which result in the breaking up of a way of life in a society. Most important is the feeling of the people that the basic values of their society have been menaced to such an extent that they appear on the verge of disintegrating.[12] Late medieval society manifested this heightened sense of insecurity in several domains: economic instability, social unrest, urban tension, national feeling. For Graus, however, spiritual values are more crucial than socio-economic factors to any analysis of the causes of crisis in a society.[13] These spiritual values were particularly threatened by the religious perplexity provoked by the Great Schism of the Western church. Thus Graus regards the crisis of the late Middle Ages as coming to a head in the crisis of confidence in the identity and authority of the church.[14]

The insights of Graus suggest why a crisis of confidence in the papacy could provoke such an intense quest for the true church in the later Middle Ages. The purpose of the present essay is to examine selected expressions of this quest from the perspective of Graus, that is, to view the ecclesiologies which arose out of this quest as responses of late medieval people to the uncertainty surrounding the church's nature and authority. Since it is impossible to deal with the whole of late medieval ecclesiology in one essay, this discussion is limited to representative samples of the quest which display both the nuances of ecclesiological answers and the continuity of ecclesiological themes which have been recognized with ever finer discrimination in recent research. From this perspective, the crisis-marred landscape of late medieval ecclesiology appears much less confused and disarrayed, since the varied contours of the quest for the true church are seen as attempts to establish a sure ecclesiological foothold in the midst of an unsure social and ecclesiastical order. Furthermore, as the concluding section will propose, the Reformation of the sixteenth century may be appropriately regarded as the concluding phase of the late medieval quest in which again a variety of ecclesiological responses are made to the last medieval crisis of papal authority.

I

In the transition from the early medieval call for reform to the late medieval quest for the true church, many critics who railed against the wealth and power of the

---

[11] F. Graus, "The Crisis of the Middle Ages and the Hussites," in *The Reformation in Medieval Perspective* (n. 8 above) 76-103.

[12] *Ibid.* 81. Hermann Heimpel summed up the peculiar crisis atmosphere of late medieval Germany in a not unrelated way as *Unentschiedenheit*; "Das Wesen des deutschen Spätmittelalters," *Archiv für Kulturgeschichte* 35 (1953) 29-51; English: "Characteristics of the Late Middle Ages in Germany," in *Pre-Reformation Germany*, ed. Gerald Strauss (New York 1972) 43-72. 43-72.

[13] Graus (n. 11 above) 91ff.

[14] *Ibid.* 88ff.

352

thirteenth-century church continued to measure that church by the standard of the *ecclesia primitiva*. In fact, this ideal persisted so strongly in the late Middle Ages that Gordon Leff was led to call the ideal of an apostolic church "the great new ecclesiological fact of the later Middle Ages."[15] For centuries, however, the apostolic ideal had been cherished and invoked in countless cloisters of western Europe without questioning the legitimacy of the church hierarchy.[16] Why, beginning with regularity in the twelfth and thirteenth centuries, were existing monastic structures no longer able to embody and nourish this ancient and revered ideal? Why did dissenting groups, such as the Waldensians and Franciscan Spirituals, give to this ideal an ever sharper polemical edge in their quest for the true church? Although the employment of the apostolic ideal *per se* was by no means a new ecclesiological strategy in the later Middle Ages, the peculiar critical intensity with which it was applied marked the first stage in the later medieval quest for the true church.

According to Leff, this intensity could be attributed to the revolutionary way in which late medieval dissenters harnessed the Bible into an historical justification for demanding a church modeled on the early Christian community.[17] This use of the Bible assumed two forms. On the one hand, Christ's words and deeds were taken as real historical events and, where necessary, were used to counter the allegedly false claims and laws of the existing hierarchy. On the other hand, the Bible became a vehicle of prophecy in which real events took on eschatological significance.

The Waldensians illustrate the first type of usage.[18] At first, their purpose was merely to embody and proclaim the apostolic ideal of poverty and simplicity. In spite of the papal prohibition against their preaching without clerical sanction, Valdes considered it more necessary to obey the biblical injunction to preach (Mark 16:15) than the injunction to be subject to authority (Romans 13:1). As a result, in 1184 the "Poor Men of Lyon" were declared heretical.[19] The Waldensians then developed their own hierarchy and employed the Bible as a blueprint for their common life together apart from the Roman Church. Indulgences, oaths, intercession of the saints and many other non-biblical practices were rejected as ecclesiastical innovations. They believed that they alone constituted the true church and that their priests alone deserved to perform sacramental functions because they were faithful to the *vita apostolica*.[20]

---

[15] Leff, "Apostolic Ideal" (n. 3 above) 71.

[16] See above n. 1.

[17] Leff, "Making of the Myth" (n. 3 above) 2-3.

[18] *Ibid.*11-15; see Leff, *Heresy* (n. 3 above) 2.452-485; Grundmann (n. 3 above) 91-100; Christine Thouzellier, *Catharisme et valdéisme en Languedoc à la fin du XIIe et au début du XIIIe siècle: Politique pontificale. Controverses* (Paris 1966). For additional information on the sources, see *Handbuch der Kirchengeschichte* (n. 4 above) 3.2.125; K.-V. Selge, *Die ersten Waldenser*, 2 vols. (Berlin 1967); *Heresies of the High Middle Ages*, ed. and trans. W. L. Wakefield and A. P. Evans (New York 1969) 50-53, 200-241, 650-651, 661.

[19] *Enchiridion symbolorum definitionum et declarationum*, ed. H. Denzinger and A. Schönmetzer, ed. 34 (Freiburg 1967) nos. 760-761; see Grundmann (n. 3 above) 67-69.

[20] Grundmann (n. 3 above) 94-96. As Grundmann points out, this position was not taken by

Since the Waldensians were early ejected from the church, they never posed as serious a threat to the hierarchy as did the Franciscan Spirituals of the later thirteenth century. The more polemical Spirituals struck at the hierarchy from within what had quickly become one of the most significant orders of the church. They read Scripture through the bifocal lens of Saint Francis's Rule and Joachim of Fiore's prophecy. Hence, they illustrate the second usage of the Bible which Leff delineates: the Bible as a vehicle of prophecy.[21] For example, the prophetic exegesis of the Apocalypse by Peter John Olivi (†1298) gave added urgency to the Spirituals' criticism of the pope. Olivi's followers, the Fraticelli, were quick to identify the carnal church of the Antichrist with the Roman Church which would soon be superseded by the true spiritual church composed of themselves. Such eschatological interpretation of current events turned the debate over apostolic poverty into a confrontation between the true and false churches.

In spite of the enthusiasm of Olivi's followers, disagreement now prevails over the question whether Olivi's *Postilla super Apocalypsim* unequivocally labeled the Roman Church as the carnal church of the Antichrist.[22] In view of this disagreement, the light which Brian Tierney has shed on the "enigmatic" Olivi has been particularly helpful.[23] As the first medieval thinker to attribute infallibility to the pope, Olivi was concerned that the papal decree *Exiit,* promulgated by Nicholas III in 1279, be observed by succeeding popes as confirming the divine authorization of Franciscan poverty and the inspired nature of the Franciscan Rule. Why then would Olivi write at times as if to extol only the followers of Saint Francis as the true church and condemn virtually the whole existing hierarchy as the carnal church?

---

all Waldensians at first; in fact it was a source of irreconcilable conflict between Italian and French Waldensians in the early thirteenth century. A letter from the Italian faction, the Poor Lombards, to some Waldensians in Germany summarizes the position of the French Waldensians and the Lombards' disagreement: "Dixerunt etiam per neminem sive bonum sive malum, nisi per eum qui est Deus et homo, i.e. Christum, panis et vini visibilis in Christi corpus et sanguinem posse transsubstantiari substantiam. Et hucusque de hac tertia sacramenti huius responsione nos et illi concordes fuimus; de hoc autem, quod addiderunt, orationem adulteri sive cuiuslibet malitiosi in hoc a Domine exaudiri et recipi, ab eis, quia a veritatis tramite deviat, dissentimus; . . . Item quod Dominus iniquorum ministrationem non recipiat et eorum orationem non exaudiat, ex subsequentibus late patet. . . ." *Rescriptum haeresiarcharum Lombardiae ad Leonistas in Alamannia* in *Beiträge zur Sektengeschichte des Mittelalters,* ed. I. von Döllinger, 2 vols. (repr. New York 1970) 2.48-49; also in Wakefield and Evans, *Heresies* (n. 18 above) 284-285. By the time the inquisitorial tract of David of Augsburg († 1271) *De inquisitione haereticorum* appeared, Waldensians (whether Lombard or French) were to be asked: "Si quilibet bonus homo possit consecrare, nisi sit ordinatus et a quo. Si malus sacerdos possit consecrare et alia sacramenta conferre ecclesiastica." *Beiträge* 2.320.

[21] Leff, "Making of the Myth" (n. 3 above) 4-11 and *Heresy* (n. 3 above) 1.51-166. For a detailed account of the impact of Joachite thought, see Marjorie Reeves, *The Influence of Prophecy in the Later Middle Ages: A Study in Joachimism* (Oxford 1969).

[22] Several recent studies have concluded that he did not. See Leff, *Heresy* (n. 3 above) 1.126, 129; Reeves (n. 21 above) 199; see also the brief summary of the debate by Tierney (n. 7 above) 108-109.

[23] "Enigmatic" seems to be a popular way of describing Olivi. See Reeves (n. 21 above) 194 and Tierney (n. 7 above) 94.

354

Such a juxtaposition would appear to undermine the very hierarchy upon which Olivi depended for the authentication of the Franciscan *usus pauper*. According to Tierney, the reason lies in Olivi's premonition that a future Roman pontiff might pervert the faith of the church and, in so doing, receive the support of almost the whole church. Thus it was necessary for a small remnant, the faithful followers of Saint Francis, to preserve the teaching of *Exiit* as the backdrop against which the coming pseudo-pope could be exposed.[24]

Tierney has demonstrated how the *Postilla* fits coherently into the total pattern of Olivi's thought. The remnant of a spiritual church is necessary in order to guard the teaching of an infallible pope (Nicholas III) against the expected sovereign claims of his successors. Vice versa, the doctrine of infallibility is necessary to ensure the divine sanction and historical irreversibility of the teaching upon which this spiritual group is based.

The implications of Tierney's argument are twofold. First, no matter how formally orthodox Olivi might be judged because he stops short of a specific identification of the Roman hierarchy with the carnal church, Olivi did store up explosive ammunition which his followers could use against the Roman Church in the name of a spiritual church. And, secondly, it appears that the Bible was not as central to Olivi's vision of an incorruptible spiritual church as Leff has argued was true for the Franciscan Spirituals. In fact, the most important document for the claims of the Spirituals was not Scripture, but a new extrascriptural revelation to the church transmitted, in this case, by Saint Francis.[25] Although the apostolic ideal formed the core of the Spirituals' concern, the scriptural basis of this concern assumed a secondary role. The primary issues became, as in the case of the Waldensians, the nature of the church and the authority to interpret Scripture. The Spirituals, like the Waldensians, eventually came to believe that they composed the true spiritual church because they alone faithfully adhered to the rule of apostolic poverty.[26] Since this belief placed both groups in minority positions, they were forced to develop remnant ecclesiologies which located the *vera ecclesia* in the faithful few opposed to the apostate many. On the question of authority, the Spirituals were even willing to endow both an extrascriptural document and an extrascriptural office with divine authority — all, of course, in the name of a scriptural ideal.

---

[24] Tierney (n. 7 above) 125-130.

[25] *Ibid.* 110-111.

[26] Leff maintains that the Spirituals did not conceive of the *ecclesia spiritualis* as separate from the *ecclesia carnalis* but as the same church in different hands, i.e., of the true followers of Christ who wished to regenerate the one church, not to replace the existing church with a new one. *Heresy* (n. 3 above) 1.176, 191. Leff himself admits, however, that this fine distinction was not always maintained. "Making of the Myth" (n. 3 above) 7. On the Waldensians, see Leff, "Apostolic Ideal" (n. 3 above) 75, and *Heresy* (n. 3 above) 2.453, 457. According to David of Augsburg, Waldensians were to be asked: "Si ecclesia Romana est ecclesia Christi vel meretrix. . . Si Pauperes Valdenses, Lombardi vel Ultramontani sint ecclesia Dei. Si congregatio Catholicorum est ecclesia Christi." *Beiträge* (n. 20 above) 2.320-321.

VI

Granted that the reading of the Bible imparted new seriousness to the apostolic ideal in the twelfth and thirteenth centuries, the question still remains: why at this particular juncture in the Middle Ages did medieval *viatores* become so serious about the apostolic ideal that, as H. Grundmann has pointed out,[27] they attempted to apply it to the entire clergy and laity? After all, the Bible had always been the source of the apostolic ideal. Cultural, social and economic factors figure significantly in the answer to this question, but to an extent as yet unclarified.[28] Additional guidance in answering the question can be gained by analyzing the crucial ecclesiological shift in the medieval landscape which occurred in the late twelfth and thirteenth centuries. This shift involved the transition from an ecclesiological stance which sought to reform the church on the model of the *ecclesia primitiva* to a remnant ecclesiology which limited the true church to a minority either outside (the Waldensians) or within (the Spiritual Franciscans up to 1322-1323) the Roman Church. What made this transition necessary? On the surface, the Roman Church was unwilling to allow such expressions of the apostolic ideal to persist unsupervised and unchecked in the church. At a more profound level, however, the transition was made necessary for the same reason that the apostolic ideal was treated with new seriousness and breadth in the first place: a heightened degree of uncertainty as to the locus of the true church.

The concept of the *ecclesia primitiva* itself can provide helpful insights into the reason why this uncertainty developed. G. Olsen has shown that the twelfth-century canonists used the term *ecclesia primitiva* to refer primarily to the pre-Constantinian church; such usage "suggested that the great divide in early church history was the reign of the first Christian emperor Constantine."[29] The canonists themselves, while not explicitly expressing distaste for the success of Christianity after Constantine, at least implicitly were concerned about the integrity of Christianity in a world which made the church materially prosperous. Moralists like Bernard of Clairvaux had no qualms about making this implicit concern explicit and bewailing the worldliness of the post-Constantinian church in which the apostolic ideal had been betrayed.[30] In a passage well known throughout the Middle Ages and quoted approvingly even by Martin Luther, Bernard noted the manifold persecutions which the pre-Constantinian church had to suffer. Consequently, he warned against the easy security which the prosperous church of his time enjoyed; this security constituted a far greater threat

---

[27] Grundmann (n. 3 above) 23, 506ff. See M.-D. Chenu, O.P., "Monks, Canons and Laymen in Search of the Apostolic Life." in *Nature, Man, and Society in the Twelfth Century,* ed. and trans. J. Taylor and L. Little (Chicago 1968) 202-238.
[28] Grundmann (n. 3 above) 34-35, 157-168, 519-524 is very reluctant to attribute the resurgence and broad application of the apostolic ideal to social causes and in particular to poverty. Chenu (n. 27 above) 230-238 assigns more importance to the social and intellectual stirrings of the twelfth and thirteenth centuries. He sees these as enhancing the "evangelical sensitivity" of the age.
[29] Olsen (n. 1 above) 86.
[30] *Ibid.* 82-84.

VI

356

to the peace of the church than open persecution, for the church's worst enemies were those who posed as her friends.[31]

A stark contrast with the worldliness of the post-Constantinian church therefore colored the concept of the *ecclesia primitiva*. It is not difficult to understand why, then, certain groups within the church invoked the ideal of apostolic poverty for everyone in order to restore the medieval church to its pre-Constantinian integrity. The Gregorian reform attempted to impress marks of the *vita apostolica* upon the clergy. Amidst the growing involvement of the medieval church in the economically and intellectually awakening world of the twelfth-century renaissance, it was only natural that this ideal would be extended by some groups to the entire church. In the case of the Franciscans, the situation was somewhat different. Here the concern was to restore their order, which had received special revelation of the divine sanction of this ideal, to its original state of strict poverty. Nevertheless, the result of both remarkably earnest applications of the ideal was the same. The concept of the *ecclesia primitiva* was transformed into a remnant ecclesiology when the demand for broader communication and stricter application of the apostolic ideal was not granted. Thus, in contrast to their status as the only ture church, the Waldensians portrayed the Roman Church as having embodied the *congregatio peccatorum* from the time of Sylvester I. And the Spirituals claimed to represent the spiritual church over against the *ecclesia carnalis* which refused to attribute due significance to the ideal of poverty.[32]

The concept of an *ecclesia primitiva* served these groups well as long as they fostered realistic hopes of reforming the Roman Church on the basis of apostolic poverty. When these hopes were dashed, however, the first in a series of spiritual crises which rocked the later Middle Ages occurred – a crisis of confidence in the church hierarchy serious enough to stimulate a quest for the true church apart from that hierarchy. This crisis was fundamentally ecclesiological in nature. In its first phase, uncertainty as to whether or not the Roman Church was living up to the ideal of the primitive church caused the biblical source of this ideal to be taken with renewed seriousness. When it became clear that the Roman Church would not allow this ideal to be expressed to the extent which these groups desired, the crisis then moved into its next phase in which a decisive shift of emphasis was made: the

[31] *Ibid.* See Bernard, *Sermones in Cantica canticorum* 33.14-16 (PL 183.958-959). Bernard writes: "Et pax est, et non est pax. Pax a paganis, et pax ab haereticis; sed non profecto a filiis" (*ibid.* 33.16; PL 183.959). For Luther's use of the passage in his first Psalms lectures (*Dictata super Psalterium* 1513-1515) see Joseph Vercruysse, *Fidelis populus* (Wiesbaden 1968) 122-123, 130-131. Olsen (n. 1 above) 84 n. 60 expresses misgivings about the allegedly excessive wealth of the papal curia which could have given moralists such as Bernard legitimate cause for concern.
[32] In the treatise of David of Augsburg, the Waldensians are to be asked: "Si ecclesia Dei defecit tempore Silvestri. Et quis reparavit eam. Si Silvester papa fuit Antichristus." *Beiträge* (n. 20 above) 320. See Leff, "Making of the Myth" (n. 3 above) 14, 15. The idea that the beginning of evil in the Roman Church went back to the wealth acquired through the Donation of Constantine seems to have entered the thought of the Spirituals later in the fourteenth century. See Reeves (n. 21 above) 411.

concept of the *ecclesia primitiva* was applied to a remnant. Without delay, this remnant began to manifest one of the essential criteria for claiming equality with the primitive church – persecution. Persecution haunted the Waldensians in the Inquisition and the Spirituals before and after their condemnation. In this radically new ecclesiological application of an old ideal, the late medieval quest for the true church was underway.

II

The ecclesiological crisis atmosphere became increasingly tense during the first half of the fourteenth century. The controversy between Boniface VIII and Philip the Fair ended in a debacle for the papacy. Strong measures had to be taken to shore up its authority and prestige. That became clear already during the course of the controversy when the curial publicists, led by Giles of Rome, articulated the hitherto most radical claims to papal sovereignty.[33] As the ecclesiastical conflict shifted from the confrontation between the papacy and the king of France to that between the papacy and the emperor (Louis of Bavaria), other champions of papal sovereignty arose to tighten the bond between membership in the true church and obedience to papal rulings. Some curialists, like Augustinus Triumphus of Ancona, used the target of thirteenth-century papal critics, the Donation of Constantine, to support the pope's authority over the emperor,[34] while others, like Guido of Terreni, adopted Olivi's concept of infallibility to preserve that papal sovereignty which it was originally intended to restrict.[35]

The radical nature of the curialist claims betrays the gravity of the situation which threatened the papacy. The seriousness of the crisis during the conflict with Louis of Bavaria was also revealed by the earnestness and intensity with which the two most significant critics of the papacy undertook their task: Marsilius of Padua and William

---

[33] For example, Giles writes: "Sic inter ipsos fideles universi domini temporales et universa potestas terrena debet regi et gubernari per potestatem spiritualem et ecclesiasticam, et specialiter per summum pontificem, qui in ecclesia et in spirituali potestate tenet apicem et supremum gradum. Ipse autem summus pontifex a solo Deo habet iudicari. Ipse est enim, ut supra diximus, qui iudicat omnia et iudicatur a nemine [I Cor. 2:15], idest a nullo puro homine sed a solo Deo." *De ecclesiastica potestate* 1.5, ed. R. Scholz (repr. Aalen 1961) 17. The application of I Cor. 2:15 was not original with Giles. Cf. S. H. Hendrix, *Ecclesia in via: Ecclesiological Developments in the Medieval Psalms Exegesis and the Dictata super Psalterium (1513-1515) of Martin Luther,* Studies in Medieval and Reformation Thought 8 (Leiden 1974) 185 n. 104. On Giles, see Scholz (n. 5 above) 32-129; Kölmel (n. 5 above) 291-360; Merzbacher (n. 5 above) 295-300.

[34] W. D. McCready, "The Problem of the Empire in Augustinus Triumphus and Late Medieval Papal Hierocratic Theory," *Traditio* 30 (1974) 325-349. Augustinus dedicated his *Summa de potestate papae* to John XXII in 1320. At the time of the controversy between Boniface and Philip, however, he had written several smaller tracts in support of the curialist position. Scholz (n. 5 above) 172-189.

[35] Tierney (n. 7 above) 238-272.

of Ockham.[36] Both men employed ecclesiological tools forged already in the preceding century in order to gauge the approximation of the Roman hierarchy to their conception of the true church. Both found the amount of deviation too great for their liking and proposed ecclesiological adjustments which would correct for the inordinate authority attributed to the papacy. For both writers, albeit in slightly differing respects, the abuse of this authority accounted for the crisis which afflicted the church.

In the case of Marsilius, the very title of his work, *Defensor pacis* (condemned in 1327), indicates that he considered himself to be the guardian of social tranquillity and peace against a "singular and very obscure cause [of strife] by which the Roman Empire has long been troubled."[37] At the end of the first discourse, Marsilius finally reveals that this singular cause is the wrong opinion of certain Roman bishops that they have coercive temporal jurisdiction over the Roman ruler and also, perhaps, their perverted desire for rulership allegedly owed to them because of the plenitude of power bestowed by Christ.[38] The source of this papal claim to authority over all other bishops and even over temporal rulers is "a certain edict and gift which certain men say that Constantine made to Saint Sylvester, Roman pontiff."[39]

Marsilius's reference to the Donation of Constantine suggests that Gordon Leff may be correct when he contends that Marsilius stood in the tradition of those seekers of the true church who invoked the pre-Constantinian apostolic ideal as the model of church reform.[40] Although, of course, he was not the first to employ that ideal, Leff claims that Marsilius "wrought it into the most devastating weapon of political criticism in later medieval ecclesiology."[41] According to Leff, this reaffirmation of the apostolic way of life is much more crucial to Marsilius's criticism of the Roman hierarchy than his use of Aristotelian political philosophy to formulate a theory of popular sovereignty.[42] Although Leff has not conclusively demonstrated what he calls the "bypassing" of Aristotle by late medieval critics of church and

---

[36] Scholz attributed both the publicist writings and the reactions of Marsilius and Ockham to far-reaching changes in church and society (n. 5 above) 458: "Beide sind der Ausdruck der grossen sozialen, politischen und kirchlichen Umwälzungen der vorangegangenen Jahrhunderte. Die mittelalterliche feodale Gesellschafts- und Staatsordnung und die alte Stellung der Kirche und ihrer Einrichtungen bilden sich um."

[37] Marsilius, *Defensor pacis* 1.1.3; trans. Alan Gewirth, *Marsilius of Padua: The Defender of Peace* 2 (New York 1956) 4-5.

[38] *Ibid.* 1.19.11-12 (Gewirth 95).

[39] *Ibid.* 1.19.8 (Gewirth 93).

[40] Leff, "Apostolic Ideal" (n. 3 above) 67, and *Heresy* (n. 3 above) 2.416.

[41] Leff, "Apostolic Ideal" (n. 3 above) 67.

[42] Specifically, Leff is arguing against the thesis of W. Ullmann and M. J. Wilks that Marsilius's use of Aristotle was the primary contributing factor to the breakdown of the Thomistic synthesis of church and state. "Apostolic Ideal" (n. 3 above) 58-65; cf. his *Heresy* (n. 3 above) 2.422: "To treat Marsilius as an anti-ecclesiastical Aristotelian is at once to remain outside his thought and to fail to recognize his vast influence upon other reformers." See M. J. Wilks, *The Problem of Sovereignty in the Later Middle Ages* (Cambridge 1963) 96-117.

society,[43] he has once again pointed to the central ecclesiological issue at stake in the crisis of the later Middle Ages. This issue is the locus of the true church and its authority, and it is discussed by Marsilius in the important chapter which follows his treatment of the early Christian church.

Marsilius raises the question, which beliefs are necessary for salvation and by whose authority are these beliefs determined.[44] He answers that it is necessary for Christians to believe as irrevocably true no writings except the canonical scriptures or those interpretations of doubtful meanings of Scripture which have been made by a general council of faithful or catholic Christians.[45] Why is this the case? Because in order to be certain of the faith, one cannot trust in writings produced by the human spirit, but only in the canonical scriptures.[46] The latter do not include "the decretals or decrees of the Roman pontiff and his college of clergymen who are called 'cardinals,' nor any other human ordinances, contrived by the human mind, about human acts or disputes."[47] A case in point is the bull *Cum inter nonnullos* of John XXII denying that Christ practiced absolute poverty. If such a papal decision were to be accepted, Marsilius says, "then the whole body of the faithful would lie in danger of shipwreck with respect to the faith."[48] Only Scripture is certain and only a general council representing all faithful Christians can claim certain revelation of the Spirit when interpreting ambiguous points of Scripture like the extent of poverty required of Christ's followers.

Marsilius found his appeal to a general council to be quite compatible with the apostolic ideal by which he measured the papacy.[49] It is well known, however, that his contemporary, William of Ockham, did not think highly enough of a general council to endow it with infallible authority.[50] In fact, it is questionable to what extent Ockham appealed to the apostolic ideal at all, although he certainly favored

---

[43] He has not satisfactorily explained, for example, why the Aristotelian element emerges more strongly in the ecclesio-political writings of Marsilius and Ockham than in the writings of the earlier publicists – a question raised long ago by M. Grabmann, *Studien über den Einfluss der aristotelischen Philosophie auf die mittelalterlichen Theorien über das Verhältnis von Kirche und Staat,* Sitzungsberichte der Bayerischen Akademie der Wissenschaften, phil.-hist. Abteilung 2 (Munich 1934) 60.

[44] Marsilius (n. 37 above) 2.19 (Gewirth 274-279).

[45] *Ibid.* 2.19.1 (Gewirth 274).

[46] *Ibid.* 2.19.4 (Gewirth 275).

[47] *Ibid.* 2.19.6 (Gewirth 276).

[48] *Ibid.* 2.20.7 (Gewirth 283). For the bull of John XXII, see Mirbt-Aland, ed., *Quellen zur Geschichte des Papsttums und des römischen Katholizismus* 1, ed. 6 (Tübingen 1967) 467 no. 754.

[49] Marsilius (n. 37 above) 2.20.5 (Gewirth 282).

[50] See n. 60 below. Leff, "Apostolic Ideal" (n. 3 above) 79-81 summarizes the main differences between Marsilius and Ockham: Ockham's denial of conciliar infallibility and his acceptance of the Petrine basis of papal primacy. These differences have long been recognized in spite of the fact that Clement VI, in his censure of Ockham in 1343, designated Ockham as the source of the errors of Marsilius. See Kölmel (n. 5 above) 517; Grabmann (n. 43 above) 58-59; G. de Lagarde, *La naissance de l'esprit laïque au déclin du Moyen Age 5. Guillaume d'Ockham: Critique des structures ecclésiales,* ed. 2 (Paris 1963) 74-76, 93-107, 126-127.

the principle of absolute poverty.[51] Rather than employing the *ecclesia primitiva* as a model for reform of the Roman Church, Ockham chose the more radical solution of locating the true church in a remnant of faithful Christians which theoretically could continue to exist apart from the Roman hierarchy if it were thought to have fallen into error.[52] In other words, though Marsilius may have employed the apostolic ideal with devastating critical effect, it was Ockham who drew out of the ecclesiological arsenal of the thirteenth century the more dangerous weapon fashioned by the Waldensians and the Spiritual Franciscans — a remnant ecclesiology — with which to confront the crisis of authority in the church. In fact, this remnant ecclesiology assumed existential proportions for Ockham when he found himself defending the true church against precisely the kind of heretical pope which Olivi had envisaged — John XXII, the censurer of the Franciscan *usus pauper*. Tierney has expressed it well: "Olivi's nightmare had become Ockham's everyday, waking world."[53]

As a true successor of Olivi,[54] Ockham sought to uphold against John XXII the claim of those Franciscans who espoused absolute poverty. To carry out his purpose, he adopted and elaborated upon Olivi's theory of the irreformability of papal decrees.[55] In pointing out this relationship, Tierney has illuminated the crisis situation which drove Ockham to such deep penetration of ecclesiological problems. At the same time, this exposure of the polemical setting of Ockham's ecclesiology has added fuel to Tierney's own negative assessment of Ockham which he first formulated in his important article: "Ockham, the Conciliar Theory and the Canonists."[56] Ockham is now faulted for plunging ecclesiology into a "morass of total subjectivity"; even worse, "there was no grain of tolerance in him; he was filled with *odium theologicum*."[57]

The charge of subjectivity is prompted by Ockham's solution to the problem of how one could decide if a papal ruling was correct and thus deserved to be stamped "irreversible." The formal principle of infallibility was not enough. After all, Ockham was confronted with the contradictory rulings of two popes — *Exiit* of Nicholas III, which he wanted to uphold, and the decrees of John XXII against the *usus pauper*

---

[51] Leff, "Apostolic Ideal" (n. 3 above) 81 attributes the similarity between Marsilius and Ockham to their common appeal to the apostolic ideal, but in his book *Heresy* (n. 3 above) 422-434 this similarity is not stressed except for Ockham's strong feelings on evangelical poverty.

[52] Tierney (n. 7 above) 210.

[53] *Ibid.*

[54] Ockham neither openly condemned nor openly endorsed Olivi. Rather, he tolerated Olivi and never set up a gulf between himself and the extreme elements in the Franciscan Order. This is judged to be a tacit endorsement of Olivi by A. S. McGrade, *The Political Thought of William of Ockham: Personal and Institutional Principles* (Cambridge 1974) 13.

[55] Tierney (n. 7 above) 210-218.

[56] B. Tierney, "Ockham, the Conciliar Theory and the Canonists," *Journal of the History of Ideas* 15 (1954) 40-70; repr. with an introduction by H. A. Oberman (Philadelphia 1971).

[57] Tierney, *Origins* (n. 7 above) 228, 235.

which made the latter a heretic in the eyes of Michael of Cesena and his followers. Ockham's task was to prove that John XXII's decrees were indeed not in accord with Christian truth. In order to do this, Ockham had to establish a criterion according to which the content of this truth could be judged. Thus he adopted the principle that "sacred Scripture and the doctrine of the universal church which cannot err is the rule of our faith."[58] By demonstrating that John XXII had transgressed this rule, Ockham could expose his papal adversary as an enemy of the faith.

There exists some degree of consensus that Ockham's criterion represents a two-source theory of Christian truth – revelation granted to the church in addition to that found in Scripture.[59] Such a position makes it all the more difficult, however, to decide who has the right and expertise to decide what the correct teaching of Scripture and subsequent revelation was. Who makes up the church which cannot err? For Ockham, it was composed of all those *fideles* who had adhered to catholic truth and never dissented from it. This body was not equivalent to a general council because a council did not fully represent the church and could err in the faith.[60] The true, infallible church consisted only of those Christians who in fact assented to the truth even if they formed a silent minority in the visible institutional church. In fact, this true church might survive in one Christian alone, if he or she preserved the faith inviolate.

In the last analysis, it is Ockham's remnant ecclesiology which appears to substantiate the charge of total subjectivity. Indeed, it does seem as if Ockham drops the responsibility of discerning truth from error into the lap of each individual Christian to an extent that would justify such a charge. The definition of the true church presupposes that each Christian has already decided which truth had to be held by the "church throughout time" without dissent. Is it accurate to say, however, that Ockham's appeal to this church "amounts to nothing but an assertion that the traditional faith of the church was to be presumed always to have been what Ockham happened to be believing in 1335"?[61] For Tierney, this is the real import of the argument of John Morrall that "adherence to tradition expressed through the historical consensus of the faithful rather than through a visible organ of church

---

[58] Ockham, *Tractatus contra Ioannem*, in *Opera politica*, ed. J. G. Sikes et al., 3 vols. (Manchester 1940-1956) 3.72; cited by Tierney (n. 7 above) 218.

[59] Tierney agrees with Oberman on this point (n. 7 above) 221. See H. A. Oberman, *The Harvest of Medieval Theology*, ed. 2 (Grand Rapids 1967) 378-382.

[60] Tierney (n. 7 above) 231. In his article (n. 56 above), Tierney established that Ockham departed from the conciliar theory as outlined by the canonists (on this point of representation, for example) and thus could not be regarded as the father of conciliarism even though many of his arguments from the *Dialogus* were to become mainstays of conciliarism. More recently, J. Miethke has carefully analyzed the concept of *repraesentatio* in Ockham's thought and warned against attributing Ockham's denial of conciliar infallibility to an inadequate understanding of the representative function of the council; "Repräsentation und Delegation in den politischen Schriften Wilhelms von Ockham," *Der Begriff der repraesentatio im Mittelalter*, Miscellanea mediaevalia 8 (Berlin 1971) 163-185.

[61] Tierney (n. 7 above) 234.

362

authority (whether papacy or council) was the keystone of Ockham's ecclesiology."[62]

Ockham's interest in justifying the correctness of his own position cannot be minimized. It is possible nonetheless to put a more charitable construction upon Ockham's remnant ecclesiology which does not presume him guilty of the basest self-interest. For example, J. Miethke has recently argued that the possible survival of the church *in uno solo* was not the reflection of a radical individualism arising out of Ockham's nominalist metaphysics. On the contrary, Ockham was appealing both to a venerable ecclesiological-liturgical tradition centered around Mary's lonely vigil at the Cross and to a theory of the canonists which has come down to us as the "corporation sole."[63]

The remnant ecclesiology which Ockham shared with the tradition has also been described by U. Bubenheimer as "Ekklesiologie der Sachautorität."[64] The emphasis here is placed upon that elaboration of the theory which says that a minority in the visible church may be in the right if it has better arguments based on Scripture. Although Tierney discounts Ockham's appeal to right reason in interpreting Scripture as "simply his own reason,"[65] Ockham earnestly sought to establish enough objective support for his arguments to obviate a charge of total subjectivity. For example, Ockham writes in the prologue to the *Dialogus* that the decisive factor in judging the truth of a statement is not *who* says it, but *what* is said.[66]

Furthermore, as A. S. McGrade points out, Ockham would rely upon the judgment of experts to decide if a particular opinion, of a pope for example, is heretical. The experts in question are the *doctores* who are to be preferred to pontiffs as long as these *doctores* have demonstrated outstanding knowledge and a laudable life.[67] Ockham thereby substitutes cognitive criteria for institutional criteria in defining the expert who is competent to pass judgment on the opinions of the holder of an ecclesiastical office. In this regard, Ockham differs significantly from Marsilius. Although the two critics are brought together by their opposition to excessive papal power, Ockham builds his challenge on a different ecclesiological foundation from Marsilius. The latter simply transfers the right to interpret Scripture from one ecclesiastical authority to another (from pope to council), whereas Ockham shifts the responsibility of judgment from authority of any kind to understanding.[68] This

---

[62] J. Morrall, "Ockham and Ecclesiology," *Medieval Studies Presented to Aubrey Gwynn S. J.*, ed. J. A. Watt et al. (Dublin 1961) 491.

[63] Miethke (n. 60 above) 172. Miethke emphasizes that Ockham employs a "korporationsrechtliches Beispiel" to illustrate how the church may survive *in uno solo*.

[64] U. Bubenheimer, "Consonantia theologiae et iurisprudentiae: Andreas Bodenstein von Karlstadt als Theologe und Iurist auf dem Weg von der Scholastik zur Reformation," Th.D. diss. (University of Tübingen 1971) 94-101.

[65] Tierney (n. 7 above) 230.

[66] "Non quis est alicuius sententie auctor, sed quid dicitur attendentes... ," *Dialogus*, in *Opera plurima* 1 (Lyon 1494-1496) fol. Ira; cited by Bubenheimer (n. 64 above) 98 n. 3.

[67] McGrade (n. 54 above) 59-61.

[68] *Ibid.* 61-63.

understanding may in some cases be only a disguise for Ockham's opinion, but at
least the precedent is set for appealing to some objective authority other than pope
or council.[69]

Although the charge of total subjectivity appears unable to be substantiated, a
final question in regard to Ockham's remnant ecclesiology may need to be reopened.
Both Tierney and McGrade concur in the judgment of the most thorough monitor of
Ockham research, H. Junghans, that Ockham's philosophical ideas had nothing to do
with his ecclesiological theory.[70] In the sense of older attempts to deduce Ockham's
doctrine of the church from Nominalist logical principles which allegedly led to
"voluntarism" or "individualism,"[71] this may well be true. In view of the recent
emphasis upon key concepts like "covenant" and "contingency" in Ockhamist
thought, however,[72] the question deserves renewed consideration. By persistently

[69] This ecclesiological *tertium quid* between papalism and conciliarism found a home in the
writings of a variety of late medieval thinkers, partly as a result of its incorporation into the
works of the widely-read canonist Nicolaus de Tudeschis († 1445). Tudeschis, who is better
known as Panormitanus, included an appeal to the best scriptural arguments in his influential
commentary on c. "Significasti" of the decretals of Gregory IX: "Nam in concernentibus fidem,
etiam dictum unius privati esset praeferendum dicto papae, si ille moveretur melioribus rationibus
et authoritatibus novi et veteris testamenti quam papa." In K. W. Nörr, *Kirche und Konzil bei
Nicolaus de Tudeschis (Panormitanus)* (Köln 1964) 105. Panormitanus himself may not have
realized the full implications of this ecclesiological standpoint; Nörr even contends that this
position remained "ein Fremdkörper in seiner Lehre." *Ibid.* 133. Nevertheless, they were
certainly recognized and appreciated by Martin Luther, who appealed to Panormitanus on three
occasions in 1518-1519: in his replies to Prierias, Cajetan at Augsburg, and against Eck at Leipzig.
Luther, *Werke: Kritische Gesamtausgabe* (Weimar 1883ff.) 1.656.30f.; 2.10.18ff.; 2.288.34f. Cf.
also 7.431.9ff. Employment of a remnant ecclesiology was not confined to Panormitanus and his
readers. It was utilized in the fifteenth century by supporters of pope and council alike, e.g., by
the propapal Heinrich Kalteisen and by the conciliarist Pierre d'Ailly. See W. Krämer, "Die
ekklesiologische Auseinandersetzung um die wahre Repräsentation auf dem Basler Konzil,"
Begriff der repraesentatio (n. 60 above) 214 n. 39. As early as the twelfth century the Decretists
used the survival of the faith in Mary alone to demonstrate the defectibility of the pope and the
Roman Church. See B. Tierney, *Foundations of the Conciliar Theory,* ed. 2 (Cambridge 1968)
44. It is necessary to distinguish, however, between remnant ecclesiology as such and "Ekklesiologie der Sachautorität," in which the minority relies not only upon its smallness but also upon
its superior arguments and understanding. Although both can be mobilized against papalism and
conciliarism, the flexibility of the latter and its employment by Luther justify a new evaluation
of the precise relationship between the ecclesiologies of Ockham (and Panormitanus) and Luther.
Perhaps the forms of their quest for the true church were more alike than has commonly been
thought. See C. Tecklenburg Johns, *Luthers Konzilsidee in ihrer historischen Bedingtheit und
ihrem reformatorischen Neuansatz* (Berlin 1966) 130ff. for the best treatment of the subject.
[70] Tierney (n. 7 above) 207; McGrade (n. 54 above) 198ff.; H. Junghans, *Ockham im Lichte
der neueren Forschung* (Berlin 1968) 262-275.
[71] By such authors as A. Dempf, *Sacrum imperium,* ed. 3 (Darmstadt 1962) 504-526; and
Lagarde (n. 50 above) 281-289.
[72] See W. J. Courtenay, "Covenant and Causality in Pierre d'Ailly," *Speculum* 46 (1971)
94-119. According to H. A. Oberman, "contingency is perhaps the best one-word summary of the
nominalist program"; "The Shape of Late Medieval Thought: The Birthpangs of the Modern
Era," *Archiv für Reformationsgeschichte* 64 (1973) 22; also in *The Pursuit of Holiness in Late
Medieval and Renaissance Religion,* ed. C. Trinkaus and H. A. Oberman, Studies in Medieval and
Reformation Thought 10 (Leiden 1974) 13. In this essay, the word "Ockhamist" is used in place

364

harnessing the ordered power of God (*potentia ordinata*) in tandem with his absolute power (*potentia absoluta*), the Ockhamists were not trying to make of God an arbitrary, playful tyrant. They were, rather, pleading for recognition of the fact that God's dealing with his world was not based on a necessary hierarchical order of being but on a covenant initiated by God himself in his love and mercy. This covenant is contingent, not in the sense of being unreliable,[73] but in the sense that God has freely committed himself to his creation and to his church.

Recently, S. Ozment has pointed to one ecclesiological implication of the Ockhamist emphasis upon God's free commitment to his covenant.[74] If God has ordained that knowledge of himself and of the way of salvation reach man through his church, then the church is just as safely ensconced in the Ockhamist soteriological plan as it is in a Thomistically arranged hierarchy of being – and just as immune to attack. Over against Thomism, the church for the Ockhamists receives its unique mediatorial role as the result of a covenant and not because of its position within a supposed metaphysical hierarchy. Compared with mysticism, however, and its emphasis upon the unmediated relationship between God and man, the covenantal foundation of the church would classify as conservative and hardly subversive of the existing ecclesiastical order.[75] In this context it appears not at all contrived for Ockham to appeal to the universal church in time as the standard of truth; such an appeal, in fact, fits naturally into a dynamic, covenantal understanding of God's historical activity. The church, although no longer confined to a static institutional representation of an eternal ecclesial ideal, remains the reliable custodian and interpreter of God's revelation.

Furthermore, for the Ockhamists God's covenant is two-sided. In the realm of

---

of "Nominalist" in order to do justice to the fluidity of meaning assigned to the latter term. For a thorough discussion of the revisions in the interpretation of Nominalism, see Courtenay, "Nominalism and Late Medieval Religion," in *The Pursuit of Holiness* 26-59. "Ockhamist" refers here to those representatives of late medieval thought (such as Ockham, d'Ailly and Biel) who placed importance on ideas of assigned value and willed verbal covenants; *ibid.* 53.

[73] Oberman, in *Archiv* (n. 72 above) 22.

[74] S. Ozment, "Mysticism, Nominalism and Dissent," *The Pursuit of Holiness* (n. 72 above) 86.

[75] *Ibid.* Ozment's concern is to show the potential for dissent inherent in mysticism. He has convincingly illustrated the impact of mystical themes on sixteenth-century dissenters in his *Mysticism and Dissent* (New Haven 1973). M. Greschat lines up the Ockhamist idea of covenant more closely with mysticism in contrast to what he terms an absorption of convenantal elements by thirteenth-century theology in which the church is viewed as "sakramentale Heilsantalt"; "Der Bundesgedanke in der Theologie des späten Mittelalters," *Zeitschrift für Kirchengeschichte* 81 (1970) 44-63. Greschat (55) agrees that ecclesiology cannot remain unaffected by the Ockhamist covenant concept. W. Kölmel has also noted some influence of Ockham's philosophical and theological principles on his ecclesio-political writings. Kölmel contends that the distinction *regulariter-casualiter*, which is parallel to the tension between God's absolute and ordered power, is an indispensable key to understanding Ockham's view of the relationship between the temporal and spiritual orders and their respective jurisdictional powers. Kölmel (n. 5 above) 534-552. Even McGrade (n. 54 above) 226 notes the contingency of institutions in Ockham's thought, without directly relating this concept to the center of his theology.

soteriology man's part is defined by the *facere quod in se est,* the expectation that man would make optimal use of his own natural powers to prepare himself for grace. A certain ecclesiological parallel to this idea may inhere in Ockham's assertion that every Christian has the right, and even the duty, to ascertain catholic truth for himself in light of the historical consensus of the faithful. This is anything but the blind fideism of which Ockhamist ecclesiology has been accused. On this basis, Ockham's argument for papal infallibility — as an attempt to check the sovereignty of a reigning pope — can be interpreted as an appeal to God's consistent and reliable revelation to his covenant people in the past in the face of apparent infidelity to this covenant by the contemporary ecclesiastical hierarchy.

In summary, it appears that neither total subjectivity nor a complete divorce between his philosophical-theological and his political-ecclesiological writings can be said to characterize Ockham's ecclesiology. In contrast to Marsilius, who relied on the *ecclesia primitiva* to serve as a model of a church to be reformed under the aegis of a general council, Ockham proposed a highly original form of Olivi's remnant ecclesiology as a theoretical solution to the crisis of the papacy in his day. This "ecclesiology of cognitive expertise," which placed understanding above institutions, was a unique contribution to the late medieval quest for the true church.

III

Ockham's contribution did not, however, become the preferred solution to the most devastating of the late medieval ecclesiological crises: the disorientation with regard to the nature and authority of the church wrought by the Great Schism (1378-1417). Those men who sought reform of the church at the turn of the fifteenth century turned instead to the ecclesiological solution proposed by Marsilius — a general council. In reality, conciliar theory was much older than Marsilius and represents a response to the crisis of the late fourteenth century which has its own ecclesiological integrity and deep roots in the earlier Middle Ages. In a landmark book, Tierney demonstrated to the satisfaction of almost everybody that the conciliar theory had its foundations in canonist thought.[76] Canonist thought, in turn, had its inception in a movement to reform the church. According to S. Chodorow, Gratian conceived of his *Decretum* as a handbook for the twelfth-century reform party with which he was associated.[77] It was only historically fitting that a finely-honed application of canonist thought be implemented in the late fourteenth and fifteenth centuries as an instrument of reform.

This concern for reform endowed conciliar theory with a more solid ecclesiological foundation than the predominantly anti-papal basis on which Marsilius's endorse-

---

[76] Tierney (n. 69 above).
[77] S. Chodorow, *Christian Political Theory and Church Politics in the Mid-twelfth Century: The Ecclesiology of Gratian's Decretum* (Berkeley 1972) 17-64.

366

ment of a council rested. As a council came to be regarded by more and more churchmen as the only solution to the schism, it received tribute in many treatises of the time as the most effective agent of *reformatio in capite et in membris.* In fact, for the later Middle Ages, R. Bäumer is willing to deem the concepts "reform" and "council" almost equivalent.[78] Reform was the primary concern of the council fathers at Pisa, Constance and Basel,[79] and it continued to enjoy a prominent place in the writings of conciliar-minded theologians of the late fifteenth and early sixteenth centuries like Ugonius and Jacobazzi.[80] The conveners of the Second Council of Pisa (1511) invoked the necessity of reform as the basis of their action. [81] At the opening of the papally approved Fifth Lateran Council in 1512, Giles of Viterbo, general of the Augustinians and loyal adherent to the papalistic traditions of his order, delivered a ringing appeal for reform under the motto: "Men must be changed by religion, not religion by men."[82]

As a result of good historical timing, the Council of Constance has nearly monopolized recent conciliar research. The 550th anniversary of this controversial gathering occurred in the wake of a council-conscious Vatican II milieu which was hypersensitive to precisely that incendiary issue of conciliar authority which dominated Constance itself.[83] The unique task of reform facing the council fathers at Constance demanded that they rethink the nature of that church for whose representation in general council they claimed such awesome, unfamiliar powers as deposing and electing popes.

The necessity for some basic ecclesiological homework was especially clear to Jean Gerson who, according to R. Bäumer, was the author to whom conciliar thinkers at the beginning of the sixteenth century were most indebted.[84] Gerson's career effectively combined his *vita activa* as an ecclesiastical reformer with his *vita contemplativa* as a mystical theologian and ecclesiological thinker.[85] Our awareness

---

[78] R. Bäumer, *Nachwirkungen des konziliaren Gedankens in der Theologie und Kanonistik des frühen 16. Jahrhunderts,* Reformationsgeschichtliche Studien und Texte 100 (Münster 1971) 245.
[79] See the remarks of K. A. Fink in *Handbuch der Kirchengeschichte* 3.2 (n. 4 above) 561ff. and 577ff.
[80] See Bäumer (n. 78 above) 244-260.
[81] *Ibid.* 253.
[82] John W. O'Malley, *Giles of Viterbo on Church and Reform,* Studies in Medieval and Reformation Thought 5 (Leiden 1968) 139ff. Sharing Renaissance expectations of a new age, Giles believed that reform in the tenth age of the church was linked to the accession of Leo X; *ibid.* 110ff.
[83] For a survey of the literature to 1965 see A. Franzen, "Das Konstanzer Konzil: Probleme, Aufgaben und Stand der Konzilsforschung," *Concilium* 1 (1965) 555-574. The debate over the binding nature of the Constance decrees is summarized by R. Bäumer, "Die Reformkonzilien des 15. Jahrhunderts in der neueren Forschung," *Annuarium Historiae Conciliorum* 1 (1969) 159-161.
[84] Bäumer (n. 78 above) 18.
[85] See G. H. M. Posthumus Meyjes, *Jean Gerson: Zijn Kerkpolitiek en Ecclesiologie* (The Hague 1963) and Louis B. Pascoe, S.J., *Jean Gerson: Principles of Church Reform,* Studies in Medieval and Reformation Thought 7 (Leiden 1973).

of this interrelation has been enhanced by a recent study which points out a common pattern of reform in Gerson's mystical theology and in his ecclesiology.[86] The key to the *via mystica* for Gerson is the *synderesis* which has been naturally implanted in the soul. As the innate point of contact between God and man, the *synderesis* becomes the home of the Holy Spirit where Christ is spiritually born into the soul. The reform of the soul takes the *synderesis* as its intrinsic point of departure. In an analogous way, the reform of the church takes as its intrinsic point of departure the *semen Dei* which is "*radicaliter* and *inseparabiliter* placed within and diffused throughout the ecclesiastical body as lifegiving blood."[87] A general council may derive from this innate divine power authority to reform the church when its head, the pope, proves incapable of governing the church. The legitimacy of the ecclesiastical hierarchy is not based on the papacy itself but on the *semen Dei*, a resource intrinsic to the body of Christ. On the other hand, the power which accrues to a council from the *semen Dei* does not establish absolute conciliar supremacy over the see of Peter; it applies only in cases where papal power is abused.[88]

Thus, in addition to the remnant ecclesiology present, for example, in Olivi and the "ecclesiology of cognitive expertise" in Ockham, it is permissible to speak of a "*semen*-ecclesiology" in Gerson. In one respect, namely in its appeal to the *ecclesia primitiva*, this *semen*-ecclesiology is related to the conciliarism of Marsilius. As the Holy Spirit itself, the reformative power of the *semen* is especially operative whenever the church is gathered in council; according to Gerson, the primitive church provides an authoritative precedent for this.[89] In quite another respect, however, Gerson's conciliar ecclesiology is considerably more sophisticated than that of Marsilius. The *semen*, received by the church in its primitive stage, establishes the hierarchy much closer to the center of his ecclesiology than is the case with Marsilius. This sanction given to the hierarchy also distinguishes Gerson's ecclesiology from that of Ockham, which "identified the true essence of the church more with belief than with hierarchical structure."[90] Gerson himself, then, proposes an ecclesiology which differs from that of his predecessors and is a shade more conservative than what is now classified as "conciliaristic" ecclesiology (absolute conciliar supremacy).

This latter position is often associated with the Council of Basel, heretofore the plain sister of Constance, which has been receiving proportionately more attention as the existential interest in Constance dwindles.[91] Among the players at the Basel

---

[86] S. Ozment, "The University and the Church: Patterns of Reform in Jean Gerson," *Medievalia et Humanistica* n.s. 1 (1970) 111-126.

[87] *Ibid.* 118. See also Pascoe (n. 85 above) 45-48.

[88] Ozment (n. 86 above) 119f.

[89] Louis B. Pascoe, "Jean Gerson: The 'Ecclesia primitiva' and Reform," *Traditio* 30 (1974) 386-387.

[90] *Ibid.* 395. In this formulation Pascoe approximates the contrast which McGrade (n. 54 above) 61-63 makes between cognition and structure in distinguishing between Ockham and Marsilius. On this basis (the superiority of institutional structures over belief and cognition) Marsilius would stand nearer to Gerson than to Ockham.

[91] For example, in the festschrift for A. Franzen, *Von Konstanz nach Trient* (n. 1 above) Basel receives attention in more essays than does Constance.

drama, there is much more ecclesiological variety than this "conciliaristic" label would lead one to expect. Basel apparently had a catalytic effect on the ecclesiologies of a number of its main characters. For example, M. Watanabe has traced the shifting views of ecclesiastical authority through the careers of Panormitanus, Aeneas Sylvius and Nicholas of Cusa.[92] The last two started out as avid supporters of the council but over the course of their conciliar journey gained an increasing appreciation for the role of papal authority in church government.[93] As Watanabe points out, it is more difficult to tell on which side Panormitanus finally came down. The various diplomatic mandates which he held required him to represent both papal and conciliar points of view.[94] In spite of the strong case which Nörr makes for the internal consistency of his thought, it remains unclear to what extent Panormitanus was willing to see papal power limited by the competencies of a council. Perhaps Panormitanus is best viewed as the outstanding canon lawyer that he was, who tried to present each side, as he was charged, as convincingly as possible. His appeal to the superiority of the best arguments may not be so foreign to his thought as Nörr has supposed.[95]

Some of the less prominent actors on the Basel stage also manifest the ecclesiological diversity and adjustment characteristic of the waning conciliar era. For example, John of Ragusa, early at Basel an opponent of the Hussites, and John of Segovia, the astute chronicler of the council, both moved from the ranks of those advocating papal primacy onto the turf of the council's supporters.[96] Consider further the surprising case of Augustinus Favaroni of Rome, general of the Augustinian Order from 1419 to 1431.[97] Favaroni came under investigation during the pontificate of Martin V (1417-1431) for statements which were allegedly similar to certain Hussite views condemned at Constance. These statements were contained in the treatise *De sacramento unitatis Christi et ecclesie sive de Christo integro* which Favaroni says he composed "many years" before the Council of Constance. He makes this claim in the preface to a defense of his views which he wrote before the

[92] M. Watanabe, "Authority and Consent in Church Government: Panormitanus, Aeneas Sylvius, Cusanus," *Journal of the History of Ideas* 33 (1972) 217-236.
[93] On Nicholas of Cusa (in addition to the publications of the Cusanus-Gesellschaft) see E. Meuthen, "Kanonistik und Geschichtsverständnis. Über ein neuentdecktes Werk des Nikolaus von Kues: De maioritate auctoritatis sacrorum conciliorum supra auctoritatem papae," in *Von Konstanz nach Trient* (n. 1 above) 147-170; K. Ganzer, "Päpstliche Gesetzgebungsgewalt und kirchlicher Konsens: Zur Verwendung eines Dictum Gratians in der Concordantia catholica des Nikolaus von Kues," *Von Konstanz nach Trient* (n. 1 above) 171-188; R. Haubst, "Wort und Leitidee der 'Repraesentatio' bei Nikolaus v. Kues," in *Der Begriff der repraesentatio* (n. 60 above) 139-162; D. Sullivan, "Nicholas of Cusa as Reformer: The Papal Legation to the Germanies, 1451-1452," *Medieval Studies* 36 (1974) 382-428.
[94] Watanabe (n. 92 above) 224-228. See Nörr (n. 69 above) 7-8.
[95] See n. 69 above. Nörr (n. 69 above) 9 portrays him as "reiner Jurist."
[96] Krämer (n. 69 above) 207-208 mentions these along with Panormitanus and Cusa.
[97] See A. Zumkeller (n. 6 above) 237-240; *idem*, "Die Augustinereremiten in der Auseinandersetzung mit Wyclif und Hus, ihre Beteiligung an den Konzilien von Konstanz und Basel," *Analecta Augustiniana* 28 (1965) 50-52.

Council of Basel had gotten underway – perhaps in 1430.[98] In this apology, Favaroni reveals that he indeed held a number of ecclesiological views which can be labeled Hussite, for example, that only the predestined are true members of the church and of Christ. Because of this position, among others, Favaroni's earlier book was condemned by the council on 15 October 1435, although his person was spared since he had submitted his teaching to the judgment of the church.[99]

Favaroni rests his case squarely on the authority of Augustine himself;[100] it is this fact which raises intriguing questions for historians. How did the general of the Augustinian Order, the order with the strongest papalist tradition, come to hold Hussite views on the church? Did he indeed arrive at these views long before Constance independently of Hus and even Wyclif? How prevalent was this strain of Augustinian ecclesiology both inside and outside the order? Did Favaroni himself have any influence on the ecclesiological tradition of his order? This last question has been tentatively answered in the affirmative with regard to the possible influence of Favaroni upon Johannes von Staupitz.[101] The final resolution of these mysteries must wait upon more detailed research into the thought and activities of Favaroni and his opponents.

One of these opponents was Heinrich Kalteisen, O.P. (†1465); he intervened in the negotiations at Basel at two significant points. Along with his better known Dominican brother, Juan de Torquemada, Kalteisen represented the propapal position and, in the opinion of K. Binder, played the key role in convincing the council to condemn the book of Favaroni.[102] Prior to the Favaroni matter, Kalteisen had acted as the primary respondent to the third article of the Hussites in their negotiations with the council between January and April of 1432. During these negotiations, the nature of the church was debated more than has been commonly acknowledged. Although ecclesiology *per se* did not constitute one of the four articles to be discussed, it became clear that the nature of the true church was the crux of the differences between Hussites and Catholics. As Peter Payne, the English

---

[98] A. Favaroni, *Contra quosdam errores hereticorum,* Basel MS A IV 17, fols. 320-328v. See Zumkeller, "Die Augustinereremiten" (n. 97 above) 50.

[99] The decision of the Council is contained in *Sacrorum conciliorum nova et amplissima collectio,* ed. J. D. Mansi (Venice 1788) 29.108-110. Juan de Torquemada made a significant ecclesiological contribution in his *Gutachten* on Favaroni's book: Mansi, 30.979-1034; see K. Binder, *Wesen und Eigenschaften der Kirche bei Kardinal Juan de Torquemada O.P.* (Innsbruck 1955) 17.

[100] Favaroni (n. 98 above) 320.

[101] By H. A. Oberman in his address to the Fourth International Luther Congress in St. Louis (August 1971) entitled "Headwaters of the Reformation: Initia Lutheri – Initia Reformationis," in *Luther and the Dawn of the Modern Era,* ed. H. A. Oberman, Studies in the History of Christian Thought 8 (Leiden 1974) 73-74. Oberman's identification of possible influences of late medieval "Augustinian" theologians on Luther has been challenged by David C. Steinmetz, "Luther and the Late Medieval Augustinians: Another Look," *Concordia Theological Monthly* 44 (1973) 245-260. Steinmetz calls for a precise definition of the term "Augustinian" in light of its manifold reference in the later Middle Ages.

[102] Binder (n. 99 above) 14-15, 16-17. See Krämer (n. 69 above) 208-213.

370

Wycliffite who was one of the Hussite representatives, formulated it: "Conveniamus in quidditate ecclesiae, quia ille dicit, illi sunt ecclesia, et ille dicit, non."[103]
An agreement on this crucial point was never reached, of course. The summons to ecclesiological consensus, however, points to the heart of the crisis which loomed large over the period of the reform councils: the uncertain locus of the true church and its authority among the competing claims of successive councils and popes. The *acta* of the Council of Basel and related documents, such as the treatises of Favaroni, Kalteisen and Ragusa,[104] constitute a rich ecclesiological lode, which, when finally brought to the surface, will in all likelihood display a considerably broader spectrum of ecclesiological responses to the Great Schism and its aftermath than was previously expected. The total effect of this severe crisis can then be more accurately assessed. It is already clear, however, that conciliarism itself can be most appropriately understood as covering a variety of ecclesiological responses in which a general council served as the agent of reform.[105] Although the ideal of the *ecclesia primitiva* certainly played a role in these conciliar ideas of reform,[106] the ecclesiological options developed in response to the Schism were considerably more varied and sophisticated than a naive call for return to the uncomplicated apostolic life. Searchers for the true church during the later Middle Ages traveled along roads much better graded than the dusty paths of the apostles and much more diverse than the main highways of papalism and conciliarism.

---

[103] Cited by K. Binder, "Der 'Tractatus de ecclesia' Johanns von Ragusa und die Verhandlungen des Konzils von Basel mit den Husiten," *Angelicum* 28 (1951) 32. Binder 35-36 demonstrates how Ragusa, speaking for the council, was led to deal with the doctrine of the church because Rokyzana, the leading Hussite representative, had introduced it in his earliest remarks. See *Concilium Basilense: Studien und Quellen zur Geschichte des Concils von Basel,* ed. J. Haller, 2 (Basel 1897 [repr. Nendeln/Liechtenstein 1971]) 337.32-37.

[104] Binder (n. 103 above) 51-52 indicates that the negotiations with the Hussites not only forced Ragusa to develop a full-bodied conciliar ecclesiology but even impelled him to include some propapal arguments and citations used later in the *Summa de ecclesia* of Torquemada. Binder suggests that the debate with Rokyzana, the Hussite leader, may have led even Torquemada to give first thoughts to a treatise on the church. This encounter well illustrates the ecclesiological interaction at Basel: an ecclesiology which was neither papal nor conciliar (Rokyzana) may have stimulated the articulation of both papal (Torquemada) and conciliar (Ragusa) positions which, in their common opposition to the Hussites, were themselves not sharply distinguished.

[105] The nuances of opinion on specific conciliar issues among theologians of the early sixteenth century have been carefully distinguished by Bäumer (n. 78 above). In his review of Bäumer's book, Paul De Vooght reemphasizes this variety: "Entre un conciliarisme extrême et un papalisme aveugle, s'ouvre pour l'immense majorité des théologiens, la voie moyenne d'un rapport dialectique fécond entre le pape et le concile." Even such a renowned papalist as Torquemada could concede the superiority of a council in certain emergency situations; *Revue d'histoire ecclésiastique* 67 (1972) 935. F. Oakley has advanced the provocative argument that conciliarism was very much alive even at the Fifth Lateran Council. That council did not condemn the decrees of Constance and only nullified those decrees of the Council of Basel which were passed after Eugene IV had transferred the council to Ferrara. "Conciliarism at the Fifth Lateran Council?" *Church History* 41 (1972) 452-463.

[106] For example, in Dietrich of Niem; see Leff, *Heresy* (n. 3 above) 2.440-442; on Gerson, see Pascoe (n. 89 above); see also Stockmeier (n. 1 above).

IV

One of these roads was the ecclesiological path along which John Hus and his
followers pursued their opposition to the Roman Church. The Hussite movement
presented a highly visible ecclesiological alternative to the Roman Church in the later
Middle Ages despite the *Compactata* arrived at with the Council of Basel (1436). In
his discussion of the spiritual crisis provoked by the Great Schism, F. Graus portrays
the Hussite movement as a response to the threat which the Great Schism posed to
the religious values of the Czech people. Exposed to the constant criticism of a
church racked by schism and moral abuse, the Czech people became uncertain about
the locus of the true church and the efficacy of its sacramental channels. In Graus's
opinion, the Hussite movement captured the enthusiasm and fantasy of the previously indifferent Czech masses because it offered to them a new concept of the
church which assured them of their status as true Christians and (in the symbol of
the chalice) of the validity of their Eucharist.[107]

Although the Hussite doctrine of the church, backed by a strong emphasis on the
Eucharist, was able temporarily to restore confidence and security to a disoriented
Czech people, Graus maintains that this concentration on the church and the chalice
was not able in the long run to satisfy the needs of late medieval people beset by
spiritual and socioeconomic uncertainty. It remained for the new humanist emphasis
on man and the religious shift from the church to personal faith to lay the
groundwork for a solution. "They were the means by which the intellectual crisis of
the late Middle Ages was overcome and a new system built upon its ruins."[108] From
the perspective of the late medieval quest for the true church, two aspects of Graus's
thesis deserve comment: first, his evaluation of the causes behind the failure of the
Hussite movement and, secondly, his brief estimate of the solution provided by the
sixteenth century to the late medieval crisis of the church. The first point will be
dealt with in the remainder of this section. The second aspect will serve as the
springboard for concluding remarks on the sixteenth century in the last section.

First, why was this emphasis on the church and the Eucharist not able to satisfy
the religious needs of the Czech people and serve as the foundation for a lasting
reformation? Graus implies that the cause of the failure lay in the appeal of the
Hussite reformers to the past, "the attempt to form a new society on a primitive
Christian model."[109] Insofar as the Hussites employed the *ecclesia primitiva* as the
model of church reform, they were simply following in the footsteps of many

---

[107] Graus (n. 11 above) 91ff. A recent well-argued contrast of the movements of Wyclif and
Hus locates the causes of Hus's success in the more mundane realm of politics. M. Wilks believes
that Wyclif's idea of reform from the top down was implemented successfully in Bohemia but
thwarted in his own homeland by the Peasants' Revolt; *"Reformatio regni:* Wyclif and Hus as
Leaders of Religious Protest Movements," *Schism, Heresy and Religious Protest,* ed. D. Baker,
Studies in Church History 9 (Cambridge 1972) 109-132.

[108] Graus (n. 11 above) 101.

[109] *Ibid.* 100-101.

another medieval reform movement.[110] Furthermore, the primitive church continued to be used throughout the sixteenth century as a criterion of reform.[111] The employment of this model was too extensive both before and after the Hussites to isolate it as the cause of their apparent failure to solve the crisis of the Middle Ages. More importantly, in what sense can they even be said to have failed? True, Bohemia did not become the launching pad for the sixteenth-century Reformation; but this does not necessarily mean that Hussite ecclesiology did not provide a viable answer to Czech people in search of the true church for the period in which they needed it. It is sufficient to regard Hussite ecclesiology as a solution to their crisis, which was only one in a series of late medieval ecclesiological crises, without blaming the Hussite doctrine of the church for not solving the crisis of the late Middle Ages viewed as a whole.

The fact remains, however, that the mainline Hussites, the Utraquists, did not establish and maintain a church completely independent of the Roman hierarchy. This was attained only after 1467 in sectarian form by the *Unitas fratrum,* who, much like the Waldensians, strictly implemented the ideal of the *ecclesia primitiva.*[112] In contrast to these Brethren, the moderate outcome of the Utraquist revolt may be explained by the intimate relation between the church and the sacraments which existed for Hus and his followers.

One way of stating the issue is this: Was the Hussite doctrine of the church subversive to the extent of constituting a theoretical basis for breaking with Rome and establishing an independent church? H. Kaminsky argues forcefully that the Utraquist revolt of 1414-1417, both as theory and as practice, imposed a duty to construct an alternative church composed of those true Christians who obeyed Christ's law, which included communion in both kinds.[113] Kaminsky also contends that the ecclesiology of Hus, following Wyclif, constituted a real threat to the authority and institutional sacrosanctity of the Roman Church.[114] W. Cook has pointed out, however, that the early Hussite emphasis on the necessity of the

---

[110] See above passim and Olsen (n. 1 above) 84 n. 59. H. Kaminsky has noted the importance of the primitive church in Hussite thought; it even served as the basis of their demand for communion in both kinds. However, the *ecclesia primitiva* was more important to Hus's followers than to Hus himself. Kaminsky, *A History of the Hussite Revolution* (Berkeley 1967) 39-40, 101-105, 116-125, 154-155. In the so-called Cheb Judge (1432), the agreement on conditions for a Hussite appearance at the Council of Basel, even the Council agreed that "God's law and the practice of Christ, the apostles and the primitive church shall be used to judge all matters, with the decrees of councils and words of doctors accepted only insofar as they are based on the above." See W. Cook, "John Wyclif and Hussite Theology, 1415-1436," *Church History* 42 (1973) 345.

[111] See John Headley, *Luther's View of Church History* (New Haven 1963) 162-194. Stockmeier (n. 1 above) 9-13 indicates how Luther imposed the criterion of reform necessary to him – correct teaching according to Scripture – upon the early church. See n. 130 below.

[112] On the influence of the Waldensians in Bohemia, see Kaminsky (n. 110 above) 171-180; Leff, *Heresy* (n. 3 above) 2.469-471.

[113] Kaminsky (n. 110 above) 121.

[114] *Ibid.* 38.

Eucharist for salvation was abandoned in the 1420s in favor of a much more superficial, but politically more satisfying, demand for the lay chalice.[115] This would mean that such Hussites as Jakoubek and Peter Payne did possess a sacramental theory different from that of the Roman Church, but that this difference was later sacrificed for the sake of reconciliation with the Council of Basel. The Utraquist wing of the Hussite movement could have espoused, at least for a time, a subversive theology. It was then defused during the Eucharistic debates of the 1420s and finally rendered harmless by the *Compactata* with Basel, which tolerated both the practice of utraquism and the Utraquists themselves in return for recognition of Roman sacramental theology.

It is questionable, however, whether this subversive potential was ever present in Hussite ecclesiology to the same degree in which it was present in some sixteenth-century Reformers, for example, in the theology of Luther. In spite of their peculiar emphasis on the Eucharist, the Hussites and the late medieval church shared belief in the necessity of sacramental grace. In fact, the net historical effect of their concentration on the Eucharist was to keep the Hussites on common theological ground with the Roman Church and smooth the path toward reconciliation with the Council of Basel. The ecclesiology of Hus himself (who never conceded that the lay chalice was necessary for salvation) was not subversive, because even his church of the predestined was dependent on sacramental grace administered through the legitimately ordained hierarchy.[116]

The Hussite movement did not fail to solve the crisis of the later Middle Ages because it offered an outdated model of reform based on an unrealistic appeal to the primitive church. Nor is it accurate to say that it became theologically superficial by giving up its earlier emphasis on the soteriological indispensability of the Eucharist in favor of a political settlement which permitted the practice of utraquism. There was more to Hussite ecclesiology than that. In their attention to the necessity of sacramental grace, even for the church of the predestined, the Hussites remained theologically profound and firmly rooted in medieval ground. Compared with the sixteenth-century Reformers, however, Hus and his mainstream Prague successors were ecclesiologically superficial – not in terms of a doctrinal comparison, but in an historical sense. That is, Hussite ecclesiology, except in its extreme sectarian form,

[115] W. Cook, in a paper entitled "The Eucharist in Hussite Theology" which was delivered at the December 1973 meeting of the American Society of Church History. For details of the period which Cook discusses, with special attention to the activities of Peter Payne, see Cook (n. 110 above) 335-349.
[116] Apparently this is what Luther suddenly realized near the end of 1520 when he protested: "Non recte faciunt, qui me Hussitam vocant." *Werke* (n. 69 above) 7.135.23. Earlier in the same year Luther had issued a ringing affirmation that he, Augustine and Staupitz were all Hussites; Luther, *Briefwechsel* (Weimar 1930ff.) 2.42.22ff. That notwithstanding, Luther dissociated himself from Hus after he was officially threatened with excommunication and realized that he would be forced out of the church. See S. H. Hendrix, " 'We Are All Hussites'? Hus and Luther Revisited," *Archiv für Reformationsgeschichte* 65 (1974) 134-161.

VI

374

did not supply an adequate conceptual framework within which to build a new church independent of the Roman hierarchy. The reconciliation with the Council of Basel tamed the mainstream Hussite movement into peaceful coexistence with the Roman Church and relegated its ecclesiology to one among many options in the late medieval quest for the true church.

V

Did the quest die with the dawn of the sixteenth century? Graus implies a positive answer to this question in his assertion that the humanist emphasis on man and the Reformers' concept of personal faith succeeded where Hussite ecclesiology failed. They allegedly rescued gasping man from the polluted late medieval crisis atmosphere and thrust him into the liberating air of the modern era where he could breathe with confidence again. Since a series of ecclesiological crises was to a great degree responsible for the predicament of late medieval man, it seems only fitting to look for his savior in non-ecclesial or anti-ecclesial concepts and forces. This emphasis on the rebirth of individualism and subjectivity has been a favorite way of defining the *novum* which the sixteenth century offered to late medieval men. Nowhere is this better illustrated than in the work of Joseph Lortz, who regards the Reformation as replacing "the basic medieval attitudes of objectivism, traditionalism and clericalism with those of subjectivism, spiritualism and laicism." [117]

It is now known that the fifteenth century, in Germany at least, was an era of exceptional piety and religious devotion. According to B. Moeller, it was also a time of greater fidelity to the church than in any other medieval epoch. [118] Moeller interprets this churchliness as the result of a spiritual and intellectual crisis similar to that which Graus has described and which Moeller himself finds illustrated in the words of an Erfurt theologian in 1466: "Mobilitas seu mutabilitas animarum et inconstantia mentis nunc in hominibus." Men sought peace and solace in what was traditional, time-proven and holy, that is, in the laws of the church. But, claims Moeller, this search was not for the church as such; rather, men yearned for the salvation which the church possessed. [119]

While this statement may pinpoint the attraction of the church for some medieval people, it is questionable whether one can distinguish so neatly between the church *per se* and its treasure of salvation. The church and salvation were bound together

---

[117] Lortz (n. 8 above) 1.10. In his study of Renaissance humanism, C. Trinkaus has reemphasized the notion of meditation and inwardness as typical of the Renaissance and parallel to the religious diversion of worship from objective and communal means to subjective and private ones; *In Our Image and Likeness: Humanity and Divinity in Italian Humanist Thought*, 2 vols. (Chicago 1970) 1.12.

[118] B. Moeller, "Frömmigkeit in Deutschland um 1500," *Archiv für Reformationsgeschichte* 56 (1965) 5-30. English versions of this article have appeared in Ozment (n. 8 above) 50-75 and in Strauss (n. 12 above) 13-42.

[119] Moeller (n. 118 above) in Ozment (n. 8 above) 60.

inseparably in the minds of late medieval people. In the exegetical tradition of medieval scholarship, for example, soteriology was intimately linked to ecclesiology. The same passages of Scripture were often applied to the church and to the individual soul.[120] If many non-scholars in late medieval Germany were searching for certitude and meaning within the established ecclesiastical structure, it was also because they felt that the Roman Church was the true church and could provide them with the salvation for which they were yearning. The ecclesiastical fidelity of the late fifteenth century in Germany does not necessarily lead one to conclude a lapse of interest in the quest for the true church. In fact, it can be read as a last attempt on the part of many *viatores* to find their earthly home in that ecclesiastical environment which they knew best – the bosom of mother Rome.

Moeller notes that devotion to the church did not by any means preclude criticism of the clergy and other church leaders. He refers particularly to the views of theologians associated with the *Devotio moderna* and to the German humanists.[121] In the first category belong such men as Wessel Gansfort (†1489), John Pupper of Goch (†1475), and John Ruchrath of Wesel († after 1479). Of these, at least Wessel appears to have proposed a view of the true church as a community of genuine Christians united in love – a view which Gerhard Ritter long ago recognized as standing squarely in the Augustinian tradition.[122] In the second category belongs a man like Erasmus, whose pen spared clerical morals as little as it seriously challenged ecclesiastical (and especially papal) authority. Typical of Erasmus's attitude is his remark in a letter to Bucer: "If the power of the pope were obstructing the gospel, his despotism should have first of all been restrained, something that was not at all difficult except that some men, as the oft-repeated saying goes, preferred the whole to the half."[123] The non-revolutionary nature of the criticism voiced by all these men does not mean that they had given up hope in the church and begun to turn toward deviant, non-ecclesial forms of spiritual satisfaction. On the contrary, by

[120] For this relationship in the medieval exegesis of the Psalms, see Hendrix (n. 33 above) 51-52.

[121] Moeller (n. 118 above) in Ozment (n. 8 above) 61-62. The name of Savonarola might be added here. His millennially inspired vision of a true Roman Catholic Church perfused with charity and flourishing under a holy pope scarcely fazed the fierce attacks which he leveled against contemporary Roman leaders. See D. Weinstein, *Savonarola and Florence: Prophecy and Patriotism in the Renaissance* (Princeton 1970) 171-174.

[122] G. Ritter, "Romantic and Revolutionary Elements in German Theology on the Eve of the Reformation," in Ozment (n. 8 above) 32f. On Pupper of Goch, see D. Steinmetz, "*Libertas Christiana*: Studies in the Theology of John Pupper of Goch," *Harvard Theological Review* 65 (1972) 191-230. Goch turns out to be an ecclesiological disciple of Jean Gerson in conceding authority to the determination of the church over the literal sense of Scripture. *Ibid.* 202-203.

[123] *Erasmus and the Seamless Coat of Jesus,* ed. and trans. R. Himelick (Lafayette, Ind. 1971) 206. C. Nauert contends that the humanist return *ad fontes* did however foster a climate in which biblical evidence was accepted as superior to, and thus able to challenge, the authority of tradition; "The Clash of Humanists and Scholastics: An Approach to Pre-Reformation Controversies," *The Sixteenth Century Journal* 4 (1973) 14-15. If such a climate existed, it affected the younger humanists more than their elders like Erasmus and Pirckheimer.

remaining within the church, they may have helped to foster a climate in which the quest for the true church could be taken up anew by the Protestant Reformers. The way in which the second generation of humanists swelled the ranks of the Reformers is indicative of their interest in the re-establishment of the church at the center of men's lives. [124]

Thus, there is as yet inadequate support for the opinions of Lortz and Graus (if the two may be associated) that the sixteenth-century Reformation, including the humanists, dealt with the crisis of the later Middle Ages by appealing to individualistic and subjective values and abandoning the church as the objective framework for the means of grace. The most damaging evidence against this view is the attention which the Reformers themselves paid to the nature of the church and its authority. This point cannot be fully developed within the limits of this essay. It can be pointed out, however, that the theology of Luther, for example, was anything but subjectively oriented and did not overshift to the side of individual faith. Ecclesiological concerns were at the center of his theological development and a correlative concept of the church grew up together with his new soteriology. [125] Luther was not interested in how the individual Christian could survive apart from the church, but in how the church properly conceived could feed the Christian faithful with the word of life in the midst of crisis and uncertainty.

Essential to Luther's reforming motivation was his conviction that the Roman Church was not performing this indispensable function of the true church. In the account of his pivotal encounter with Cajetan at Augsburg in 1518, Luther is concerned, but not overly surprised, at what he labeled Cajetan's "distortion of the Bible," because "it has long been believed that whatever the Roman Church says, damns or wants, all people must eventually say, damn or want, and that no other reason need be given than that the Apostolic See and the Roman Church hold that opinion. Therefore, since the sacred scriptures are abandoned and the traditions and words of men accepted, it happens that the church of Christ is not nourished by its own measure of wheat, that is, by the word of Christ, but is usually misled by the indiscretion and rash will of an unlearned flatterer. We have come to this in our great misfortune that these people begin to force us to renounce the Christian faith and deny Holy Scripture." [126] Luther's mature ecclesiology continued to stress the

---

[124] See B. Moeller, "Die deutschen Humanisten und die Anfänge der Reformation," *Zeitschrift für Kirchengeschichte* 70 (1959) 46-61; also in *Imperial Cities and the Reformation*, ed. and trans. H. C. Erik Midelfort and Mark U. Edwards, Jr. (Philadelphia 1972) 19-38.

[125] See Hendrix (n. 33 above) 178, 212. Two studies which emphasize the objective frame of reference in Luther's theology are: S. E. Ozment, *Homo spiritualis: A Comparative Study of the Anthropology of Johannes Tauler, Jean Gerson and Martin Luther (1509-1516) in the Context of Their Theological Thought*, Studies in Medieval and Reformation Thought 6 (Leiden 1969); K.-H. zur Mühlen, *Nos extra nos: Luthers Theologie zwischen Mystik und Scholastik*, Beiträge zur historischen Theologie 46 (Tübingen 1972).

[126] Luther, *Acta Augustana*, in *Werke* (n. 69 above) 2.17.12-20. English rendition from *Luther's Works*, American ed. 31 (Philadelphia 1957) 276.

dependence of the church on the word of Scripture and the definition of the church by that word. This definition meant that the locus of the true church could in no way be circumscribed by any particular city or by obedience to any one hierarchy (especially Rome); the true church could exist wherever the word of Scripture was truly proclaimed and was nourishing the church.[127]

Luther's Reformation, and indeed the entire withdrawal from the papacy in the sixteenth century, is not correctly understood if it is read as the result of the personal spiritual crisis of an overzealous Augustinian monk. Quite the contrary is true: Luther's Reformation is best explained as an ecclesiological response to the last great medieval crisis of the church's identity and authority. Other factors played important roles in the popular support and political breathing room which the nascent Reformation churches received. Nevertheless, the crucial factor was their own ecclesiological support base, the ability of the Reformers to maintain confidence in their churches as new manifestations of the true church over against the papacy and the Roman hierarchy. This crucial role played by ecclesiology is illustrated by the failure of Protestant and papal negotiators at the Colloquy of Regensburg (1541) to agree on the nature of the church and its authority after they had reached a consensus on justification.[128] In the dissenting Protestant statement submitted to the emperor, Philip Melanchthon based the authority of the true church on the genuine understanding and interpretation of Scripture which was not bound to any persons or places but belonged to the "living members of the church."[129]

Not all sixteenth-century men were convinced that the churches of the magisterial Reformers were in fact distinct enough from Rome to claim the title of the true church. Thus, additional ecclesiological options were offered by Anabaptists and other radical Reformers who drew more directly on medieval patterns of reform like the *ecclesia primitiva.*[130] One desideratum of Reformation research is a detailed investigation into the ecclesiologies of both major and minor Reformers which would trace the interaction between their concepts of the church and the way in which

[127] Luther articulated these views in such works as *Von dem Papsttum zu Rom 1520, Werke* (n. 69 above) 6.285-324; *Ad librum Ambrosii Catharini . . . responsio 1521, ibid.* 7.705-778.

[128] See *Handbuch der Kirchengeschichte* 4 (n. 7 above) 289.

[129] *Corpus reformatorum* (Halle 1834-   ) 4.350-351: "Secundo tribuenda est autoritas verae Ecclesiae, quod penes eam est verus intellectus seu interpretatio scripturae . . . . Porro omnia, quae dicta sunt de vero intellectu et dono interpretationis, pertinent ad eos solos, qui sunt viva membra ecclesiae, in quibus spiritus sanctus accendit veram lucem et fidem." Melanchthon's statement also contains features of the medieval remnant ecclesiology (the gift of interpretation is present "alias in pluribus, alias in paucioribus") and an appeal to the consensus of the early church ("ecclesia prima").

[130] F. Littell calls the recovery of the life and virtue of the early church "the dominant theme" in the thinking of the mainline Anabaptists; *The Origins of Sectarian Protestantism* (New York 1964) 79. The theories of the fall of the church and the restitution of the true church are treated in detail, 46-108. See also C. Bauman, *Gewaltlosigkeit im Täufertum,* Studies in the History of Christian Thought 3 (Leiden 1968) 198-199. On Menno Simons, see John Tonkin, *The Church and the Secular Order in Reformation Thought* (New York 1971) 152-155.

VI

378

their reforming activity met the needs of men still affected by the crises of their late medieval environment. As this data is more fully evaluated in light of the variety in late medieval ecclesiology, it will become increasingly difficult to contrast "Reformation" and "medieval" ecclesiology as if they were two relatively homogeneous entities. [131] Rather, the development of various ecclesiologies during the Reformation period will be more suitably viewed as the continuation of the late medieval quest for the *vera ecclesia*. As in the case of the Anabaptists, some sixteenth-century ecclesiologies will appear to have medieval counterparts. Upon investigation, other ecclesiological responses to the last great medieval crisis of the papacy may reveal features sufficiently unique to help explain why this crisis would no longer be called medieval at all, but would mark the beginning of a new era. With the advent of the Reformation, the crises of medieval ecclesiology may have ceased, but the quest for the true church continued.

[131] Tonkin 158-159 is aware of the dangers in speaking collectively of the medieval tradition or of the Reformers on the crucial issue of ecclesiology; but he still regards the Reformation as "a struggle between two opposing understandings of the church" (35).

VII

"We Are All Hussites"?

Hus and Luther Revisited

I.

Early in 1520 Martin Luther reacted to John Hus' tract *De Ecclesia* in a letter
to Spalatin with the following words: "Up until now I have held and espoused
all the teachings of John Hus without knowing it. Johann von Staupitz has
unwittingly done the same. In short, we are all Hussites without realizing it.
Even Paul and Augustine are literally Hussites. Look, if you will, what we
have come to without the Bohemian leader and teacher. I am dumbfounded
when I see such terrible judgments of God upon men. The most obvious
evangelical truth, which was publicly burned more than one hundred years ago,
is condemned and no one is allowed to confess it. Woe to us!"[1] Contributors to
the revival of interest in the relationship between Luther and Hus[2] have duly
taken note of this ringing affirmation of unity among Luther, his spiritual

---

1. *WABr* 2, 42.22 ff. (no. 254). Cf. *WA* 6, 588.4 f. (*Von den neuen Eckischen Bullen
und Lügen* 1520): "Es sein nit Johannis Husz artickel, szondern Christi, Pauli, Augustini, auffs aller sterckist gegrundt und unwidderstoszlich beweret, ..." Luther received a
copy of *De Ecclesia* on October 3, 1519 from two Prague Utraquists who had heard
of his approval of Hus at Leipzig. Cf. *WABr* 1, 514.27 ff. (no. 202).
2. The beginning of this "revival" dates from back to back articles in vol. 36 (1965)
of *Luther. Zeitschrift der Luthergesellschaft* by Ingetraut Ludolphy: "Johann Huss,"

Originally published in *Archiv für Reformationsgeschichte/Archive for Reformation History* 65
(Gütersloh, 1974), pp. 134–161, used by permission.

VII

fathers Paul and Augustine, and the Czech reformer. To most of them, however, Luther's unequivocal stance has proved a source of embarrassment. How can historical relationships be explained that simply, especially by one who stood so close to the actual events? How could Luther judge his own reformation with proper objectivity?

Taking advantage of the historian's distance from his subject, recent research has attempted to qualify Luther's statements by pointing up the differences, primarily theological, between Hus and Luther. For Ingetraut Ludolphy, their *Ansätze* are totally different. Internal reasons caused Luther to become a reformer against his will. His struggle for the proper understanding of justification led him step by step to new theological insights and forced him to take a stand on matters of practical reform. In contrast, Hus was first and foremost a practical reformer. Spurred on by Wyclif's reform ideas, Hus' first concern was to implement change in the life of the church even when he had no solid theological grounds for doing so. He was not a forerunner of Luther and we cannot agree with Luther "that all of us Protestants are Hussites."[3]

Bernard Lohse is inclined to see more validity in Luther's self-identification with Hus. To posit an essentially formal agreement between Luther and Hus, as Walter Köhler did,[4] is to say too little. Hus' ideas on the lordship of Christ and the authority of scripture place him in Luther's camp. Still, neither Hus' criticism of abuses in the Roman church nor his own theology originated in a Reformation understanding of justification. In this respect, Hus never left the territory of medieval catholicism. Luther overestimated how much he had in common with Hus, even though Luther picked up certain ideas from Hus and integrated them with his own views.[5]

97–107; and B. Lohse: "Luther und Huss," 108–122. Also included are I. Kiss: "Luther und Hus," *Communio viatorum* 8 (1965), 239–250; F. M. Dobiáš: "Hus – Luther – Calvin," *Mitteilungen der Johannes-Mathesius-Gesellschaft* 5/6 (1969/70), 23–34; O. Sakrausky: *Hus und Luther heute. Studien und Dokumente 3*, ed. E. Turnwald (Kirnbach über Wolfach, 1969); Walter Delius: "Luther und Huss," *Luther-Jahrbuch 1971*, 9–25. Three earlier articles stressed in a less critical manner Luther's identification with Hus and the Czech reformation: J. Pelikan: "Luther's Attitude toward John Hus," *Concordia Theological Monthly* 19 (1948), 747–763; F. M. Bartoš: "Das Auftreten Luthers und die Unität der böhmischen Brüder," *ARG* 31 (1934), 101–120. Bartoš' plea for seeing direct influence of the Czech reformation on Luther's reforming activity was followed up by S. H. Thomson: "Luther and Bohemia," *ARG* 44 (1953), 160–181.
3. Ludolphy, p. 107.
4. *Luther und die Kirchengeschichte nach seinen Schriften* (Erlangen, 1900), 162 to 236. On Köhler, cf. Lohse, p. 109, n. 1, and p. 118.
5. Lohse, pp. 117–118. Specifically for Lohse, the agreement between Hus and Luther

Oskar Sakrausky is ready to admit that Hus qualifies as a Reformer if one regards the sole authority of scripture as the formal principle of the Reformation. This principle, however, can be traced back to the Waldensians. It formed only the basis upon which Luther established his genuine Reformation insight: the total inability of man before God to produce good works. Hus, on the other hand, built his reform program on the optimistic assumption that man can recover his original sinless state when he tenaciously keeps the law of God. Such an assumption places Hus in the ranks of the humanists rather than in the camp of Luther. Between them extends a yawning anthropological chasm.[6]

Finally, Walter Delius concedes that there does exist at points formal agreement between Luther and Hus, but in substance their ideas are quite different. Not only did Hus never abjure the doctrine of transubstantiation; even in the crucial area of ecclesiology, Hus based membership in the church on predestination whereas Luther, whose theology was minted in the struggle over justification, attributed membership to personal faith. Although their conceptions of the *communio sanctorum* differed significantly, Luther did align Hus on the side of the gospel and divine truth. Still, Luther was not intentionally a Hussite. In contrast to Hus, Luther moved decisively away from the territory of medieval catholicism toward a church based solely on the gospel.[7]

It is hardly surprising that recent research has responded "yes-but" to the question of agreement between Hus and Luther. The same paradoxical attitude can be found in the writings of Luther himself. He affirmed his identification with the Czech reformer on several occasions other than the one recorded at the beginning of this essay.[8] In 1531 Luther even applied the so-called prison prophecy of Hus to himself: "They will roast a goose now (for 'Hus' means 'goose'), but after a hundred years they will hear singing a swan which they will have to endure."[9] At other times Luther expressed himself more cautiously. For

consists in their common advocacy of the "Sache Christi gegen Menschensatzungen" and Luther's designation of the true church as the body of the predestined (*ibid.* p. 117).

6. Sakrausky, pp. 7–8, 13. Sakrausky places not only Hus at the opposite pole from Luther, but also later Hussites, the Unitas Fratrum, humanism and catholicism (*ibid* p. 14).

7. Delius, pp. 24–25.

8. E.g., *WA* 6,587.21 ff. (*Von den neuen Eckischen Bullen und Lügen* 1520); *WA* 5, 451.29 ff. (*Operationes in psalmos* 1519–1521).

9. *WA* 30/III, 387.6 ff. (*Glosse auf das vermeinte kaiserliche Edikt* 1531). This prophecy appears to be a conflation of a prison utterance of Hus with the last appeal of Jerome of Prague in 1416. For details, cf. Adolf Hauffen: "Husz eine Gans – Luther ein Schwan," in: *Untersuchungen und Quellen zur Germanistischen und Romanischen Philologie: Johann Keller dargebracht von seinen Kollegen und Schülern.* Zweiter Teil (Prague, 1908), 1–28.

example, in his *Address to the Christian Nobility*, Luther remarks that whether Hus was a heretic or not, he was executed unjustly because heretics are to be refuted with arguments and not with fire.[10] Months later, Luther asserted that he had done five times more than Hus, who did not go far enough. Hus did not ultimately deny that the pope was supreme in all the world. Luther would even deny that St. Peter was pope if he sat in Rome, because the papacy was a human invention of which God knew nothing.[11]

Luther's ambivalent attitude is best illustrated by his remarks on Hus recorded in the *Table Talk*.[12] On the positive side, the *causa* of both Luther and Hus stemmed from the issue of indulgences (no. 488), although Hus wrote against them before the time was ripe (no. 3846). Still, he precipitated the decline of the papacy (no. 1529). A powerful impetus of the Spirit prevailed in Hus (no. 3495). He was a learned man, fit to be compared with Christ; "ego amo eum" (no. 4922). On the other hand, Hus taught that works justified along with faith, though he was liberated from this error before his death (no. 2926 a). He also clung to the superstition of the private mass (no. 6035). Most importantly, Hus only opposed the bad life of the papists (no. 624): "Doctrine and life must be distinguished. Life is bad among us, as it is among the papists, but we don't fight about life and condemn the papists on that account. Wyclif and Hus didn't know this and attacked the papacy for its life. I don't scold myself into becoming good, but I fight over the Word and whether our adversaries teach it in its purity. That doctrine should be attacked – this has never happened. This is my calling."[13]

How could Luther say that "we are all Hussites" while at the same time establishing a difference between himself and Hus as decisive and clearcut as this? One solution, of course, is to say that Luther simply made a mistake in one or the other of his assertions.[14] On the other hand, if one takes into account all

---

10. *WA* 6, 455.11 ff. Luther is not too cautious here. He says he has found nothing erroneous in Hus and that his executioners were inspired more by an evil spirit than by the Holy Spirit. However, he has no intention of making a martyr out of Hus (*WA* 6,454.35 ff.; cf. *WA* 6,588.9 ff.).

11. *WA* 7,431.31 ff. *(Grund und Ursach aller Artikel* 1521).

12. These remarks can be conveniently assembled by referring to the entries under "Huss" in the index to vol. 8 of *Luthers Werke in Auswahl*, ed. O. Clemen, 3rd ed. (Berlin, 1962), p. 367, together with the *Nachträge* in the same volume, pp. 346–347. In the following we give only the numbers of the *Table Talk* entries, according to which they can be found in any edition.

13. Clemen, ed. 8,79.17 ff. (= *WATR* 1,294.19 ff.). English translation in *Luther's Works*, vol. 54 (Philadelphia, 1967), p. 110. Cf. also nos. 92, 880, 6421.

14. E.g., on Luther's relegation of Hus to the status of a moral reformer, Ernst Wer-

of the sources, is it accurate to say "yes-but"; to say Luther exaggerated the degree of agreement or that only formal agreement existed alongside significant theological deviation? If their *Ansätze* really were poles apart, as Luther himself implies, is there still a meaningful and legitimate way in which one could second Luther's exclamation of unity between himself and Hus? In the following we will attempt to answer these questions. As indicated, our emphasis will be more on Luther's view of Hus than upon Hus himself as such. The examination of Luther's affirmation "we are all Hussites" sheds significant light on the relationship between late medieval reform and its early sixteenth century manifestation in Martin Luther.

II.

There is general agreement as to the significance of the Leipzig Disputation (1519) for Luther's attitude toward Hus.[15] Even prior to Leipzig, Luther's most ardent opponents[16] had pronounced him guilty of mental association with the Czech reformer. This early sniping indicated that Luther would have to come to grips with his relationship to Hus and that the battle would not be fought over the superficial issue of indulgences. The fundamental issue would be ecclesiological – the nature of the church and ecclesiastical authority.[17]

This was indeed borne out by the events at Leipzig in July, 1519. In the course of his argument for the divine right of papal primacy, Eck remarks that among the pestiferous errors of Wyclif condemned at the Council of Constance (1415) was the assertion that belief in the supremacy of the Roman church was

---

ner claims: "Hier täuschte sich Luther" (*Der Kirchenbegriff bei Jan Hus, Jakoubek von Mies, Jan Želivský und den linken Taboriten* [Berlin, 1967], p. 25). Gordon Leff would be forced to reject outright Luther's identification of himself with Hus after writing: "That was his [Hus'] great difference from Luther; he sought reconciliation and looked to the reform of the church as it stood. He was challenging not institutions or the authority of the hierarchy, as such, but their misuse. He was therefore never an extremist, like Wyclif, nor a rebel like Luther" (*Heresy in the Later Middle Ages*, vol. II [Manchester, 1967], p. 631).

15. Cf. Thomson, pp. 168–169; Pelikan, pp. 752 ff.; Lohse, p. 115; Delius, pp. 12 ff.

16. Tetzel, Prierias and Eck. Cf. the summary of these remarks in Delius, p. 12. For Prierias, cf. *WA* 2, 51.22 f.; for Eck, cf. *WA* 1, 302.11 ff.

17. H. A. Oberman formulates it well: "Nicht erst Eck in Leipzig zwingt Luther dazu, die ekklesiologischen Komponenten seines Rufes zur Reformation zu bedenken, sondern schon Prierias; und auch er findet ihn nicht unvorbereitet, da Luther – wie sich zeigen läßt – bereits in seiner ersten Psalmenvorlesung (1513–1515) begonnen hat, Rechtfertigung und Kirche in enger Verbindung miteinander neu zu verstehen" ("Wittenbergs Zweifrontenkrieg gegen Prierias und Eck," *ZKG* 80 [1969], p. 339). For Prierias' position, which cannot be dealt with here, cf. *ibid.* pp. 335 ff.

VII

not necessary for salvation. Eck immediately adds three propositions of Hus condemned at the same council which militate against papal primacy: 1. Peter never was head of the Catholic Church; 2. there has never been any evidence that only one head ought to govern the church in spiritual matters; 3. the popes owed their dignity and origin to the emperors.[18] To refute these "errors" Eck cites the bull *Unam sanctam* (1302) of Boniface VIII: it is necessary to salvation for every human creature to be subject to the Roman pontiff.[19]

At first, Luther reacted horrified to the implication that he might share the errors of Hus. Even if the Bohemians held the divine right of the papacy, their schism would be evil because the supreme "divine right" is charity and unity of the spirit.[20] Luther firmly denies that he has any intention of protecting the Bohemian schismatics. He only wishes to uphold the legitimacy of the Greek church which has never conceded primacy to Rome. Nevertheless, many of the condemned propositions of Hus are clearly most Christian and evangelical: for example, that there is only one universal church. This the whole church could not condemn, especially since it is confessed in the Creed.[21] It is immaterial whether Wyclif or Hus thought it unnecessary to believe that the Roman church was superior. Certainly the Greek bishops who did not believe in Roman superiority were saved. In any case, the Roman pontiff has no power to establish new articles of faith. The faithful Christian cannot be forced to go beyond sacred scripture, which is properly "divine right," unless new, approved revelation has been received.[22]

In this defense of the Greek fathers, which is tantamount to an attack on papal supremacy, Luther makes two loaded observations: first, many of Hus' propositions were Christian and evangelical; secondly, true divine right is sacred scripture. These assertions do not appear to be directly related in Luther's mind. Instead, it is Eck who brings these two observations together. He calls it *verum Bohemicum* to wish to understand scripture better than the popes, councils, doctors and universities. It would be amazing if God had hidden that truth from so many saints and martyrs prior to the coming of the "Reverend

---

18. *Der authentische Text der Leipziger Disputation 1519*, ed. Otto Seitz (Berlin, 1903), pp. 81–82 (hereafter cited: Seitz). For the condemned propositions of Wyclif and Hus, cf. *Enchiridion Symbolorum*, ed. H. Denzinger and A. Schönmetzer, 34th ed. (Freiburg, 1967), nos. 1191, 1207, 1209, 1227 (hereafter cited: DS).
19. Seitz, p. 82. Cf. DS no. 875.
20. Seitz, p. 82.
21. Seitz, p. 87.
22. *Ibid.* The last sentence reads: "Nec potest fidelis Christianus cogi ultra sacram scripturam, quae est proprie ius divinum, nisi accesserit nova et probata revelatio."

Father" Luther.[23] Eck realizes more clearly than Luther which proposition of Hus had the most far-reaching implications. Indeed, the fifteenth article of Hus condemned at Constance defined ecclesiastical obedience as obedience according to the invention of the priests of the church apart from the express authority of scripture.[24] Luther, however, does not cite this proposition among the evangelical articles of Hus. Most important for him is Hus' assertion that the one universal church is the totality of the predestined – a definition which he traces back to Augustine.[25]

The remainder of the debate reveals that Luther does not attempt to reinforce his appeal to the supremacy of scripture by reference to Hus. Consistent with his ecclesiological presuppositions, Luther admits that a council is able to err since it is a creature of the word of God.[26] Luther also defends himself against the alleged statement of Hus that a sacrament administered by a priest in mortal sin is invalid.[27] It is Eck, however, who hammers home the Hussite nature of any rejection of papal primacy by referring to the fifteenth article of Hus which deprecates ecclesiastical obedience. Although Eck claims that Luther denied the heretical nature of this article when it was called to his attention, Luther never explicitly made such a denial. Eck may have been right, however, in accusing Luther of "mixing up" this article of Hus with another on the nature of human works. Confronted by Luther's counterchallenge to prove that a council could not err, Eck calls Luther a gentile and a publican, not to mention a Hussite. What might be heretical, Eck says, we will not discuss at this moment.[28]

The Leipzig Debate thus leaves it unclear precisely how Luther understood the support of his dubious new ally. The fact that Hus was unfairly condemned provided Luther with an illustration of the way in which councils could make mistakes. This illustration itself seemed to be more important to Luther than the content of those articles of Hus with which he agreed. He made no enthusiastic

---

23. Seitz, p. 91. The Weimar Edition reads *virus Bohemicum* in place of the less exciting *verum Bohemicum* (*WA* 2, 282.12).

24. DS no. 1215: "Oboedientia ecclesiastica est oboedientia secundum adinventionem sacerdotum Ecclesiae praeter expressam auctoritatem Scripturae." The condemned articles with Hus' comments on them are given in Matthew Spinka: *John Hus' Concept of the Church* (Princeton, 1966), pp. 401 ff.

25. Seitz, p. 98. Cf. *infra* n. 91. Although Luther speaks of two articles here, they appear together as the first of Hus' condemned articles (DS no. 1201). Luther enumerates two other articles of Hus as Christian and evangelical (Seitz, p. 98; DS nos. 1204, 1216).

26. Seitz, pp. 99–100; 119.

27. Seitz, p. 117. DS no. 1230.

28. Seitz, p. 129. Cf. *ibid.* p. 126.

VII

appeal to Hus' biting dissociation of ecclesiastical obedience from the authority of scripture. This may be explained by Luther's understandable reluctance to become identified with Hus anymore than necessary at that point. However, it may also be explained by the fact that Luther was not consciously seeking backing to flaunt in the face of ecclesiastical authority. Luther came to Leipzig as a disputant with a cogently worked out ecclesiology which he was prepared to defend. He did not come as a rebel mustering support for a full-fledged attack on the church. In order properly to assess Luther's attitude toward Hus at Leipzig and thereafter, it is imperative that we examine Luther's ecclesiological stance and reforming motivation during the crucial years 1518–1520.

III.

As early as his first Psalms lectures (1513–1515) Luther worked out an ecclesiological position which was no longer dependent upon the sacramental-hierarchical structure of the Roman church. Faithful Christians were no longer defined by their possession of the *gratia creata* or *caritas* dispensed in the sacraments. Rather, by 1515, Luther regards faithful Christians as "creatures made in the spirit through faith." They do not depend upon a repeated infusion of grace and *caritas*, but live as spiritual men in the knowledge and love of invisible things. True Christians do not confine themselves to this earthly, fleshly existence but live in faith and the spirit.[29] Their faith need no longer be nourished by the sacramental grace dispensed by the Roman hierarchy. Faith relies only upon the word; and where Christians are fed and fortified by the pure word of God, there also the church is nourished and flourished.[30]

29. Cf. *WA* 4,450.33 f. and *WA* 3,150.27 ff. For a detailed delineation of the way in which Luther worked out his new ecclesiology in the *Dictata*, cf. S. H. Hendrix: *Ecclesia in Via: Ecclesiological Developments in the Medieval Psalms Exegesis and the Dictata super Psalterium (1513–1515) of Martin Luther*, vol. 8 of *Studies in Medieval and Reformation Thought* (Leiden, 1974), esp. ch. 5. For a discussion of the literature, cf. ch. 4 of the same work.
30. In the *Dictata*, cf., e.g., *WA* 3,259.18 ff.; 3,454.24 ff.; 4,415.21 f. Cf. also *WA* 4,475.18 ff. In his subsequent exegetical works on Romans, Galatians, the Penitential Psalms, and Hebrews (1515–1518), Luther continues to emphasize the dependence of the church and faithful Christians upon the word. The gospel established the church (*WA* 56, 165.26 f.); Christians are able to have only the word, not the thing itself [*res*] (*WA* 56,103.13 f.); Christ feeds his faithful with his words (*WA* 57/II,60.13 ff.); only faith and the hearing of the word make one worthy of the name Christian and the ears alone are organs of the Christian man (*WA* 57/III, 222.5 ff.); "die stat gottis, die heylige Christenheit" is built only with the word and grace of God (*WA* 1,202.7 f.); Christ rules the church by no power other than the word (*WA* 57/III,108.17 ff.).

Such is the origin of Luther's well-known linkage of the church to the word. The potential of this new ecclesiological standpoint is readily apparent. If the *fideles* in the church are no longer being fed with the word, if the gospel is being suppressed or stifled, then it may become necessary to protest this suppression in order to prevent the starvation of faithful Christians. In fact, it may become necessary to establish an alternate podium for the word if it appears in danger of being snuffed out.

With this ecclesiological and soteriological concern in mind, Luther's progress to Leipzig and his reaction to Eck's incriminating association of himself with Hus come into sharper focus. Luther's initial involvement in the indulgence controversy and his stubborn refusal to retreat in the face of mounting ecclesiastical pressure are best explained by his conviction that the word was being smothered by the intensified hawking of indulgences. As a result, his flock and Christians everywhere were unable to receive the nourishment they needed to be faithful Christians. In the *Ninety-five Theses* Luther wrote that "every true Christian, whether living or dead, shares by the gift of God in all the goods of Christ and the church even without indulgences."[31] In the *Resolutiones* of 1518 Luther specifies how this happens. Participation in the goods of Christ is the unique result of faith apart from the power of the keys or indulgences. In order for the Christian to be certain that he is forgiven and enjoy the blessings of Christ, it is necessary only that he believe the words of absolution. It is immaterial who speaks these words: "The judgment of the keys is necessary so that man will not believe himself but rather the key, i.e., the priest. But I do not care whether he is an ignorant or even an insincere 'keyholder.' For [forgiveness is granted] not on account of the priest or his power, but on account of the word of him who spoke without lying: 'Whatever you loose, etc.' [Matth. 16:19]."[32] The office of the keys is retained, but only as a vehicle for the word. The relative unimportance of the vehicle is underscored by Luther: "Neither the sacrament, nor the priest, but faith in the word of Christ through the priest and his office justifies you. What difference would it

---

31. *WA* 1,235.9 ff. (Thesis no. 37). According to E. Kähler, when Luther asserted that indulgences were beneficial only weaker Christians, he broke the hold of traditional church authority, since his "true" Christians did not need what the church offered them ("Beobachtungen zum Problem von Schrift und Tradition in der Leipziger Disputation von 1519," in *Hören und Handeln. Festschrift für Ernst Wolf* [Munich, 1962], p. 229). Oberman has correctly observed that this implies Luther was fomenting schism for the sake of the *perfecti* ("Wittenbergs Zweifrontenkrieg," p. 358, no. 6). A better formulation, which circumvents this implication, is to say that the church was not offering what *all* Christians needed – the word to nourish their faith.

32. *WA* 1,594.31 ff. Cf. the explanation of Thesis no. 7 (*WA* 1,540.41 ff.).

make if the Lord spoke to you through a he-ass or a she-ass as long as you hear the word in which you can hope and believe?"[33]

Luther's concern for the feeding of his people, coupled with his disgust at the abuse of sacerdotal power caused by indulgences, leads him to stress the necessity and accessibility of the word at the expense of its priestly mediator. The priest is not unnecessary, of course. The Christian must hear the word from some external source. The sensitive point underlying Luther's emphasis on the word, however, is that the priestly mediator could be anyone, not just a member of the Roman hierarchy. Since the gospel is the true treasure of the church,[34] and not the Roman ecclesiastical warehouse of accumulated merits and grace, no necessity prevails that the mediator of the word be empowered to tap that source of grace. As Luther ludicrously implied, Christians could live without the Roman hierarchy as long as someone feeds them the word. The sacred authority of the reigning hierarchy is thus seriously impugned. Even worse, its members could become enemies of Christ if they stifle the word to make room for indulgences. The fact that Luther places the pope on the side of Christ in this 53rd thesis does nothing to diminish the import of this statement.[35] By early 1518, Luther has made it painfully clear that for him the word is the only truly indispensable food of the faithful: "It is better to omit the sacrament than not to proclaim the gospel; the church has decreed that the mass is not to be celebrated without reading the gospel. God puts more weight on the gospel than on the mass, because without the gospel man does not live in the spirit; he does live, however, without the mass. For man will live in every word that proceeds from the mouth of God [Matth. 4:4], as the Lord himself says in more detail in John 6 [26 ff.]."[36]

It is no wonder that Luther's most astute theological opponent, Thomas de Vio (Cajetan), picks out precisely this complex of themes on which to challenge Luther at their historic meeting in Augsburg in October, 1518. Cajetan clearly recognizes the threat that Luther's new soteriological and ecclesiological position posed to the established hierarchy and sacramental structure of the church. According to Luther, Cajetan attacked him on two points: 1. his assertion that the merits of Christ did not constitute the treasury of merits of indulgences (in

33. WA 1, 595.33 ff.
34. WA 1, 236.22 f. (Thesis no. 62).
35. WA 1, 236.3 ff. (Thesis no. 53): "Hostes Christi et Pape sunt ii, qui propter venias predicandas verbum dei in aliis ecclesiis penitus silere iubent."
36. WA 1, 604.35 ff. Note the explicit congruence between Luther's emphasis on men living "in the spirit" and his definition in the Dictata of faithful Christians living in faith and the spirit (supra n. 29).

opposition to the bull *Unigenitus* [1343] of Clement VI); 2. his teaching in the explanation of thesis seven that faith made the sacrament of penance efficacious.[37] It has been frequently noted how Luther anguished over the second objection because he scarcely feared anything less than that this doctrine would be called into question.[38] More significant, however, is the result of this anguish: the way in which Luther was forced explicitly to set the word of God over the pope. "The pope is not above, but under the word of God."[39] In other words, Luther was now compelled to draw the unpleasant consequences of the ecclesiological stance he had developed beginning with the *Dictata* – the exclusive reliance of the church on the word. If faithful Christians could not have their faith nourished by the word in the Roman ecclesiastical structure, then it would be necessary to oppose even that structure: "It has long been believed that whatever the Roman church says, damns, or wants, all people must eventually say, damn, or want, and that no other reason need be given than that the Apostolic see and the Roman church hold this opinion. Therefore, since the sacred Scriptures are abandoned and the traditions and words of men are accepted, it happens that the church of Christ is not nourished by its own measure of wheat, that is, by the word of Christ, but is usually misled by the indiscretion and rash will of an unlearned flatterer. We have come to this in our great misfortune that these people begin to force us to renounce the Christian faith and deny Holy Scripture."[40] Luther's motivation for drawing these explicit conclusions is the same as that which compelled him earlier in 1518 to exalt the word over indulgences, the mass and the hierarchy: his concern for the feeding of the faithful.

When Luther arrived in Leipzig in July 1519, he was well aware that the issue between him and the papacy was primarily ecclesiological – the nature of ecclesiastical authority. Wilhelm Borth has recently called attention to the

---

37. *WA* 2,7.26 ff. (*Acta Augustana*). In regard to the second point, Cajetan had written prior to their meeting that such a position was tantamount to "constructing a new church." Cf. G. Hennig: *Cajetan und Luther* (Stuttgart, 1966), p. 56.
38. *WA* 2,8.16 ff.
39. *WA* 2,11.2 f.
40. *WA* 2,17.12 ff. English translation in *Luther's Works*, vol. 31 (Philadelphia, 1957) p. 276. As early as the *Dictata*, Luther had envisioned in theory that *doctores* and prelates may be regarded as enemies of the church if they exalt "human traditions" over the faith of true Christians who are taught by the anointing of the Spirit (I John 2:27) and who are able as spiritual men to judge all things and be judged by no one (I Cor. 2:15). Cf. *WA* 4,353.5 ff. For the astounding application of I Cor. 2:15 to the Christian instead of to the pope, cf. Hendrix: *Ecclesia in Via*, pp. 184–187, and Oberman, "Wittenbergs Zweifrontenkrieg," pp. 340–342.

crucial nature of the decision which Luther had to make in late December, 1518 or early January, 1519.[41] On November 9, 1518 at the urging of Cajetan, Leo finally issued the bull *Cum postquam* in which he required that everyone accept his teaching on indulgences. The bull, published by Cajetan at Linz a. d. Donau on December 13, 1518, was designed to force Luther's hand. Luther submitted his reply in a letter to Frederick between January 13 and 19, 1519. Luther asserts that *Cum postquam* offers nothing new and, most importantly, does not offer biblical, patristic or even canonical support for its assertions. Since the church ought to give a basis for its doctrine, Luther could not acknowledge such a decretal as a firm and sufficient doctrine of the holy church. He must obey God's commandments and prohibitions. Although he will not reject it, Luther says, he will not bow down before it.[42] As he staked out this position, Luther set himself in unambiguous opposition to an official papal pronouncement.

Luther was, however, not yet convinced that he must immediately envision a new church to be constructed out of the building blocks of his ecclesiology which had been maturing since 1513–1515. As he stated prior to the disputation: "I seek nothing except to shut up those who dare to imprison behind the word of men and pontiffs the free understanding of scripture given by Christ. They wish to judge the words of God by the words of men, although the reverse is true: the words of men ought to be judged by the word of God which judges all things."[43] Luther is still concerned that the word of God be allowed to feed the faithful. Wherever that can happen, the church can exist. Luther wrote further in the *Resolutio:* "Wherever the word of God is preached and believed, there is true faith; that rock is immovable. Moreover, where there is faith, there is the church. Where the church is, there is the bride of Christ, there are all things which belong to the bridegroom. So faith has in itself everything which follows upon faith: the keys, the sacraments, authority, and all other things."[44] If the word and faith can freely exist in the Roman *ecclesia* where, Luther concedes still at Leipzig, the pope enjoys a certain primacy by human right, then a new *ecclesia* is not necessary.

---

41. Wilhelm Borth: *Die Luthersache (Causa Lutheri) 1517–1524. Historische Studien,* Heft 414 (Lübeck and Hamburg, 1970), p. 62.
42. *WABr* 1, 307.37 ff. (no. 136). For *Cum postquam,* cf. DS nos. 1447–1449. Hennig has shown that Cajetan himself was the real author of the bull (*Cajetan und Luther,* pp. 90 ff.).
43. *WA* 2, 225.24 ff. (*Resolutio Lutheriana super propositione XIII* 1519). Luther's play on I Cor. 2:15 is certainly intentional.
44. *WA* 2, 208.25 ff.

Such is the ecclesiological and ecclesiastical situation which Luther faced at Leipzig when Eck charged him with the taint of Hussitism. Luther had opposed a specific ruling of the pope; he had stated that the pope and the council were neither ultimate nor infallible authorities.[45] However, Luther had not yet deemed it necessary voluntarily to break with the church. It was still possible for the pope himself to submit to scripture or for a council to take the side of scripture and overrule the pope.[46] For this reason, it appears entirely reasonable that Luther did not want to be unequivocally identified with the schismatic Hussites. He did not yet consider himself separated from the *ecclesia romana*. As he writes in September 1519 in his lectures on Galatians, no one should consider him an opponent of the Roman church. Love forbids him to break the unity of the spirit and secede from the church even though he must bear "the burdens and the truly intolerable abominations of the Roman curia." The separation of the Bohemians from the Roman church can in no way be condoned; it is an impious act contrary to all the laws of Christ.[47]

In late 1519 and early 1520 Luther became increasingly enthusiastic about Hus and dropped the reservations he had retained at Leipzig. Even before he had had time to read *De Ecclesia*, he informed Eck that he could ascribe to many more articles of Hus.[48] And after studying *De Ecclesia*, he made his euphoric endorsement of Hus quoted at the beginning of this essay in which he claims to have defended "all the teachings" of Hus. Why this relatively sudden upsurge of feeling for Hus? Did Luther discover something in Hus' *De Ecclesia* with which he could fully identify? The letter to Spalatin indicates that Luther saw in Hus an ally against those who would suppress evangelical truth and, perhaps specifically, against the pope. Later in 1520 Luther will advise the Bohemians how Christians can (and now perhaps *should*) survive without the pope: "The prime concern should be that [the Bohemians] live sincerely in faith and in accordance with Holy Scripture. For Christian faith and life can well exist

---

45. Cf. *supra* n. 39. Cf. also Luther's response to Prierias, citing Panormitanus (*WA* 1, 656.32): "... tam Papa quam concilium potest errare." Also *WA* 2, 18.2 f.: "Veritas divina est etiam domina Papae; ..."

46. Remigius Bäumer has asserted that the incongruence of Luther's positive and negative remarks about the papacy in the years 1518–1520 indicate insincerity, vacillation and tactical maneuvring on Luther's part (*Martin Luther und der Papst*, 2nd ed. [Münster, 1970], pp. 25 f., 33 f., 38 f., 53, 61). A fairer and more defensible explanation is that Luther had not yet begun to consider himself separated from the church and hoped to the end that the word would be allowed free rein in the *ecclesia romana* by the pope or a council.

47. *WA* 2, 605.12 ff.

48. *WA* 2, 702.2 f. (*Ad Ioh. Eccium ... epistola* 1519).

without the intolerable laws of the pope. In fact faith cannot properly exist unless there are fewer of these Romanist laws or unless they are abolished altogether."[49]

No wonder, then, that Luther extols Hus so enthusiastically in the *Operationes in psalmos*. The ecclesiologically rich context of Luther's remarks demonstrates that he is most concerned to show that the church can exist apart from Rome. Luther rebukes the "Roman impiety" which attempts to tie the church to Rome, permitting no one to be Christian unless he is Roman. For Luther the church is a spiritual congregation, a *communio sanctorum*, not a *communio Romanorum*.[50] Since we live in the last times about which Christ spoke, when the fury of Roman impiety so openly resists the gospel, we must arm our minds, firmly believing the word of God and knowing without doubt that "the church of Christ is nothing other than a spiritual assembly of the faithful wherever they be on earth; and whatever is of flesh and blood, whatever has to do with person, place, time and those things which flesh and blood can make use of, does not belong to the church of God."[51]

In this antipapal context, Luther recalls his confrontation in Leipzig and, in order to clear his conscience, staunchly embraces the articles of Hus which he had defended at Leipzig – specifically, the definition of the church universal as the totality of the predestined. Luther labels the Council of Constance a *conciliabulum Satanae* and damns and "excommunicates" all those who were present or acquiesced and still acquiesce in its decisions, be they popes, bishops, kings or whoever. If Hus and Jerome of Prague were burned only for those articles, then the pope and his cohorts were, and are, the cruelest and most impious murderers, enemies of Christ and his church.[52] Luther then concludes his excursus on Hus: "At Leipzig I was completely ignorant of the meaning of those articles, whose words I saw to be most Christian. Thus I was not able to refute the sense which that fan of the pope [Eck] gave to them. But now that I have at hand the book of John Hus [*De Ecclesia*], I see from the context of the articles that also their meaning is most Christian. What is the pope, what is the world, what is the prince of this world, that on his account I should deny the truth of the gospel for which Christ died? Let prevail who will, let perish who will, with God being merciful I shall always feel this way!"[53]

In 1520 Luther realized that he might have to implement the longstanding

49. *WA* 6, 456.22 f. (*An den christlichen Adel* 1520).
50. *WA* 5, 450.24 ff.
51. *WA* 5, 450.38 ff.
52. *WA* 5, 451.29 ff.
53. *WA* 5, 452.3 ff.

potential of his ecclesiology and, in opposition to Rome, support an independent church based solely on the word. Most of the evidence cited so far indicates that Luther may have seen in Hus a personal and theological precedent for the task at hand. In late 1520 and early 1521, however, Luther again becomes cautious about a total identification between himself and Hus. By the end of June 1520, Luther had been threatened with excommunication in the bull *Exsurge domine* (June 15, 1520) and had written in the foreword to his publication of Prierias' *Epitoma:* "And now farewell, unhappy, hopeless, blasphemous Rome! The wrath of God has come upon you as you deserved."[54] The thirtieth article condemned in *Exsurge domine* was Luther's advocacy of the truest, most Christian, evangelical nature of some of Hus' articles.[55] Now in reply to this condemnation, Luther reaffirms that he erred by not asserting that all of the articles of Hus were most Christian and evangelical.[56] But he continues, surprisingly, that "they do not act rightly who call me a Hussite."[57]

Luther states his reasons for this unexpected disavowal. If Hus was a heretic, then Luther is ten times a heretic, because Hus said considerably less (than he, Luther) as if he were only beginning to let in the light of truth.[58] Perhaps Hus was burned because he did accuse the "Roman idol and his satanic statutes and deeds" of not a little error. Indeed, Hus was striving to do what Luther himself was after at first: to save some credibility for the papal decrees. But the credibility gap had grown too wide and, in order to save the decrees, Hus had to perish, and with him Christ and faith and truth.[59] Luther labels the papal decretals "impious and contrary to Christ," not just "apocryphal" as Hus and Wyclif did.[60] Thus, in Luther's eyes, Hus did not really fight to abolish the monarchy of the pope. He *only* denied that an impious pope was a member of the church, or even pope; nevertheless, Hus felt such a pope should be endured like any other tyrant. Luther, for his part, is ready to deny the existence of the papacy *in toto,* because all churches and sees are equal.[61]

---

54. *WA* 6, 329.17 f. In the same context Luther writes that if Rome believes what Sylvester (Prierias) believes, then blessed be Greece and blessed be Bohemia and all those who cut their ties with Rome (*ibid.* 4 ff.). Further on he writes: "Extincta est in ea [Roma] iam dudum fides, proscriptum Evangelium, exul Christus, Mores plusquam barbarici" (*ibid.* 12 f.).

55. DS no. 1480. Cf. *supra* n. 21.

56. *WA* 7, 135.15 ff. (*Assertio omnium articulorum* 1520). Cf. *supra* n. 52.

57. *WA* 7, 135.23: "Secundo, non recte faciunt, qui me Hussitam vocant."

58. *WA* 7, 135.24 f.

59. *WA* 7, 135.28 ff.

60. *WA* 7, 136.9 f.

61. *WA* 7, 135.34 ff.: "Igitur Ioannes Huss non repugnare videtur, quo minus sit

149

Although we are now familiar with the ecclesiological foothold supporting Luther's steps in 1518–1520, we are still confronted by an apparent inconsistency in his opinion of Hus. What aroused now this sudden reservation in his attitude toward Hus? Why did Luther begin to doubt that Hus' ecclesiology would be able to support his earlier exuberant embrace? Luther's avowal of Hus' definition of the church as most Christian implies that he regarded it as consonant with his own *spiritualis fidelium collectio*. Did Luther and Hus in fact have the same understanding of the church? What is the relationship between their ecclesiologies and Luther's sudden change in attitude? What could Luther have seen in Hus' *De Ecclesia* which would have prompted him late in 1520 to shy away from adopting the Hussite label? Was Luther's later slant on Hus as a moral reformer more accurate – a view which was simply submerged in the first flush of enthusiasm for the Czech reformer as a defender of evangelical truth? The answers to these questions must await an examination of Hus' ecclesiology itself.

IV.

What was Hus after: a reform of morals or a reformation of the church? In a recent essay, Jan Smolík offers an impassioned plea for seeing in Hus a defender of the truth instead of a spiritualizer or moral crusader. The truth which Hus championed is the truth of God embodied historically in the *congregatio praedestinatorum:* "With the concept of the congregation of the predestined Hus defends the thesis that in the world God will always have his church in which the truth cannot perish."[62] This view of Hus as the champion of God's truth – also shared by Luther in early 1520 – has been echoed or at least complemented by other recent appraisals which see in the Czech reformer a true

---

Monarchia Papae: hoc tantum agit, impium pontificem non esse Membrum Ecclesiae, multo minus Papam, ferendum tamen sicut quemvis alium tyrannum. ... Papa enim res ficta est in mundo, neque fuit neque est neque erit sed fingitur esse. Quare ipsam sedem Bestiae nego, nihil moratus, sit ne bonus an malus, qui in ea sedet. Sedes, inquam, quae sit super omnes sedes, nulla est in Ecclesia super terram iure divino, sed omnes sunt aequales, ..."

62. J. Smolík: "Die Wahrheit in der Geschichte: zur Ekklesiologie von Jan Hus," *Evangelische Theologie* 32 (1972), p. 271. Cf. *ibid.* p. 273, n. 20. H. Riedlinger has recently argued that Hus' concept of the church of the predestined is in no way time-bound or perfected in history and thus results in an "Entleerung der Geschichte der Kirche" ("Ekklesiologie und Christologie bei Johannes Hus," in *Von Konstanz nach Trient. Festgabe für August Franzen,* ed. R. Bäumer [Munich, Paderborn, Vienna, 1972], pp. 47–55). According to Riedlinger, this ahistorical concept of the church is a unique consequence of Hus' traditional refusal to allow any room in his Christology for the development of wisdom and knowledge in the historical Jesus (*ibid.* pp. 51 ff.).

Reformator of the church. Ernst Werner is convinced that Hus' concept of the church undermined the dogma of papal primacy and "all the consequences which followed therefrom."[63] By combining the doctrines of predestination and the church, Hus robbed the papacy and the Roman hierarchy of their right to exist by setting up moral criteria with which they could not comply without dismantling their institutional structure.[64] Howard Kaminsky has argued that the ecclesiological factor was basic to the case of Hus because of the subversive nature of a doctrine of the church based on predestination. As in Wyclif's case, the effect of such an ecclesiology was "to deny the actual Roman church its title to institutional holiness, and hence to deny its final authority in matters of doctrine."[65]

These authors have pointed to the central problem of Hus' thought: behind Hus' pleas for moral reform did there lurk a potentially subversive theology (in particular: ecclesiology), or was Hus the theologian harmless compared with Hus the reformer? There is now sufficient evidence to conclude that Hus was neither a superficial moral crusader nor a theological lightweight. Even the scholarly work of the Hus apologist, Dom Paul de Vooght, recognizes that Hus' advocacy of a church of the predestined threatened both papal primacy and conciliar supremacy, although de Vooght still believes Hus was a more proficient reformer than theologian.[66] But one does not have to concentrate on the

---

63. Werner: "Der Kirchenbegriff," p. 25.

64. *Ibid.* pp. 22–23.

65. H. Kaminsky: *A History of the Hussite Revolution* (Berkeley, 1967), p. 38. Kaminsky is of course aware of the work of Sedlák and others who have demonstrated subsequent to Loserth (in his *Hus und Wiclif,* 1st ed. [Prague and Leipzig, 1884]) that Hus did not slavishly copy Wyclif but skillfully used his works. Nevertheless, Kaminsky believes Hus did not vary significantly from Wyclif in the adoption of the latter's predestination-based ecclesiology (*History,* p. 36, n. 109). Cf. Paul De Vooght: "Hus et Wyclif: État de la question," in *Hussiana* (Paris and Louvain, 1960), pp. 1–6.

66. De Vooght attempts to show that until 1413 Hus' ecclesiological position remained catholic in its entirety, esp. his inclusion of the *praesciti* in the *congregatio fidelium.* Thus, when Hus adopted Wyclif's concept of the church as the *universitas praedestinatorum,* Hus not only created confusion in the traditional terminology, but also introduced a contradiction into his own ecclesiology. According to De Vooght, the notion of an *ecclesia praedestinatorum* does not affect Hus' understanding of sacramental absolution or religious obedience. Cf. "'Universitas praedestinatorum' et 'congregatio fidelium' dans l'ecclésiologie de Jean Huss," in *Hussiana,* pp. 9–65. De Vooght has been challenged on these points by Matthew Spinka: *John Hus' Concept of the Church* (Princeton, 1966). Spinka believes that the church of the predestined was an integral part of his thought prior to *De Ecclesia* and that Hus never denied the existence of a congregation of the faithful embracing both predestined and *praesciti* (*ibid.* pp. 68 f.). Spinka would agree, however, that Hus' church of the predestined challenged the legal concept

church of the predestined to discover possible subversive elements in his ecclesiology. One can point to his "semi-Donatist"[67] conclusion that a priest or pope is a true (*verus*) vicar of Christ if he has been properly ordained but not truly (*vere*) a successor of Christ and Peter unless he follows them in morals.[68] Consequently, it could become necessary publicly to resist one's ecclesiastical superior when he acts contrary to divine counsels and precepts.[69] Although the transgressing prelate's ordination (*potestas ordinis*) cannot be challenged,[70] his jurisdictional authority (*potestas iurisdictionis*) may legitimately be ignored. Or one may point to the way that Hus grants to the Christian the right to assume that his priest is an enemy of Christ if he is explicitly aware of the priest's *crimen*.[71] Further, there is the way in which Hus challenges the supremacy claim of *Unam sanctam* by inserting Christ in place of the pope as Roman pontiff.[72] Like Eck, one can point to Hus' scripture principle, where ecclesiastical obedience is set in opposition to "spiritual obedience" to the law of God and attributed to the "inventions of the priests of the church apart from the express authority of scripture."[73] Finally, one can appeal to the right given by Hus to every Christian to judge his superiors according to the law of Christ. In

of a *congregatio fidelium* held by both papalists and the conciliarists who condemned Hus (*ibid*. pp. 394 f.).

67. The term is Heiko Oberman's. Cf. his *Forerunners of the Reformation* (London, 1966), p. 210.

68. *Tractatus de Ecclesia* (hereafter cited *DE*) c. 9 (ed. S. H. Thomson [Cambridge, 1956], p. 70). Cf. *DE* c. 14 (Thomson, p. 112).

69. *DE* c. 19 (Thomson, p. 177). Cf. *DE* c. 11 (Thomson, pp. 92–93).

70. *DE* c. 10 (Thomson, p. 88). It is clear that Hus did not hold a fully Donatist position on the unworthiness of an evil priest as the propositions condemned at Constance led Luther at Leipzig to believe. Cf. *supra* n. 27 and De Vooght, *Hussiana*, pp. 211 ff. Spinka believes that Hus "indeed skated on the thin ice of Donatism. ..." (*John Hus' Concept of the Church*, p. 232).

71. *DE* c. 5 (Thomson, p. 38). G. Leff raises the pertinent question how Hus can logically assert ignorance of who is damned and saved (e.g. *DE* c. 5 [Thomson, p. 36]) and simultaneously damn those who contravene Christ's laws (*Heresy in the Later Middle Ages*, II, p. 664). This certainly mitigates the threat of Hus' doctrine of predestination; at the same time, it enhances his moral demands.

72. *DE* c. 12 (Thomson, pp. 96 ff.).

73. *DE* c. 17 (Thomson, p. 156). Cf. *supra* nn. 23, 24. Oberman believes that it was "probably due to [Hus'] opposition to the authority of extrascriptural canon law" that Luther could exclaim that "we are all Hussites" (*Forerunners of the Reformation*, p. 212). According to Hus, the Christian is required to believe explicitly or implicitly every truth which the Holy Spirit has put in scripture, but not the words of the saints or papal bulls unless they are based explicitly or implicitly on scripture (*DE* c. 8 [Thomson, p. 56]).

this context, Hus quotes, among other passages, I Cor. 2:15: "The spiritual man judges all things." Hus anticipates Luther by applying this verse, not to the pope as was traditional (e. g. in *Unam sanctam*), but to the individual Christian's right to judge his ecclesiastical superiors.[74]

In the face of these examples, there can be little doubt that Hus' ecclesiology contains sufficient incendiary material to ignite both papal and conciliar opposition. On this basis it is impossible to support any contrast between Hus and Luther which reduces Hus to a theological pygmy alongside a Wittenberg giant. Although Luther certainly must have realized that his spiritual assembly of truly faithful Christians was not precisely the same as Hus' *universitas praedestinatorum*, it is easily understandable how Luther could see in several of the above points an ecclesiological platform from which the evangelical truth could be proclaimed. In his letters especially, Hus continually casts himself in the role of a defender of the "truth of God," the "law of God," or the "gospel." In 1410 Hus defends himself against the charge of heresy by accusing his opponents of wishing to stifle the gospel. Hus declares that he will not be intimidated from obeying God and publicly proclaiming the truth of the gospel.[75] Much later, from Constance just before his death, Hus beseeches his Bohemian friends to uphold the truth of God which he has drawn from the law of God. This appeal for steadfastness in the law and truth of God resounds constantly from Hus' prison cell.[76]

Could it be that Hus was a genuine *Reformator* of the church and defender of the truth as Luther pictured him early in 1520? Formally, there appears to be no obstacle to such an assertion. If we ask the crucial question, however, whether Hus in fact thought it necessary to establish a new church and, if so, on what basis he would legitimize its existence, then the identification between Luther and Hus becomes tenuous. There is a significant gap between allowing

74. *DE* c. 19 (Thomson, pp. 180–181). Cf. *supra* n. 40.

75. Cf. the timely English translation by Matthew Spinka: *The Letters of John Hus* (Manchester, 1972), pp. 38–39 (= V. Novotný ed., *M. Jana Husi, Korespondence a dokumenty* [Prague, 1920] no. 18). Hus writes that the will of God and scripture teach that superiors should be obeyed only in things lawful (Spinka, *Letters*, p. 53 [= Novotný, no. 28]). Furthermore, "everyone, whether priest or layman, who knows the truth, ought to defend it to death; otherwise he is a traitor of the truth and thus of Christ as well" (Spinka, *Letters*, p. 62 [= Novotný, no. 35]).

76. Spinka, *Letters* p. 165 (= Novotný, no. 129). Cf. Spinka, *Letters*, pp. 182, 197, 198, 202, 209 (= Novotný, nos. 141, 154, 155, 160, 164). Cf. also Hus' appeals to the Praguers, from his earlier exile in 1412, praising their progress in the law of God and giving thanks for the spread of the truth in spite of attempts to suppress it (Spinka, *Letters*, pp. 79 83 f. [= Novotný, no. 49]).

the possibility of rebellion against one's ecclesiastical superiors and providing an ecclesiology capable of supporting an autonomous church cut off from the Roman hierarchy. Although Hus' ecclesiology contained some theoretical potential for elevating the authority of individual Christians over that of the Roman institution, was it necessary for Hus to take that step in order for the true church as he conceived it to survive? Could Hus' church of the predestined support itself?

The answer to this question must remain negative. The reason for this answer is hinted at in a letter which Hus wrote to the preachers and brethren at Bethlehem in the autumn of 1412. In this letter he agonizes whether or not to acquiesce in the exile imposed upon him.[77] Hus reports having pondered a letter of Augustine in which the bishop of Hippo advised his fellow bishop Honoratus that a pastor is allowed to flee persecution if his flight does not deprive the church of the "necessary ministry." But the pastor who flees in such a way that Christ's flock is deprived of that by which it lives spiritually is a hireling.[78] Against this backdrop Hus reveals his own feelings: "Let me know, therefore, if you can acquiesce in Augustine's advice. For my conscience urges me not to cause offence by my absence, even though the necessary food of God's word is not wanting the sheep. On the other hand, I fear lest my presence – because of the damnedly acquired interdict – would afford an occasion for the withholding of that food, i.e. the communion of the venerable sacrament and the other means to salvation."[79] The key factor here, as with Luther, is the feeding of the Christian people. Hus admits that the word of God is part of the necessary food of God's flock;[80] but Hus is reluctant to return because an even more important conduit of nourishment for the people would be turned off – the sacraments which supply grace. Judging from Hus' decision not to violate his exile and thus bring down the interdict upon the heads of his people, sacramental grace is more essential to the Christian's diet than the word. Granted, the word was still being preached in Hus' absence.[81] If however, faith in the word of God *with or without* sacramental grace had been the mark of

---

77. Spinka, *Letters*, pp. 75–77 (= Novotný, no. 47).
78. *Ibid*. p. 75. For Augustine, cf. *Epist*. 228.14 (Migne, *PL* 33,1019).
79. Spinka, *Letters*, p. 76 (= Novotný, no. 47).
80. In the same letter Hus asks that prayers be made for him "in order that my hunger after the word of God be satisfied; and then also that the others like me be nourished" (*ibid*. p. 77).
81. When Hus heard that the order had been given to tear down Bethlehem Chapel, he wrote to the lords and masters at Prague: "... they wish to suppress his holy word, to destroy the chapel useful for the preaching of God's word, and thus to obstruct the salvation of the people" (Spinka, *Letters*, p. 77 [= Novotný, no. 48]).

true Christians for Hus as it was for Luther, then the interdict would have not been sufficient reason for Hus not to return to Prague and feed the people himself.

Hus' self-justification for remaining in exile receives significant support from the ecclesiological theory which he elaborated in *De Ecclesia*. At this point, the question of the true impact of the *universitas praedestinatorum* on Hus' ecclesiology must be raised. Did it really undermine the sacramental structure of the church and serve Hus as a foundation for a church detached from the papal hierarchy? If we look closely at what Hus requires for a Christian to attain salvation, then it is clear that the grace of predestination does not cancel the need for sacramental grace. Hus explicitly affirms that the only faith which saves is *fides caritate formata* coupled with perseverance.[82] The faithful Christian (*fidelis*) is one who has faith infused by God.[83] In fact, together with Christ, the *fides formata* can be considered the foundation of the church.[84] Hus holds the traditional medieval view of sacramental grace consisting of the infused virtues formed by *caritas*. The Christian who will emerge as a true member of the heavenly as well as of the earthly church is the one whose predestination enables him to continue in this grace to the end.

Even when Hus speaks of predestination, he employs such terms as the "grace of predestination" and the "*caritas* of predestination." The mystical garment which makes one a true son and friend of the church is the *caritas* of predestination.[85] Because they lack this *caritas* of predestination, the foreknown do not really belong to the church (*de ecclesia*), although they may be in the church (*in ecclesia*) according to the grace of present righteousness.[86] For Hus to make his congregation of the predestined totally independent of the contemporary institution, he would have to define the grace of predestination as something entirely different from the grace and *caritas* which come through ordinary

82. *DE* c. 8 (Thomson, pp. 53–54): "Unde quicunque habuerit fidem caritate formatam in communi sufficit cum virtute perseverancie ad salutem. ... Ubi sciendum quod duplex est fides: una informis, cum credunt demones et contremiscunt [Iac. 2:19]; alia est fides caritate formata. Ista cum perseverancia salvat sed non prima."
83. *DE* c. 8 (Thomson, p. 54).
84. *DE* c. 7 (Thomson, p. 51): "... non locus sive antiquitas sed fides formata fundet Christi ecclesiam." *DE* c. 9 (Thomson, p. 57): "Fundamentum, a quo primo, et fundamentum in quo primo fundatur sancta ecclesia katholica, est Christus Ihesus, et fundamentum quo fundatur est fides, que per dilectionem operatur, quam Petrus proposuit dicens: 'Tu es Christus, filius dei vivi' [Matt. 16:16]."
85. *DE* c. 5 (Thomson, p. 31). The church as *sponsa* is joined to her head by *caritas perpetua* (*DE* c. 4 [Thomson, pp. 22,23]).
86. *DE* c. 3 (Thomson, p. 15). Cf. *DE* c. 4 (Thomson, p. 26).

sacramental channels. Hus does take a step in this direction. He unequivocally states that there are two kinds of grace – the grace of predestination which cannot be lost, and the grace according to present righteousness which is only temporary.[87] This distinction must be more than a mere temporal one, however, if Hus is to show that a *praescitus*, as long as he possesses the *caritas* of present righteousness, does not in fact simultaneously possess the grace of predestination and for that precise period is a member of the true, holy, catholic church (= body of the predestined).

Hus confronts this dilemma headon in chapter four of *De Ecclesia*,[88] and approaches a terminologically workable solution. Building on the two kinds of grace and *caritas* already distinguished, Hus implies that it is possible to have the grace of predestination for a time without possessing the grace of present righteousness. For this reason, it is possible to say that a man is simultaneously righteous and unrighteous. Prime examples here are Peter and Paul, who were always righteous through the grace and *caritas* of predestination even while they were committing the mortal sins of persecuting Christ and denying him. One can even say "Paul was *fidelis* according to predestination and *infidelis* according to persecution, an Israelite according to predestination and a blasphemer according to present righteousness; he was in the *caritas* of predestination and he was *accaris*, i.e., without the *caritas* of present righteousness."[89] It would seem that two kinds of *caritas* are clearly distinguished here. The crucial test, however, is whether or not a faithful Christian could acquire and maintain the *caritas* of predestination without ever possessing in addition the *caritas* of present righteousness, i.e., whether or not the *caritas* of predestination is available totally apart from the sacramental grace of present righteousness. This would be absolutely necessary if Hus were to set up his own church solely on the foundation of predestination. Hus clearly implies a negative answer. Although the predestined retain the grace of predestination which cannot be lost, they may be deprived temporarily *(ad tempus)* of the grace of present righteousness.[90] The word "temporarily" indicates that the predestined are expected normally to possess the grace of present righteousness in addition to their omnipresent *caritas* of predestination.

Hus is concerned to show that foreknown Christians cannot ever belong to

---

87. *DE* c. 3 (Thomson, p. 17).
88. Thomson, pp. 27–28.   89. *Ibid*. p. 28.
90. *Ibid*. p. 27: "Praedestinati vero, licet ad tempus priventur fluente gracia, habent tamen radicalem graciam a qua non possunt excidere." The contrast *fluens – radicalis* picks up the previous analogy with the human body which has some fluids which flow in and out *(fluens)* and others which circulate permanently within the body.

the church qua society of the predestined, whether they possess temporary grace or not. To do this, he shows that the grace of predestination is to some extent qualitatively different from the grace of present righteousness. Hus is not concerned to show that the faithful Christian can be saved without ever belonging to the church qua sacramental institution. Conceivably, his grace and *caritas* of predestination could be made to support an independent church of the predestined. Hus gives no hint, however, that he anticipated this ecclesiological possibility. In fact, the reverse is true. He gives every indication that the *caritas* of predestination cannot exist totally independent of sacramental grace and that the latter, if not absolutely equivalent to the former, is a necessary partner of the former in the process of salvation. In this respect, Hus does not differ from Augustine and the mainstream medieval tradition, regardless of the emphasis placed on predestination.[91]

In 1886 J. Gottschick argued for a similar interpretation of Hus as the one presented here.[92] Gottschick pointed out how, for Hus, one can never be certain that one is predestined.[93] Therefore, one is driven to the means of grace to obtain the *caritas* which makes predestination efficacious. In Hus' system, predestination only leads to an *Aufwertung*, not an *Entwertung*, of the means of grace, since the traditional understanding of the *gratia infusa* remains in force. Consequently, predestination is not the key to the novelty of Hus' ecclesiology.[94] Rather, Gottschick finds this key in the right accorded every Christian by Hus to hold up the scripture as an authority over the prelates of the church and judge them accordingly. The motivation to overrule one's ecclesiastical

---

91. On the basis of a detailed study of Augustinian texts cited by Hus, De Vooght concludes: "Son ecclésiologie ne reproduit pas celle de saint Augustin" ("La part de Saint Augustin dans le *De Ecclesia* de Huss," in *Hussiana*, p. 92). De Vooght claims that Augustine integrated the predestined into the structure of the visible church while Hus, by starting with the church of the predestined, was not able to salvage the reality or necessity of the militant church embracing both *boni* and *mali* (*ibid.* pp. 88–91). Our investigation has led to the opposite view that Hus was in fact not able to sever the *universitas praedestinatorum* from the visible church of the sacraments. It is possible to argue on slender evidence that Augustine's understanding of predestination undermined the sacramental community. Much stronger evidence shows, however, that Augustine bequeathed to the Middle Ages the ecclesiological concept of an inner circle of *sancti* and *boni* living in *caritas*. Cf. Hendrix, *Ecclesia in Via*, ch. 1.

92. "Hus', Luthers und Zwinglis Lehre von der Kirche," *ZKG* 8 (1886), 345–394 and 543–616 (on Hus: pp. 345–394).

93. Cf. *DE* c. 5 (Thomson, p. 38): "Racionem autem predestinacionis vel caritatis, que non excidit, que est vestis nupcialis distinguens membrum ecclesie a membro dyaboli non hic sensibiliter intuemur." Cf. *ibid.* p. 36.

94. Gottschick, pp. 362 ff.

superior was given when his conduct conflicted with the supreme criterion established for the church: the *lex Christi*. According to Gottschick, Hus did not quite attain the later Protestant scripture principle because, though formally the same, their content was as different as law and gospel. Nevertheless, Hus' achievement was to call into question the medieval assumption of an authoritative ecclesiastical hierarchy.[95]

More profoundly than some of his successors, Gottschick focused attention on the pivotal question of Hus' motivation and the theological base from which his reform was implemented. He never quite touched, however, the crucial matter of how the faithful are nourished. Even with a suprainstitutional criterion for reform like the *lex Christi*, there would be no reason for Hus to push his reform to the point of ecclesiastical schism unless the true Christians (= *praedestinati*) could no longer survive in the Roman institutional framework. As we have seen, however, the society of the predestined could not survive – at least not longer than temporarily – without the traditional food of sacramental grace. The potential for a new ecclesiastical authority was certainly present in the *lex Christi* as a kind of proto-*sola scriptura*. Hus was condemned because this authority not only offended papalists but also threatened conciliarists. Nevertheless, Hus could never have carried out the threat to the extent of institutional separation because, in the end, his concept of the *universitas praedestinatorum* did not make the prevailing sacramental system expendable.

V.

We can now return to the question posed at the beginning of this essay: how accurate is Luther's observation that he, Paul, Augustine and Staupitz were all Hussites? Based on his situation in early 1520, it is understandable how Luther could make such a claim. Several of the points recounted above – the authority of scripture, the spiritual man's right to judgment, the apparent independence of the *universitas praedestinatorum* – might have prompted Luther at first to see in Hus a champion of God's truth and defender of the gospel against a repressive church hierarchy. Hus' correspondence reveals that he saw himself in just that light. We must move beyond abstract stylized comparisons of theological points, however, and ask the historical question what motivated each of these men to attack the existing ecclesiastical authorities. Why did they believe reform was necessary and to what extent could their respective theologies support them if a formal break with the church became necessary?

---

95. Gottschick, pp. 374 ff.

When the motivation and ecclesiological support base of each man are examined, the contrast between Hus and Luther becomes pellucid. Hus desired reform because he thought the church of his day had to be brought in line with the *lex Christi*. By not adopting the Donatist solution of a separate church hierarchy, however, Hus was compelled to seek his reform within the ecclesiastical structure and sacramental channels of the Roman church. Like Augustine, he sought ecclesiological refuge in a church of the predestined which ultimately remained tied to the militant church. As long as Hus regarded the sacramentally dispensed *gratia infusa* as the food of the faithful and refused to take the radical Donatist way out, there was no alternative but to promote reform from within the bosom of the existing church.

Luther, on the other hand, sought reform because the faithful were not being fed with what he considered to be the indispensable food: the word of God. By radically redefining the *fideles* of the church in terms of their faith in the word, Luther fashioned an ecclesiology which could exist independently of the Roman sacramental structure and subsist on its own proclamation of the word. Luther's later statement that Hus and Wyclif attacked only the bad life of the papacy while he reproached their doctrine contains at least this much truth: Hus' ecclesiology never moved beyond the traditional medieval framework in spite of the emphasis he placed on predestination. For this reason, his reform program could not be implemented on the basis of predestination alone. Hus' concept of the *universitas praedestinatorum* was not really subversive; Luther's *spiritualis fidelium collectio* was. Luther states why, in that same *Tischrede* in which he distinguishes between doctrine and life: "It all depends on the word; the pope suppressed the word and created another one. Therefore, I have won, and won nothing except that I teach correctly."[96] Thus does Luther sum up both the cause of his reformation and the reason for its success.

Our answer, then, is not "yes-but" but "no-but." No, Luther was not a Hussite, although Hus was certainly Augustinian. Luther's enthusiastic endorsement of Hus in February 1520 can be explained, but not accepted as either theologically or historically accurate. Luther's own reappraisal of his relationship to Hus in December 1520 was right on target: "They do not act rightly who call me a Hussite."[97] In early 1520 it was possible for Luther to regard Hus as an undisputed ally in the defense of divine truth and the word. By the end of 1520, however, when Luther realized fully that he would have to stand on his own ecclesiological feet and break with the papacy, he had to accept the

---

96. Clemen, ed. 8, 79.26 ff. (= *WATR* 1, 295.3 ff.).
97. Cf. *supra* n. 57.

fact that he was moving beyond Hus. He was making a break which Hus had not been prepared to make. Luther does not say that Hus could not have made such a break. According to the results of our investigation, however, Luther's conclusion accurately reflects the ecclesiological potential (or lack of same) in Hus' work. We do not know whether Luther reread the *De Ecclesia* in late 1520 before he altered his opinion of the reforming precedent which Hus had set. Thus, we cannot say whether Luther's retreat from Hus was the immediate conscious result of the same kind of analysis to which we have subjected Hus' ecclesiology. If Luther did not restudy *De Ecclesia*, he retained enough of it to reflect critically on his relationship to Hus when confronted with article 30 of *Exsurge domine*. This critical reflection resulted in Luther's final decision that ultimately he could not wear the Hussite hat and thus resolves, for us, the conflict in Luther's statements about Hus.

But, there is one sense in which Luther and Hus belong in the same camp – a way more significant than the formal points of agreement mentioned above. For both of them, ecclesiological concerns were paramount. A comparison of the two men highlights the importance of ecclesiological factors in the transition from late medieval reform to the Reformation. It is tempting to point to the failure of competing late medieval doctrines of the church to attain reform and conclude that Luther's soteriological innovations (justification by faith, etc.) did the trick. Even Gottschick, after his insightful analysis, was driven to this conclusion: because Luther's ecclesiology was a direct result of his soteriology (which differed so fundamentally from Hus), Luther was able to dispense with the existing hierarchy.[98] And F. Graus, who has recently written so perceptively on the crisis of the late Middle Ages, concludes that the Hussite concentration on the traditional doctrine of the church was not capable of answering the thorny problems raised by such a crisis. It remained for the new humanist concentration on man and nature and the religious shift from the concept of the church to the concept of faith to lay the groundwork for a solution.[99]

Such attempted explanations of the enigmatic relationship between late medieval reform and sixteenth century reformation fail to take adequate account of the intimate relationship between ecclesiology and soteriology which existed in the medieval tradition. This interrelationship is responsible for the failure of Hus' ecclesiology to establish an autonomous base of operations for his reform efforts as well as his retreat to a church of the predestined.[100] The

---

98. Gottschick, pp. 551 f., 574.
99. F. Graus: "The Crisis of the Middle Ages and the Hussites," in *The Reformation in Medieval Perspective*, ed. Steven Ozment (Chicago, 1971), p. 101.
100. The accent here is on *Hus'* ecclesiology. In this essay we have not been able to

VII

spontaneous interaction between ecclesiology and soteriology *mutatis mutandis* enabled Luther to establish the church upon the word of God and thus to give his new soteriology simultaneously a lasting ecclesiological and ecclesiastical foundation. Both Hus and Luther were *simul* reformers of the church and of the individual Christian. It is misleading to type Hus and late medieval reform as ecclesiocentric while relegating ecclesiology to a mere sidelight of the novel soteriology of Luther and the sixteenth century reformers. For both Hus and Luther, the nature of the church and of the church's role in the salvation of each faithful Christian was a key factor in the impact of their reform efforts. Judged by the importance of their respective ecclesiologies for the impetus and outcome of their reform programs, the swan of Wittenberg was not far amiss in claiming the Bohemian goose as a close relative.

ZUSAMMENFASSUNG

In einem Brief an Spalatin Anfang 1520 verglich Luther unzweifelhaft sich und Staupitz, ja selbst Paulus und Augustinus, mit Johannes Hus und seiner Lehre. An anderen Stellen bekundete Luther allerdings eine ambivalentere Einstellung zu Hus. Neuere Untersuchungen haben denn auch gezeigt, daß trotz mancher formaler Ähnlichkeiten wesentliche theologische Unterschiede zwischen beiden bestanden. Nicht geklärt wurde bisher jedoch, wie Luther sich schon Ende 1520 ausdrücklich dagegen verwahren konnte, ein Hussit genannt zu werden. Gibt es eine historische und theologische Erklärung für Luthers offensichtliche Kehrtwendung in dieser Frage während des genannten Jahres? Eine Untersuchung von Luthers Entwicklung in den Jahren 1518–1520 läßt erkennen, daß ihm, obwohl er schon vor dieser Zeit über eine klar formulierte Ekklesiologie verfügte, nur sehr allmählich bewußt wurde, damit die theologischen Grundlagen für eine neue Kirche außerhalb der *ecclesia romana* gelegt zu haben. Solange er nur gegen die Unterdrückung des Wortes durch die römische Kirche protestierte, konnte er Hus enthusiastisch als Verbündeten für seine Sache reklamieren. Als es jedoch zum Bruch zwischen ihm und seiner alten Kirche kam, mußte sich – gegen Ende 1520 – auch sein Verhältnis zu Hus einschneidend ändern.

deal with the ecclesiology of Hus' more radical successors and their relationship to Hus. Nor can we broach the broader question of whether the Hussite movement should be termed revolt, revolution or reformation. There is substantial disagreement over the influence which Hus' ecclesiology had upon his successors and the role which the ideas of Hus himself played in the movement which took his name. In lieu of a detailed treatment, cf. the moderate position of Kaminsky: Hus' own theoretical work was only partly responsible for the revolution that emerged after his death. His ideology "encouraged others to revolt, but it led him to Constance – to submission and martyrdom." The ideology of his successors actually justified the resulting schism (*History*, p. 55). Kaminsky's position is plausible, although not thoroughly consistent with his appraisal of Hus' ecclesiology (cf. *supra* n. 65).

Ein Blick auf Hus' Ekklesiologie zeigt, daß Luther die Unterschiede zu ihm durchaus richtig einschätzte. Obgleich sie verschiedene Punkte enthielt, mit denen er sich einverstanden erklären konnte, war sie doch weit davon entfernt, die Einheit der römischen Kirche als Gnadeninstitution grundsätzlich in Frage zu stellen. Demgegenüber mußte sich Luthers *spiritualis collectio fidelium* außerhalb der römischen Kirche zusammenfinden, um das Wort zu hören, das für ihn die Grundlage des Lebens war. Obgleich Luther daher schließlich doch darauf verzichten mußte, sich auf Hus zu berufen, macht die Tatsache, daß die Abgrenzung von ihm durch den unterschiedlichen Kirchenbegriff beider bedingt war, ein weiteres Mal deutlich, in wie hohem Maße ekklesiologische Fragen für die spätmittelalterliche wie für die reformatorische Kirchenreform bestimmend waren.

VIII

CONSIDERING THE CLERGY'S SIDE:
A MULTILATERAL VIEW OF ANTICLERICALISM

My approach to the topic of anticlericalism is, as far as I know, different from those which have been applied heretofore to the sources of the Protestant Reformation in Germany. By "a multilateral view" I mean an approach to anticlericalism that tries to see and to appreciate the different sides of the parties involved in anticlerical disputes. Since anticlericalism is a social form of blame, the sources usually present grievances or charges against the clergy that arise out of anger or disappointment. For that reason, we cannot assume that the sources present a fair view of the clergy's side or, for that matter, an accurate picture of what motivates the attacks. By "multilateral", therefore, I mean an approach to the sources that will utilize them to construct a fairer and more balanced picture of the two (or more) sides in controversy.

The specific identities of these sides change as the Reformation unfolds. In particular, I am interested more in the *target* of early Reformation attacks than in the attackers, i.e., I want to investigate the side of the Catholic clergy who were attacked by early Protestants, whether lay or clerical. By the "side" of Catholic clergy I mean three things: 1) to what extent the attacks upon them were fair or unfair; 2) how they would defend themselves against those attacks which they felt were unjust; and especially 3) what were the frustrations, disappointments and resentments that the clergy suffered and that caused them to feel unfairly treated?

Several kinds of sources provide insight into the side of early sixteenth-century Catholic clergy. First are the records that enable us to reconstruct the actual historical context of late medieval clergy. Second are treatises of Catholic theologians which defend the case of the clergy and reveal some of their motives. And, third, are the Protestant pamphlets that disclose, sometimes inadvertently, the frustrations of the clergy that led to the very behavior which Protestants were attacking. In the following I will offer samples of each kind of source and show, in a preliminary way, how they can contribute to a more balanced historical understanding of anticlericalism.

The prerequisite for representing fairly the side of any party is to understand as accurately as possible who belonged to that party and what circumstances governed their thinking and their actions. Applied strictly to the clerical context, this prerequisite would require a comprehensive history of the late medieval clergy — an enormous task which has yet to be accomplished. Two ways of focusing the sources, however, make the task more manageable: studies of the clergy in one local area and portraits of the clergy that are sketched from a cross section of similar records. One example of each — neither the most recent nor necessarily the most intensive such study — will illustrate the relevance of such work to the evaluation of anticlericalism.

The first example is the examination by Rolf Kießling of church and society in pre-Reformation Augsburg.[1] Clerical privileges were a prominent source of the laity's resentment in German cities. Prior to the Reformation in Augsburg, however, Kießling demonstrates that the city council was able to make inroads into the special rights and benefits of the clergy. The council adopted measures that reduced clerical advantages in matters of taxation, business competition, and juridical competence — all matters that were of utmost importance to Augsburg's citizens.[2] Later, therefore, when Protestant laity in Augsburg expressed resentment of clerical immunity in their town, the clergy scarcely needed to feel guilty since they had already lost some of their significant privileges. They were entitled to protest further infringement of their historic rights and benefits, as Bishop Christoph of Stadion did on their behalf in 1537.[3]

A second example comes from the German Protestant church orders of the sixteenth century as analyzed and summarized by Ernst Walter Zeeden.[4] Zeeden's intent was to point out the continuity between late medieval and sixteenth-century Lutheran worship and practice. Given the nature of church orders and visitation records, the continuities which he found accentuated the inadequacies and hardships of the clergy. Instead of blaming them, however, Zeeden was able to recognize and to credit the burdens under which the late medieval and Reformation clergy both labored. For example, in North Germany, out of economic necessity the pastors had to tend their own fields in spite of the fact that church orders prohibited such labor or at least tried to save Saturday for the clergy to carry out their pastoral duties. Zeeden concluded that poor remuneration, which was carried over from the Middle Ages into the Reformation, continued to be a liability for the clergy, both

---

[1] Rolf Kießling, *Bürgerliche Gesellschaft und Kirche in Augsburg im Spätmittelalter. Ein Beitrag zur Strukturanalyse der oberdeutschen Reichsstadt* (Augsburg, 1971).
[2] Kießling, 97-8.
[3] Herbert Immenkötter, "Die katholische Kirche in Augsburg in der ersten Hälfte des 16. Jahrhunderts", in *Die Augsburger Kirchenordnung von 1537 und ihr Umfeld. Wissenschaftliches Kolloquium*, ed. R. Schwarz (Gütersloh, 1988), 9-31, here 31. Without acknowledging the losses suffered by the Catholic clergy in the city, Immenkötter is quick to criticize Bishop Christoph for ignoring the legitimate need for reform of the church.
[4] Ernst Walter Zeeden, *Katholische Überlieferungen in den lutherischen Kirchenordnungen des 16. Jahrhunderts* (Münster, 1959).

for their pastoral work and for the reputation of their office.[5] Underpaid Catholic and Protestant clergy justifiably felt resentment when they were attacked for not being good pastors, for reading their sermons out of the *postilla*, or for selling beer in the village to make additional money. Why should they work harder for nothing?

A second kind of source that raises the side of clergy are the tracts of the Catholic controversialists. Their theological replies to Protestant works on such topics as ordination and celibacy do not necessarily yield the most relevant material. As a rule, they provide arguments from Scripture and tradition that defend Catholic practice or engage in polemic against Protestant authors.[6] On occasion, however, these Catholic theologians express dissatisfaction with their own clergy. In so doing, they reveal motives that led people to become priests and confirm the ill-preparedness of the clergy which Protestants criticized.

For example, in his reply to Luther's *Schmalkald Articles*, the Colmar Augustinian prior Johann Hoffmeister (ca. 1510-1547) agreed that the negligence of the bishops was responsible for what he called the "jamer der secten".[7] Their main failure consisted of not regulating the caliber and motives of candidates for the priesthood. As a result, laments Hoffmeister, men are transferred directly from the plow to the altar and the coarsest wild asses (*waldesel*) occupy the richest benefices, while those who could and would best serve the church are left to go begging. Even worse, he continues, the priesthood has become a career opportunity; those who cannot earn a living for themselves become priests even though they are not dedicated to the ministry. When teachers notice a lazy student who will not study, they say: "He will make a fine priest."[8]

It is not surprising to find an Augustinian prior expressing criticism of the secular clergy. His own standards aside, however, these non-polemical remarks identify some of the burdens which were imposed on Catholic clergy. They confirm, first of all, what we already suspect and in some cases know: the lack of preparation and the poor academic qualification of many priests. But, second, they also testify indirectly to the professional injustice and resentment that many qualified priests must have experienced, when they saw less qualified colleagues — even upstarts and newcomers —

---

[5] Zeeden, 69-70.

[6] For example, Johann Eck in his *Enchiridion* [German edition: Augsburg, 1530], ed. Erwin Iserloh (Münster, 1980), 28-31, 59-62.

[7] Johann Hoffmeister, *Warhafftige endeckung unnd widerlegung deren artickel, die M. Luther auff das concilium zu schicken und darauff beharren fur genummen*, in *Drei Schriften gegen Luthers Schmaldkaldische Artikel von Cochläus, Witzel und Hoffmeister (1538 und 1539)*, ed. Hans Volz (Münster, 1932), 116-187, here 175,22-24: "Ich halt warlich dafür, das dise hinlessigkeit nit die kleinest ursach sey, das wir in solchen jamer der secten kummen sind."

[8] Hoffmeister, 175,24-176,3.

452

receive the best-paid and more prestigious positions. Add to this resentment the poor reputation that the priesthood enjoyed with teachers and educated laypeople, and it becomes more understandable why the priesthood neither attracted more qualified candidates nor inspired those who did serve to perform their duties with zeal and devotion. As Hoffmeister himself asks: "When such circumstances force one into the priesthood and the regular authorities do not provide better oversight, what good can finally come out of that?"[9]

The writings of the controversialists further illuminate the side of the clergy when they challenge directly the anticlericalism of Protestants or reflect the experience of their authors. Even that toughened opponent of Protestantism, Johann Cochlaeus (1479-1552), allows attacks against Catholics and their clergy to get under his skin. In his reply to the articles of the Münster Anabaptists (1534), Cochlaeus bristles at the notion that Catholics along with Protestants should be addressed as "the godless". If, says Cochlaeus, "you include among the 'godless' also those Christians who have stayed with the old faith and with the pope, then you talk like other faithless heretics; [you] have learned it from that rowdy Lutheran crowd which haughtily and maliciously label us such, against all Scripture, justice, honor, and propriety." Even though he blames it on the Lutherans, we can hear in the indignation of Cochlaeus the injury and insult that the unjust label "godless" also inflicted on him and on other Catholic clergy.[10]

In his response to Johann Bugenhagen's epistle to the English people (1526), Cochlaeus shows specific sensitivity to the charges against Catholic clergy. He accuses Bugenhagen of stirring up the Catholic laity against their clergy by attributing to the priests what Christ said about the scribes and the Pharisees "as if the clergy of the church were not a Christian but a Jewish people." When by such slander, he continues, the people have been inflamed with envy and hatred against the priests, the evangelicals serve up their own impious teachings while the people cheer them on.[11] Cochlaeus not only argues that Catholic clergy are different from the scribes and Pharisees; he

---

[9] Hoffmeister, 176,4-6: "Wo dan einen ein solche ursach zu dem preisterthumb zwingt unnd die ordentliche obergkeit nicht bass sorget, was solt dan entlich guts darauss erwachsen?"

[10] Johann Cochlaeus, *XXI Artickel der Widderteuffer zu Munster durch Doctor Johan Cocleum widerlegt*, in *Die Schriften der Münsterischen Täufer und ihrer Gegner*, vol. 2: *Schriften von katholischer Seite gegen die Täufer*, ed. Robert Stupperich (Münster, 1980), 101: "Wo sie aber durch die gottlosen wöllen versteen die gemeinen christen, die es im alten glauben der kirchen mit dem babst halten, so reden sie wie andere abtrünnige ketzer und habens auch vom Lutherischen hauffen gelernt, die uns also heissen wider alle schrifft, recht, eher, und zucht aus ubermessiger hoffart und eigenwilliger bossheit."

[11] Johannes Cochlaeus, *Responsio ad Johannem Bugenhagium Pomeranum*, ed. Ralph Keen (Nieuwkoop, 1988), 107,1-8.

also testifies to the investment that he and other clergy had made in the Church as the guarantor of the old (and still for them) true faith: "So you will not scare us away from our ancient faith, even if ten thousand times over you call us hypocrites, Pharisees, apostles of the Antichrist, the kingdom of Satan, and the like."[12] The anger of Cochlaeus is not the detached polemic of a theological debate, but personal hurt and indignation aroused by the criticism of his own allegiance to the "ancient faith". His anger also stems from the Protestant dismissal of himself and of other Catholic clergy as (to use a word of the young Luther) *antichristiani*.

Another interesting insight into the side of the clergy can be gleaned from the blame which Cochlaeus places upon the laity. Although he holds both secular authorities and evangelical preachers responsible for the laity's defection, he also faults the people for so easily falling away from the old faith. They too readily believed the strange itinerant preachers rather than adhering to their regular bishops and pastors.[13] Cochlaeus' blame extends to the way the laity treat their clergy after they have become Lutheran. They refuse to pay their pastors what they owe them, deny them the customary tithe, contribute no offerings or anything else that is justly required of them.[14] Cochlaeus' defense of the clergy exposes the loss of secure income which pastors and priests might suddenly suffer. His criticism of the laity, I suspect, also exposes a kind of *clerical anti-laicism* that crossed confessional lines and arose from a common resentment of the laity's disrespect and disregard for clerical sustenance.

A third kind of source which reveals the side of the Catholic clergy is the Protestant pamphlet. It may seem an unlikely source from which to learn more about the Catholic side, since it will often contain just the opposite —

---

[12] Cochlaeus, *Responsio ad Johannem Bugenhagium*, 107,34-109,1. Cf. the translation on 106 and 108.

[13] Cochlaeus, *XXI Artickel der Widderteuffer zu Munster*, in *Die Schriften der Münsterischen Täufer und ihrer Gegner*, 2: 97: "Das volck aber darumb, das sie so leichtfertig sind und von altem glauben so liederlich abfallen und gleuben mehr den losen frembden landtleuffern dann yren ordentlichen bischoffen und pfarherrn und lassen sich äffen und umbher führen von itzlichem winde newer leere wider manigfeltige warnung Christi, Pauli und aller heyligen väter."

[14] Cochlaeus, *Responsio ad Johannem Bugenhagium*, 109,9-11: " ... non reddentes Clero census debitos, non decimas consuetas, non oblationes, non alia quae iuste ab eis exiguntur." A similar complaint about the support of evangelical preachers is offered in 1538 by Urbanus Rhegius, *Wie man die falschen Propheten* ... (n. 15 below), D^y-Dii: " ... da hat man wider korn noch gelt/ das die armen prediger vor hunger entrinnen müssen/ und da die undanckbar welt zuvor hat mit aller volle/ mehr denn 400. Baals Propheten können erneeren/ Da kann und wil man itzt schwerlich wenig rechte Propheten/ mit wasser und brot erhalten." Rhegius claims that the monasteries which formerly could support forty or sixty monks now cannot support one evangelical preacher. Why? Because God's Word does not appeal to the "old Adam" (ibid.).

VIII

a strong polemic against the old clergy. But consider an obvious example of such a pamphlet: *Wie man die falschen Propheten erkennen ia greiffen mag*, based on a sermon delivered in Minden in 1538 by the Protestant preacher Urbanus Rhegius.[15] The false prophets are the cathedral clergy in Minden who, together with the rest of the clergy, receive a bitter scolding from Rhegius. The keynote of his polemic is the charge that the Catholic clergy are responsible for the terrible state of the church. Instead of being our faithful fathers and pastors, the bishops and the priests [*seelsorger*] are now our greatest enemies and slayers of souls [*seelmörder*].[16] "Summa summarum", he concludes, "if you examine the clerical estate inside and outside, you will find nothing but a facade with nothing behind it."[17]

The same polemic, however, contains evidence of Rhegius' own disappointment in that clergy to which he too once belonged. Several times he flashes back two decades, to the year prior to his own ordination (1518), and expresses his amazement that the clergy could have turned out so badly. "Twenty years ago who would have believed that monks and nuns would deny Christ. . . . [or] that our clergy and pastors would be such devouring wolves?"[18] Yet, of all people, Rhegius should have believed it; for in this same pamphlet he recalls the time when "I was one of your preachers."[19] Rhegius agreed to the printing of his sermon so that the angry canons of Minden would become even angrier at their apostate Rhegius, who fifteen years earlier in Augsburg had been a member of their order. He hopes, however, that their anger will force them to realize the error of their ways. If Urbanus passed up the opportunity to become a rich canon and a prominent papist, and fled in the nick of time out of Sodom and Gomorrah, then they too might recognize the danger of their estate and turn to Christ.[20]

More evident here than the anger of the Minden canons is the anger of Rhegius himself, which arises out of his disappointment at the profession

---

[15] It is extant in three printed editions: 1) s.l., 1538; 2) Wittenberg: Hans Frischmut, 1539; 3) Brunswick: Anders Goldbeck, 1539.

[16] *Wie man die falschen Propheten* ... (Brunswick, 1539), Eiv^v: "Die Bischoff und geistlichen die unsere trewen Veter und seelsorger sein solten/ die sind itzt unsere grösten feind und seelmörder."

[17] Ibid., Fiii: "Summa summarum/ ersuch den geistlichen stand inwendig und auswendig/ so findstu nichts anders denn einen schein/ und nichts darhinter."

[18] Ibid., Giv^v: "Wer hete fur 20 jar gleubt/ das pfaffen/ Mönch und Nonnen solten Christum verlaugnen?" Cf. ibid., H: "Wer hett aber vor zwentzig jaren geglaubt? Das unsere Geistlichen und Hirten solch reissend Wolff weren?"

[19] Ibid., Jiii: "Ich bin ewer prediger auch gewesen/ aber es wolt mir mein Bisschoff zu Brixen fur xiiij jaren einbinden/ Ich solt menschen lehr predigen und bekennen/ das menschen lehr die conscientz möge billich verstricken/ do ichs nicht einrümen wolt/ richt er mir ein solche persecution an bey der Oberkheit/ das ich meins lebens weder tag noch nacht sicher was."

[20] Ibid., Aii-Aii^v.

VIII

that he chose and wanted to improve. That disappointment must have deeply penetrated the soul of this illegitimate son of a priest whom Johann Eck once called a "priestly whore's son".[21] From the time of his ordination, whether as Catholic priest or as Protestant preacher, Rhegius sought to improve the quality of the clergy; it was the leitmotif of his career. When, in 1538, Rhegius wonders who could have believed that the clergy would become such ravenous wolves, he is still wrestling with his own disappointment. At the same time, I think, he exposes the frustration of the very Catholic clergy whom he was attacking. Why should the canons of Minden have shared the ideals of Rhegius? Why should they not have expected to become guardians of the church's assets and to live comfortably in exchange for their vows? They certainly had a right to be angry at Rhegius, because he threatened their wealth and prominence and because they felt just as betrayed by him as he still felt by them. The canons of Minden may also have felt unfairly treated by being lumped together with the monks and all the secular clergy. Seventeen years earlier Rhegius did not make that mistake. Instead, he singled out for recognition the clergy whom he called "die frummen priester", who would be better off, he said, if it were not for the Roman clergy and the courtesans.[22]

In the early Reformation, Rhegius was not the only evangelical author to remind his readers that devoted Catholic priests did exist. On the title page of his 1522 pamphlet written in Wittenberg, Johann Eberlin von Günzburg placed the following admonition: "There are still many pious priests, and for their sake the laity should refrain from undertaking anything against the clergy, so that the innocent do not have to *pay* for the guilty."[23] This pamphlet, entitled *Seven Pious But Disconsolate Priests Bewail their Distress* ... , is one of a pair which present the conflicts that beset the Catholic clergy in the early stage of the reform movement. Its companion, which offers consolation to the priests through Eberlin's spokespersons, the

---

[21] Maximilian Liebmann, *Urbanus Rhegius und die Anfänge der Reformation* (Münster, 1980), 70.
[22] In the context of denying that Luther was simply against the priesthood; *Anzaygung/ dasz die Romisch Bull mercklichen schaden in gewissin manicher menschen gebracht hab/ und nit Doctor Luthers leer* (s.l., 1522), Aiv^v: "Do schryen etlich der Luther sy gar wider de priesterschafft/ das thond allain die/ die nitt verston wellen/ was mainung der Luther von semlichen dingen redt. Er hat wol wider die Romischen gytigkait und die Kurtisanen geredt/ denen niemantz hold ist dann jr brotmaister der teüfel/ wann die selben nit weren/ die frummen Priester kemen basz herfür/ er beriert niendert anders/ dann allain die böse myszbreijch und zaigt an die rechten wirdigkait der priester/ ..."
[23] *Syben frumm aber trostloss pfaffen klagen ire not, einer dem anderen, und ist niemant der sye tröste, Gott erbarme sich jre*, in Ludwig Enders, ed., *Johann Eberlin von Günzburg*, vol. 1: *Ausgewählte Schriften*, vols. 2-3: *Sämtliche Schriften*, Flugschriften aus der Reformationszeit 11, 15, 18 (Halle, 1896, 1900, 1902), 2: 57-77, here 2: 57.

456

Fünfzehn Bundesgenossen, also adds insight into the mentality of the priests, even though it offers mainly, as expected, evangelical solutions.[24] Together the pamphlets form a remarkable expression of what I have called the *side* of the Catholic clergy, which Eberlin, a former Franciscan monk and preacher, knew from experience and, despite his sympathy for the Wittenberg movement, was still able to credit.[25]

Each of the seven *Pfaffen* describes the dilemma which faces him. These descriptions are not without comic elements and they certainly have an edge that is critical of the clergy and of the hierarchy in particular. But Eberlin is not sarcastic, and the dilemmas contain a genuine element which many a priest must have faced. The general tone is set by the first priest who has to ask a layperson which book of the Bible he should read first. The layman replies that he will find everything a priest needs to know in the three letters to Timothy and Titus. After having read and reread them, the priest exclaims in frustration: "If a pastor has to be like what is taught there, then God help me!"[26]

As portrayed by Eberlin, however, the challenge to the clergy is greater than living up to the ideal described in Scripture. They are also caught in real dilemmas which seem insoluble. For example, the priest who struggles with the requirement of celibacy describes his dilemma this way:

> So I am caught [*Also binn ich verwickelt*]. I cannot be without a wife. If I am not permitted to have a wife, then I am forced to lead publicly a disgraceful life, which damages my soul and honor and leads other people, who are offended by me, to damnation. How can I preach about chastity and unchastity, adultery and depravity, when my whore comes openly to church and my bastards sit right in front of me? How shall I conduct mass in this state?[27]

His options are either to remain chaste as well as celibate or to leave the priesthood, both of which he considers. If he tries to be chaste, then he fears that God will give him up to the desire of his heart and he will fall into even worse sins, as described in the first chapter of Romans. If he leaves the priesthood, he says, he cannot support himself, and if he stays [with a

---

[24] *Der frummen pfaffen trost. Ein getrewer glaubhaffter underricht unnd antwort uff der syben trostlossen pfaffen klagen, Newlich durch die Fünfftzehen Bundsgnossen beschriben, uff die hye vertzeychneten artickel*, in Enders (n. 23 above), 2: 79-93.
[25] For a summary of his Wittenberg pamphlets and commentary on his place among the Wittenbergers, see Martin Brecht, "Johann Eberlin von Günzburg in Wittenberg 1522-1524", *Wertheimer Jahrbuch 1983* (1985): 47-54.
[26] *Syben frumm aber trostloss pfaffen*, in Enders 2: 59.
[27] Ibid., 2: 63: "Also binn ich verwickelt, ich kan on weyb nitt sein, so lässt man mir kein eeweib, also würd ich gezwungen zu eim offentlichem schandtlichem [*sic*] leben, zu schaden meiner seelen und eeren, ja zu verdamnüss viler menschen, die sich an mir ergeren, wie soll ich predigen von unkeüscheit unnd keüscheit, von Eebruch, von buberey etc. so mein hur zu kirchen und strass gat, so meine bastart mir vor augen sitzen, wie soll ich mess lesen in diesm standt."

VIII

CONSIDERING THE CLERGY'S SIDE   457

concubine], he will be caught as described.[28] The dilemma is enough, he concedes, finally to make him believe that the pope and the bishops are the Antichrist. And he concludes: "No state in Christendom is so scandalous and desolate as the priesthood."[29]

While the first priest deplores the current frustration of the Catholic clergy, the second and third priests illuminate the disappointment that must have sprouted among clergy when they realized that a career in the priesthood would not fulfill their expectations. The second priest is disturbed by the fact that clergy do not have to earn their support but receive it from the tithes and donations of the laity. They are hungry, he says, while we sit around full, they are busy while we play, they have worries, while we whistle a merry tune and make love to our mistresses. And this sin [of not working], he continues, is so ingrained and callous that people think it is right, and parents raise their children to become priests so that they will have a good life.[30] The career of this priest, however, and perhaps for the Franciscan Eberlin and colleagues whom he knew, was not the good life which they had been raised to expect. The sixth priest calls anyone an archfool who believes that priests have a good life. Even though he became a priest unawares and now cannot escape, he warns other young men to avoid this life of misery.[31]

The conscience of the third priest is bothered by the superficiality, deceit, and pompousness of the vigils and masses at which he presides. He voices a theme that commonly appears in the literature of reform: the longing for the way things used to be. I would like to be a priest, he says, if the priestly office were godly as it was in earlier times, when a priest would preach, administer the sacraments, and consecrate.[32] The fifth priest, who fears an uprising of the laity, mourns the loss of his honor and reputation with God and with the people: "Before God, in my conscience, I am ashamed of my soulless, godless life; I lack the knowledge and honor of God in myself, and people will add me to that godless crowd which they are now calling *pfaffen*

---

[28] Ibid., 2: 64.
[29] Ibid., 2: 64: "So ist kein standt der christenheit ergerlicher und wüster dann pfaffenstandt."
[30] Ibid., 2: 65: "Und ist dise unser sünd so tieff und hart worden, das sye für gut und recht wird geachtet, also, das die elteren ire kind darumb uff pfaffheit ziehen, das sye gut tag haben, und man für ubel achtet, wann ein pfaff solt arbeiten."
[31] Ibid., 2: 75: "Aber wiewol ich in die pfaffheit binn kommen, wie Contz hinder das vyhe, und nit wol mag davon kommen, so wolt ich doch gerne andere junge knaben wären trewlich gewarnet, das sye nit in diezen jamer kämend. Man sagt, wir pfaffen haben gut leben, ja einer ist ein ertznarr, welicher unser leben für gut haltet."
[32] Ibid., 2: 68: "Ich wolt gern priester sein, wann priester ampt göttlich were als vorzeiten, do ein priester predigt, sacrament reicht, und consecriert, etc."

458

und münch.[33] Eberlin does not blame Luther for the loss of priestly status, but Luther is blamed in another document which voices the same regret. In a pamphlet, called bluntly *Lamentation of the Priests*, Haug Marschalck has the clergy intone:

> Vor waren wir all inn grossen ehren,
> das thustu, Luther al[le]s verkeren
> mit deinem schreyben und auch leren.[34]

Much is being exaggerated here — the prestige which a career in the priesthood allegedly used to carry, and the ideal of the priesthood as a ministry of Word and sacrament. Despite this exaggeration and its anti-clerical tone, and regardless of who receives the blame, I still suspect that a genuine loss for the clergy is being mourned. That loss is not just the loss of respect and prestige, but it is also the loss of an ideal, the disappointment of hopes, and the realization that expectations of what the priesthood would be cannot be fulfilled. That loss and disappointment had been accumulating over generations. The sixth priest claims that his great uncle, who was a priest himself, told his father: "If you were to drown your son, it would be better for him and for you than if he became a priest."[35]

When all that loss is combined with the dilemmas facing the priesthood, then the burden borne by conscientious priests must have been heavy. The consolation offered by Eberlin, I doubt, could scarcely have offset the weight of that burden. The consequences of turning evangelical do not appear especially attractive. If he preaches God's Word, the pastor will be a "man of death", who has to risk everything he has and can expect to lose his friends and his life. And even death would be better than being locked up, forced to recant, or sent into exile.[36] The compensation for such a risk might seem inadequate. Eberlin argues that God has not made a mistake by calling them to the priesthood. Although they are lumped together with their scurrilous brethren, there are still many good priests and pious, insightful

---

[33] Ibid., 2: 72: "Ich klage sonderlich den verlust meiner eeren und rhum vor gott unnd den menschen, ich schäme mich vor gott in meinem gewissen, meines seelosen gottlosen lebens, das ich in mir selbs mangel Gottes erkantnisz und eere, auch vor den menschen erkannt würd als ein zusatz des gottlosen hauffen, welche man yetzund pfaffen und münch nennet."

[34] Marschalck, *Der Pfaffen Klage*, in Laube 1: 570,5-7.

[35] *Syben frumm aber trostloss pfaffen*, in Enders (n. 23 above), 2: 75.

[36] Ibid., 2: 71: "Soll ich aber sagen gottes wort, so binn ich ein mann des tods, wie will ich blyben vor pfaffen, münchen, fürsten, ja vor bischoffen, Babst, Keyser, deren aller bann, Acht, gebott, verbott, in allen landen, stetten, kirchen gezeigt und gelesen werden, ich muss eer und gut dran wagen, ja aller meiner freund verlust. zuletzt grifft man mir nach dem leib und erwürgt mich, das ich nit so gross achte, als ob man mich würff in einen thurn, wie vilen geschehen ist, oder zwüng mich zu einem wideruff, oder vertrib mich vom land."

laypeople who recognize that no field is without its weeds. They should preach the truth and suffer for it, and God will sustain them.[37]

Observed from the side of the laity, early Reformation anticlericalism might look like an issue of power, as Bob Scribner proposes.[38] Seen from the side of the Catholic clergy, however, it was more an issue of justice. For urban clergy it was unjust to be asked to surrender more privileges when they had already been eroded by the city. For rural clergy, it was unfair to labor all week for practically nothing and then have to work on Sunday as well, and even worse to be told you could not earn a few extra pfennig. It was insulting for your allegiance to the ancient faith of the church to be despised and to be labeled godless as well. It was disappointing to sacrifice family for a good benefice and then be told you had no right to a comfortable life. It was even more painful to wake up one day with an enlightened but stabbing conscience that would not let you enjoy the benefits to which you thought you were entitled by your sacrifices. You received no credit for what you did. And it was most distressful of all to realize that, instead of seeing your expectations fulfilled, you confronted a dilemma with no simple solution and faced massive losses. I imagine that the clergy felt just as angry and cheated as the laity; and, consequently, some of the clergy did abuse their power. But, as often happens in cases of abuse, the sources recount the injuries of the abused more readily than they reveal the side of the abusers.

---

[37] Ibid., 2: 90, 91.

[38] "Anticlericalism and the Reformation in Germany", in R. W. Scribner, *Popular Culture and Popular Movements in Reformation Germany* (London, 1987), 243-256, here 244.

IX

LUTHER ET LA PAPAUTÉ

« La malheureuse attitude politique qui désire renverser le pape, c'est ce qu'il y a de si troublant chez Luther [1]. » Bien que ces mots de Sóren Kierkegaard traduisent avant tout sa manière particulière de concevoir un réformateur, ils n'en signalent pas moins un difficile problème d'interprétation de Luther qui depuis quelques années attire de plus en plus l'attention : celui de l'attitude de Luther vis-à-vis de la papauté. Les luthérologues se sont consacrés en priorité au sujet insaisissable de la découverte de la réforme par Luther et à la série complexe d'événements qui se produisirent après que Luther fut l'accusé dans un procès ecclésiastique. Cependant, aucune des deux manières (point de vue théologique prédominant ou ecclésiopolitique) d'envisager l'apparition de Luther comme réformateur n'a pu fournir

1. *The Journals of Kierkegaard*, trad. A. Dru, New York, 1959, 164.

50

une explication convaincante de la relation entre la découverte de la réforme par Luther, d'une part, et son activité réformatrice de l'autre. Devant cette aporie, l'attitude de Luther vis-à-vis de la papauté mérite l'attention qu'on lui accorde. L'enquête sur l'attitude de Luther requérant une analyse de son évolution théologique aussi bien que des tactiques légales et politiques mises en œuvre par ses partisans comme par ses adversaires, ce thème promet de jeter utilement quelque lumière sur l'évolution du jeune Luther.

Mais notre compréhension du jeune Luther ne sera pas seule à profiter d'un nouvel examen de sa relation avec le pape. Depuis longtemps Hans Preuss a montré comment Luther résumait sa vie entière comme une lutte contre la papauté[2]. Certes Luther affronta d'autres adversaires au cours de son orageuse carrière, mais sa permanente opposition à la papauté, probablement exprimée jusque dans la nuit de la mort[3], fournit un continuum, suivant lequel on peut vérifier la fermeté de la vision de Luther aux points clefs de sa carrière, notamment dans la région moins explorée qu'est la fin de sa vie. Les préoccupations théologiques et politiques étaient inextricablement mêlées dans l'attaque corrosive de 1545 (Contre la papauté de Rome, institution du démon), tout comme elles l'étaient dans l'éloignement progressif de Luther par rapport au pape avant 1521.

L'intérêt pour notre thème a été stimulé par l'ouvrage de l'érudit catholique romain Remigius Bäumer. En 1969, Bäumer, passant en revue la littérature sur le sujet[4], constatait qu'aucune monographie n'avait été, du côté catholique, consacrée à Luther et au pape, depuis les travaux de Paulus et Grisar au tournant du siècle. Bäumer se mit immédiatement en mesure de combler cette lacune en éditant lui-même sa brève étude de 1970[5]. Du côté protestant, ce point n'a pas été traité sous forme de monographie depuis le petit livre d'Ernst Bizer en 1958[6]. Depuis lors, un certain nombre d'études significatives[7], en particulier celles consacrées à l'ecclésiologie de Luther, ont jeté

---

2. H. PREUSS, Die Vorstellungen vom Antichrist im späteren Mittelalter, bei Luther und in der konfessionellen Polemik (Les représentations de l'Antéchrist dans le bas Moyen Age, chez Luther et dans la polémique confessionnelle), Leipzig, 1906, 146.
3. Cf. C.R.S. LENZ, « A Recently Discovered Manuscript Account of Luther's Last Prayer » (Un compte rendu manuscrit récemment découvert de la dernière prière de Luther), in Archiv für Reformation 66, 1975, 79-92.
4. R. BÄUMER, « Der junge Luther und der Papst » (Le jeune Luther et le pape), in Catholica 23, 1969, 392-420.
5. R. BÄUMER, Martin Luther und der Papst (Kath. Leben u. Kirchenreform 30), Münster, 1970 ([2]1971).
6. E. BIZER, Luther und der Papst (Theol. Existenz heute 69), Munich, 1958.
7. Cf. notamment K.V. SELGE, Normen der Christenheim im Streit um Ablass und Kirchenautorität 1518 bis 1521, I : Das Jahr 1518, thèse de doctorat, Heidelberg, 1968.

quelque lumière sur les rapports de Luther avec la papauté, mais aucune ne s'est exclusivement appliquée à cette question. C'est le travail de Bäumer qui a attiré sur elle l'attention des œcuménistes et des savants. Dans sa réponse indignée à l'article de Bäumer de 1969, F. W. Kantzenbach reprochait à l'auteur de confondre le dialogue œcuménique avec la volonté de faire rentrer Luther dans le bercail catholique [8]. Dans sa réfutation incisive [9], Bäumer montrait clairement qu'il n'était pas dans son intention d'ignorer, en vue d'une réunion œcuménique superficielle, les obstacles présentés par les rapports de Luther avec la papauté. Face à Kantzenbach, Bäumer réitérait son opinion que la question de la primauté papale demeure la pierre d'achoppement entre les confessions. Il renforçait sa position en invoquant les remarques de plusieurs spécialistes protestants et se déclarait entièrement d'accord avec Kantzenbach pour dire que l'historien ne peut pas reconstruire la société pour rendre vrais les rêves œcuméniques.

Cette escarmouche confessionnelle a, ainsi que d'importants dialogues œcuméniques sur la question, rendu absolument nécessaire un nouvel examen des données historiques, d'autant que la réponse de Kantzenbach laisse de côté l'interprétation historique de Bäumer. Un essai récent de Gerhard Müller a apporté une utile contribution dans ce sens [10]. Le reste du présent article dégage une tentative de réponse à l'une des questions majeures qui ont surgi durant la recherche, dans l'espoir de susciter de nouvelles réflexions sur le sujet.

La question à débattre est de savoir si Luther fut mené par un souci théologique constant qui motiva tout au long de sa carrière son attitude vis-à-vis de la papauté. Une réponse affirmative à cette question suppose un résultat positif dans trois cas déterminés.

I. L'ATTITUDE DE LUTHER VIS-A-VIS DU PAPE DURANT LES ANNÉES CRUCIALES JUSQU'A 1521

Selon l'interprétation de Bäumer, Luther changea de position vis-à-vis de l'autorité ecclésiastique selon le processus suivant : après avoir été convaincu de l'autorité papale et avoir à l'occasion exprimé sa foi, au cours de l'an 1518, Luther devint en 1518-1519 partisan discret des vues conciliaristes et finalement, à partir de 1519, rebelle à toute

8. F.W. KANTZENBACH, « Die ökumenische Relevanz historischer Forschung » (Intérêt œcuménique de la recherche historique), in Catholica 24, 1970, 214-217.
9. R. BÄUMER, « Antwort an Kantzenbach » (réponse à K.), in Catholica 24, 1970, 218-223.
10. G. MUELLER, « Martin Luther und die Papsttum » (Martin Luther et la papauté), in G. DENZLER (éd.), Das Papsttum in der Diskussion, Ratisbonne, 1974, 73-101.

52

autorité autre que l'Ecriture [11]. Certaines déclarations de Luther ne cadrant pas avec ce tableau chronologique, Bäumer taxe Luther d'affirmations contradictoires et de comportement incohérent pour des raisons tactiques. Ainsi, l'affirmation de Luther répondant à Cajetan que le pape n'est pas au-dessus de la Parole de Dieu mais soumis à elle (WA 2. 11. 2-3) semble à Bäumer en incompatibilité flagrante avec la volonté exprimée par Luther d'accepter le verdict du pape après la rencontre d'Augsbourg. D'autres essais de conciliation de la part de Luther, tels ses appels à un concile de l'Eglise en 1518 et 1520, ne peuvent, selon Bäumer, être prises argent comptant si Luther avait déjà absolument renoncé à toute autorité hormis celle de l'Ecriture.

S'il est vrai que les partisans de Luther ont préconisé des tactiques défensives, la position de Bäumer repose encore sur un principe inutilement rigide : toute déclaration positive à propos d'une source d'autorité dans l'Eglise doit, ou bien signifier que Luther accorde une autorité absolue à cette source (c'est-à-dire qu'il doit être papaliste, conciliariste ou bibliciste à l'époque de la déclaration), ou bien traduire une inconséquence de la part de Luther. En posant ce principe, Bäumer a trop tôt fermé la porte sur une perspective de l'évolution de Luther où l'on reconnaîtrait qu'il était guidé par une constante préoccupation théologique et pastorale au cours des années 1517-1520 tout en se cramponnant à l'espoir d'obtenir du pape la reconnaissance de cette préoccupation, malgré la constatation répétée du contraire.

En fait, depuis l'époque de ses premiers commentaires sur les *Psaumes* (1513-1515) et durant les années cruciales de 1517-1520, Luther embrassa une ecclésiologie ferme qui définissait l'Eglise comme la congrégation des chrétiens fidèles nourris et fortifiés par la Parole de Dieu, et qui attribuait l'autorité dans cette Eglise à la Parole et à ceux qui la proclament fidèlement [12]. Tant que le pape, les évêques et les prêtres nourrissaient le peuple de la pure Parole, il n'y avait aucune raison de récuser leur autorité. Mais une fois que Luther fut convaincu que l'on refusait aux fidèles l'accès à cette Parole, il lui devint nécessaire de mettre cette autorité en question. Si ce défi devait aboutir à une excommunication par l'Eglise de Rome, alors la véritable Eglise continuerait à vivre en dehors du pape aussi longtemps que l'on proclamerait l'Evangile et que les fidèles s'en nourriraient. Le traité de Luther, *la Papauté à Rome,* de 1520, contient la prise de conscience définitive, quoique faite à contrecœur, de cet état de choses imminent et l'application à la situation de son ecclésiologie antérieure.

11. BÄUMER, *Martin Luther und der Papst,* 44-45.
12. Cf. S.H. HENDRIX, « We Are All Hussites ? Hus and Luther Revisited », in *Arch. f. Ref.* 65, 1974, 141-149 ; K.H. ZUR MUEHLEN, *Nos extra nos. Luthers Theologie zwischen Mystik und Scholastik* (Beitr. z. hist. Theol. 46), Tübingen, 1972, 231-235.

Cette position ecclésiologique explique sans doute les appels de Luther aux décisions conciliaires et son intention expresse de reconnaître un jugement papal entre 1518 et 1520, alors qu'on ne peut le qualifier de papaliste ou de conciliariste absolu. Il n'y a pas de contradiction entre l'invocation par Luther de l'autorité de la Parole et son intention d'accepter une décision papale ou conciliaire, s'il avait vraiment l'espoir, même faible, que le pape ou un concile se prononcent conformément à sa conception de la Parole de Dieu. Au milieu de l'année 1520, Luther acquit la conviction que cet ultime espoir ne serait pas réalisé par le pape et il fit ses adieux à Rome (*WA* 6. 329. 12-34). Cependant, pressé par ses amis et ses conseillers, il fit un dernier appel au pape et au concile. Dans sa *Lettre ouverte à Léon X* [13], la distinction que fait Luther entre la papauté en tant qu'institution de l'antéchrist et le cas personnel de Léon X prouve que son rejet de la papauté procédait de sa conviction constante qu'elle avait usurpé la suprématie du Christ et de sa parole dans l'Eglise, et non d'une quelconque vengeance personnelle contre les titulaires de la charge papale. Luther voyait concrétisé chez Léon X le danger d'un vicaire du Christ méconnaissant la propre présence du Christ dans l'Eglise (*WA* 7. 10, 17-25), danger contre lequel il avait explicitement mis en garde en 1515 (*WA* 4. 403. 29 sqq.), puis en 1519 au commencement de sa polémique avec Eck (*WA* 2. 257. 9-23).

II. DÉBUT DE L'OPPOSITION DE LUTHER A LA PAPAUTÉ
ET DE SON INNOVATION THÉOLOGIQUE

Dans son étude de 1958, Ernst Bizer soutenait déjà que l'attitude de Luther vis-à-vis du pape durant la période de 1518 à 1521 était cohérente et fondée sur sa perception nouvelle de la nature de la foi et de l'importance de l'Ecriture [14]. Pour Bizer, cependant, Luther en vint pour la première fois à cette manière de voir durant l'année 1518. Cette année-là, son attitude à l'égard de l'Ecriture subit une transformation totale qui eut pour résultat de changer ce moine jadis fidèle en contestataire de l'autorité papale [15]. Ainsi, l'étude de Bizer, comme il le dit dans l'avant-propos, est la conséquence logique de son analyse révolutionnaire de la découverte de la Réforme par Luther, qu'il trouve articulée pour la première fois après les *Quatre-vingt-quinze Thèses.*

L'interprétation de Bizer ne donne aux *Thèses* qu'une fonction de catalyseur qui provoqua la Réforme à faire fonds sur la Parole comme

13. Cf. H.G. LEDER, *Ausgleich mit dem Papst?* (Accord avec le pape ?) (Arb. z. Theol. 38), Stuttgart, 1969, 40-63.
14. BIZER, *op. cit.,* 30-35.
15. *Ibid.,* 9.

54

l'autorité pour la foi et le cœur des sacrements. Cependant, les premiers adversaires de Luther pensaient à coup sûr différemment et leur sensibilité à la critique indirecte du pape par Luther montre que les *Thèses* sont plus qu'une anomalie dans sa carrière réformatrice ou, au maximum un catalyseur dont on n'a pas suffisamment tenu compte. Les *Thèses* elles-mêmes suggèrent que, sous-jacente à leur composition, il y avait la même motivation qu'aux attaques ultérieures de Luther contre la papauté. Luther craignait que la Parole ne soit étouffée par le trafic des indulgences et que son propre troupeau ne s'égare en mettant sa confiance dans des lettres de pardon plutôt que dans cette Parole (thèse 52-54). Le souci primordial de Luther pour l'exaltation de l'Evangile en tant que vrai trésor de l'Eglise (thèse 62) s'explique mieux s'il avait déjà adopté une théologie où la Parole et la foi étaient les éléments indispensables d'une vie chrétienne authentique.

L'absence de critique directe de la papauté avant 1518 n'implique pas nécessairement une position théologique papaliste ou pré-réformatrice de la part de Luther. Plutôt, Luther n'avait tout simplement aucune raison de croire que le pape ait effectivement l'intention de faire obstacle à la proclamation de la Parole, ni donc de mettre son autorité en question. Les protestations bien connues d'allégeance antérieure au pape de la part de Luther et son hésitation sur la question de l'autorité papale sont une preuve évidente de son intention de rester loyal. En outre, elles démontrent la répugnance et l'angoisse qui accompagnèrent la prise de conscience croissante de son éloignement par rapport au pape : « Ceux qui ensuite commencèrent à attaquer arrogamment la majesté blessée du pape n'avaient pas idée de ce que mon cœur souffrit durant cette première et cette seconde année, ils ignoraient combien grande était mon humilité et comme j'étais proche du désespoir ! » (*WA* 39/I. 6. 16-19). C'est à regret que Luther entreprit de s'opposer au pape, par besoin d'être fidèle à ce qu'il estimait indispensable aux chrétiens dans l'Eglise.

Le même engagement qui amena Luther aux *Thèses,* il le formulait dans ses *Explications des Thèses* et dans la lettre de dédicace à Léon X qui les accompagnait. Dans ces deux documents, Luther se défend de l'accusation de porter atteinte à l'autorité papale. Dans la lettre, il rejette la responsabilité de la controverse sur les prédicateurs des indulgences qui opprimaient les gens avec des fausses espérances et déchiraient la chair du peuple pour s'engraisser (*WA* 1. 527. 7-10). Peu après cette lettre, Luther accuse encore les prédicateurs de terrifier les gens en proclamant que leurs propres paroles sont la Parole de Dieu (*WA* 1. 387. 14-16). Dans les *Explications* mêmes, le fameux appel de Luther pour une réforme de l'Eglise s'inspire de son désarroi devant la dissimulation dans l'Eglise qui rendait les bons prédicateurs

IX

eux-mêmes inefficaces et qui empêchait Dieu, dans sa colère, de donner des pasteurs selon son cœur qui, au lieu d'indulgences, nourriraient le peuple avec une mesure de froment (*WA* 1. 628. 1-8).

La soumission de Luther à l'autorité papale au milieu de l'année 1518 ne diminue en rien la substance ecclésiologique de son propos. Depuis ses premières remarques critiques sur les indulgences, avant 1517, jusqu'à son discours de Worms en 1521 (*WA* 7. 833. 8-834. 2), Luther avait à cœur la conscience de tous les chrétiens fidèles autant que la sienne. Il plaidait pour la nécessité commune à tous les fidèles d'entendre la Parole de Dieu sans laquelle ils ne pouvaient survivre. Quand on voit les *Quatre-vingt-quinze Thèses* comme la première expression publique de ce souci de réforme — qui eut à la vérité une publicité beaucoup plus grande que ne l'avait souhaité Luther —, alors, elles apparaissent comme beaucoup plus qu'un catalyseur. Elles deviennent la première salve tirée contre une obstruction spécifique de la Parole qui, prenant de la force, va ricocher de défenseur en défenseur jusqu'à ce qu'elle frappe au cœur la papauté elle-même.

L'insistance de Luther sur l'autorité de la Parole s'est certainement accentuée au fur et à mesure qu'il rencontrait de nouveaux refus. Pourtant, il n'est pas nécessaire de postuler que Luther se soit armé d'une théologie définitivement nouvelle dès le début de 1518 pour expliquer sa désillusion croissante à propos du pape et la fin de tout espoir de réconciliation en 1520.

III. DURES ATTAQUES DE LA PAPAUTÉ VERS LA FIN DE LA VIE DE LUTHER

L'attaque de Luther en 1545, *Contre la papauté,* renforcée par les illustrations vulgaires auxquelles il fait allusion dans son traité [16], a discrédité son opposition à la papauté aux yeux mêmes de ses interprètes les plus sympathiques. Pour les autres, elle a été taxée de « haine invétérée » de la part de Luther [17]. On a expliqué, sinon excusé, les vitupérations de Luther, en invoquant sa peur de voir bientôt s'effondrer l'œuvre de sa vie en raison d'un échec ou d'un compromis politique. Comme explications de sa contestation polémique, on a de même invoqué son âge, son état de santé, sa vision du conflit eschatologique entre la véritable Eglise et la fausse. Si certains de ces facteurs ont contribué à l'aigreur de Luther, ils n'ont fait qu'ajouter à la force de son refus de la papauté sans changer fondamentalement la motivation de ce refus. L'intérêt porté aux invectives de Luther

16. Cf. *WA* 54. 346-373. H. GRISAR - F. HEEGE, *Luthers Kampfbilder,* IV (Luther-Studien 6), Fribourg, 1923, 16-63.
17. BÄUMER, *Martin Luther und der Papst,* 99-100.

56

a empêché de voir les affirmations de son dernier traité qui confirment que son souci premier restait inaltéré.

Luther avait tout à fait conscience d'utiliser des « mots méprisants, blessants et cinglants » vis-à-vis du pape. Mais il croyait ces mots nécessaires car « nul ne peut se figurer quelle abomination est la papauté » et pour que « ceux qui vivent aujourd'hui et ceux qui viendront après nous puissent savoir ce que je pensais du pape, le maudit Antichrist, et que quiconque veut être chrétien soit mis en garde contre cette abomination » (*WA* 54. 215. 11-25). Dans ce traité tout comme dans l'important traité ecclésiologique de 1541, *Contre Hans Wurst*, Luther ne cesse de répéter son dévouement foncier à la liberté de toutes les consciences chrétiennes qui étaient encore retenues prisonnières des lois de la papauté (*WA* 51. 492. 14-493. 8 ; 54. 268. 20-26). On continuait de laisser le peuple dans l'incertitude, ne sachant si « le pape se montrerait en serviteur empressé pour la consolation et le bénéfice des pauvres gens » (*WA* 54. 272. 9-10 ; 250. 23-25). Là où jadis Luther avait exprimé avec courtoisie et prudence son souci de la survivance des fidèles, il traduisait désormais sa grande angoisse en termes pesants, avec la confiance que le Christ le pardonnerait (*WA* 54. 277. 23-24).

Dans son dernier traité, la façon de s'exprimer de Luther est devenue hardie jusqu'à l'impudence, mais son angoisse et son tourment n'ont fait que croître. Ils n'ont pas changé de base ecclésiologique. Le critère par quoi tout vrai chrétien peut juger le pape et les évêques demeure leur fidélité à la mission de nourrir le peuple de la Parole sans laquelle l'Eglise ne peut survivre (*WA* 54. 280. 1-9 ; 294. 20-31). Si Luther avait acquis la conviction de quelque chose de nouveau durant ses dernières années, c'était que l'inanition dont souffrait le troupeau du Christ n'était pas due à la simple négligence mais à une malice criminelle. Son ultime protestation est amère ; certains pourront dire qu'elle est d'antipathie. On peut même la dire haineuse. Il ne s'agit cependant pas d'une haine autojustifiée, née de « furieuses réactions d'émotivité » personnelle, mais d'une aversion anxieuse de celui qui « blasphème le seigneur » et asphyxie son peuple (*WA* 54. 262. 12-22).

*   *
*

L'opposition passionnée de Luther à la papauté a été, on le comprend bien, quelque chose d'embarrassant pour les *conversations œcuméniques du XX*e *siècle*. D'où la tendance à minimiser l'attitude intransigeante de Luther lui-même en faveur de la disposition expresse de Melanchthon à concéder une autorité limitée au pape. Ce genre de stratégie semble avoir prévalu dans les récentes déclarations communes issues du dialogue entre luthériens et catholiques romains sur la primauté papale aux USA [18]. On se contente d'y faire appel aux remarques positives éparses où Luther se déclarait prêt à reconnaître la papauté si elle était réformée selon l'Evangile.

Manifestement, certains luthériens ne sont pas disposés à aller aussi loin qu'Erwin Mülhaupt et à affirmer que les arguments théologiques de Luther contre la papauté demeurent des raisons valables pour attribuer à cette dernière les caractères de l'Antéchrist [19]. Inversement, négliger comme périmée l'attitude de Luther à l'encontre de la papauté ne fait pas justice au souci fondamental que les chrétiens fidèles soient nourris de la Parole de Dieu, souci qui a dicté l'attitude de Luther à l'égard du pape à tous les stades de sa vie. Selon l'ecclésiologie de Luther, assurer cette nourriture était la fonction indispensable de toute structure ecclésiastique, et nulle structure, papale ou autre, ne se légitimait à moins de s'acquitter fidèlement de cette mission. Le propre combat de Luther se dirigeait contre la papauté parce que, à son avis, elle n'accomplissait pas cette tâche à son époque. Pour la continuation du dialogue œcuménique, plus important que le jugement spécifique de Luther sur la papauté au XVIe siècle est sa vision de la tâche pastorale essentielle de toute structure ecclésiastique légitime. Cette vision peut encore servir de critère vital pour la recherche de structures plus adaptées pour notre temps.

(Traduit de l'américain par André Divault.)

18. *Lutherans and Catholics in Dialogue V : Papal Primacy and the Universal Church,* P.C. EMPIE et T.A. MURPHY éd., Minneapolis, 1974.
19. E. MUELHAUPT, « Vergängliches und Unvergängliches an Luthers Papstkritik » (Transitoire et permanent dans la critique du pape par Luther), in *Luther-Jahrbuch* 26, 1959, 73.

X

Urbanus Rhegius and the Augsburg Confession

The significance of the Augsburg Confession for the shape and identity of German protestantism after 1540 is undeniable. This significance is tied to political decisions in the Empire like the Peace of Augsburg (1555), which established the legal force of the Confession, and to formal resolutions of theological conflicts, like the Formula of Concord (1577), which made a certain interpretation of the Confession normative for Lutheran identity in those territories which subscribed to it. The immediate impact of the Confession on the teaching and practice of Protestant territories during the 1530s, however, is not so clear. Did the Confession influence the way in which Protestant preachers interpreted the evangelical message to their hearers? Did these preachers invoke the Confession when changing the religious practices of the Roman church to conform to their message

During the decade after it was submitted to Emperor Charles V at the Diet of Augsburg, the Augsburg Confession underwent an important change of status. It gradually became a normative document for German Protestantism instead of the descriptive document which Charles V had called for and its authors had presented to him at Augsburg.[1] The rejection of the Confession by Charles in the Edict of Augsburg[2] made affirmation of the Confession a political hallmark of those cities and territories which formed the Smalcald League in order to defend themselves against the consequences of non-compliance with the Edict. At the order of these same princes and city councils, Protestant theologians subscribed officially to the Confession and to Melanchthon's Apology when they signed Melanchthon's Treatise on the Power and Primacy of the Pope, at Smalcald in 1537.[3] The Confession began also to be invoked as a norm for Protestant teaching and practice in formal ecclesiastical documents. For example, a church order in Hesse (1532) which regulated liturgical matters appealed to the Confession and the Apology as guides for celebration of the Lord's Supper because the documents contained nothing improper or objectionable.[4] And, at a conference held in Hamburg on April 15, 1535,

[1]See Karl Förstemann, *Urkundenbuch zu der Geschichte des Reichtages zu Augsburg im Jahre 1530* (2 vols.; 1833; rpt. Hildesheim: Olms, 1966). I. 7-8, 308-309. See also Brück's preface to the Augsburg confession in *Die Bekenntnisschriften der evangelisch-lutherischen Kirche (BSLK)* (6, ed.; Göttingen: Vandenhoeck & Ruprecht, 1967), pp. 45-46.
[2]Förstemann, *Urkundenbuch*, II, 474-478.
[3]*BSLK*, pp. 496-498.
[4]*Ordenung der Christlichen kirchen in furstenthumb zu Hessen* in Emil Sehling, ed., *Die evangelischen Kirchenordnungen des XVI. Jahrhunderts (= KOO)*, vols I-IV (1902-1913; rpt. Aalen: Scientia, 1970-1978), vols. VI-XV (Tübingen: Mohr [Siebeck], 1955-), VIII, 76.

preachers from six Hanseatic cities agreed that the Augsburg Confession of 1530 would be the norm for their teaching and that no one would be permitted to preach in their cities unless he had first been examined on the basis of the Confession.

At least on occasion, therefore, formal appeal was being made to the Augsburg Confession in a normative sense in church orders and political charters of the 1530s. To what extent, however, did this formal appeal mean that the Confession directly influenced the preaching and practice of Protestants in northern Germany? Did preachers invoke the Confession frequently and explicitly in those literary works which provide clues to their day-to-day reforming activity?

The work of Urbanus Rhegius (1489-1541), pastor and eventually superintendent of the churches in the Duchy of Lüneburg from 1530 to 1541, affords an instructive case study of the actual use of the Confession during the first decade of its existence. If any Protestant outside the Wittenberg circle was likely to make the Confession the polestar of his work, it was Rhegius. Prior to his departure from Augsburg in 1530, Rhegius had been a Protestant preacher in that city for seven years.[6] He had mediated between Zwinglian and Lutheran factions in Augsburg and was rewarded by the city council for his opposition to the Anabaptists. In a public demonstration of his break with the papacy in 1525 Rhegius married an Augsburg native and, at Christmas of the same year, together with his colleague Johannes Frosch, he presided over the first public celebration of the Lord's Supper in Augsburg in which both elements were offered to the laity.[7]

As a consequence of his career in Augsburg, Rhegius was well-versed in both the theological and the practical issues which dominated the diet. He was an active participant in the discussions which accompanied the preparation of the Confession. Before the Diet began, Rhegius reported enthusiastically to Luther on his daily association with the Saxon theologians, adding that Luther's own presence would make his joy complete.[8] In all likelihood Rhegius was among the twelve theologians who attended the formal session of the territorial representatives on June 23 to give final approval to the Confession.[9] Indeed, the presence of Philip of Hesse at that final session might have been due to the influence of Rhegius

[5]Sehling, *KOO*, V, 541. The cities were Lübeck, Bremen, Rostock, Stralsund, Lüneburg, and Hamburg.

[6]The standard biography of Rhegius has been: Gerhard Uhlhorn, *Urbanus Rhegius: Leben und ausgewählte Schriften*, Leben und ausgewählte Schriften der Väter und Begründer der lutherischen Kirche, VII (Elberfeld: Friderichs, 1861). For the period to 1530 Uhlhorn has now been supplemented by the thorough new study of Maximilian Liebmann, *Urbanus Rhegius und die Anfänge der Reformation*, Reformationsgeschichtliche Studien und Texte, 117 (Münster: Aschendorff, 1980). For Rhegius' career as a reformer in Augsburg, see Liebmann, pp. 174-200.

[7]*Ibid.*, pp. 194-200.

[8]*D. Martin Luthers Werke: Kritische Gesamtausgabe: Briefwechsel* (= *WABr*) (Weimar: Böhlau, 1930ff. &, 5, 334.5-9 (May 21, 1530).

[9]Liebmann, p. 259.

himself. One month earlier Rhegius had dined with Philip and discussed theological issues at length, spending two hours alone on the Eucharist. Rhegius reported to Luther that Philip did not agree with Zwingli on that nettlesome subject, and it may well have been Rhegius, therefore, who helped persuade Philip to sign the Augsburg Confession.[10]

Rhegius was active and influential as well in the negotiations which followed the submission of the Confession to Charles V. In discussions with the Catholic party Rhegius supported the conciliatory stance taken by Philip Melanchthon and John Brenz instead of the harder line advocated by Justus Jonas.[11] Intra-Protestant dialogue was also facilitated by Rhegius. It was due to the efforts of Rhegius that Melanchthon finally agreed to meet with Martin Bucer on August 22, 1530. Four days later, Rhegius was able to leave Augsburg with a mail pouch containing letters of Melanchthon and Bucer to Luther and theses on the Eucharist which both had formulated in consultation with each other.[12] Rhegius himself was prepared to plead the case for concord before Luther. The submission of separate confessions by the Lutherans and by the South German cities had not cooled the ardor for a solid Protestant front which Rhegius had manifested in Augsburg before the diet and which the rejection of both confessions by Charles V made more attractive than ever.

Rhegius left Augsburg on August 26, 1530, en route to his new field of activity in the Duchy of Lüneburg under Dukes Ernest (the "Confessor") and Francis, both of whom signed the Confession.[13] During his stopover at the Coburg Rhegius saw Luther for the first time and came away deeply impressed by the Wittenberg leader. He later recalled the entire day which he spent with Luther as the happiest day of his life and praised Luther as a theologian without equal in any age.[14] Rhegius' enthusiastic account of his experience at the Coburg has suggested that he underwent a conversion

---

[10]*WABr* 5, 334.11-25. Rhegius told Luther that he rejoiced to see that Philip of Hesse was much less prone to discord than rumor had indicated before his arrival in Augsburg. Rhegius now hoped that Philip would not spurn the advice of Melanchthon and the others. *Ibid.*, p. 334.21-25. See Liebmann, pp. 242-244, 264-265.

[11]Liebmann, pp. 272-302; Uhlhorn, pp. 158-159. On the negotiations in August 1530, see Herbert Immenkötter, *Um die Einheit im Glauben: Die Unionsverhandlungen des Augsburger Reichstages im August und September 1530* (2. ed.; Münster: Aschendorff, 1973), pp. 28-67.

[12]Liebmann, pp. 251-256.

[13]*BSLK*, p. 137.

[14]These comments were excerpted from letters addressed by Rhegius from Lüneburg to friends in South Germany in 1534, and the excerpts were published independently in 1545 under the title: *Iudicium D. Urbani Rhegii de D. Martino Luthero.* The *Iudicium* was printed at the end of a collection of theological sources used by Rhegius and published posthumously: *Loci theologici* (Frankfurt: Peter Braubach, 1545), lvs. 251v-252r. This first printing of the *Iudicium* needs to be added to the citation of the *Iudicium* in the first critical bibliography of Rhegius' works published by Liebmann in his study (p. 390). The numbers which Liebmann assigns to the manuscripts (= Ms.) and to the printed editions (= D) of Rhegius' works will be cited in this essay to indicate where full bibliographical information may be found. The *Iudicium* corresponds to D99 and D100 in Liebmann's bibliography. It is also contained in the collected Latin works of Rhegius: *Opera Urbani Regii latine edita* (Nuremberg: Johannes Montanus and Ulrich Neuber, 1562), II, LXXXr.

from the independent and conciliatory Protestantism of his Augsburg period to a stricter adherence to Luther's theology which shaped the last eleven years of his activity in northern Germany.[15] This apparent new devotion to Luther would help to explain the importance which the Augsburg Confession, in the eyes of some interpreters, assumed for Rhegius during the 1530s. Uhlhorn, for example, claimed that Rhegius frequently appealed to the Confession and that it remained a firm support for him in his later years.[16]

In fact, the writings of Rhegius between 1530 and 1541 contained only occasional references to the Augsburg Confession; it did not have an explicit influence on the shape of his theology. Furthermore, the works of Rhegius do not support a direct correlation between his use of the Confession and a stricter devotion to Luther or a stronger Lutheran identity during the 1530s. It would be important to Lutherans of a later generation to draw such a correlation over against Melanchthon and his use of the Confession. But the fluid situation of the 1530s in both intra-Protestant and Protestant-Catholic relations prevented one's attitude toward the Confession from assuming as much stigmatic quality as it would later possess.

Rhegius spent his years in northern Germany organizing the Reformation in the territory of Lüneburg and travelling from his home in Celle to cities which requested his assistance in consolidating the nascent Protestant movement. He was a key figure in both the territorial and the urban Reformation of northern Germany. In the territory of Lüneburg itself the instruction of pastors and the resistance of the cloisters to the takeover by Protestantism occupied most of his time. Rhegius had correspondence with a number of cities both inside and outside the boundaries of Lüneburg, but he was most directly involved in the Reformation of Lüneburg (city) and Hannover. Outside Celle Rhegius spent more time in Lüneburg than in any other single city. Rhegius entered the scene in Lüneburg before the Reformation had completely taken hold, and he faced tenacious opposition there. Despite the report of a later historian of the Reformation in that city,[17] however, the Augsburg Confession did not directly shape Rhegius' reform work in that urban setting.

[15] According to Karl Keim, Rhegius received at the Coburg "die Weihe des Lutheraners" for his work in North Germany: *Schwäbische Reformationsgeschichte bis zum Augsburger Reichstag* (Tübingen: Fues, 1855), p. 235. Cf. Uhlhorn, p. 160. Liebmann, p. 302, seems to agree.

[16] Uhlhorn, p. 157. For the North German period (1530-1541) Uhlhorn's work has been supplemented by the dissertation of Richard Gerecke, *"Urbanus Rhegius: Studien zu seiner Kirchenregimentlichen Tätigkeit in Norddeutschland"* (unpublished Dr. theol. dissertation, University of Göttingen, 1976). Part of the dissertation has been published under the title: "Studien zu Urbanus Rhegius' kirchenregimentlicher Tätigkeit in Norddeutschland: Konzil und Religionsgespräche," *Jahrbuch der Gesellschaft für niedersächsische Kerchengeschichte* (= *JGNKG*) 74 (1976), 3-49. According to Gerecke, the Confession retained special significance for Rhegius during his career in North Germany: "Studien," p. 14.

[17] Rhegius supposedly instructed the citizens of Lüneburg according to Scripture and the Augsburg Confession: Johann Georg Bertram, *Das Evangelische Lüneburg: Oder Reformations-und Kirchen-Historie der Alt berümten Stadt Lüneburg* (Braunschweig: Schröder,

In Hannover the situation was different. In contrast to Lüneburg the Reformation had been adopted when Rhegius arrived in the city for the first time during the fall of 1535.[18] A Protestant church order composed for the city had, however, been rejected by Nikolaus von Amsdorf when it was referred to him by Luther and Melanchthon for publication in Magdeburg.[19] That rejection and a meeting of the Smalcald Diet set for December 1535, which would rule on the admission of Hannover to the Smalcald League, prompted the city council to invite Rhegius to Hannover. Because the territory of Calenberg had remained Catholic under Duke Erich I, it was important for Hannover to legalize and to consolidate its Protestantism as quickly as possible and to ally itself with other Protestants. After spending several weeks in the city, Rhegius wrote a new church order for Hannover and sent it to the council in January 1536. At the Diet of Smalcald in 1537 Rhegius represented the city of Hannover as well as his home territory of Lüneburg.

As Rhegius read the struggle between Protestants and Catholics in the mid-1530s, it had already come down to the question of which side was the true church. In the long preface to his church order for Hannover, Rhegius argued that the decision should be based on the definition of the church in article seven of the Augsburg Confession: true Christians were those among whom the right understanding of the gospel and the right use of the sacraments were found.[20] After listing sixteen items which the gospel clearly taught, Rhegius claimed that those items and "everything which was confessed by our side before the emperor at the Diet of Augsburg was the truth."[21] That teaching published at Augsburg proved that in all their articles Lutherans believed and taught just as the church taught in apostolic times and just as orthodox Christians in the whole world believed.[22] Lutherans had not abolished all the old ceremonies of the church, nor had they left the papal church because they were scandalized by the presence of evil Christians. In accord with articles fifteen and eight of the Confession, Rhegius argued that Lutherans had kept those ceremonies which promoted good order and did not bind the conscience and that Lutherans recognized the right of both good and evil Christians to remain in the church.[23] In sum, those who now called themselves Lutheran and who confessed their faith at Augsburg in the Diet had never deviated from the true church.

1719), p. 54. The church order which Rhegius composed for Lüneburg in 1531 does not mention the Augsburg Confession: *Christlyke ordenynghe van der scholen und kercken sacken der stadt luneborch*, in Sehling, *KOO*, VI / 1, 633-649.

[18]On the Reformation in Hannover and Rhegius' role in it, see Waldemar Bahrdt, *Geschichte der Reformation der Stadt Hannover* (Hannover: Hahn, 1891); Gerecke, "Urbanus Rhegius" (diss.), pp. 141-176.

[19]Gerecke, "Urbanus Rhegius" (diss.), p. 160. Amsdorf's letter was published in Möhlmann, "Beiträge zur Geschichte der Hannoverschen Reformation,"*Hannoversches Magazin* (Hannover, 1843), p. 408. Amsdorf was afraid that any new order would become a snare for consciences and lead to a "new papacy."

[20]*Kirchenordnung der statt Hannofer durch D. Urbanum Regium*, in Sehling, *KOO*, VI / 2, 949.

[21]*Ibid.*, p. 965.   [22]*Ibid.*, p. 949.   [23]*Ibid.*, pp. 998-999.

X

In defending the establishment of Protestantism against Catholic opposition, Rhegius made use of the same arguments for the legitimacy of a Protestant ecclesiastical structure which the Augsburg Confession itself had used. Although Rhegius could not appeal to the Confession as a legally valid document within the empire, he could invoke it as public evidence for the teaching which he defended. The fact that the emperor had listened to the Lutherans' account of their faith at the "excellent Diet of Augsburg"[25] enhanced the public and official stature of the Confession. In 1535 he appealed to that stature as proof that the teaching in his *Small Catechism for Children* "sincerely presented the gospel according to the ecclesiastical sense of the orthodox fathers and of the 'old church.' "[26] In the same *Catechism* Rhegius cited article seven of the Confession almost verbatim to demonstrate where the holy, catholic church of the Creed was to be found.[27] After he had summarized how faith was attained, Rhegius advised the child to study articles four and five of the Confession which he then quoted for convenience in the Catechism itself.[28]

As public evidence of the catholicity and orthodoxy of Lutheran teaching the Augsburg Confession did function in a normative capacity for Rhegius. Except for a few passages in the Catechism of 1535, however, the Confession did not serve as an explicit source or model for the content of Rhegius' teaching.[29] The Augsburg Confession was not mentioned at all in

[24]*Ibid.*, p. 944: "Das die, so man itzt lutherisch nennet und ihren glauben zu Augspurg im reichstag bekent haben, niemals von der waren kirchen abgewichen seien, sondern allein nach dem gebot Christi Matth. 16 [6] sich fur unserer phariseer und saduceer saurteig, soviel müglich, hüten."

[25]*Ibid.*, p. 996.

[26]*Catechismus minor puerorum, generoso puero Ottoni Furster, dicatus* (Wittenberg: Hans Lufft, 1535), lvs. FIV / v-FV / r (Liebmann D103): "Nos autem contra Evangelium nihil adserimus sed Evangelium synceriter docemus iuxta sensum Ecclesiasticum Orthodoxorum et veteris Ecclesiae, nostraeque fidei confessionem Anno domini .1530. exhibuimus Carolo .5. Romano Caesari et Romani imperii proceribus, In comiciis Augustae frequentissimis."

[27]*Ibid.*, lf. Fiiv. Rhegius used article seven in a different work to argue that any jurisdictional authority which Protestants might accept would have to teach the gospel, administer the sacraments according to the word of God, and not establish other novel forms of worship. *Libellus consolatorius ad pios in Hannovera, contra Papistarum tyrannidem & blasphemias* (Frankfurt: Peter Braubach, 1545), lf. 16r (Liebmann D109: this Latin translation of his letter of consolation to Christians in Hannover is part of a larger Latin composite which alone is cited here by Liebmann).

[28]Rhegius, *Catechismus minor*, lf. Fviir-v.

[29]Similarities between statements of Rhegius and the Confession do exist, especially in his satirical work against monastic practice, *Eine ungehewre wunderbarliche Absolution der Closterfrawen jm Fürstenthumb Lüneburg mit jhrer auslegung durch Urbanum Regium* (Wittenberg: George Rhau, 1532) (Liebmann D88). On the subject of good works, Rhegius cited Luke 17:10 just as in article six of the Augsburg Confession. See *Absolution*, lf. Cir-v; *BSLK*, p. 60. Rhegius also recalled the former role which monasteries played as schools. See *Absolution*, lf. Hiiir; article twenty-three of the Confession, *BSLK*, p. 112. Rhegius made reference to Augsburg in his 1538 treatise on both kinds in the Eucharist: *Confutatio libelli, cuiusdam Luneburgi occulto adfixi . . .* (Wittenberg: Josef Klug, 1538), lf. Eviiir (Liebmann D127).

the ordination examination for pastors in the Duchy of Lüneburg which Rhegius wrote in 1536. Candidates were to be tested on law and gospel according to the order transmitted by Scripture in Luke 24:47: ". . . repentance and forgiveness of sins should be preached in his name . . ."[30] The same verse played an important role in the homiletical handbook which Rhegius prepared for young preachers in Lüneburg. Sermons were to manifest the proper balance between repentance and faith instead of emphasizing one at the expense of the other and leaving the people in despair or presumption.[31] Rhegius expressed this balance in words reminiscent of the Augsburg Confession. Both texts, however, had a common ancestor in Melanchthon's *Instruction for the Visitors of Parish Pastors in Electoral Saxony* (1528), which also cited Luke 24:47 as the basis for understanding the full thrust of the gospel message.[32]

The priority which Melanchthon's *Instruction for Visitors* assumed for Rhegius over the Augsburg Confession was due to the kind of work which Rhegius did as a reformer in northern Germany. His doctrinal concerns were governed by the necessity of spelling out in clear and balanced form the implications of the Protestant message for the lives of people who were changing their religious tradition. Practice and conduct which reflected a proper understanding of the message took precedence over theological purity on controverted issues. When Rhegius instructed his preachers how to handle the mass, for example, he concentrated on the elimination of the idea of sacrifice and did not dwell at all on the issue of the presence of Christ.[33] Rhegius' writings did occasionally deal with the same practical issues which were treated under the rubric of abuses in the second part of the Augsburg Confession. But he made little attempt to demonstrate doctrinal conformity with the Confession in his practical works since that demonstration was necessary only for formal political purposes and not for the instruction of the people. The Confession was invoked as a public witness rather than as a guide to the content of the Protestant message.

[30]*Examen episcopi in ducatu Luneburgensi* (Erfurt: Wolfgang Stürmer, 1538), lvs A2v-A3r (Liebmann D126).

[31]Rhegius, *Wie man fürsichtiglich und ohne Argerniss reden soll von den fürnemesten Artikeln christlicher Lehre (Formulae quaedam caute et citra scandalum loquendi)*, ed. Alfred Uckeley (Leipzig: Deichert [Böhme], 1908), pp. 31, 41-45 (Liebmann D101).

[32]*Wie man fürsichtiglich*, p. 42; article twelve of the Augsburg Confession in *BSLK*, pp. 66-67; Melanchthon, *Unterricht der Visitatoren*, in *Melanchthons Werke in Auswahl*, ed. Robert Stupperich (Gütersloh: Bertelsmann, 1951), I, 221.8-222.27, 244.1-3. Cf. Rhegius' discussion of repentance in *Absolution der Closterfrawen*, lf. Jiv. See Ferdinand Cohrs, "Urbanus Rhegius' 'Examen episcopi in ducatu Luneburgensi,' 1536 (?): Ein Beitrag zur Geschichte des Prüfungswesens in der evangelischen Kirche," in *Studien zur Reformationsgeschichte und zur praktischen Theologie: Gustav Kawerau an seinem 70. Geburtstage dargebracht* (Leipzig: Heinsius, 1917), pp. 57-69.

[33]*Wie man fürsichtiglich*, pp. 49-53. For the distinctiveness of Rhegius' theology in the context of his reforming work, see Hans-Walter Krumwiede, "'Vom reformatorischen Glauben Luthers zur Orthodoxie: Theologische Bemerkungen zu Bugenhagens Braunschweiger Kirchenordnung und zu Urbanus Rhegius' *formulae quaedam caute et citra scandalum loquendi*," *JGNKG* 53 (1955), 33-48.

The Augsburg Confession did play a small role in Rhegius involvement in Protestant politics during the 1530s. He may have consulted the Confession in advisory documents which he prepared for Duke Ernest on the calling of a church council to settle the religious disputes. In the first of these documents, written in early 1531, Rhegius supported the right of Protestants to appeal to a council as Chancellor Brück of Electoral Saxony had provided for that eventuality in his preface to the Augsburg Confession[34] Article twenty-eight of the Confession also served Rhegius as a source for discussing the role of bishops in the church.[35] In 1533 Rhegius was asked by Duke Ernest to respond to the conditions under which Pope Clement VII declared himself willing to call a council. Rhegius rejected the conditions because he was convinced they would prevent a free council from taking place. "There is no other way," he admonished Duke Ernest; "we must remain confessors of Christ and enrage the world!"[36]

At the Diet of Smalcald in February 1537 Rhegius emerged as a spokesman for the assembled theologians.[37] Melanchthon's *Treatise on the Power and Primacy of the Pope* was discussed at a meeting of theologians on February 17, and Luther's *Smalcald Articles* were presented to the same assembly. After discussion of the Articles was delayed due to Luther's illness, Rhegius wrote to Melanchthon in the name of the brethren and asked him to take charge and push for action so that all of them could leave the "workhouse" of Smalcald and no longer have to consume the "dirt and refuse of the Franconians."[38] Rhegius urged Melanchthon to have the South German theologians sign the Articles of Luther and the Augsburg Confession so that "we might know how they feel about the Eucharist and certain other controversial points."[39] The most prominent South German in attendance was Martin Bucer. In the Wittenberg Concord of 1536 Bucer had just reached the agreement on the Eucharist which he had pursued so eagerly ever since the Diet of Augsburg and the mission of Rhegius to the Coburg. Now Rhegius was ostensibly pushing Bucer even further in the direction of Luther's view of the real presence by requiring Bucer's subscription to the Smalcald Articles as well as to the Augsburg Confession. Was Rhegius advocating a strict interpretation of article ten of the Confession in the sense of Luther over against Melanchthon and his own earlier conciliatory stance?[40] Was the divisive effect of the Confession among later Lutherans already foreshadowed in the action of Rhegius?

[34]For a detailed discussion of this document (Liebmann Ms. 48), see Gerecke, "Studien," pp. 18-30. Cf. *BSLK*, pp. 48-49.

[35]Gerecke, "Studien," p. 30.

[36]This letter (Liebmann Ms. 62) was published in Uhlhorn, p. 211. See Gerecke, "Studien," pp. 31-33.

[37]*Urkunden und Aktenstücke zur Geschichte von Martin Luthers Schmalkaldischen Artikeln (1536-1574)*, ed. Hans Volz (Berlin: de Gruyter, 1957), pp. 165, 167 n. 16. Ernst Bizer, "Zum geschichtlichen Verständnis von Luthers Schmalkaldischen Artikeln," *Zeitschrift für Kirchengeschichte* 67 (1955 / 56), 86.

[38]This letter (Liebmann Ms. 75) was published by Hans Volz, "Ein unbekannter Brief des Urbans Rhegius aus dem Jahre 1537," *JGNKG* 65 (1967), 270-271.

[39]*Ibid.*, p. 271.

[40]See the interpretation of Gerecke, "Studien," pp. 40-42.

Since Protestants needed as much solidarity as possible in order to back up their refusal to attend the council called by Pope Paul III, Rhegius hardly intended to cause a split among the Wittenbergers. In the same letter Rhegius clearly identified himself and his colleagues from Lower Saxony with the theological positions of Melanchthon.[41] Rhegius gave no indication, moreover, that Melanchthon himself might have reservations about Luther's Articles or that any real difference of opinion existed among the North Germans.

At the same time Rhegius may still have desired a clearer reading on Bucer and his South German colleagues. Rhegius' encounter with Luther in 1530 did leave behind a more guarded attitude on Rhegius' part toward Bucer's efforts at compromise.[42] Even though Bucer reported that he and Luther had practically reached agreement on the Supper when Bucer himself visited the Coburg in late September 1530,[43] Rhegius followed Luther's lead in rejecting Bucer's freshly written effort at concord which Bucer sent to Luther and to Duke Ernest of Lüneburg in late December 1530 and early January 1531. Luther reported his rejection of Bucer's work to Duke Ernest, and Duke Ernest in turn used Luther's own words to convey his reservations about Bucer's positions to Strassburg. A draft of the letter from Duke Ernest to Strassburg was written by Rhegius himself after his arrival in Celle; still no evidence indicates that Rhegius regarded his adherence to Luther's position in 1531 as a departure from Melanchthon or from his earlier endorsement of negotiations between Wittenberg and Strassburg.[44]

[41]Volz, "Ein unbekannter Brief," p. 271: "Saxones mei synceri sunt, illi non vel syllaba una a te et nobis unquam dissentient."

[42]After Rhegius conveyed Bucer's offer to Luther at the Coburg, Luther wrote Melanchthon that he would not respond to Bucer and that he hated the tricks and craftiness of Bucer and his colleagues. *WABr* 5, 617.15-16 (September 11, 1530). Luther probably conveyed this feeling to Rhegius along with his notion that Bucer's efforts posed a threat to the Confession. *Ibid.*, 617.19-21: "Sic Diabolus undique nostrae Confessioni insidiatur, quando vi nihil potest, veritate superatus." After he had met with Philip of Hesse in May 1530, Rhegius promised Philip to work as hard as possible for concord. *WABr* 5, 334.18-20: ". . . votis tamen ardentissimis exoptat [Philip of Hesse] doctorum hominum concordiam, quantum sinit pietas, ad quam rem promisi operam mean omnem charitatis" (Rhegius to Luther, May 21, 1530). Luther's attitude at the Coburg, however, must have put a damper on Rhegius' enthusiasm, and he did not report to Bucer on their encounter.

[43]In Bucer's letter to Rhegius, January 3, 1531, published in Albert Meno Verpoortenns, *Commentatio historica de Martino Bucero eiusque de coena Domini . . . sententia* (Coburg: Pfotenhauer, 1709), pp. 187-192. Having assumed that Rhegius did not meet with success at the Coburg, Bucer wrote: "Attamen contra spem sperans, ipse te secutus, D. Doct. conveni, humanioremque multo quam ante repperi." *Ibid.*, p. 187.

[44]Luther's rejection of Bucer's effort in *WABr* 6, 25-26 (January 22, 1531); Luther's letter to Duke Ernest, *WABr* 6, 28-29 (February 1, 1531); Bucer addressed his proposed new statement of concord to Duke Ernest and Strassburg endorsed Bucer's effort in a letter to Duke Ernest. See Henricus Philippus Gudenius, *Dissertatio saecularis de Ernesto Duce Brunsvicensi et Luneburgensi* (Göttingen: Hager, 1730), pp. 116ff., 129-130. In his reply to Strassburg Duke Ernest wrote of Bucer and his colleagues: ". . . so wird GOTT Gnade geben, dass sie kein Scheuen werden haben, das auch nachlassend gleicher Weise die Gegenwärtigkeit des Leibes dem Mund oder eusserlich ins HERRN Brod, welches unsers Bedünckens den euren als

The Wittenberg Concord of 1536 must have encouraged Rhegius; it could scarcely have impressed him as a dilution of the Augsburg Confession.[45] With his Articles prepared for Smalcald, Luther did not intend to sabotage the agreement reached between the Wittenbergers and Bucer in 1536.[46] In spite of Melanchthon's misgivings about the Articles, Rhegius did not necessarily have to regard them as objectionable to Bucer. In fact, Bucer declared his willingness to sign Luther's Articles were it not for the effect that his signature might have on the acceptance of the Wittenberg Concord by the Swiss and others.[47] The mention of the Smalcald Articles in the same breath with the Augsburg Confession by Rhegius did not mean that Rhegius was attempting to raise Luther's Articles to the level of a confessional statement and thereby give an extra "Lutheran" significance to the Augsburg Confession. The Articles had been submitted to the assembly of theologians for discussion and the question of subscription was raised. The theologians had not discounted the Smalcald Articles on the basis of a prior political decision,[48] and Rhegius was not trying to resurrect them from political oblivion in order to intimidate Bucer.

Rhegius' letter at Smalcald, therefore, need not be read as a Lutheran manifesto which either reflected special fidelity to Luther over against Melanchthon or which anticipated a gnesio-Lutheran interpretation of the Confession. Rhegius certainly understood himself to be Lutheran, and he appreciated the different positions on the presence of Christ in the Supper which had prevented Luther from adopting Bucer's first efforts at concord. At Smalcald, however, Rhegius was not attempting to force Bucer out of the Lutheran camp or to refine, as it were, Lutheran teaching to its greatest purity, free of all political contamination, in preparation for a head-on conflict with Rome.[49] The Augsburg Confession remained for Rhegius the public witness of Protestant teaching for all members of the Smalcald League. At Smalcald Bucer signed along with Rhegius the statement of allegiance to the Augsburg Confession and to the Apology at the end of Melanchthon's treatise on the papacy.[50] The fact that Rhegius signed the Smalcald Articles as the first of the non-Wittenbergers did not symbolize any new level of allegiance to Luther or to the Confession.

gelahrten hochverständigen Leuten nicht so gahr beschwerlich seyn mag, dieweil sie wol mercken, dass nichts desterweniger des Luthers Gedancken in dem Fall und der Papisten Gedancken gantz ungleich sind." Gudenius, *Dissertatio*, p. 132. Cf. the wording in *WABr* 6, 28.22-29.26. The draft of the letter from Duke Ernest to Strassburg in Rhegius' handwriting is contained in a volume of correspondence in the Kirchen-Ministerial-Bibliothek, Celle, 2 Z 100, No. 7. Appreciation is expressed to Herr Rüggeberg at the Theological Academy in Celle for his guidance in the use of this material.

[45]The Wittenberg Concord contained an endorsement of the Augsburg Confession and of the Apology. Ernst Bizer, *Studien zur Geschichte des Abendmahlstreits im 16. Jahrhundert* (1940; rpt. Darmstadt: Wissenschaftliche Buchgesellschaft, 1962), pp. 118-119.

[46]Bizer, "Zum geschichtlichen Verständnis," pp. 73-80, 90-91.

[47]*Ibid.*, p. 87.

[48]*Ibid.*, pp. 88-89.

[49]See Gerecke, "Studien," pp. 41-42.

[50]*BSLK*, p. 497.

X

Rhegius did become more pessimistic than Bucer about the success of religious colloquies with the Catholic side as the 1530s wore on, and this pessimism did color his remarks on Augsburg. In 1532 Rhegius had already described the conflict between Protestants and Catholics in polarized fashion. He labeled the two sides Christians and papists, the Christian realm and the world, and Christ and Belial. Similar terminology employed by Rhegius in his advisory paper on the colloquy scheduled for Nuremberg in 1539 was therefore not new.[51] The use of exclusive language which divided the two sides into opposing churches did not reflect so much a new hardline stance on Rhegius' part as it did the fact that his patience was running out. As his perspective lengthened, the event of the Diet of Augsburg assumed more significance than the confessional document itself. In his preface to the church order of Hannover (1536), Rhegius wrote: "We have delayed implementing the Reformation for so long because we hoped that with so many diets agreement could be reached on how one should teach and live correctly; but our hope is in vain."[52] Just prior to the Diet of Smalcald Rhegius wrote that the Protestants had made a sufficient and fair offer at Augsburg. If the "clear gospel" were permitted them, the Protestants would help faithfully to uphold the jurisdiction of the bishops and the reverence which they deserved. As far as faith allowed, Protestants would not omit any zeal for agreement, but the Catholics were too embittered against them.[53]

By 1539 the diet of Augsburg had become an event which in the eyes of Rhegius could not be reversed. His reforming labor had taught him that there was little hope of reconciliation with the Roman church no matter how well the theologians debated in their colloquies. In a sermon delivered

[51]Rhegius to Philip of Hesse, June 19, 1532: ". . . aut quae concordia Christo cum Belial? aut quae pars fideli cum infideli? Was das christlich wesen betrifft, kan man sich mit der Welt nymmermehr vereinigen. Wir müssen das Evangelion rein, den Glauben unverruckt, die Liebe frey und ungebunden behalten, Wollen wir Christen pleiben, dan es muss in unss nit der Welt geist, sonder Christus leben." C. G. Neudecker, ed., *Urkunden aus der Reformationszeit* (Cassel: Krieger, 1836), p. 214. Cf. *WABr* 5, 576.13-16 (Luther to Spalatin; August 26, 1530). For Rhegius' remarks in 1539, see *Iudicium Urbani Regii de Doctorum Conventu Noribergae habendo, Opera*, III, IXv-XIIIr. For interpretations which stress Rhegius' unyielding stance in 1539, see Gerecke, "Studien," pp. 45-49, and Liebmann, p. 302.

[52]Sehling, *KOO*, VI / 2, 999.

[53]*Dialogus. Ein lüstig und nützlich Gesprech vom zukünfftigen Concilio zu Mantua Zwisschen einem Weltfromen und einem Epicureer und einem Christen* (Wittenberg: Josef Klug, 1536), lf. Hiir (Liebman D114): "Orthodoxus: Wir haben uns zu Augspurg jhe gnugsamlich / zu aller billigkeit erboten / Man lasse uns nur das klare Evangelium / so wollen wir den Bisschoven jr iurisdiction und debitam reverentiam / ob Gott wil / mit aller trew helffen erhalten. Gedenck aber selbs mein Pharisee / wenn man uns will dringen wider Gottes wort / und unser gewissen zu handeln / Wer kan sich denn jnn dem fhal zun füssen werffen? Man mus jhe Gott mehr gehorsam sein / denn den menschen / Sie seien hoch oder nider / Act. 5. Es sol jnn aller billigkeit / was der glaub jmer erleiden mag / an uns zur eintrechtigkeit kein mangel haben / Sie sind aber gar zuverbittert wider uns." Gerecke, "Studien," p. 48, stresses the importance which "perseverance in doctrine" had for the consciences of all Christians in the view of Rhegius.

74

in Minden, where he had little success, Rhegius asserted that Scripture and the ancient church taught that faith alone made one godly. This was such a monstrous doctrine to the papists, however, that they publicly prohibited it in the Edict of Augsburg.[54] The Augsburg Confession itself served only infrequently as the explicit source for his teaching and practical reforms. But the submission of the Confession at Augsburg did provide public testimony to the catholicity and orthodoxy of those new ecclesiastical structures which Rhegius labored to establish and which looked more and more permanent as the first decade of the Confession's life drew to a close.

[54]*Wie man die falschen Propheten erkennen ia greiffen mag* (Braunschweig: Anders Goldbeck, 1539), lf. Fiir (Liebmann D129).

HISTORIA

Der Augspurgischen

Confession:

Wie sie erstlich berahtschlägt/ verfasset/ vnd Keiser Carolo V. vbergeben ist/ sampt andern Religions Handlungen/ so sich dabey auff dem Reichs= tag zu Augspurg / Anno M.D.XXX.jU getragen: Durch

D. DAVIDEM CHYTRAEVM erstlich zusammen geordnet/vermehret/ vnd nun endtlich widerumb durchsehen.

Gedruckt zu Franckfurt am Mayn/
M. D. LXXX

XI

Toleration of the Jews in the German Reformation: Urbanus Rhegius and Braunschweig (1535-1540)[1]

Interest in the relationship between the German Reformation and Judaism has for the most part been dominated by Luther's attitudes.[2] Even when other sources and figures from the Late Middle Ages and the Reformation have been studied, they often serve to create a backdrop for a discussion of Luther. For

1. Research for this article was made possible by a guest scholarship from the Herzog August Bibliothek, Wolfenbüttel, in the summer of 1988. I would like to thank the following members of the Library staff: Frau Dr. Sabine Solf, director of the Research Division, for her support of the project; Herr Hogrefe and his staff in the catalogue; Herr Dr. Niewöhner and Prof. Dr. Milde for their specific suggestions and assistance. In addition, I would like to thank the staffs of the Stadtarchiv Braunschweig and the Niedersächsisches Staatsarchiv, Wolfenbüttel, for their courteous and efficient help. – Abbreviations: Liebmann: Maximilian Liebmann: *Urbanus Rhegius und die Anfänge der Reformation* (Münster, 1980). Liebmann Bibliography: Liebmann, 341-416 (H = Handschrift; D = Druck). NStAWf: Niedersächsisches Staatsarchiv Wolfenbüttel. StABS: Stadtarchiv Braunschweig. *WA: D. Martin Luthers Werke. Kritische Gesamtausgabe* [Schriften] (Weimar, 1883-). *WABr: Martin Luthers Werke. Briefwechsel* (Weimar, 1930-). – After this manuscript was completed, Ms. Rotraud Ries, Münster, kindly shared with me excerpts from her unfinished dissertation entitled "Soziale und politische Bedingungen jüdischen Lebens in Niedersachsen im 15. und 16. Jahrhundert." Because her work directly supports and supplements my conclusions at important points, I have added references to it in several notes below.
2. The literature is voluminous. For older scholarship, see Johannes Brosseder: *Luthers Stellung zu den Juden im Spiegel seiner Interpreten. Interpretation und Rezeption von Luthers Schriften und Äußerungen zum Judentum im 19. und 20. Jahrhundert vor allem im deutschsprachigen Raum* (Munich, 1972). Brosseder has also analyzed more recent literature: "Lutherbilder in der neuesten Literatur zum Thema: Martin Luther und die Juden," in *Europa in der Krise der Neuzeit. Martin Luther: Wandel und Wirkung seines Bildes*, ed. Susanne Heine (Weimar, Cologne, Graz, 1986), 89-111. See also Kurt Meier: "Zur Interpretation von Luthers Judenschriften," in *Vierhundertfünfzig Jahre lutherische Reformation 1517-1967. Festschrift für Franz Lau*, ed. Helmar Junghans et al. (Berlin, 1967), 233-251. Two significant studies since 1983 have treated the influence of Luther's views: *Die Juden und Martin Luther – Martin Luther und die Juden: Geschichte, Wirkungsgeschichte, Herausforderung*, ed. Heinz Kremers (Neukirchen-Vluyn, 1985); and Johannes Wallmann: "The Reception of Luther's Writings on the Jews from the Reformation to the End of the 19th Century," *Lutheran Quarterly* 1 (1987): 72-97. Current literature can be followed in section B 5 h) of the annual Luther bibliography in *Lutherjahrbuch*.

Originally published in *Archiv für Reformationsgeschichte/Archive for Reformation History* 81 (Gütersloh, 1990), pp. 189-215, used by permission.

XI

example, in his nuanced study of the roots of anti-Semitism,[3] Heiko Oberman
has shown that the anti-Judaism of Luther both belonged to the general anti-
Jewish climate of Reformation Europe and assumed a character of its own.
Although sharing the concern of Reuchlin and Erasmus that the legalistic spirit
of "Judaism" be expunged from sixteenth-century life and thought, Luther valued the Old Testament more than Erasmus, and he remained more sceptical
than Reuchlin about the conversion of the Jews.[4] Luther's colleague, Justus
Jonas, who translated Luther's works on the Jews into Latin, stressed the common heritage of Jews and Christians and the common future that converted
Jews would share with Gentile believers. In contrast to Jonas, Luther regarded
the mass of the Jews as lost and viewed them, together with Turks and "papists," through the spectacles of apocalypticism as enemies of the gospel in the
last days.[5]

Although Oberman does not regard Luther's views as typical of the Reformation, the roots of enlightened toleration are traced neither to Luther's colleagues nor to urban reformers like Andrew Osiander and Wolfgang Capito
who were influenced by the Hebraic tradition or by humanism. Instead, Oberman credits the "Third Reformation" of the Calvinist refugees, who came to
know firsthand the age-old Jewish fate of exile, with spreading sympathy for
the Jews to Holland, France, the British Isles, and North America.[6] Only
through this "Third Reformation" were the positive ideas of Reuchlin, Erasmus, and Luther separated from their anti-Judaism. While a nod is given to the
forward-looking theology of Justus Jonas,[7] positive attitudes of other sixteenth-
century reformers toward the Jews are dismissed.[8]

An even more negative view of the Reformation's relationship to Judaism
maintains that Protestant anti-Judaism was encouraged by the fear that Jewish
studies would undermine Christian faith and lead to a Judaization of Christianity. Using the Hebraist Sebastian Münster and the reformer Martin Bucer as
primary examples, Jerome Friedman has argued that Protestants, under the
pressure of that fear in the 1530s, abandoned their positive attitudes toward the

3. *Wurzeln des Antisemitismus: Christenangst und Judenplage im Zeitalter von Humanismus und Reformation* (Berlin, 1981). English trans. by James I. Porter: *The Roots of Anti-
Semitism in the Age of Renaissance and Reformation* (Philadelphia, 1984).
4. *Roots*, 45–50.
5. *Roots*, 47–49, 118–122.
6. *Roots*, 139–142.
7. *Roots*, 141.
8. *Roots*, 140–141.

Jews.[9] According to Friedman: "As it became increasingly clear that Hebraica was not making Jewish converts, many Protestant leaders anxious over religious irregularity in Protestant areas became fearful of the very opposite phenomenon: the Judaization of Protestantism."[10] Münster, for example, who had written two mission tracts in 1529 and 1537, ceased both his collaboration with the scholar Elias Levita and his own Jewish studies and turned his attention to geography.[11]

Two patterns of the Reformation's relationship to Judaism have thus been proposed: (1) the uniqueness of Luther's apocalyptic outlook within a culture that made no genuine contribution to toleration (Oberman); and (2) the initial concern of Protestant Hebraists for conversion of the Jews that turned into strong anti-Jewish, even anti-Semitic, sentiment out of fear of possible Judaization (Friedman). Neither pattern, however, does justice to the German Reformation when one considers the example of another Lutheran reformer, Urbanus Rhegius (1489–1541),[12] who is mentioned neither by Oberman nor by Friedman. Rhegius shared Luther's sense of living in the last days and he was a Christian Hebraist who tried to convert the Jews. Nevertheless, he never gave up his Hebrew studies or his hope for Jewish converts; more importantly, in 1539 and 1540 he argued fervently for toleration of the Jews against the Lutheran clergy in Braunschweig. Rhegius' apologetic writings and his contacts with rabbis and Jewish communities reveal a more consistent and tolerant attitude toward Judaism than either Oberman or Friedman was able to find.

Rhegius, who was born in Langenargen on the Bodensee, was trained as a humanist as well as a theologian. He studied the liberal arts, philosophy and theology first at the University of Freiburg (1508–1512) and then at Ingolstadt (1512–1518). His most influential teacher was Johannes Eck, who became Dean of the Liberal Arts Faculty in Freiburg during Rhegius' tenure and whom Rhegius followed to Ingolstadt in 1512.[13] From Eck, who had ties to the humanist

---

9. Jerome Friedman: "Sebastian Münster, the Jewish Mission, and Protestant Antisemitism," *Archiv für Reformationsgeschichte* 70 (1979): 238–259.

10. Ibid., 252.

11. Ibid., 255–256.

12. This South German period of Rhegius' life, including his conversion to Lutheranism, has been studied in detail by Liebmann. The old standard biography is by Gerhard Uhlhorn: *Urbanus Rhegius: Leben und ausgewählte Schriften* (Elberfeld, 1861). The most recent biographical overview appears in *Contemporaries of Erasmus*, 3 (Toronto, 1987): 151–153.

13. Joseph Schlecht: "Dr. Johann Ecks Anfänge," *Historisches Jahrbuch* 36 (1915):

circle in Alsace, Rhegius imbibed a mixture of scholastic theology and humanist concern for classical texts and practical application. His humanist studies, however, seem to have taken precedence over theology during these university years. In Freiburg, Rhegius heard the lectures of the humanist, Rhagius Aesti-campianus (Johannes Rack from Sommerfeld, d. 1520), whose words still rang in his ears seven years later.[14] In Ingolstadt, where he received the Master of Arts degree in 1516, Rhegius lectured on the letters of the Italian humanist, Franciscus Philelphus (d. 1481), and on the commentary on Aristotle's *Politics* by the French reform-minded humanist, Jacques Lefèvre d'Etaples. Like many humanists, Rhegius belonged to a literary circle, this one gathered around the historian Johannes Aventinus (d. 1534). Moreover, in 1517 during a stopover in Ingolstadt, Emperor Maximilian I bestowed on Rhegius the title of poet laureate.[15] While he lived with Johannes Fabri in Constance (1518-1520), Rhegius conducted an extensive correspondence with South German and Swiss humanists.[16]

During his humanist studies, in addition to Greek, Rhegius began to learn Hebrew, a language that he had mastered at least by 1530 but probably much earlier. We have no precise information about how he learned Hebrew, but several opportunities were available to him while he studied in South Germany. For example, he could have been exposed to the language in Freiburg, where Eck studied Hebrew with the Carthusian prior Gregor Reisch (d. 1525),[17] or in Ingolstadt, where Reuchlin lectured on the grammar of Kimchi and named Eck

6, 8-10; Walter Moore (ed.): *In Primum librum sententiarum annotatiunculae D. Iohanne Eckio Praelectore* (Leiden, 1976), 10-12.

14. Liebmann, 84. On Aesticampianus, see the article by Heinrich Grimm in *Neue Deutsche Biographie* 1 (Berlin, 1953): 92-93.

15. Liebmann, 88-102. In a letter dated May 1, 1520, the *sodalitas* in Schlettstadt included Rhegius in a list of *duces meliorum studiorum* along with Erasmus, Capito, Zasius, Luther, Melanchthon, Mosellanus, and Eobanus Hessus. *Correspondance de Martin Bucer*, ed. Jean Rott (Leiden, 1979) 1, no. 13. 29-32 (pp. 111-112). See also Ortwin Rudloff: *Bonae litterae et Lutherus: Texte und Untersuchungen zu den Anfängen der Theologie des Bremer Reformators Jakob Propst* (Bremen, 1985), 131, n. 7.

16. Liebmann, 112-118. See also Conradin Bonorand: *Personenkommentar III zum Vadianischen Briefwechsel* (St. Gallen, 1985), 173-175. Rhegius is among the Swiss and South German humanists praised by Friedrich Nausea in 1519 in the dedication accompanying his poems (*ibid.,* 59, 173). Erasmus sent greetings to Rhegius through Eck just before Rhegius left for Constance in 1518 (May 15, 1518): "Urbanus Rhegius I know as a learned man from the letter he himself wrote me and suppose him a civilized one from the service he did me: pray, give him my warmest greetings." *Correspondence of Erasmus* 6 (Toronto, 1982): 36. 317-319.

17. On Reisch, see *Correspondence of Erasmus* 3 (Toronto , 1976): 37.

as one of his students.[18] Rhegius might have learned Hebrew from Matthäus Adrianus, who taught the language in Heidelberg from 1513 to 1516 and had Johannes Oecolampadius and Wolfgang Capito as his students.[19] Or possibly Rhegius studied with Capito himself, his former fellow student in Freiburg, while Capito was the cathedral preacher in Basel from 1515 to 1519.[20]

During the first stage of his career as a Protestant preacher in Augsburg (1524–1530), there is little direct evidence that the study and use of Hebrew occupied much of Rhegius' attention. One indication that he did use the language is the reputation of his wife, Anna Weissbrücker (an Augsburg woman whom he married in 1525), who was said to be learned in the Old Testament and the Hebrew language.[21] A significant meeting with a Jewish rabbi during the Diet of Augsburg indicates that Rhegius had already studied rabbinic exegesis, direct evidence for which would appear frequently after 1530. During the Diet of 1530, Rhegius, together with Melanchthon and Johannes Brenz, met with Rabbi Isaac Levi from Prague, with whom they debated for six hours the exegesis of Isaiah 53 and Daniel 7. According to his later account of the debate,[22] Rabbi Isaac argued that Isaiah 53 referred not to the Messiah but to the Jews who were dispersed throughout the world among the Gentiles.[23] Rhe-

18. Beate Stierle: *Capito als Humanist* (Gütersloh, 1974), 30; Ludwig Geiger: *Das Studium der Hebräischen Sprache in Deutschland vom Ende des XV. bis zur Mitte des XVI. Jahrhunderts* (Breslau, 1870), 30. Reuchlin, however, did not live in Ingolstadt until late 1519 when Rhegius had left the city; see Ludwig Geiger: *Johann Reuchlin: sein Leben und seine Werke* (Leipzig, 1871), 461–462.

19. Geiger, *Das Studium,* 41–48, 109. See James Kittelson: *Wolfgang Capito: From Humanist to Reformer* (Leiden, 1975), 21–22; see also Stierle, *Capito,* 34–35. On Adrianus, see *Correspondence of Erasmus* 4 (Toronto, 1977): 301.40 (n); 5 (Toronto, 1979): 191.11 (n).

20. It appears, however, that Rhegius arrived in Basel in early July, 1520, about two months after Capito had left Basel for Mainz. See Liebmann, 106, and Stierle, *Capito,* 192.

21. Both Rhegius and Melanchthon allegedly praised Anna's knowledge of the Old Testament and she appeared in a later list of learned women skilled in Hebrew. See *De Foeminis ex Hebraea gente Eruditis Dissertatio Prima, exposita a Joh. Conrado Zeltner* (Altdorf Noricorum: Typis Jodoci Wilhelmi Kohlesii, 1708), 5. See also *Hebraeische Bibliographie: Blätter für neuere und ältere Literatur des Judenthums* 20 (Berlin, 1880): 66.

22. The account appears in Rhegius' *Dialogus von der schönen Predigt die Christus Luc. 24. von Jerusalem bis gen Emaus den zweien Jüngern am Ostertag aus Mose und allen Propheten gethan hat* (2nd ed. Wittenberg: Josef Klug, 1539), 78ᵛ, 181ᵛ; see also Liebmann Bibliography, H 72 and D 115.

23. Rhegius, *Dialogus,* 181ᵛ: "Der Koheleth von Prag / wolt Magistro Philippo Melanthoni / Joanni Brentio / und mir zu Augspurg auff dem Reichstag das Capitel [Isaiah 53]

XI

gius countered that Jewish exegetes themselves had interpreted the chapter as a reference to the Messiah; as examples he listed the Targum of Jonathan and the "alten Hebreer."[24] Rhegius also criticized Rabbi Isaac for citing an interpretation of Daniel 7 from the *Nizzahon*, which in its best-known form was an anthology of Jewish anti-Christian apologetic compiled by Lipmann Mühlhausen at the beginning of the fifteenth century.[25] Although it is not certain that Rhegius had read the *Nizzahon* prior to the encounter with Rabbi Isaac, he was already acquainted with various forms of rabbinic literature.[26]

At the Diet of Augsburg Rhegius was invited by Duke Ernest of Lüneburg to accompany him back to Celle in order to solidify the evangelical reform which Ernest had initiated in his duchy. In 1530 Rhegius and his family moved to Celle, and Rhegius began a wide-ranging reforming career in northern Germany that lasted until his death in 1541. In letters Rhegius advised pastors, princes, and city councils on the tactics and theology of reform; he also represented Lüneburg at political diets, and he wrote church orders for the cities of Lüneburg and Hannover, where he spent months helping with the Reformation. From 1530 on, however, his facility in Hebrew and his contact with rabbis and Jewish writings became an important dimension of Rhegius' work in north-

---

auslegen von den jtzigen Jüden / die jnn aller welt unter den Heiden zerstrewet / veracht und geplagt sind / Er redet aber solch ungereimt / ungegründ / erlogen ding / das er darob für uns allen offentlich zu schanden ward."

24. *Ibid.,* 182ʳ.

25. *Ibid.,* 78ᵛ: "Er brachte her für ein ungegründte / tölpische rechnung / aus seinem Nezachon / das war ein lauter fabel / Denn die Jüden sind der Historien unerfaren / und lauter kinder / darumb bestund er ubel / Und fande bey jm / der doch für einen grossen Rabbi gerechnet wird / weder grund noch warheit." On the *Nizzahon* see W. Horbury: "The Basle Nizzahon," *Journal of Theological Studies* 34 (1983): 497–514; see also David Berger: *The Jewish-Christian Debate in the High Middle Ages* (Philadelphia, 1979), 32–37, 373–382. On Lipmann Mühlhausen, see *Encyclopaedia Judaica* 12 (Jerusalem, 1971), 491–502.

26. Rhegius must have read the *Nizzahon* in manuscript since the first printed edition of Lipmann's version appeared in Nürnberg in 1644. An earlier compilation, first edited as *Nizzahon Vetus* by Joh. Christoph Wagenseil, appeared in *Telea Ignea Satanae. Hoc est: Arcani, & horribiles Judaeorum adversus Christum Deum, & Christianam Religionem Libri ANEKDOTOI* (Altdorf: Schönnerstadt, 1681) and has been re-edited and translated by Berger (see above, n.25). According to Horbury ("Basle Nizzahon," 513), the Basel manuscript, which dates from the early sixteenth century and contains a fuller version of the *Nizzahon Vetus* than a manuscript in Rome, passed through the hands of "great Hebraists" in the sixteenth and seventeenth centuries. One of these Hebraists was Sebastian Münster (Berger, 377). Perhaps Rhegius saw this manuscript during his stay in Basel in 1520; he was certainly one of the Protestant Hebraists who made use of Münster's contributions to Jewish studies (see Friedman, "Sebastian Münster," 241).

194

ern Germany. He found time to compose apologetical and exegetical works, to debate with rabbis in Hannover and Braunschweig, to lobby for the teaching of Hebrew, and, finally, to intercede on behalf of the Jews in Braunschweig. This dimension of Rhegius' work is a significant and hitherto unrecognized contribution to the relationship between the Reformation and Judaism. His contacts with the Jewish community in Braunschweig are especially noteworthy and will occupy most of our attention.

To begin with his literary production: the *Nizzahon*, regardless of when he first read it, formed in all probability the model for one of Rhegius' most popular and novel works: the *Dialogus von der schönen Predigt*.[27] In the *Dialogus*, Rhegius explains to his wife Anna how a multitude of passages from the Old Testament pointed to the identity of Jesus as the Messiah. Rhegius claims to make explicit what Jesus himself allegedly did on the first Easter, when, "beginning with Moses and all the prophets," he explained to the disciples on the road to Emmaus "in all the scriptures the things concerning himself" (Luke 24:27). Although the *Dialogus* is constructed as a dialogue with his wife that contains that first Easter exegesis, in fact the *Dialogus* is a work of Christian apologetic that is strikingly similar to the *Nizzahon*. While the *Nizzahon* argues against the Messianic interpretation of Old Testament passages and treats some New Testament passages as well, the *Dialogus* argues for the Messianic interpretation of even more Old Testament passages. In other words, the *Dialogus* is a massive answer to Jewish exegetical apologetic in general and probably to the *Nizzahon* in particular. What other reason could there be for such an enormous collection of material that could serve only as a reference? Rhegius says that he published this material, which he had discussed at home with Anna, for the sake of those who had been requesting it for five years.[28] In all likelihood, Rhegius had been preparing a response to the *Nizzahon* at least since he encountered Rabbi Isaac in 1530, and he may well have discussed various texts

---

27. See above, n.22. The manuscript, dated March 18, 1536, is in the Herzog August Bibliothek in Wolfenbüttel: Cod. Guelf. Helmst.610. The first printed edition of almost 500 pages was issued in 1537 by Joseph Klug in Wittenberg, who also published a second revised edition in 1539. Reprinted many times thereafter, the *Dialogus* also appeared in Latin, Low German, Dutch, Danish, English and Czech translations; see Liebmann Bibliography, D 115 and D 115.1.

28. *Dialogus* (1539), *iii^r: "Derhalben scheme ich mich nicht / sondern frewe mich von solcher reichen gnade Gottes jnn Christo / zu reden mit meiner lieben Hausfrawen / Und wie ichs mit jr zu haus geredt / hab ichs auch öffentlich im druck ausgehen lassen / umb der willen / die solchs nu wol fünff jar von mir begert haben." At least since 1532, therefore, five years prior to the first edition of 1537, others had expressed interest in Rhegius' work.

XI

with Anna over the years. But the interested audience probably consisted not of Apollonia, the sister of Duke Ernest to whom the *Dialogus* is dedicated, nor of other members of the ducal household, but of pastors and theologians who knew about Rhegius' special interest in refuting Jewish exegesis of the Old Testament.[29]

The *Dialogus* is also the source of our information about the contact which Rhegius had with Jewish communities and rabbis in Hannover and Braunschweig. According to Anna's report, a rabbi in Hannover told Rhegius that he would not ask forgiveness from the Messiah even if he should appear.[30] This encounter with the rabbi probably took place in the Fall of 1535, while Rhegius was spending a month in the city in support of the Protestant movement.[31] It is unclear on whose initiative Rhegius visited the synagogue in Hannover or what the purpose of his visit was. At most a very small number of Jews lived in the city in the 1530's,[32] and Anna's report in the *Dialogus* seems to be the only basis for assuming that a synagogue existed in Hannover at that time.[33] Indeed, this report may stand behind the doubtful but repeated assertion that Rhegius conducted a Christian mission to the Jews in Hannover.[34] The most that one can

---

29. Friedman is probably correct in assuming that "missionary tracts" like Münster's *Matthew* were directed more at Christians than at Jews; the *Dialogus* is certainly directed to Christians as well as perhaps to Jewish scholars, but it gives no evidence that Rhegius fears a Judaization of Protestantism or is aiming at a "growing number of Protestants concerned with 'Jewish policy'" (Friedman, "Sebastian Münster," 252).

30. *Dialogus* (1539), 182ᵛ: "Ich habe aber kein gröbere blindheit nie jnn den Jüden gesehen / als da der Rabbi zu Hannopher jnn der Synagoge zu euch sprach / Wenn schon der Messiah keme / So wolte er dennoch bey jm kein vergebunge der sünde noch frömkeit suchen. O der greulichen blindheit."

31. See Waldemar Bahrdt: *Geschichte der Reformation in der Stadt Hannover* (Hannover, 1891), 95-96. Rhegius was in Hannover a second time in November, 1537; but since Anna's report appears in the manuscript of the *Dialogus* (Helmst. 610, 196ᵛ), which is dated 1536, the encounter must have taken place during Rhegius' first visit to the city in 1535.

32. See *Germania Judaica* 3.I (Tübingen, 1987): 515-517; *Encyclopaedia Judaica* 7 (Jerusalem, 1971): 1277-1278.

33. See Peter Aufgebauer: "Judenpolitik im Zeitalter der Reformation, vornehmlich in Norddeutschland," *Die Diözese Hildesheim in Vergangenheit und Gegenwart* 51 (1983): 40.

34. Aufgebauer (ibid.) dates this mission in 1533, citing Meir Wiener: "Geschichte der Juden in der Residenzstadt Hannover," *Monatsschrift für Geschichte und Wissenschaft des Judenthums* 10 (1861): 132. Wiener's information is based on a source which he identified as "Redecker in seinen historischen Collectaneen von der königlichen und churfürstlichen Residenzstadt Hannover p. 441." This source is an unpublished chronicle in the Stadtarchiv Hannover (B 82879). Rotraud Ries, to whom I owe this information (see above, n. 1), reports that the passage on p. 441, to which Wiener refers, reads as follows:

196

say for certain is that Rhegius conducted a disputation with a rabbi in Hannover in 1535 much as he and his colleagues had done in Augsburg in 1530. We know much more, however, about his contacts with the Jews in Braunschweig. In 1535 Rhegius wrote a letter in Hebrew to the Jewish community in that city. The original Hebrew letter is not extant, but a Latin version of the letter was published in 1591 in Hamburg.[35] The letter contains an invitation to dialogue as well as a challenge to be saved by converting to Christianity. Although by his own admission he is not personally acquainted with the Jewish community in Braunschweig, Rhegius seeks to convince them that Jesus was indeed the expected Messiah. He proceeds on the assumption that the faith of Jews and Christians has the same basis *(fundamentum)*, namely, Moses and the prophets. If that is true, asks Rhegius, why have we disagreed with each other for so many centuries?[36] Rhegius requests the Jewish community to explain to him what they find lacking in the Christian faith and what Messiah they still expect, since Jesus the Nazarene fulfilled such clear prophecies as Genesis 49 and Daniel 7. Rhegius dissuades them, however, from citing the *Nizzahon* as their authority. He read that work long ago, says Rhegius directly, and it contains nothing but impious fables. Its author, foolish and ignorant of Scripture

---

"Urbanus Rhegius ging fleissig in die Juden Schule (welche in der Juden-Straße war) und suchte die Bekehrung der Ungläubigen, hatte aber kein Gehör, wie denn einst in derselben Schule der Rabbi zu ihm sagte: Wenn schon der Messias käme, so wolle er dennoch bey ihm keine Vergebung der Sünden noch Gerechtigkeit suchen." If Redecker was correct in reporting a second visit of Rhegius to the synagogue in Hannover, it must have occurred during November, 1537, when Rhegius was again in the city (Bahrdt, *Geschichte,* 127–130). Without corroborative evidence for a second visit, however, I suspect that Redecker's interpretation of Rhegius' activity in Hannover as proselytization, as repeated by Wiener and Aufgebauer, is based mainly on Rhegius' own *Dialogus.* In her dissertation (see n. 1, above) Ries argues that Redecker's location of a synagogue in the Judenstrasse is probably false; if existed at all, it stood in the Neustadt where the majority of Jews lived. The *Encyclopaedia Judaica* (see above, n.32) states even more discrepantly: "... in 1553 *[sic]* the Jews were compelled to listen to the court preacher Urbanus Rhegius in the synagogue."

35. *Epistola D. Urbani Rhegii ad totam Iudeorum Synagogam Brunsvici habitantem, ex Ebrae in sermonem latinum conversa* (Hamburg: Jacobus Wolff, 1591); see also Liebmann Bibliography D 104. The Latin version existed prior to 1562 when it was included in the collected Latin works of Rhegius: *Opera Urbani Regii latine edita* (Nürnberg: Montanus & Neuberus, 1562) 3:XCII^r–XCIII^r. In his note to the reader in the 1591 edition, the printer Wolff says he would have published the Hebrew original if he had access to it; he requests any reader who has a copy of the letter in Hebrew to notify him without delay: *Epistola* (1591), A 1^v.

36. *Opera* 3:XCII^r: "Cum igitur fides nostra idem habeat verbum, idem fundamentum, cui innititur, cur tot saeculis sumus discordes?"

and history, has deceived you more than Rabbi Schlomoh, even though the latter also seduces you just as the Roman pope seduced us.[37]

In spite of his willingness to hear their arguments, Rhegius hardly regards the Jews in Braunschweig as entitled to the same consideration before God as Christians claim. Even though their faith may have the same basis in the Old Testament, Rhegius warns them that they cannot be saved by the Mosaic law.[38] Rhegius nevertheless reveals that he is willing to hear their side. He even attempts to make the concept of a crucified Messiah less offensive by arguing that the Targum of Jonathan and the early Hebrews *(prisci Hebraei)* applied the humiliation of the servant described in Isaiah 53 to the Messiah and foretold his exaltation as well.[39] As a believer in Jesus as the Messiah, Rhegius obviously feels that he is in a superior position and his words sometimes smack of condescension. Nevertheless, when compared with the harsh statements of the later Luther, Rhegius' moderation and willingness to debate are notable. So it must have appeared already in 1710 to the Braunschweig church historian Philipp Julius Rehtmeyer, when he described Rhegius' appeal as *sehr bescheidentlich.*[40]

During the next five years Rhegius maintained contact with the Jews in Braunschweig even though his letter of 1535 did not have the effect for which he had hoped. We do not know if the Jewish community answered his letter, but we do know that Rhegius visited the Jewish community in Braunschweig in 1538. In the spring of that year, despite the strong opposition of Duke Henry of Braunschweig-Wolfenbüttel, the Smalcald League met in the city and Rhegius attended the Diet as the theological advisor of Duke Ernest.[41] In the 1539 edition of the *Dialogus,* Rhegius reveals the fact that he had visited the syn-

---

37. *Opera* 3:XCII^v. The identity of Rabbi Schlomoh is uncertain. It seems unlikely that he is the same person as Rabbi Samuel in Braunschweig, on whose behalf Rhegius would intercede in 1540 (see below, p. 199).

38. *Opera* 3:XCIII^r.

39. *Opera* 3:XCII^v–XCIII^r. Rhegius continues: "Cum igitur post humiliationem Messiae audiatis eius glorificationem, quaeso cur vos tantopere scandalizat voluntaria crux Messiae, quam non necessitate, sed voluntate pertulit, ut ipse innocens nostras culpas hac sua passione expiaret, & verum sacrificium pro peccatis nostris offerret ...?"

40. Philipp Julius Rehtmeyer: *Der berühmten Stadt Braunschweig Kirchen-Historie* (Braunschweig: J. G. Zilliger, 1707–1720), III:92–93: "Damit sie sich aber zum Christenthum bekehren möchten / so schrieb D. Urbanus Rhegius von Cölln *[sic]* aus An. 1535 an die gantze Jüdische Synagoge hin in Braunschweig einen Hebräischen Brieff / und zeigte ihnen sehr bescheidentlich, dass der Messias müsse gekommen seyn."

41. For a description of the Diet, see Werner Spiess: *Geschichte der Stadt Braunschweig im Nachmittelalter* (Braunschweig, 1966) 1:69–72. Documents pertaining to Rhegius' visit in 1538 are found in StABS B IV 11:10.

agogue in Braunschweig during the previous year. After Anna's report of the Hannover rabbi's rejection of the Messiah, Rhegius adds that he had recently heard the same scandalous error from the Jews in Braunschweig in their synagogue; and he cites Paul's judgment on the Jews (I Thess. 2:16) that the wrath of God has come upon them at last.[42] From Rhegius' comment we can conclude that, to his great disappointment, the Jewish community in Braunschweig had rejected both his letter and the appeal that he brought in person.

In spite of this rejection, Rhegius interceded for the Jews in Braunschweig in two cases during 1539 and 1540. The first case involves a rabbi named Samuel or Schmuel, who taught Hebrew in the city. According to a letter which Rhegius sent to the mayor and council of Braunschweig on September 27, 1540, more than a year earlier he had requested the council to allow Rabbi Samuel to live outside the city "on the hill" and teach within the city.[43] Now, a year later, Rhegius asked the council to permit Rabbi Samuel to move into town because it was a hardship to commute during the winter, and because Samuel was afraid of Duke Henry, to whom "some clergy" had complained about him.[44] Since the complaint was made to Duke Henry, who was Catholic, and since Samuel lived "on the hill" ("auff dem Berg"), the clergy in question were probably Catholic clergy at the Stift of St. Cyriacus. It was located on a hill just south of the city and in 1540 still existed as a Catholic insitution under the jurisdiction of Duke Henry.[45]

In support of his request, Rhegius tries to anticipate and defuse two possible objections from the council. First, he personally recommends the rabbi, whom he apparently had met and whose letter of recommendation from "the most

---

42. *Dialogus* (1539), 182ᵛ: "Eben diesen schendlichen jrthumb höret ich auch neulich von den Jüden zu Braunschwick jnn jrer Synagoga / Paulus redet .j. Thessalon. am 2. cap. ein erschrecklich wort von Jüden / Nemlich / das der zorn schon endlich uber sie komen sey." Neither the manuscript of the *Dialogus* nor the first printed edition of 1537 contains this passage.

43. Original manuscript: StABS B IV 10 a:5 no. 10. The letter was published by Meir Wiener: "Die Kenntniss der hebräischen Sprache verschafft im 16. Jahrhundert mehreren Juden die Erlaubniss, sich in Niedersachsen niederlassen zu dürfen," *Zeitschrift des historischen Vereins für Niedersachsen* (1861): 371-372.

44. StABS B IV 10 a:5 no. 10, 1ʳ (Wiener, "Die Kenntniss," 371).

45. At the end of August, 1540, the citizens of Braunschweig were still protesting against the "blasphemy" being perpetrated "in de borch [i.e., the Domstift St. Blasii in the old town] und up den berge [i.e., the Stift St. Cyriaci]." See, e.g., the Ratsprotokollbücher for 1540: StABS B I 5 1,1, 191ʳ. See also Gustav Hassebrauk: "Heinrich der Jüngere und die Stadt Braunschweig 1514-1568," *Jahrbuch des Geschichtsvereins für das Herzogtum Braunschweig* 5 (1906): 24-26.

prominent people" in Strasbourg he had read.[46] Rhegius assures the council that Samuel was not a difficult man like some Jews he knew, but "a learned, quiet Jew who attends to his books and faithfully teaches the holy language to others."[47] Because he is dedicated to that task, adds Rhegius, Samuel has to study so much that he does not have time to practice usury.[48] These remarks divulge that Rhegius shared some of his contemporaries' prejudice against the Jews and was not above using it in order to gain the sympathy of council members. This prejudice, however, did not lead him to recommend action against either the worship or the instruction of the Jewish community.

Second, Rhegius supports Rabbi Samuel's request by arguing that the council should allow Jews to live in the city and to receive instruction from teachers like Samuel. They should be tolerated because of the hope that some will be converted to Christianity; such toleration is a work of Christian love that would draw them toward the truth.[49] Furthermore, implies Rhegius, if the Jews learned Hebrew and could read the Old Testament, Christian teachers could more easily convince them that Jesus was the Messiah promised in their own scriptures.[50] As was the case just five years earlier, Rhegius' main interest was the conversion of the Jews; and, despite the rejection he suffered in Braunschweig just two years earlier, he still had hope for their conversion if they were moved by Christian example and patience. Part of this patience, however, was toleration by the council of both the community and of teachers like Samuel. In order to lend more force to his plea on behalf of Samuel, Rhegius sent a similar letter to Mayor Cord von Damm,[51] with whom he was in all likelihood

---

46. StABS B IV 10 a:5 no. 10, 1ᵛ (Wiener, "Die Kenntniss," 372).
47. StABS B IV 10 a:5 no. 10, 1ʳ (Wiener, "Die Kenntniss," 371).
48. StABS B IV 10 a:5 no. 10, 1ᵛ (Wiener, "Die Kenntniss," 372).
49. StABS B IV 10 a:5 no. 10, 1ᵛ (Wiener, "Die Kenntniss," 371): "Wenn wir nü ain mitliden mit Inen haben, der hofnung, das noch under Inen seyen, die Gott In sein gnad werde uffnemen, so thun wir ain loblich werck christlicher liebe und muss sie dennocht der Christen exempel und güllt bewegen, das sie dester leichter mit der Zit vom Irthumb Zur Warheit mögen gebracht werden, So ist der Christenheit grosser nutz, das etlich under Inen die heilige sprach lernen, welchs dann seer wol kan geschehen, so E. E. W. disem Juden die Wonung In der Statt vergonnt und Zulasst, ..."
50. These letters make clear that Rabbi Samuel was teaching Hebrew to the Jews in Braunschweig and not to the pastors or Christian laypeople of the city. This false assumption was first made by Wiener ("Die Kenntniss," 369–370), and has been repeated by Aufgebauer ("Judenpolitik," 38) and by Hans-Heinrich Ebeling: Die Juden in Braunschweig (Braunschweig, 1987), 96.
51. September 27, 1540: StABS B IV 10 a:5, no. 9 (Wiener, "Die Kennntiss," 372–373). Cord was a younger brother of the Braunschweig doctor and humanist poet, Bertram von

acquainted, and he also had Duke Ernest of Lüneburg write a letter of recommendation to the Braunschweig council.[52]

We do not know whether Rhegius' letters on behalf of Rabbi Samuel achieved their purpose. But another letter written just prior to them does reveal in more detail Rhegius' attitude toward the Jews. This letter, dated September 22, 1540, and addressed to superintendent Martin Görlitz and the other pastors in Braunschweig, is found in the Staatsarchiv Wolfenbüttel and until now has escaped the notice of Rhegius' biographers and Reformation historians.[53] The occasion for this letter is not a plea for Rabbi Samuel. Instead, Rhegius is concerned about the possible expulsion of the Jews from Braunschweig because of charges that they have blasphemed both Christ and Christian people.[54] In spite of these charges (which he does not discuss), Rhegius makes a strong theological case for toleration of the Jews and asks the clergy to intercede with the magistrates on their behalf. The case for toleration elaborates a point which Rhegius will make several days later in his letter to the Braunschweig council on behalf of Rabbi Samuel. Because Rhegius makes his case for the Jews so thoroughly and urgently and because the letter also reveals the attitude of Braunschweig's Lutheran clergy toward the Jews, this letter deserves closer study.

Not all of Rhegius' remarks about the Jews are positive. He claims that the Jews, "on account of certain misdeeds," have in some places been sent into perpetual exile. And in Hesse, he observes, "they are oppressed with a very hard lot which their stiff neck deserves."[55] Here Rhegius is referring to the new *Judenordnung*, decreed only one year earlier by Landgraf Philip of Hesse, that severely restricted Jewish life in that territory. The Strasbourg theologian, Mar-

---

Damm, who supported the Protestant movement and in 1539 published a Latin translation in verse of Paul's letter to the Romans. He dedicated this work to Duke Ernest of Lüneburg, and Rhegius praised it in a letter to Bertram. See Richard v. Damm: "Bertram v. Damm, ein braunschweigischer Zeit- und Streitgenosse Luthers," *Zeitschrift der Gesellschaft für niedersächsische Kirchengeschichte* 18 (1913): 160–205, esp. 176–177, 191–193.

52. September 29, 1540: StABS B IV 10a:5 no. 8 (Wiener, "Die Kenntniss," 373). Wiener may have received his mistaken impression that Samuel was teaching Hebrew to the pastors in Braunschweig (see above, n. 50) from a passage in the letter of Duke Ernest, which advises the council that their pastors and preachers might wish to study Hebrew with Rabbi Samuel.

53. NStAWf 2 Alt 13155. It is printed for the first time in the Appendix below. Neither Wiener ("Die Kenntniss") nor Ebeling *(Die Juden in Braunschweig)* mentions this letter, but in her dissertation (see n. 1, above) Ries does make use of the letter.

54. NStAWf 2 Alt 13155, 2^r. Appendix, lines 8–11.

55. Ibid. Appendix, lines 11–14.

XI

tin Bucer, and his colleagues in Hesse had helped to prepare the way for this decree.[56] While the pastors in Hesse favored expulsion, Bucer argued for punishment of the Jews by having severe restrictions imposed on their life and work. In his *Commentary on Romans* Bucer had supported a Christian mission to the Jews; but in his *Judenratschlag* of 1538 Bucer stressed the right of magistrates to impose God's punishment on the Jews here and now.[57] Bucer's proposal to allow Jews access only to the lowliest jobs was not incorporated into the *Judenordnung* of 1539; the Landgraf was more tolerant than Bucer and the Hessian clergy.[58] Nevertheless, tight restrictions were placed on their business transactions, especially the charging of interest. The Jews were also forbidden to construct new synagogues or to debate religion with anyone but the clergy, and they were required to attend special sermons.[59]

Within a year of its publication, Rhegius has become acquainted with the Hessian *Judenordnung* and thinks that it is not unfair. He is not surprised that some godly people burn with such hatred "against these traitors" that they think [the Jews] should not be tolerated in "our commonwealths and territories."[60] In spite of this opinion, however, Rhegius proceeds to argue in his letter for the toleration of the Jews in Braunschweig. He has apparently reckoned with resistance from the clergy, since he assures them that nothing but a pious intention lies behind his arguments. Then he appeals to "certain reasons and Scripture passages" in order to exculpate those magistrates who have decided to tolerate the Jews.[61]

The long discussion of Scripture passages that follows is explained by the fact that Rhegius was addressing theologians from whom he expected resistance to his case for toleration. The structure for the body of his letter is provided by three texts, carefully selected to convey maximum authority from three different parts of Scripture: one text from the Old Testament, one from the words of Jesus, and one from the apostle Paul. First, Rhegius cites Hosea

---

56. The *Judenordnung* and related documents are printed in *Martin Bucers Deutsche Schriften* 7 (Gütersloh, 1964): 320–394.

57. For a description and evaluation of Bucer's attitudes toward the Jews, see Ernst-Wilhelm Kohls: "Die Judenfrage in Hessen während der Reformationszeit," *Jahrbuch der Hessischen Kirchengeschichtlichen Vereinigung* 21 (1970): 87–100, esp. 94.

58. Ibid., 99. Cf. Bucer's *Ratschlag* (*Deutsche Schriften* 7:116.5–12) with the *Judenordnung* (*Deutsche Schriften* 7:391.25–31).

59. *Deutsche Schriften* 7:391–393. See Friedrich Battenberg: "Judenordnungen der frühen Neuzeit in Hessen," in *Neunhundert Jahre Geschichte der Juden in Hessen* (Wiesbaden, 1983): 83–121, esp. 90–92.

60. NStAWf 2 Alt 13155, 2^r. Appendix, lines 15–16.

61. Ibid. Appendix, lines 17–20.

202

3:4–5 as the promise that after many years of decline at least some of the Jews will be converted to Christ, the "true David," in the last days.[62] Rhegius believes that he is living in "these very last times" and that the Jews have already suffered the calamities that Hosea predicted. Hence it is time for Christians to recall the wayward Jews to the truth and salvation through "teaching, a blameless life, and acts of kindness."[63] To the charge that the Jews are "scoundrels, blasphemers, despisers, and enemies of Christ," Rhegius responds that regretably these terms can be applied to some of the Jews and that he himself detests their "stiff necks." Nevertheless, he does not want the Jews to be alienated from the gospel by hatred or persecution and thus to become embittered against Christianity.[64]

Second, from Luke 21:32 Rhegius cites the prediction of Jesus that the present generation would not pass away until all was fulfilled. That present generation was made up of the Jews, who consequently have to abide somewhere until the end of the world. There is no better place for the Jews to live than among Christians where there is hope for their conversion. Among the Turks they would have no such hope.[65]

Third, Rhegius cites as his most powerful authority the eleventh chapter of Romans, in which Paul says many things that command Christians to treat the Jews with clemency and not haughtily to reject them. First of all, Paul testifies that some of the Jews are among the elect and will be saved by the grace of Christ.[66] Second, the metaphor of the wild olive branch (the Gentiles) grafted onto the olive tree (the Jews) shows that Christians cannot boast of their faith. In spite of their rejection of the gospel, God will have regard for the Jews again and will graft some of them anew, also through grace, onto their own olive tree. Therefore, Christians cannot treat as unsavable those Jews to whom divine promises have given the hope of salvation.[67] Finally, though Paul says that the Jews are to be regarded as enemies for the sake of the gospel which they reject, they are friends on account of election and the patriarchs. "For Christ is from their fathers according to the flesh and many of them are elect." Thus, they will be converted and we "from the Gentiles" ought to mourn their lot and in every way we can call forth the Jews to repentance.[68]

---

62. Ibid. Appendix, lines 24–32.
63. Ibid., 2ᵛ. Appendix, lines 47–50.
64. Ibid. Appendix, lines 59–65.
65. Ibid. Appendix, lines 66–70.
66. Ibid. Appendix, lines 71–75.
67. Ibid., 2ᵛ–3ʳ. Appendix, lines 75–93.
68. Ibid., 3ʳ. Appendix, lines 93–99.

XI

On the basis of these arguments, Rhegius beseeches the clergy in Braunschweig to abandon their hatred of the Jews and to work for their conversion
through "clemency, charity, mercy, and the other fruits of Christian teaching."
If the Jews would see these, they would be drawn more easily to the faith.[69]
Paul was willing to be made anathema in order for the Jews to be saved. "It is
necessary," urges Rhegius, "that we also be endowed with this same zeal toward
a blind people. Let them be our enemies insofar as they persecute the truth of
the gospel with blind zeal, but let us love them on account of their holy fathers
to whom the saving promises were made."[70] Paul commended the Jews earnestly and diligently to us and in this way taught that they ought to be tolerated. Rhegius then employs a brief historical argument: the early church tolerated the Jews and even "our elders" did likewise because Jews have lived in
Braunschweig for 300 years.[71] As for charges of usury and blasphemy, the
magistracy can easily control such matters; it is their job to punish blasphemers
and to forbid any unsound comments about Christianity even in private.[72]

   After making his case, Rhegius then asks the clergy to inspire in the magistrates hope for the conversion of the Jews so that no more harsh measures
would be inflicted upon them.[73] Was it, however, the magistrates who needed
this inspiration or was it not much more the clergy themselves? Rhegius' letter
does not make clear whether in Braunschweig members of the council were
incensed at the Jews and charging them with blasphemy or whether the clergy
and other citizens were making the charges.[74] Hans-Heinrich Ebeling has main-

---

69. Ibid. Appendix, lines 100–107.
70. Ibid. Appendix, lines 109–113.
71. Ibid. Appendix, lines 117–119.
72. Ibid. Appendix, lines 119–123.
73. Ibid. Appendix, lines 123–127. Restrictions had been placed upon the Jews in
Braunschweig in 1532: StABS B I 5 1,1, 273 f. This record is summarized by Rotraud
Ries: "Zum Zusammenhang von Reformation und Judenvertreibung: Das Beispiel
Braunschweig," in *Civitas Communitas, Studien zum Europäischen Städtewesen.* Festschrift
Heinz Stoob, ed. Helmut Jäger, Franz Petri, Heinz Quirin (Cologne and Vienna, 1984),
630–654, esp. 636. The restrictions aimed at reducing the number of Jews in the city, iso-
lating them from Christians, closing the synagogue and forbidding their festivals and ceremonies, curbing the practice of usury and trading money. The final restriction pertains
to the occasion for Rhegius' letter (Ries, 636): "... sollten 'alle Joden einen geborlicken
eidt doen, dat se seck der lesteringe jegen Cristum unsen verlosser und salichmacker
hemelicken und openbar gentzlicken willen enthalden.'" See also Ebeling, *Die Juden in
Braunschweig,* 103. Ries (636) cautions that Rehtmeyer's account of the council's action
(*Der berühmten Stadt Braunschweig Kirchen-Historie,* III:92) distorts the record.
74. The unclarity results from two considerations: 1) Whom did Rhegius intend to
designate with the word *dominationes* at the beginning of the letter (Appendix, line 8)?

204

tained that in 1540 an alliance of guild members and clergy were demanding that the council punish "Juden und Judengenossen."[75] Ebeling's assertion is based, as far as I can tell, on only one passage from the minutes of the council; but this passage does not unequivocally state that the preachers called for punishment of the Jews.[76] It is unlikely, however, that council members themselves had charged the Jews with blasphemy. The council had consistently refused to give in to demands that the Jews be driven from the city, although it had promised in 1532 to banish them "soon."[77]

Therefore, the most feasible scenario, into which the letter of Rhegius fits, looks as follows: some preachers were indeed charging the Jews with blasphemy and thus stirring up the citizenry and putting pressure on the council to banish the Jews. Rhegius heard about these charges (from Rabbi Samuel or another acquaintance in Braunschweig) during August, 1540. As a consequence, he wrote to Görlitz and to the clergy in order to persuade them, despite the charge of blasphemy, to be tolerant of the Jews in Braunschweig and not to demand their exile from the city. Although Ebeling's hypothesis of an "alliance" between the preachers and the guilds is not conclusively documented, Rhegius in fact heard correctly that some pastors had preached against the Jews; and with his theological arguments he was trying to persuade them to change their stance and to support the council in tolerating the Jews instead of fanning the flames of anti-Jewish feeling in the guilds.[78]

The most probable designation is the pastors themselves. 2) How accurate was the information that Rhegius had about anti-Jewish sentiment in Braunschweig and from whom did he get his information? I was unable to find a letter to Rhegius from Braunschweig that would answer the second question.

75. Ebeling, *Die Juden in Braunschweig*, 107.

76. StABS B I 5 1,1, 191ʳ. This passage from the Ratsprotokollbücher is part of the guilds' answer to the council on August 28, 1540, i.e., just one month before Rhegius' letter. Specifically, it is included in the answer of the "Wantsnider in Hagen" and asks the council to consider "de velen vormanunge der predicanten." After demanding that the blasphemy "in der borch und up den berge" (see above, n.45) finally be taken seriously and stopped, the passage continues as if listing a second demand: "Sunde und schande wokerie ebrekerie Jodden Joddengenoten tho strapfen und upsehent tho hebben und dar inne neyne latferdichkeit tho hebben." Cf. ibid., 196ʳ, where the same demand is paraphrased by a different hand but without mentioning the Jews.

77. Ebeling, *Die Juden in Braunschweig*, 103-104. Describing the same decision of the council in 1532, Ries ("Reformation und Judenvertreibung," 636) cites the council's feeling "dat men se gentzlicken uth der stadt nicht wol verwissen mag" (StABS B I 5 1,1, 273) and stresses the determination of the council to keep its agreements with the Jews.

78. In her dissertation (see above, n.1) Ries also believes that the ministers in

We do not know if Rhegius' plea to the clergy in Braunschweig was successful. If so, its only effect was to forestall the banishment of the Jews as long as
Görlitz remained in his post. After a new superintendent, Nikolaus Medler,[79]
assumed office in 1545, the ministerium publicly called for the banishment of
the Jews. One year later the council took this step, and about one hundred people finally left the city in December, 1546.[80] By this time Rhegius had been dead
for five years and the strident anti-Jewish tracts of Luther had appeared. While
Luther's writings probably influenced the action of Medler and the Braunschweig ministerium in 1545,[81] the letter of Rhegius obviously lay forgotten. It
had no lasting effect on the policy of the city of Braunschweig or later on the
policy of the Protestant territory of Wolfenbüttel.[82]

In contrast, Luther's tract *Von den Juden und ihren Lügen* (1543)[83] did continue to affect the clergy in Braunschweig. In 1578 the Protestant Duke Julius
issued an edict that permitted Jews to settle again in the territory of Wolfenbüttel. Immediately after the edict was posted on the door of St.Blasius, the city
council of Braunschweig posted its own protest against this violation of its
autonomy and asked the ministerium of the city for its opinion of the Duke's
action.[84] The ministerium opposed the decree of Duke Julius, and the author of

Braunschweig were preaching against the Jews. In addition to the letter of Rhegius, Ries
cites the same text upon which Ebeling relies (see above, n.76) and another document
from StABS (B IV 10 a:5, 4) that records a meeting between the preachers and the council
during the period from 1540 to 1546.

79. Medler (1502–1551), who had served as chaplain to Elisabeth of Brandenburg and
as a reformer in Naumburg (1536–45), was recommended for the post by Luther, Bugenhagen, and Melanchthon; he remained superintendent in Braunschweig until 1551; see
WABr 11: 180–181 (September 25, 1545); see also Johannes Beste: *Album der evangelischen Geistlichen der Stadt Braunschweig* (Braunschweig and Leipzig, 1900), 10, and the
article on Medler by O.Albrecht in *Realencyklopädie für protestantische Theologie und
Kirche* 12 (Leipzig, 1903): 492–497, esp. 496–497. Together with Hieronymus Weller,
Medler had been promoted to the doctorate by Luther in 1535; see *WABr* 12: 441.6–10;
7,222.22–223.29.

80. Rehtmeyer: *Der berühmten Stadt Braunschweig Kirchen-Historie,* Supplementa: 83.
See Ries, "Reformation und Judenvertreibung," 638–639; see also Ebeling, *Die Juden in
Braunschweig,* 105.

81. Ebeling, *Die Juden in Braunschweig,* 105–106. For Luther's most influential anti-
Jewish tract, see n.83. See also below, n.86.

82. In her dissertation (see above, n.1) Ries cites indirect evidence for the possibility
that Rhegius' letter had temporary influence on the council before 1546.

83. *WA* 53:417–552; *Luther's Works,* American Edition 47 (Philadelphia, 1971):
121–306.

84. Ebeling, *Die Juden in Braunschweig,* 114–118. The edict is printed in *Tractatio iuri-*

its response, superintendent Martin Chemnitz, invoked for his stance the authority of two of Luther's treatises, *Von den Juden und ihren Lügen* and *Schem Hamphoras*, which he described as "fine, useful, and well-grounded in Scripture." Chemnitz recommended that the council read the third section of *Von den Juden*, precisely that part in which Luther called for sharp measures against the Jews.[85] Chemnitz also reminded the council of the stand which the preachers had taken against the Jews some 30 years earlier. They had, said Chemnitz, admonished the council to use its office in order to warn and punish the Jews as it befitted zealous Christians to do. The clergy, he said, still thanked the council for having freed the church and the city from blasphemy and from the irritating company and injurious dealings of the stubborn Jews. Furthermore, emphasized Chemnitz, the council could not defend its conscience before God or its sister churches if it now reinstituted what it had abolished thirty years earlier on good grounds according to God's Word and the counsel of Luther.[86]

In Chemnitz' *Gutachten* there is no hint of the completely different position that Rhegius had taken in favor of tolerating the Jews. The only trace of Rhegius' influence is found in the publication of his 1535 letter to the synagogue in Braunschweig.[87] The printer, Jacobus Wolff, gave two reasons for publishing the letter: (1) because of its author, all of whose works were "outstanding and almost unique"; and (2) because of its usefulness to many people, "especially in those places where the blind Jewish people still practice their blasphemy."[88] Ironically, the letter appeared in 1591 – the same year in which Duke Heinrich Julius reversed the decree of his father and once again banished the Jews from Wolfenbüttel.[89] Rhegius' attempt to convert the Jews, as exemplified in his 1535

---

dica de Iure Recipiendi Iudaeos ... subiicit Joannes Henricus Jung auctor (Göttingen: Abram. Vandenhoeck, 1741), 87–94.

85. The original of Chemnitz' *Gutachten* is found in StABS B IV 11,20:16. Two copies are extant and both are contained in codices of the Herzog August Bibliothek, Wolfenbüttel: Cod. Guelf.14.6 Aug 4 and Cod. Guelf. 64.21 Extrav. 2. It has been published by Ries: "Reformation und Judenvertreibung," 649–654; Chemnitz' recommendation: 650. On Chemnitz, see the article by Theodor Mahlmann in *Theologische Realenzyklopädie* 7 (1981): 714–721.

86. Ries: "Reformation und Judenvertreibung," 651, 653. Ries (640–641) argues that these passages prove that Luther's anti-Jewish writings did influence the action of the Braunschweig council in 1546 – probably through the urging of Medler.

87. For this letter, see above, n.35.

88. *Epistola,* A 1ᵛ.

89. Ebeling, *Die Juden in Braunschweig,* 118–120; Jung, *Tractatio iuridica* (see above, n.84), 95–103.

XI

letter, still seemed useful in 1591, but his arguments for toleration remained unheeded.[90]

The attitudes of Urbanus Rhegius toward the Jews were certainly not those of a modern ecumenically-minded Christian theologian, but that is not the standard by which he should be judged. Rhegius' strong plea for toleration of the Jews, however, does stand out among his contemporaries. Granted, he did share some of the anti-Jewish prejudice of other sixteenth-century theologians, and his call for conversion of the Jews was not unique. Nevertheless, his fervent advocacy of Rabbi Samuel and his rebuke of the anti-Jewish clergy in Braunschweig stand in sharp contrast to Bucer's reluctant and punitive tolerance of the Jews and even moreso to the intolerance and rejection shown by the later Luther and by Chemnitz. Clearly, no fear of Judaization compelled Rhegius to abandon his support of Jewish studies or his desire for conversion of the Jews.

The roots of enlightened toleration need not be sought first in the "Third Reformation" of the Calvinist refugees. These roots are already visible on the ground of the Lutheran Reformation in the fervent plea of Rhegius to the pastors in Braunschweig. The German Reformation sometimes demonstrated a kinder face toward the Jews than the severe and dominant frown of Luther has allowed to appear. The assumption that one was living in the last days did not necessarily result in rejection of the Jews as it did for Luther. Instead, this eschatological awareness could also prompt persistent hope and inspire toleration as the rediscovered letter of Rhegius forcefully demonstrates. While Rhegius might be regarded as the exception that proves the rule, he also shows that, in their relationship to Judaism, Protestant reformers defy easy categorization.

90. Rhegius was also known as an advocate for toleration among his contemporaries. He was cited as such by Sebastian Castellio in his collection entitled *De haereticis an sint persequendi* ([Basel], 1554): 211. (I owe this information to Hans R. Guggisberg, Basel.)

ZUSAMMENFASSUNG

Die jüngere Forschung hat die Beziehung zwischen der deutschen Reformation und den Juden meistens negativ aufgefaßt. Man hat entweder den Blick hauptsächlich auf Luther gerichtet, oder man hat behauptet, die evangelischen Theologen hätten sich gegen die Juden und ihre Schriften gewendet, weil sie eine Judaisierung der Kirche und der Theologie gefürchtet hätten. Der Reformator Urbanus Rhegius (1489–1541) hat sich aber in seiner Einstellung von Luther, Bucer, und von anderen erheblich unterschieden. Dies zeigt sich am besten in seinen Beziehungen zu den Juden und zu den Geistlichen in Braunschweig. Er hat sich um ein Gespräch mit der jüdischen Gemeinde bemüht und sich auch für einen Rabbi eingesetzt, der Hebräisch in Braunschweig unterrichtete. Besonders bemerkenswert ist sein Einsatz für die Duldung der Juden in der Stadt im Jahre 1540. In einem Brief, der hier zum ersten Mal veröffentlicht wird, hat Rhegius den Superintendenten und die Geistlichen in Braunschweig darum gebeten, sich bei dem Rat dafür einzusetzen, daß die Juden nicht aus der Stadt vertrieben würden. Seine Begründungen zeigen, daß Rhegius, wie andere Theologen im 16. Jahrhundert auch, an einer Bekehrung der Juden interessiert war, daß er aber anderen Geistlichen und Laien gegenüber auch bereit war, die Juden als Mitbürger rechtlich zu tolerieren.

APPENDIX

Niedersächsisches Staatsarchiv Wolfenbüttel 2 Alt 13155
Urbanus Rhegius to Superintendent Martin Görlitz and the
Ministers of Braunschweig
Celle, September 22, 1540

The letter is known to be extant only in the original manuscript of Rhegius. It is reproduced here according to the guidelines in *Archiv für Reformationsgeschichte* 72 (1981): 299–315; 73 (1982): 319. Note: "ae" appears where Rhegius used e-caudata or himself wrote "ae"; otherwise, "e" has been retained. Capitalization has been normalized at the beginning of sentences; otherwise Rhegius' use of capital letters has been retained. Punctuation has been normalized except where noted. The Latin text is severely abbreviated. All abbreviations have been deciphered except for the names of Biblical books and "c." (for "caput" or "capitulum").

1. Folio 1ʳ contains a brief summary of the letter and designates it as number 10 of a collection of documents in a *Sammelband.* A note at the bottom of 1ʳ identifies the document as a "Geschenk des Auditoris A. Nolte November 1878." In all probability this letter

XI

[2ʳ]¹ Ihesum Christum nostram unicam Iustitiam.
Ornatissimi viri et fratres in Domino charissimi.

Inofficiosum omnino me esse arbitrarer, si hoc morbido et calamitoso tempore sine arduis causis ad vos scriberem et vestros labores sanctos interturbarem, at causae inciderant quae me plane urgebant ut vel pauculis verbis cum 5 vestris humanitatibus commentarer; quae ut pro vestra erga me et charitate et observantas boni consulatis, diligenter obsecro.

Audio vestras dominationes nonnihil in Iudaeos urantes incanduisse et eis duo² impegisse crimina minime levia, nempe quod et christianos et nostrum caput maiestatis Regem Christum in Synagoga acerbius blasphemarint, unde eis 10 exicialis[?]³ aliqua calamitas aut grave reifamiliaris dispendium immineat. Et scio ob quaedam Iudeorum facinora eos alicubi in exilium perpetuum proscriptos esse. In Hassia⁴ dura admodum sorte premi ut dura eorum cervix commeretur. Indormit enim gens ipsa miseria miserior suis malis nimis prohdolor altum. Hinc non mirum est pios aliquos odio in hos desertores[?]⁵ incalescere, ut 15 etiam existiment eos in Rebuspublicis et Ducatibus non esse tolerandos.

Qua de re nunc familiariter vobiscum loquar, sed nolim putetis haec⁶ adfectu aliquo minus pio a me scribi. Moveor enim rationibus quibusdam et scripturis ut credam Magistratus nostros facile excusari posse, sicubi in territoriis ac urbibus suis toleraverint Iudaeos. Immo christianam clementiam dedecere autumo 20 ut ex omni loco eam gentem miseram pellat.

Non gravabor autem rationes meas adnotare. Principio, Iudaei habent in script[uris] sanctis promissiones, quod sint tandem relicturi errorem et ample-

---

belonged to a collection of letters in the Herzog August Bibliothek Wolfenbüttel: Cod. Guelf. 503 Nov. A note below the table of contents in that volume says that it belonged to "Herrn Superintendent Nolte" in Amtleben and was bought from him in 1871 for 25 taler. Number 9 in the collection (fol. 27ʳ-30ᵛ) designates two copies of another letter from Rhegius to Martin Görlitz dated September 14, 1538, and the table of contents indicates that letter number 10 is also by Rhegius. But number 10, together with several other letters, is missing from Cod. Guelf. 503 Nov. Apparently, therefore, Nolte removed several letters from the volume before selling it in 1871 and then gave number 10 to the Staatsarchiv in 1878.

2. It is uncertain what the second crime is, since only blasphemy is specified at this point. The second crime may be usury, which Rhegius mentions later in the letter (see line 120 below).

3. The reading "exicialis" (= "exitialis" or "exitiabilis") is a conjecture based on spelling and appropriateness of meaning.

4. A reference to the 1539 *Judenordnung* in Hesse (see above, n. 56).

5. The word has been corrected by writing over it.

6. After this word "a me" has been deleted, apparently to be relocated later in the sentence.

210

xuri Christianismum, verum post multos annos Iudaici lapsus. Nota enim omni-
25 bus[?][7] est prophetia Hoseae c. 3[8] ["]Filii Israel sedebunt dies multos sine lege,
et sine principe et sine sacrificio et sine altari et sine Ephod et sine theraphin. Et
post haec revertentur filii Israel et quaerent dominum deum suum. Et David
Regem suum et stupebunt cum pavore super dominum et super bonum eius IN
NOVISSIMIS DIEBUS.["][9] Haec prophetia ab orthodoxis concorditer exponi-
30 tur de poenitentia et conversione Iudaeorum ad Christum verum David in ulti-
mis hisce seculis in quibus et nos sumus. Id quod et Moses indicat in Deut. c. 4[10]
ubi eodem verbo utitur[:] ["]bĕ'aḥărît hayyāmîm [wĕ]šabta 'ad yhwh.["][11]
Nunc autem haec aerumnosa gens mille et quingentos annos, gemina captivitate
miserabilis, spirituali et corporali carcere detenta, in certibus sedibus[12] per
5 totum orbem vagatur. Ex eius stirpe nec Rex ullus nec princeps nec Sacerdos
comparet, habent tamen promissionem infallibilem, quod post exilium illud diu-
turnum, multi ex eis ad Christum sint convertendi et reversuri ad hunc verum
David et ad illud inaestimabile Bonum nimirum Evangelium gratiae dei, pudebit
eos erroris horrendi, propriam cecitatem execrabuntur et cum stupore quodam
10 ac pavore venient ad Ecclesiam, quando videbunt iudicia dei iusta in contemptores et longanimitatem dei, agent gratias pro dei misericordia in Christo.

Profecto qui hanc Iudaeis gratiam promisit et verax et potens, quod promisit,
praestare. Et nisi Dominus de ultima illa Israelis conversione paternas cogitatio-
nes cogitasset, impossibile esset Iudaeos tamdiu mansisse superstites inter tot
exilia, caedes et iniurias, quibus [2v] ubique terrarum assidue et crudeliter di-
vexati et apflicti [sic] sunt.

Iam cum Christus suum ovile ex Iudaeis et gentibus constituat testibus pro-
pheticis et Evangelicis scripturis, christianae pietatis fuerit, Iudeos errantes, doc-

---

7. The text reads "omnius." My emendation of this word is similar to that made by an
earlier hand at n. 12 below.
8. Hos. 3:4-5.
9. The last three words are printed in capital letters by Rhegius without abbreviation.
In *Biblia Sacra iuxta Vulgatam Versionem*, ed. Robertus Weber OSB 2 (Stuttgart, 1969):
1376, the last phrase of Hosea 3:5 reads "et pavebunt ad Dominum et ad bonum eius in
novissimo dierum."
10. Deut. 4:30.
11. This passage is written in Hebrew. The "same word" that Rhegius says is used in
both Hos. 3:5 and Deut. 4:30 is the phrase "bĕ'aḥărît hayyāmîm." As indicated by the
brackets, the Hebrew text of Deut. 4:30 that Rhegius cites differs slightly from the text in
Biblia Hebraica, ed. Rud. Kittel (Stuttgart, 1963), 269. In the left margin another hand has
supplied the Latin translation of the Hebrew: "Hoc est: Reverteris ad dominum in novissimis diebus."
12. The text reads "sedius"; "b" has been inserted by another hand above the text line.

trina, vitae innocentia, beneficiisque ab errore ad veritatem, a perditione ad
salutem revocare! Nonne Christus mandat ut et inimicos diligamus, non qui- 50
dem verbo solum et lingua sed opere et veritate, ut iubet Ioannes.[13] Certe hoc
Hoseae vaticinium praebet nobis spem conversionis multorum ex Israel iuxta
carnem. ["]Iudicia dei abyssus multa.["][14] Si quidam nostratium Iudaeorum
etiam sunt filii promissionis, quare nos eos prorsus abiiceremus![15] et non potius
quaerimus et observamus omnes occasiones et vias serviendi eis ad poeniten- 55
tiam ipsorum? Charitas enim christiana bonitatem illam patris caelestis imitatur
et eius longanimitatem, quae non vult mortem peccatoris sed magis ut converta-
tur et vivat. Quod si ex animo volumus eorum conversionem, cur sic eos tracta-
mus quasi Deus totum hunc populum sine omni spe reversionis repulerit? Dicet
aliquis, ["]Nebulones sunt, blasphemi,[16] contemptores, hostes Christi.["] Doleo 60
haec de quibusdam nimis vere dici, detestor et ego omnium maxime duras has
cervices, ut Moses appellat,[17] et errores Iudaeorum. Non patrocinor eorum vel
caecitati vel malitiae, sed nolim intempestivo odio, et persecutione immoderata,
eos a nostra sacrosancta religione abalienari et in gloriosum Christi nominem et
christianos exacerbari.

Dein videmus Luc. 21[18] Christum verbis minime obscuris, addito etiam iura-
mento,[19] dixisse Hanc Generationem nimirum Iudaeorum mansuram usque in
finem. Necesse est ergo ut usque ad saeculi consummationem haec gens maneat
et alicubi moretur. Nusquam autem morantur melius quam apud christianos
propter spem conversionis eorum, nam apud Turcos nulla talis spes est Iudaeis.

Et fortissime omnium munit hanc meam sententiam Apostolus ad Ro. 11, qui
in Hosee Oraculum respiciens[20] multa in eo c. dicit, quae nos iubent Iudaeos
christiana mansuetudine tolerare et non fastuose abiicere. Primo enim clare
dicit, Non totum populum a deo reiectum esse, sed quosdam esse electos ex gratia Christi salvandos. Deinde reprimit nostram arrogantiam similitudine valde
apposita de olea vera et oleastro naturali. Iudaei sunt Caro et sanguis Patriar-
charum ex sancta Patrum radice tanquam rami progerminantes, et quamvis per
incredulitatem sint defracti et nos ex gentibus velut ignobiles rami ex oleastro

---

13. 1 Jn. 3:18.
14. Ps. 36:6 (Ps. 35:7 Vulg.).
15. The exclamation points here and in line 50 above were set by Rhegius.
16. Just before "contemptores" the letters "conpte" have been struck through; Rhegius
apparently misspelled the word on his first try.
17. E. g., Ex. 34:9; cf. Acts 7:51.
18. Lk. 21:32.
19. This oath is apparently the introduction to the saying of Jesus: "Amen dico vobis."
20. There is no evidence of Paul's use of Hosea 3:4–5 in Romans 11.

rudi tandem desumpti et in veram patrum oleam per fidem insiti, Tamen glo-
riari contra naturales ramos prohibemur, quia si naturalibus ramis divina seve-
ritas non pepercit, cur nobis gentibus aliunde insitis parceret? Nos sine meritis
nostris ex mera et insperata gratia sumus Patribus insiti et in gratiam evangeli-
cam vocati. Quid igitur superbimus? Nonne Deus pater illos denuo respiciet[?].
Imo vult (promisit enim Isa.59²¹ Iere. 31²² Hose.3²³ et alias)²⁴ eos denuo per
gratiam inserere propriae oleae. Et hac spe minime vana non dubito Iudeos
inter nos, certis legibus, tolerandos esse. Nam caecitas qua nunc percussi sunt
Iudaei in illa ultima captivitate, ex parte accidit Israeli, donec plenitudo gentium
advenerit, Ro.11.²⁵ Hoc est, caecitate percussi sunt [3ʳ] aliquandiu Iudaei,
donec Ecclesia id est numerus Electorum ex gentibus compleatur. Sed tandem
Iudaei respicientur a deo et ad Christum convertentur Dominum nostrum
numero ut speramus non poenitendo. Cur igitur nos Christiani eos, quibus
divina oracula spem salutis praebent, tanquam desperatos et insanabiles sine
omni misericordia repelleremus? Postremo dicit Apostolus Iudaeos inimicos
quidem nobis haberi causa Evangelii, quod etiamnum ex caecitate oppugnant,
caeterum amicos esse habendos propter Electionem et patres. Nam Christus est
ex patribus eorum secundum carnem Et multi ex eis sunt Electi. Ergo tandem
convertentur nam qui Electi sunt et vocantur et iustificantur etc. Ro.8.²⁶ Nos
igitur ex gentibus doleamus eorum vicem et omnibus modis quibus licet provo-
cemus miseros Iudaeos ad poenitentiam.

Obsecro fratres charissimi quorsum spectat implacabile illud in Iudaeos
odium, qui inde omnium hominum sub sole sunt calamatosissimi? Nonne dum
nulla erga eos misericordia movemur, sed tantum persequimur, maledicimus,
offendimus et omnibus iniuriis afficimus, hac asperitate eos a christianismo
absterremus, ut incipiant a religione nostra vera abhorrere, quando putant hoc
vicium esse Religionis, non personarum? Si autem cernerent nostram mansuetu-
dinem, charitatem, misericordiam et reliquos doctrinae christianae fructus, hac
ratione facilius ad fidem nostram allicerentur. Si Christiani haberi volumus
quare non zelo quodam christiano et dolore pro eis oramus ut convertantur et
vivant? Id quod Apostolus tanto aestu facit Ro.10. Et c.9²⁷ optat ἀνάθεμα²⁸

---

21. Is.59:20-21.
22. Jer.31:31-34.
23. Hos.3:4-5.
24. The parentheses are Rhegius' own.
25. Rom.11:25.
26. Rom.8:30.
27. Rom.9:3.
28. This word is written in Greek.

pro Iudaeis fieri, ut ipsi salventur. Hoc animo et nos praeditos esse oportebat 1
erga cecam gentem. Sint igitur Iudaei inimici nostri quatenus adhuc caeco zelo
persequuntur veritatem Evangelii, sed diligamus eos propter patres eorum
sanctos quibus promissiones salutiferae factae sunt. Nam in ea gente utcumque
nunc misera electum semen superest quod a nobis non hostiliter tractandum,
sed dicendo, monendo, arguendo, tolerando et pro eis orando ad veram salutem 1
in Christo permovendum est, quemadmodum ad Ro.11[29] apostolus nobis
Iudaeos serio et diligenter commendat. Et hac spe apostolus docet Iudaeos
tolerandos esse, primitiva Ecclesia toleravit, Et seniores nostri similiter tolera-
verunt, audio enim Iudaeos Brunsvici trecentos annos habitasse. Quod autem
obiicitur usura, et blasphemia eorum, facile haec Magistratus coercebit, cuius
est in[30] blasphemos animadvertere, et edicto statuere, ne Iudaei vel verbulum de
religione nostra cum quoquam indocto misceant, et etiam privatim sub poena
perpetui Exilii ab omni blasphemia abstineant. Haec optimo animo ad vos cha-
riss[imos] fratres Urbanus frater et servus vester scribit, per Christum Ihesum
obsecrans vos ut miseris Iudaeis sitis misericordes et vestro intercessu spe con- 2
versionis efficiatis apud Magistratum, ne quid durius in ignorantissimos et
infoelices homines statuatur. Quod si hasce preces meas pro solita humanitate
vestra exaudieritis, praebebo et ego me vicissim in omnibus vestris petitionibus
benevolum et ex animo promptum. Dominus vos omnes in sana doctrina, fide et
spe conservet, dona spiritus augeat et Ecclesiam vestram indies locupletet et a
tyrannide vicini Antiochi[31] praeservet. Datum Cellae 22. September anno 40.

D. Urbanus Rhegius
frater et servus vester
fidelis

29. Rom. 11:13-14.
30. "in" has been inserted below the line.
31. A reference to Duke Henry of Wolfenbüttel as the Seleucid king Antiochus
Epiphanes (175-163 B.C.E.), whose persecution of the Jews led to the Maccabean revolt.
Duke Henry, who kept his territory Catholic, was a constant threat to the Protestant city
of Braunschweig until he was driven from his territory by the Smalcald League in 1542.
See Hassebrauk, "Heinrich der Jüngere und die Stadt Braunschweig 1514-1568" (see
above, n.45), 14-37.
32. ="maesta"
33. Rhegius and his wife, Anna Weissbrücker from Augsburg, had eleven children
according to a chart entitled "Genealogia D.Urbani Regij" that is written in another
hand at the very end of his manuscript (fol.323r) of the Dialogus von der schönen Predigt
(1536: Cod. Guelf. 610 Helmst.). From left to right four sons are named, followed by
seven daughters. The sons are: Paulus, Urbanus, Ernestus, and Franciscus Otto. The

214

35 Orate dominum pro moesta[32] familiola nostra, decumbunt duo filii mei,[33] Paulus dysenteria gravissima, Franciscus Ottho alio quodam morbo flet iugiter dies et noctes.

[3v] "Praestantissimis ac pientissimis Viris ac Dominis, Magistro Martino Gorolitio Ecclesiae Brunsvicensis: Episcopo fideli ac caeteris omnibus gloriosi
40 Verbi Dei in ea urbe Ministris vigilantissimis Dominis et Fratribus suis in Christo dilectis."[34]

---

daughters are Sophia, Anna, Appollonia, Maria, Ursula, Margareta, and Euphrosina. The chart may or may not be accurate, but to my knowledge it is the fullest description of his family that we possess and has not been utilized before by Rhegius' biographers.

34. This address is written very distinctly and does not appear in Rhegius' hand.

XII

Christianizing Domestic Relations
Women and Marriage in Johann Freder's
Dialogus dem Ehestand zu Ehren

Johann Freder (1510-1562) composed his *Dialogue in Honor of Marriage* (1545) as a rebuttal to the damaging impression of women and marriage that he thought had been left by the *Sprichwörter* of Sebastian Franck. Although Freder's dialogue belongs to a broader class of Renaissance and Reformation treatises on marriage, it has special significance for our understanding of the Reformation. The work by Freder, both a Lutheran pastor and a skilled student of the classics, makes two important contributions to the learned mentality of the German Reformation. First, in his defense of marriage, Freder advocates a parity between women and men that stretches the limits set by better-known and more influential reformers. Second, Freder proposes a consciously Christian ethic of domestic relations which he contrasts with pagan antiquity. Freder's recognition of the equality of women and men in sin prevented him, however, from making the full realization of these ideals criteria by which the success of the Reformation should be judged.

THE DIALOG IN HONOR OF MARRIAGE, composed by Johann Freder (1510-1562) first received this title in its High German edition, which was published with a preface by Martin Luther in 1545.[1] Freder's express reason for composing the dialogue was to challenge the negative impression of women and marriage that he felt had been left by the *Sprichwörter* of Sebastian Franck.[2] In this respect, Freder's work belonged to a broad genre of Renaissance and Reformation literature that defended the integrity of marriage and instructed women about how properly to fulfill the role of wife. Protestant reformers, in particular, were quick to extol marriage over celibacy and to elaborate upon the divine purpose of matrimony and the mundane responsibilities of both marital partners. Moreover, humanists such as Cornelius Agrippa of Nettesheim praised the excellence of the female sex and illustrated its virtue through historical examples of famous

---

[1]*Ein Dialogus dem Ehestand zu ehren geschrieben. Durch M. Johan Freder. . . . Mit einer Vorrede D. Mart. Luth.* (Wittenberg: Nickel Schirlentz, 1545).

[2]Sebastian Franck, *Sprichwörter. Schöne Weise Herzliche Clugreden unnd Hoffsprüch Darinnen der alten und nachkommenen aller Nationen unnd Sprachen gröste vernunfft unnd klugheyt. . . .* (Frankfurt: Christian Egenolff, 1541).

XII

women.[3] A Lutheran pastor and a skilled student of the classics himself, Freder readily utilized both Reformation ideas and humanist examples in his response to Franck.

The way in which Freder combined the concerns and the sources of both reformers and humanists makes the *Dialogue* worthy of special attention. In fact, Freder's work illustrates two aspects of a learned Protestant mentality that was fostered by the German Reformation. These aspects are two attitudes, one specific and the other more general: first, Freder's advocacy, within a defense of marriage, of the integrity and, to some extent, the equality of women; and, second, a consciously Christian ethic which is contrasted with pagan antiquity. Each of these attitudes will be discussed in turn. But, first, who was this relatively obscure contributor to the formation of Reformation mentality and what might have prompted him to compose such a dialogue?

I

In 1543, when his *Dialogue* first appeared, Johann Freder (1510-1562) was a thirty-three year old Lutheran pastor and teacher in Hamburg. He grew up in Pomerania and his father had been a mayor of the town where he was born.[4] From 1524 to 1537 Freder studied in Wittenberg; for some of that time he lived together with Veit Dietrich in Luther's house. Freder earned the Master's degree in 1534 and soon thereafter married Anna Falck, a first cousin of the first wife of Justus Jonas.[5] From a letter written to Jonas we know that Freder owned a house in Wittenberg which in 1543 he was trying to sell.[6]

After his tenure in Hamburg, controversy stalked Freder wherever he went. In Stralsund, where he served as superintendent from 1547 to 1549, Freder refused to stop criticizing the *Interim* which the Pomeranian princes had accepted. As a result, he was fired and had to move to Greifswald, where he was appointed Professor of Theology and Superintendent of

[3]*Henrici Cornelii Agrippae de nobilitate et praecellentia foeminei sexus* (Antwerp: Michaelis Hellenius, 1529). This treatise was translated into several languages and frequently reprinted; see Ruth Kelso, *Doctrine for the Lady of the Renaissance* (Urbana: University of Illinois Press, 1956), 327. See also Charles G. Nauert, *Agrippa and the Crisis of Renaissance Thought* (Urbana: University of Illinois Press, 1965), 26-27.

[4]For his life, see the article on Freder by Herrmann Müller in *Allgemeine Deutsche Biographie* (1877; reprinted Berlin: Duncker & Humblot, 1968), 7:327-31, and the article by Ernst Kähler in *Neue Deutsche Biographie* (Berlin: Duncker & Humblot, 1961), 5:387-88. See also Gottlieb Mohnike, *Des Johannes Frederus Leben und geistliche Gesänge,* 3 vols. (Stralsund: C. Löfflersche Buchhandlung, 1837, 1840); *Lexikon der Hamburgischen Schriftsteller bis zur Gegenwart,* ed. Hans Schröder (Hamburg: Verein für Hamburgische Geschichte, 1854), 2:354-62.

[5]Jonas described Anna Freder as a quiet woman, who excelled in handwork and did not like to quarrel: *Der Briefwechsel des Justus Jonas,* ed. Gustav Kawerau, 2 vols. (Halle: Otto Hendel, 1884, 1885), 1:404 (no. 509: 17 August 1540).

[6]*Briefwechsel des Justus Jonas,* 2:99-100 (no. 679: 31 March 1543).

Rügen, an island off the coast of Pomerania. In Greifswald a controversy flared over Freder's ordination because he had not received the imposition of hands. After losing that battle, Freder went to Wismar as pastor and superintendent. There he fought Anabaptists, Calvinists and Zwinglians until he died, four days after his wife, in 1562. His friend, David Chyträus, said of Freder that he often changed his residence but always found his new situation more uncomfortable than the last.[7]

Among the Wittenbergers, Jonas knew Freder best. In 1540, he recommended Freder to the princes of Anhalt for a position in Dessau; Jonas reported that Freder would take a cut in salary in order to leave Hamburg, where the sea air did not suit him or his wife, to be closer to Wittenberg.[8] Jonas later admitted to Prince George of Anhalt that Freder, like all outstanding artists, had his weaknesses. But, alongside his homiletical ability and attention to Scripture, Jonas extolled Freder's education in the classics, his Latin style, and his facility for translating German tracts into Latin. Indeed, translations, which he published under the Latin cognomen, Johannes Irenäus, made up the bulk of his literary output and provided extra income.[9] By far the most original and widely-circulated of his literary works, however, was his dialogue in defense of women and marriage.

Freder composed the dialogue in 1542 or 1543 in reaction to Franck's *Sprichwörter.* At the time of its publication (1541), the *Sprichwörter* was the most comprehensive collection of proverbs to appear in German.[10] It contained about seven thousand proverbs which Franck took from other collections, most notably from the *Adagia* of Erasmus in the 1539 edition of Eberhard Tappe.[11] Franck's *Sprichwörter* must have come to Freder's attention soon after its publication in 1541, for the first edition of his defense was published in 1543.

Although the *Sprichwörter* contained a substantial number of proverbs about women and marriage, this theme was only one among many in the topically organized collection. Nevertheless, Freder seized on this topic in

[7]Cited by C. H. W. Sillem, *Briefsammlung des Hamburgischen Superintendenten Joachim Westphal aus den Jahren 1530 bis 1575,* 2 vols. (Hamburg: Lucas Gräfe & Sillem, 1903), 1:135.

[8]*Briefwechsel des Justus Jonas,* 1:401, 403.

[9]According to Mohnike (*Des Johannes Frederus Leben* 1:40-45), Freder translated into Latin nine works of Luther, nine works of Urbanus Rhegius, and one work of his Hamburg colleague Aepinus. Jonas noted that Freder's translation of Luther's *Eine einfältige Weise zu beten* was so good that people thought Jonas himself had done it or had assisted Freder: *Briefwechsel des Justus Jonas,* 1:402. For a list of translations and editions by Freder, see *Lexikon der Hamburgischen Schriftsteller,* 2:358-60. In 1543 Freder complained to Jonas that he had not been paid by the dukes of Lüneburg for his translation of Rhegius' *Dialogus von der schönen Predigt: Briefwechsel des Justus Jonas,* 2:99.

[10]Ulrich Meisser, *Die Sprichwörtersammlung Sebastian Francks von 1541* (Amsterdam: Rodopi, 1974), 436-37.

[11]*Adagiorum Epitome* (Cologne: Johannes Gymnicus, 1539); see Meisser, *Sprichwörtersammlung,* 22-25.

order to defend a Christian view of marriage and women against what he considered to be its derogation by Franck. In his dedication of the work to Queen Dorothea of Denmark,[12] Freder places Franck in the category of those who "in our time" not only take pleasure in the shameful and blasphemous proverbs which degrade the image of women, but also speak and write contemptuously about women just as the pagans did.[13] According to Freder, Franck translated many shameful proverbs of the pagans and added to them some proverbs "of the godless world" that insulted the female image and scorned marriage to the utmost. Franck then dressed up these proverbs with the name of *Klugreden* and gathered them into one book. There could exist no more insulting and filthy proverbs, laments Freder, than most of the ones that pertain to women.[14]

Franck, of course, did not in the least intend to belittle marriage or to insult women. Although he was, for reformers, a pesky critic of the Lutheran Reformation, he was mainly a proponent of the spiritual church, of the inner word, and of the ethical integrity of the religious life.[15] Franck held an exalted view of marriage and never identified himself with negative proverbs about women.[16] It is even possible that the extensive discussion of women and marriage in Part II of his *Sprichwörter* was intended as a composite *Ehespiegel* for his new wife whom he married in 1541.[17] Insofar as Franck had an agenda for his section on women and marriage, it was to reverse the collapse of marital commitment which he described as a "...rampant state of divorcing and running away...where one partner abandons the other in exigencies just when they need each other the most."[18]

[12]Dorothea (1511Ø1571), who was married to Christian III, King of Denmark and Duke of Schleswig-Holstein, was the daughter of Magnus I of Sachsen-Lauenburg; see Wilhelm von Isenburg, *Stammtafeln zur Geschichte der europäischen Staaten,* 5 vols. (Marburg, 1953-1978), 1:89.

[13]*Dialogus* (1545), Biiiᵛ.

[14]Ibid. Freder's *Dialogus* is mentioned only as a response to Franck by Waldemar Kawerau, *Die Reformation und die Ehe: Ein Beitrag zur Kulturgeschichte des sechzehnten Jahrhunderts* (Halle: Verein für Reformationsgeschichte, 1892), 58.

[15]See Horst Weigelt, *Sebastian Franck und die lutherische Reformation* (Gütersloh: Gerd Mohn, 1972), 20-62; see also Steven Ozment, *Mysticism and Dissent* (New Haven: Yale University Press, 1973), 137-67.

[16]Meisser, *Sprichwörtersammlung,* 255-56, 366-70, 424-25. Cf. Alfred Hegler, *Geist und Schrift bei Sebastian Franck* (Freiburg: Mohr [Siebeck], 1892), 181.

[17]*Sprichwörter* (1541), II:199ᵛ-205. After the death of his first wife, Ottilie Beham (sister of the Nürnberg painters Sebald and Barthel), in 1541, Franck moved from Basel to Strasbourg and married Margaretha Beck, the daughter of a publisher. See Meisser, *Sprichwörtersammlung,* 21, 423; Weigelt, *Sebastian Franck,* 19.

[18]*Sprichwörter* (1541), II:204ᵛ-205: "Diss zuschreiben hat mich für nötig angesehen in disem wilden wesen/ ehe scheyden und von einander lauffen ... und bleibt schier ietz in nöten keins bei den andern / da man einander am besten bedarff."

Freder might have chosen to respond to Franck's alleged derogation of marriage for several reasons. As a former Wittenberger, Freder probably shared the distaste that Luther had for Franck. In 1540, advising against reading the books of Franck, Luther described him as an evil, malicious man and a vain fugitive.[19] In 1545, Freder approved a more vivid condemnation of Franck that Luther rendered in his preface to the *Dialogus*.[20] The death of Franck four years earlier was Luther's license to attack him in writing, something Luther says he was loath to do while Franck was still alive.[21] As if making up for lost time, Luther then pilloried Franck as a blowfly which buzzed behinds in the privy and then, after it had soiled its nose and feet, flew in your face as if it had just flown out of a fragrant garden or apothecary.[22]

Freder also admitted that he was encouraged to write against Franck by "other prominent, well-informed persons," among whom were probably some of the Wittenbergers.[23] In particular, Freder might have been put up to the task by his fellow Pomeranian and "dear father in Christ," Johann Bugenhagen, nicknamed Pomeranus. According to Freder, Bugenhagen sang to him the praise of Queen Dorothea of Denmark, to whom Freder dedicated the *Dialogus*.[24] Freder knew Bugenhagen not only from his Wittenberg days; he surely also talked with Pomeranus after 1537 when Bugenhagen traveled through Hamburg on his way to and from Copenhagen and Schleswig-Holstein. Bugenhagen had completed his own tract on marriage and divorce in 1539 just before he left Denmark, and on his return to Wittenberg he preached in Hamburg.[25] Bugenhagen might also have seen

---

[19]*WATR* 4, 671.21-25 (no. 5121).

[20]*Dialogus* (1545), Ri^v.

[21]*WA* 54, 171.2-9.

[22]*WA* 54, 174.6-12.

[23]*Dialogus* (1545), Rii: "Wiewol ich auch nicht aus eigenem furnemen / sondern mit rat und anreitzen anderer grosser hochverstendiger Leute jn gestraffet habe / Auff das etliche gute Leute mit fursichtigkeit seine Bucher lesen / oder ungelesen lassen mochten."

[24]*Dialogus* (1545), Biv: "Dieweil ich aber / Durchleuchtigste Königin / Gnedigste Fraw / von vielen grossen Leuten / und sonderlich von dem Ehrwirdigen Herrn D. Johan Bugenhagen / meinem lieben Vater in Christo / berichtet werde / Das E.K.M. mit sonderlichen hohen gaben und tugenden reichlich gezieret sey / . . ."

[25]On June 26, 1539, according to *Dr. Johannes Bugenhagens Briefwechsel*, ed. Otto Vogt (1910; reprinted Hildesheim: Georg Olms, 1966), 596, 597. See Karl August Traugott Vogt, *Johannes Bugenhagen Pomeranus: Leben und ausgewählte Schriften* (Elberfeld, R.L. Friderichs, 1867), 395. Bugenhagen's tract, *Vom Ehebruch und Weglauffen,* was published with a new edition of Luther's *Von Ehesachen* in 1540 in Wittenberg. For a discussion of Bugenhagen's view of divorce see Steven Ozment, *When Fathers Ruled: Family Life in Reformation Europe* (Cambridge: Harvard University Press, 1983), 85-92.

256

Freder on his way to Schleswig-Holstein in 1542,[26] just one year before the first edition of Freder's *Dialogus* appeared. At this time the two Pomeranian natives and Wittenberg theologians could have agreed that a response to Franck's *Sprichwörter* was needed.

II

In his dedication of the dialogue to Queen Dorothea, Freder reveals the strategy that he will use to defend marriage and that will lead him to advocate the integrity and limited equality of women. After declaring that marriage is God's good order and a holy estate, Freder accuses the devil of attacking that order throughout history by causing women to be disparaged.[27] By citing proverbs from reputedly the wisest authors of classical antiquity, Franck endorsed misogynous attitudes that were also held by many heretics and especially by the Antichrist at Rome.[28] Because the devil in this way keeps many people from marrying and traps them in other sins, Freder has decided to refute Franck's nasty proverbs and to turn his own weapon against him. Not only will he employ Scripture against Franck, says Freder, but he will also cite examples of many virtuous, praiseworthy women from pagan histories themselves.[29]

The body of the dialogue composed by Freder proceeds to execute this strategy of defending marriage by praising women. The two speakers are Johannes and Antonius. Johannes, the defender of marriage and women, reproaches Antonius for his immoral life and asserts that he ought to marry in order to save his soul. Marriage is a remedy provided by God for our weakness and it is better to marry than to burn for whoremongering.[30] Antonius, however, is not readily convinced. He replies that he is held

[26]*Bugenhagens Briefwechsel,* 601; K.A.T. Vogt, *Johannes Bugenhagen Pomeranus,* 397-398. See Martin Schwarz Lausten, "König und Kirche: über das Verhältnis der weltlichen Obrigkeit zur Kirche bei Johann Bugenhagen und König Christian III. von Dänemark," in *Johannes Bugenhagen: Gestalt und Wirkung,* ed. Hans-Günter Leder (Berlin: Evangelische Verlagsanstalt, 1984), 144-167, here 160; see also Friedrich Bertheau, "Bugenhagens Beziehungen zu Schleswig-Holstein und Dänemark," in *Wirkungen der Deutschen Reformation bis 1555,* ed. Walther Hubatsch (Darmstadt: Wissenschaftliche Buchgesellschaft, 1967), 493-511, here 507-510.

[27]*Dialogus* (1545), Biii-Biii^v: "Unter andern aber beweiset er solche seine kunst auch damit / das er vom Weibs geschlecht / in gemein seer gifftig und schmelich redet / und sie also feindselig zu machen unterstehet."

[28]*Dialogus* (1545), Biii-Biii^v.

[29]*Dialogus* (1545), Biv: ". . . und dieweil der böse Geist / damit viel vom Ehestand abhelt / das er sie in ander sunde müge füren / und darin behalten / So habe ich solche Schandsprüche widerlegt / nicht allein mit Göttlicher schrifft / sondern auch mit Exempeln vieler tugentsamer / löblicher Weiber / aus heidnischen Historien / Auff das die Heiden mit jren eigenen Exempeln lügen gestraffet mügen werden."

[30]*Dialogus* (1545), C^v: "Und weil ir euch an Himel nicht halten konnet / wie ir sagt / So begebt euch in Ehestand / Diese artzney ist unser schwacheit von Gott gegeben / Denn es je besser ist freien / den brennen. Und Hurerey zu meiden / sol ein jeglicher sein eigen Weib haben / j. Cor. vii. [1 Cor. 7:2,9]."

XII

back from marrying by the smartest and wisest people on earth, who have earnestly advised against matrimony. These same authors have written such terrible things about women that it makes his skin crawl whenever he thinks of marriage. When Johannes asks who these allegedly smart and wise authors are, Antonius maintains that it would take too long to name them all. Nevertheless, he offers to name a few,[31] and the simulated debate begins over the correctness of these classical deprecations of women and marriage.

Several examples will illustrate how Freder, in the person of Johannes, defends marriage by defending women. Among classical authors, Cato is quoted as saying that man's life would be blessed if he could live without women. Johannes responds that most murders and quarrels occur among men when no women intervene; and, furthermore, if it were not for women, there would be no love and friendship such as one finds between parents and children, spouses, and siblings.[32] Another author warns that if a man takes a pretty wife, she becomes common property and he will not be able to keep her; but if he marries an ugly woman, he will grow old with her. Against this argument that women make marriage a no-win situation for men, Johannes declares that even beautiful pagan women have proved how they loved their honor more than their life.[33] Furthermore, not all women are either beautiful or ugly; in fact, most women have average looks (*sind mittelmessiger gestalt*). In the end, beauty is not decisive, because love, fidelity, and friendship between spouses–good-looking or not–depends on God's blessing and on their fear and knowledge of God.[34]

In fact, argues Freder, many women, beautiful or not, have loved their honor more than their life. Among the sayings of antiquity cited by Franck is a statement attributed to Secundus that woman is an insatiable beast, the

[31]*Dialogus* (1545), Cii.

[32]*Dialogus* (1545), Civ - Civᵛ: "Das Cato sagt / es were ein selig leben unser leben / wenn wir on Weiber lebeten / Das ist nicht war / Denn es ist je trawen grosse uneinigkeit / zwitracht / mord / und ander unlust unter den Mennern / da auch keine Weiber da zwischen komen / ja die meisten mord und unlust / erheben sich unter den Mennern / wenn sie zusamenkomen ... Die gröste liebe / gunst / neigung und freundschafft / ist je zwischen Eltern / Kindern / Eheleuten / Brudern / Schwestern / Blutsfreunden und Schwegern etc. Wenn nu keine Weiber weren / so were auch solche liebe und freundschafft nicht / ..."

[33]*Dialogus* (1545), D: "Das Bias sagt / Nimpstu ein schöne / so hastu ein gemeine / und wirst sie nicht alleine behalten. Nimpstu eine hesliche / so wirstu bey jr alt werden etc. Dis ist auch nicht war / denn es hat manch schon Weib / jre Ehr wol so lieb / das sie lieber jr Leben / denn jre Ehre verlieren wolte / Wie das viel Exempel zeugen / auch der Heidnischen weiber."

[34]*Dialogus* (1545), D - Dᵛ: "Auch sind die Weiber nicht alle gleich schon / sind nicht alle eitel Sara / Rahel / Judith / Lucretien etc. Auch sinds nicht alle gleich heslich und ungestalt. Der meiste teil / sind mittelmessiger gestalt / ... Aber wie gesagt / Es ist an der schonheit allein nicht gelegen / wo Gott sein segen und gnad gibt / wo Gottes furcht und erkentnis ist / da ist auch liebe / trew und freundschafft unter Eheleuten / sie seien schon oder nicht / ... "

shipwreck of a lusty man, and a vessel of adultery. Freder, in the guise of Johannes, protests that such an opinion does injustice to all honorable, chaste women; there are some unchaste women, to be sure, just as there are many unchaste men, but all women are not such.[35] As an example, Freder retells the story of Brasilla Dirachina. When she was threatened with rape by an enemy soldier, she told her attacker that she knew of an herb that had the power to make him invulnerable. He allowed her to demonstrate the herb's power by rubbing it on her neck and then submitting to a blow from his sword. When her head came off, not only was the would-be rapist deprived of his prey, but Brasilla preserved her honor by surrendering her life.[36]

Citing examples of honorable and virtuous women is only one device that Freder uses to defend women and marriage. Another argument he employs is to advocate a limited equality of women and men. Sometimes this argument finds the least common denominator between men and women: whatever can be said negatively about women can apply equally or even more aptly to men. For example, Freder claims that men cause more quarrels and strife than women, but women end up taking the blame.[37] If two men lived together, Freder presumes, they would not get along as well as husband and wife. Just look at Paul and Barnabas. They were pious, godfearing men, but they had to separate because they disagreed so much.[38] In marriage men are often just as guilty of provoking strife as are women.[39]

A vulgar proverb cited by Franck elicited from Freder a positive statement about the equality of women that deepens the argument that men can be just as bad as women. The proverb says: "All women are alike with the lights out."[40] Freder wasted a great opportunity to respond: "So are all men." Martin Luther, however, did not. In his preface to the *Dialogus*

[35]*Dialogus* (1545), Div^v: "Antonius: Zum anderen saget er / ein Weib sey ein unersetliche Bestie / ein Schiffbruch des geilen Mannes / und ein Vas oder Werckzeug des Ehebruchs . . . Johannes: Damit thut er allen ehrlichen / züchtigen Weibern / gros gewalt und unrecht / Denn ob wol etliche Weiber unzüchtig gnug sind (wie denn auch viel unkeuscher Menner sind) sind darumb nicht alle Weiber unzuchtig etc."

[36]*Dialogus* (1545), Eii - Eii^v.

[37]*Dialogus* (1545), Fiii^v: "und zwar wenn man es beim liecht wolte ansehen / so halt ichs dafur / das wol so viel unlust / zanck und hadder durch Menner sich verursache / als durch Weiber. Aber was die Menner böses thun / das ist alles wol gethan / da sagt man nichts von. Die arme Weibere mussen es alles auff sich nemen / allein die schuld und die last tragen / und die nachsage haben / das sie allen hadder und zanck anrichten."

[38]Ibid.

[39]*Dialogus* (1545), Fiv: "Denn das unterweilen hadder und zwitracht unter Eheleuten ist / ist nicht allwege den Weibern die schuld allein zu geben / sondern auch wol den Mennern / die offt so grosse schuld haben als die Weiber und mehr/. . ."

[40]*Dialogus* (1545), H: "Einer lautet also / Lessche das Liecht aus / so sind die Weiber alle gleich."

(1545), Luther took Franck to task for insulting with this proverb his own mother and wife and asked why the same proverb did not also apply to men.[41] Freder offers a more interesting theological response. Before God, he argues, men and women are alike because they are all sinners.[42] As far as this life is concerned, however, there are pious and evil men just as there are pious and evil women. One can draw the same distinction among women as among men, because both men and women manifest the work of the devil as well as the work of God.[43] Freder thus defends the equality of men and women at both the theological and at the practical level. In the eyes of God, all men and women are equally sinners, while in the eyes of the world both men and women display good and evil conduct.

What about the Fall, however? Was it not a woman who was responsible for the first sin? Not as far as Freder was concerned; in his mind Eve was no guiltier than Adam. Eve should not be counted among the deceitful women of Scripture because she did not intentionally trick Adam. She did indeed sin, because she believed the serpent more than she believed God. But insofar as she thought she could make Adam great, like God, she actually intended good for Adam and acted toward him out of a special kind of love.[44] This appraisal of Eve's role in the story of the Fall is more sympathetic and positive than the view espoused by many reformers. For example, both Luther and Calvin assigned to Eve responsibility for the Fall, and Luther even claimed that all women inherited their gullibility from Eve.[45] Freder's assessment of Eve is also more positive than the view

---

[41]*WA* 54, 174.34 - 175.4

[42]*Dialogus* (1545), H: "Fur Gott sind beide Menner und Weiber gleich / da ist ein Mensch wie der ander / nemlich / allzumal Sunder / Wie Paulus sagt Ro. 3 (Rom. 3:10). Es ist keiner der guts thut / auch nicht einer/ ..."

[43]*Dialogus* (1545), H - Hᵛ, Hii.

[44]*Dialogus* (1545), Lii: "Sie hat zwar wol greulich gesundiget wider Gott / das sie der Schlangen mehr glaubte denn Gott. Aber weil sie dem Adam den apffel gab aus keinem bosen willen / noch arger list / sondern aus hertzlichem wolmeinen / aus sonderlich lieb (welches sie gleichwol fur Gott nicht entschuldiget / weil sie sein Gebot ubertrit) das sie jn gros mochte machen / So kan man sie warlich nicht zelen unter die hinderlistige schendliche Weiber / die aus bosem willen und fursatz / umb jres forteils willen jemand betriegen und beschedigen."

[45]On Calvin, see Claude-Marie Baldwin, "Marriage in Calvin's Sermons," in *Calviniana: Ideas and Influence of John Calvin,* ed. Robert V. Schnucker (Kirksville, Mo.: Sixteenth Century Journal Publishers, 1988), 121-29, here 124. For a mitigation of this view, see Jane Dempsey Douglass, *Women, Freedom and Calvin* (Philadelphia : Westminster, 1985), 60. On Luther, see Ingetraut Ludolphy, "Die Frau in der Sicht Martin Luthers," in *Vierhundertfünfzig Jahre lutherische Reformation 1517-1567: Festschrift für Franz Lau zum 60. Geburtstag,* ed. Helmar Junghans, Ingetraut Ludolphy, Kurt Meier (Berlin: Evangelische Verlagsanstalt, 1967), 204-21; Merry Wiesner, "Luther and Women: The Death of Two Marys," in *Disciplines of Faith: Religion, Patriarchy, and Politics,* ed. Jim Obelkevich, Lyndal Roper, Raphael Samuel (London and New York: Routledge & Kegan Paul, 1987), 295-308, here 300. See also Merry Wiesner, "Women's Response to the Reformation," in *The German People and the Reformation,* ed. R. Po-Chia Hsia (London: Cornell University Press, 1988), 148-71, here 150-51.

XII

260

of medieval biblical exegetes such as Hugh of St. Victor, who held Eve more guilty than Adam because she sinned out of voluntary wickedness.[46] The equality of men and women in sin does not, however, presuppose that they were created with equal opportunity and the same calling. Although women are endowed with the same noble and rational soul as men,[47] Freder still believes that women were created for women's work and men for men's. Woman's place is in the home; man's place is in the courthouse, the military, the pulpit, and the university. This division of labor does not mean that women are less competent or that their work is less important than men's. Without the fulfillment of childraising and household responsibilities by women, the world would collapse just as surely as it would if men did not perform their tasks.[48]

Although Freder accepts a social order of distinct estates and assigns women to the household, his intention is to defend women against the charge (allegedly by Franck) that they can be called irrational beasts. To reinforce his argument that women are comparable to men, he cites numerous examples of female rulers and women who have performed great deeds that are normally reserved for men.[49] His list of outstanding women is so long that these women seem more like the rule than the exception.[50] It comes as no surprise, therefore, that Freder concludes his historical evidence with a quote from Socrates that surpasses his own previously stated position: women do not only possess sufficient intelligence for their own work, but women's intelligence is just as sharp and capable *for any purpose* [italics mine] as are the minds of men.[51]

Freder's strategy of defending marriage by defending women seems to anticipate the tendency of modern historians to treat women mainly in the

[46]Joan M. Ferrante, *Woman As Image in Medieval Literature from the Twelfth Century to Dante* (1975; reprinted Durham, NC: Labyrinth Press, 1985), 34.

[47]*Dialogus* (1545), Jii^v: "Denn es hat Gott den Weibern je so wol eine edle and vernunfftige Seele gegeben als den Mennern. Auch hat er jnen je so viel verstand / sinne und Weisheit verliehen das auszurichten / was jrem Ampt zustehet / als den Mennern zu jrem Ampte."

[48]*Dialogus* (1545), Jii^v-Jiii: "Ein Weib / sol nicht das Rathaus regiern / nicht am Gerichte sitzen / nicht in Kriege ziehen / nicht predigen / nicht auff Hohenschulen lesen / und dergleichen Menner werck thun. Sondern sie ist von Gott dazu geschaffen / das sie sol Kinder tragen / sie auffziehen / in der narung und allem anliegen des Mannes gehulffe sein / und das haus helffen regieren. Diese wercke sind nötige / und ja so nötig werck als der Menner. Denn on solche Werck die Welt eben so wenig bestehen / und ein Haus auffgehalten kan werden / als on der Menner werck etc. Zu diesen wercken sind sie beruffen / dazu haben sie auch so viel verstand als ein Man zu seinen wercken."

[49]*Dialogus* (1545), Jiii - Kiv.

[50]Some examples are obvious exceptions, however, like Pope Joan, the legendary female pope of the ninth century: *Dialogus* (1545), Kiii^v.

[51]*Dialogus* (1545), Kiv: "Socrates / der zu seinen zeiten der Weiseste war geachtet / sagt in Symposio Xenophontis / Das der Weiber verstand zu allen dingen / nicht weniger tüchtig und geschickt sey / denn der Menner verstand. Desgleichen meint auch Plutarchus." Cf. above, n. 47.

context of family history.[52] The history of the publication of Freder's dialogue already exhibited this tendency. The title of its first, Low German edition, *Praise and Innocence of Women,* published in 1543,[53] accurately shows that the dialogue is more about women than about marriage. After 1543, however, the translators and publishers of the pamphlet apparently could not decide whether it should be marketed under the theme of women or of marriage. The Latin version that appeared in 1544 included both topics in its title: *Defense of the Female Sex Written to the Glory of God and in Honor of Sacred Matrimony.*[54] In one form or another, that policy was followed by the editors of the High German editions that appeared in 1568, 1569, and 1573.[55] By highlighting the dual theme of women and marriage, these editors and translators probably hoped they would attract more readers and thus enhance the dialogue's popularity.[56] When they reissued this lively treatise, pious and clever editors also seized an opportunity to promote Christian discipline and to flatter potential patronesses, just as the original author had done.[57]

Regardless of how his dialogue was marketed, Freder's dedicated defense of women emphasized their dignity and capability more forcefully than other reformers were wont to do. Some of Freder's views were comparable to those of more prominent reformers. For example, his restriction of women's public roles and his subordination of them to men in marriage

[52]The danger of subsuming women's history under family history has been lamented by Merry E. Wiesner, "Beyond Women and the Family: Towards a Gender Analysis of the Reformation," *Sixteenth Century Journal* 18 (1987): 311-21, here 316.

[53]*Loff und Unschuldt der Frouwen. Und wedderlegginge der Sproke / darmede de Frouwesbylde / dorch de Philosophos / edder werltwyse Heyden / und etlicke vormeynde Christen geschmehet werden* . . . (Rostock: Ludowich Dyetz, 1543).

[54]*Apologia pro sexu foemineo ad Dei gloriam et sacri coniugij honorem scripta per M. Ioan. Irenaeum, & versa nunc per Ioannem Broscium Christi ministrum.* . . (Frankfurt: Peter Braubach, 1544).

[55]*Lob und Unschuldt der Ehefrawen* . . . *Gott und dem heiligen Ehestande zu ehren geschrieben* . . . *Jetzt aus Pommerischer Sprache in Meissnische gebracht* . . . *Durch Andream Hondorff.* . . (Leipzig: Jacobus Herwaldt, 1568). *Lob und Unschuldt der Ehefrauwen* . . . *Gott und dem heyligen Ehestande zu ehren geschrieben* . . . *Jetzt auss Pommerischer Sprache in Meissnische gebracht und mit etlichen schönen Historien und Exampeln gemehrt. Durch Andream Hondorff.* . . (Franckfurt am Mayn: Peter Schmid in verlegniss Hieronymi Feyerabends, 1569). *Lob und Unschuld der Frawen. Ein Dialogus dem Ehestand zu Ehren geschrieben.* . . (Rostock: Johan. Stöckelman und Andreas Gutterwitz, 1573).

[56]A Czech translation of the 1544 Latin edition appeared in 1584 and 1585. See *Knihopis Českých A Slovenských Tisků,* II:3 (1946), 446 (no. 3389). For this reference I am indebted to Dr. Mirjam Bohatcová, Prague.

[57]In 1573, Johann Freder, Jr., dedicated the new edition of his father's treatise to Princess Sophia of Denmark on the occasion of her marriage. He described the princess as the image of her mother who shone like the sun with all noble virtues: *Lob und Unschuld der Frawen* (1573: see above, note 55), Aiii-Aiii[v]. According to Freder, Jr., through marriage God had set boundaries around the relationship of man and woman so that they would not go astray like cattle but remain chaste and live together honorably: ibid., Aiii[v].

echoed the views of both Luther and Calvin.[58] In respect to their roles, however, Freder took pains to stress the equal worth of women's contribution and to curb the abuse of men's authority. The role of women in maintaining the household and in raising children was just as important to society as preaching, teaching, and ruling.[59] And in marriage, even though women were subject to their husband's authority and admonition, men who did not love and honor their wives, but abused them even verbally, acted in unchristian and tyrannical fashion.[60] There is no hint in Freder's dialogue of belittling remarks about women, either married or single, such as Wiesner has found in Luther's writings.[61] Ozment's description of the dignity which the Reformation conferred upon married women captures the view of Freder better than the sentiments of some other reformers: "A wife's subjection to the rule of her husband was not the subservience of a serf to a lord, or a maid to a master, or a child to a parent; despite male rule an ordered equality existed between husbands and wives."[62]

Although the structure of Freder's *Dialogus* links women and marriage, the dignity and equality of women are not compromised by Freder's avowal of the theology of marriage as it was taught by sixteenth-century reformers. In fact, Freder's *Dialogus* supplies important evidence against the unnecessarily categorical judgment of Ian Maclean about the influence of Renaissance ideas of marriage on women: "Marriage is an immovable obstacle to any improvement in the theoretical or real status of woman in law, in theology, in moral and political philosophy."[63] For Freder quite the contrary is true. His praise of women as a means of advocating marriage for men turns marriage into a help rather than a hindrance to the standing of women during the Reformation. Lutheran theology of the divinely-intended order

---

[58]See Wiesner, "Women's Response to the Reformation," 150-152; see also Wiesner, "Luther and Women: The Death of Two Marys," 298-300, and Douglass, *Women, Freedom and Calvin,* 62-65.

[59]See above, n. 48.

[60]*Dialogus* (1545), Fiii: "Die nun solchs nicht thun (i.e., lieben) / sondern jre Weiber geringer denn jre Dienstmegde achten / ja schier fur ein unsauber Fustuch halten / geschwind mit jnen faren / und on not und ursach schelten und fluchen / alles / wens nicht schnur gleich nach jrem tollen kopff gehet / . . . Solche unmenschen handeln nicht allein unchristlich / sondern Tyranisch / geben aus lauterm mutwillen ursach dazu / das ewiger unfriede und unruge im hause ist / on der Weiber schuld etc."

[61]Wiesner, "Luther and Women: The Death of Two Marys," 298-301. For a defense of the historical relativity of Luther's views, even of his patriarchalism, see Ludolphy, "Die Frau in der Sicht Martin Luthers," 214-16.

[62]Ozment, *When Fathers Ruled,* 99. Citing Luther as an example, Robert Stupperich argued similarly that the reformers imparted a new dignity to women and to their roles as wives and mothers: "Die Frau in der Publizistik der Reformation," *Archiv für Kulturgeschichte* 37 (1955): 204-233, here 206.

[63]Ian Maclean, *The Renaissance Notion of Woman* (Cambridge: Cambridge University Press, 1980), 85.

of marriage, as reflected in Freder's dialogue, did not aim at defending the status quo or at preventing change.[64] Instead, it sought to provide the basis for an improvement, both in theory and in practice, of domestic relations by stressing the value of marriage and of women within an intentionally conceived Christian ethic.

III

That conscious Christian ethic, which is contrasted with the values of pagan antiquity, is the second attitude that is characteristic of Freder's reforming mentality. True, Freder does cite pagan sources in a positive manner, for example, Socrates and historical examples of outstanding non-Christian women. There, however, Freder is executing his stated strategy of employing Franck's own evidence against him; and the use of pagan sources does not blur, in his mind, the sharp distinction between pagan and Christian attitudes. His purpose, less conspicuous perhaps than his defense of women, is to Christianize the minds of his readers, teaching them a Christian ethic of domestic relations. This purpose presupposes that for Freder all baptized Christians are not truly Christian and that the society which he is addressing is not thoroughly Christianized. Freder's conviction that his society is not thoroughly Christian is reflected in his use of language. For example, women who neglect their household duties and defy their husbands are labeled godless and not Christian women.[65] And a husband *who would be Christian* [italics mine] should not love his wife any less for all her faults and imperfections.[66]

The words pagan and Christian have two distinct meanings for Freder. On the one hand, pagans are non-Christians, that is unbaptized and unbelieving people, such as the authors and protagonists of classical antiquity. In contrast to these pagans in the strict sense of the word, the name Christian applies to all baptized believers. On the other hand, the word pagan characterizes an attitude or an action that contradicts Freder's definition of a Christian stance. So, for example, the disparagement of women, as illustrated in the proverbs collected by Franck, is a pagan attitude, even if this stance against women is taken by nominal Christians. By the same token, even genuine pagans like Socrates and the women who sacrificed their lives for their honor exhibit a Christian mindset. Freder does not call

---

[64]Cf. Maclean, *Renaissance Notion,* 85: "Even if the injustice of certain aspects of the institution (of marriage) is recognized, the status quo is still generally defended in the name of religious orthodoxy or a conservatism based on the belief that change in itself is bad."

[65]*Dialogus* (1545), F: "Solche Weiber lobe ich warlich nicht / sie sind auch nicht lobens werd / Denn sie sind nicht Christliche / sondern Gottlose Weiber / die gottes straffe / wo sie sich nicht bessern / nicht entgehen werden."

[66]*Dialogus* (1545), Fiv^v: "Wenn sie gleich nicht schon / nicht von grossem stande / nicht reich / nicht gesund ist / oder sonst etliche gebrechen und feile an sich hette / sol ein Eheman gleichwol nichts dester weniger sein Weib lieben / der ein Christ sein wil."

these pagans Christian, but they certainly manifest Christian attitudes and conduct. While Freder does not propose the existence of a hidden church in antiquity, he is concerned to make the nominal Christians of his day genuinely Christian. In the matter under discussion, to be genuinely Christian is to hold both women and marriage in honor and to live accordingly.

Freder's concern for instilling genuinely Christian attitudes was prompted also by his assessment of how easily common people could be deceived by what he considered to be Franck's false use of Scripture. Freder had consulted other books by Franck and found in one of them[67] the following proposition: "Women are by nature evil and a cause of all sin; therefore we should avoid them, leave them alone, hate and flee them."[68] Following a *sic et non* method, Franck had placed a counterproposition opposite the first and supported both propositions with statements and examples from Scripture. That balance did not, however, satisfy Freder. He complained that Franck did not demonstrate which proposition was true and which was false. In Freder's opinion, therefore, Franck was abusing Scripture.[69]

Freder feared that the simple reader would draw the wrong conclusions from Franck's method of presentation. The average reader could not look up every Scripture passage in order to discover its true meaning in context. Hence, the reader would be left with the impression that Scripture, since it could be cited in support of contrary propositions, contradicted itself.[70] Instead of being a Christian exercise, as Franck had claimed, the study of such antinomies supported by Scripture could lead only to a confusion of consciences.[71] In contrast, claims Freder, the exercise which the Holy Spirit intends is a correct, clear exposition of Scripture, the confession of God's

[67]*Das verbüthschiert mit siben Sigeln verschlossen Buch* (Augsburg: Heinrich Steiner, 1539); see Weigelt, *Sebastian Franck,* 78 (no. 20).

[68]*Dialogus* (1545), Piii^v: "Die Weiber sind von Natur bose / und aller sunde ein ursach / derhalben zu meiden / lassen / hassen und fliehen."

[69]*Dialogus* (1545), Piii^v·

[70]*Dialogus* (1545), Qi^v - Qii: "Solches aber kan der gemein Man nicht wol mercken / Ja es ist ummüglich (sic) / das ein schlecht Mensch nicht solt jrrige / ungereimbte und ferliche dancken aus demselbigen seinem Buche schepffen / und seer daraus geergert werden. Es kan sich ein Idiot nicht daraus entrichten / weil er nicht sihet / was vor oder hernacher stehet im Text. Auch kan er alles nicht nachsuchen / weil er auch kein Dialecticam weis / so kan er nicht sehen / wie es folge oder nicht. Weil es aber stracks gegeneinander gestellet ist / also das wo ein Spruch ja ist / da ist der ander Nein / so lesst sichs ansehen als were die Schrifft gantz und stracks wider einander."

[71]*Dialogus* (1545), Qii: "Das kein Spruch / ja kein buchstaben (wie er thar sagen / doch mit keinem grunde) drinnen ist / der nicht ein widersprechen und gegen buchstaben habe / das ist warlich nicht eine Christliche ubung / sondern eine verwirrung der gewissen."

word, and a godfearing life.[72] Freder the pastor and paedagogue stood hand in hand with Freder the defender of women and marriage. Freder's goal of reforming Christian attitudes was one of the Reformation's agendas that historians have increasingly acknowledged and debated. In reference to Luther, Helmar Junghans has called this agenda the "Christianization of culture." Junghans defines Luther's goal as penetrating culture with the gospel and he describes how Luther pursued that goal in the realms of politics, education, and art.[73] Freder's treatise demonstrates how the goal of Christianizing attitudes was also pursued in the realm of domestic and gender relations. Freder's view of what needed to be changed was more radical, however, than the typical attack of reformers on celibacy and on the marital provisions of canon law.[74] Freder was not so much advocating a change from one kind of Christian piety to another. Instead, he was asking for a conversion of unchristian or pagan attitudes into Christian ones.

In this respect, Freder's agenda was closer to the hypothetical agendas proposed for the Catholic and Protestant Reformations by Jean Delumeau, namely, that both were processes by which the masses were to be Christianized and religion spiritualized.[75] Delumeau's testing of this hypothesis for the Catholic Reformation focused on the relics of paganism in religious practice and on their repression by a diligent and worthier clergy. Freder's goal of substituting Christian attitudes for pagan ones was more demanding and elusive; not only practice, but also hearts and minds had to be changed if one would be Christian.

To what extent he or any other reformers expected to succeed is highly controversial.[76] That judgment depends partly upon whether the sin which made women and men equal before God also included their failure to attain

[72]*Dialogus* (1545), Qii:"Die ubung so der heilig Geist uns furstellet / stehet nicht in solchen gesuchten / und on not gemachten Antinomiis / dadurch arme gewissen seer verworren und beschweret werden / sonder ein richtiger / klarer auslegung der Schrifft / in bekentnis Göttliches worts / und in einem Gottfurchtigen leben."

[73]Helmar Junghans, "Luther und die Kultur," *Lutherjahrbuch* 52 (1985): 164-83, esp. 172-79.

[74]Ozment, for example, discusses the Protestant defense of marriage under the heading of celibacy, the liberation of women from the nunnery, and the critique of canon law: *When Fathers Ruled*, 1-49.

[75]Jean Delumeau, *Catholicism between Luther and Voltaire: A New View of the Counter-Reformation*, trans. Jeremy Moiser (French ed. 1971; London: Burns & Oates, and Philadelphia: Westminster, 1977), 161.

[76]The catalyst for this controversy was the thesis of Gerald Strauss that the Reformation failed insofar as it tried to make people think and act as Christians: *Luther's House of Learning: Indoctrination of the Young in the German Reformation* (Baltimore: Johns Hopkins University Press, 1978), 307-308. For responses to Strauss, see James M. Kittelson, "Successes and Failures in the German Reformation: The Report from Strasbourg," *Archiv für Reformationsgeschichte* 73 (1982): 153-75; Scott H. Hendrix, "Luther's Impact on the Sixteenth Century," *Sixteenth Century Journal* 16 (1985): 3-14.

XII

266

the Christian ideal which Freder espoused. On the one hand, Freder
certainly wanted Christians to honor and respect women as partners in a
marital relationship of affection and fidelity. Ironically, despite his attack
on Franck, Freder would have supported Franck in deploring the breakdown
of marital commitment.[77] On the other hand, his Protestant recognition
of the serious impact of sin on human attitudes and conduct would have
prevented Freder, as it did Luther and other reformers,[78] from expecting
the perfect realization of his ideal. The acceptance of divorce by Protestant
theologians, though they disagreed on what constituted licit grounds,[79]
demonstrates that they did not expect all Christians to have successful
marriages which corresponded to their model. In the realm of domestic
relations, as in education and the practice of piety, the Reformation intensified
Christian standards while it simultaneously acknowledged and provided
for human limitations.

[77]See above, n. 18.
[78]See Hendrix, "Luther's Impact," 7-8.
[79]See Thomas Max Safley, "Protestantism, Divorce, and the Breaking of the Modern
Family," in *Pietas et Societas: New Trends in Reformation Social History. Essays in Memory of
Harold J. Grimm,* ed. Kyle C. Sessions and Phillip N. Bebb (Kirksville, Mo.: Sixteenth Century
Journal Publishers, 1985), 35-56, here 38-40.

XIII

LUTHER'S LOYALTIES AND THE AUGUSTINIAN ORDER

Scholars who have found a positive correlation between Luther and Augustine or between Luther and late medieval Augustinianism have been forced either to contradict Luther's own assessment or to rely on indirect evidence for their conclusions. Those scholars who have focused on the immediate significance that Augustine's writings had for the young Luther have been confronted by Luther's own disavowal of this significance in his *Table Talk*. For example, analyzing Luther's use of the *Confessions*, Pierre Courcelle took exception to the notion, promoted at table by Luther himself, that Augustine's *Confessions* did not teach doctrine but instead provided inspiration and example.[1] According to Courcelle, the *Confessions* did in fact provide a doctrinal basis which Luther was able to elaborate into his new theology.[2]

Pursuing Luther's use of Augustine's *De spiritu et litera* in careful textual studies, both Bernhard Lohse and Leif Grane have argued that Augustine served Luther as the gateway to a new understanding of Paul's letter to the Romans and thus brought Luther to the threshold of his new evangelical theology.[3] In the same excerpt from the *Table Talk* in which he minimized the doctrinal content of

---

[1] *Luthers Werke, Kritische Gesamtausgabe, Tischreden*, Weimar, 1912-1921 [= WATR], 1, 140.10-11 (no. 347): "Libri Confessionum nihil docent, sed tantum accendunt, continent tantum exemplum, sed leren nichts." The following additional abbreviations are used for the collected works of Luther: WA = *Luthers Werke. Kritische Gesamtausgabe. [Schriften]*, Weimar, 1883 ff. WABr = *Luthers Werke. Kritische Gesamtausgabe, Briefwechsel*. Weimar, 1930 ff. LW = *Luther's Works, American Edition*. ed. Jaroslav Pelikan and Helmut Lehmann, Philadelphia and St. Louis, 1955-1986.

[2] Pierre Courcelle, "Luther interprète des Confessions de Saint Augustin," *RHPhR* 39 (1959), pp. 235-250, esp. 236, 248-249.

[3] Bernhard Lohse, "Die Bedeutung Augustins für den jungen Luther," *KuD* 11 (1965), 116-135; reprinted in *Evangelium in der Geschichte: Studien zu Luther und der Reformation*. ed. Leif Grane, Bernd Moeller, Otto Hermann Pesch, Göttingen, 1988, pp. 11-30. Leif Grane, *Modus Loquendi Theologicus: Luthers Kampf um die Erneuerung der Theologie (1515-1518)*. Leiden, 1975.

XIII

the *Confessions*, however, Luther acknowledged that at first he devoured Augustine; but, as soon as he began to understand from Paul what justification by faith meant, then his infatuation with Augustine was over.[4] While this statement can be interpreted to mean what Lohse and Grane plausibly concluded, Luther himself remembered a much sharper disjunction between his devouring of Augustine and his new appreciation of Paul.

For Courcelle, Lohse, and Grane, Augustine was more important for Luther than the Augustinian theology of the Middle Ages. Other scholars have attempted to isolate a late medieval Augustinian[5] school of theology and to demonstrate how this theology was mediated to Luther through members of his own order. For this task Luther has been of little direct help. Heiko Oberman has proposed an elaborate and controversial form of this approach to the impact of Augustine on Luther. According to Oberman, a modern Augustinian school of theology, which contained elements of nominalism, humanism and Augustine and whose father was Gregory of Rimini, was transmitted to Luther through sources in the library at Wittenberg, through Johannes von Staupitz, and possibly through Luther's elder colleague, Andreas Bodenstein von Carlstadt.[6]

Oberman's thesis has been forcefully criticized by David Steinmetz, who argues that theological influence does not necessarily mean theological agreement and that Staupitz had to correct the theology which Luther had learned in Erfurt from teachers of his own order.[7] In his study of Luther and Staupitz, Steinmetz argues further that in the final analysis Luther's new theology of Word and faith was not decisively influenced by Staupitz, who "was content to follow a more traditional and wellmarked path established by

---

[4] *WATR* 1, 140.5-7 (no. 347): "Principio Augustinum vorabam, non legebam, sed da mir in Paulo die thur auffgieng, das ich wuste, was iustificatio fidei ward, da ward es aus mit ihm."

[5] For a helpful distinction among the possible meanings that the term Augustinian might have for late medieval historians, see David C. Steinmetz, *Luther and Staupitz: An Essay in the Intellectual Origins of the Protestant Reformation*, Durham, NC, 1980, pp. 13-16.

[6] Heiko A. Oberman, "Headwaters of the Reformation: *Initia Lutheri—Initia Reformationis*," in *Luther and the Dawn of the Modern Era*, ed. Heiko A. Oberman, Leiden, 1974, pp. 40-88.

[7] David C. Steinmetz, "Luther and the Late Medieval Augustinians: Another Look," *Concordia Theological Monthly* 44 (1973), pp. 245-260, esp. 254-259. Cf. Steinmetz, *Luther and Staupitz*, pp. 4-9, 27-34.

generations of conservative Augustinian theologians."[8] Steinmetz is left to conclude, with only Luther's indirect support, that Staupitz' influence on Luther was mainly pastoral. He helped Luther conquer his anxiety by helping Luther to conquer the source of that anxiety—his bad theology—with a "therapeutic combination of traditional pastoral advice and sound Augustinian theology."[9]

It is not my intention to argue that the above interpretations are flawed either because they contradict Luther's own memory or because they rely indirectly on his statements. Luther's evaluation of his relationship to Augustine and to the Augustinian order should not be taken at face value anymore than, as Steinmetz points out, Luther's evaluations of his own contemporaries should be accepted without question.[10] In fact, I want to take Luther's personal statements very seriously and read them imaginatively in order to interpret such elusive historical categories as influence, relationship, motivation and loyalties. Careful and imaginative reading, informed by categories of interpretation that illuminate the text, is necessary in order to appreciate Luther's reevaluation of his monastic and Augustinian heritage. Such a reevaluation is stated forcefully and personally in the letter of 1521 in which Luther dedicated the treatise *De votis monasticis iudicium* to his father Hans.[11] The purpose of this essay is to investigate how Luther's loyalty to his father and mother and the loyalty to his monastic vows interacted to liberate him from his initial religious commitment and to shape his new self-understanding as "a monk and not a monk, a new creature, not of the pope, but of Christi."[12]

According to Luther, he is not dedicating the treatise to his father, whom he adresses as "dearest parent," in order to glorify the family name; but, by using the conflict between them over his entrance into the monastery, he intends to illustrate the point of the treatise for his readers.[13] In fact, Luther is doing much more. He is

---

[8] Steinmetz, *Luther and Staupitz*, p. 141.
[9] *Ibid.*, p. 143.
[10] *Ibid.*, p. 142.
[11] *WA* 8, 573-576. Reference will also be made to the English translation of this letter in *LW* 48: *Letters I*, ed. and transl. by Gotfried G. Krodel, Philadelphia, 1963, pp. 329-336.
[12] *WA* 8, 575.28-29: "Itaque iam sum monachus et non monachus, nova creatura, non Papae, sed Christi."
[13] *WA* 8, 573.6-12: "Hunc librum tibi, parens carissime, nuncupare consilium fuit, non ut nomen tuum ferrem in orbem et in carne gloriaremur adversus

also settling accounts with his father in the sense that he reevaluates the impact of his father's expectations in both his decision to become a monk and in his decision as of 1521 to reject his monastic vows. The dynamics of this reevaluation of what he owed his parents is, in my opinion, the key to understanding how Luther was able to free himself from his monastic vows and to shape a new religious loyalty.[14] A careful summary of his developing views on monastic vows, although helpful, does not adequately explain how Luther was able to take this personal step.[15] By dedicating this treatise to his father, Luther himself unwittingly provides the key to his own reverse conversion, that is, his free choice to move from the cloister into the world.

Raising the question of Luther's relationship to his father immediately raises the specter of psychohistory and the controversial interpretation of the young Luther proposed by Erik Erikson.[16] Most of the reasons for being critical of Erikson's book have been pointed out by scholars.[17] Neither Erikson's historical errors,[18] however, nor the assertion that his method is not scientific[19] disqualifies

---

doctrinam Pauli, sed ut occasionem apprehenderem, quae sese inter te et me opportune obtulit, brevi prologo et causam et argumentum et exemplum huius libelli piis lectoribus enarrandi." Cf. *LW* 48, 331.

[14] When Luther describes himself as a new creature of Christ, he says that he both is a monk and not a monk (above, n. 12). This description appears to reflect the ambivalence about monastic vows that he harbored some three months earlier (August 1, 1521; *WABr* 2, 371.29-31), but instead Luther is declaring the newly-acquired freedom from vows which he documents in this letter.

[15] Such summaries have been written by Bernhard Lohse, *Mönchtum und Reformation: Luthers Auseinandersetzung mit dem Mönchsideal des Mittelalters*, Göttingen, 1963; and, more recently, by Heinz-Meinolf Stamm, *Luthers Stellung zum Ordensleben*, Wiesbaden, 1980. Neither author attributes significance to Luther's letter or to the relationship between Luther and his father.

[16] Erik H. Erikson, *Young Man Luther: A Study in Psychoanalysis and History*, New York, 1958.

[17] For important critiques of Erikson, see the following collections of essays: *Psychohistory and Religion: The Case of the Young Man Luther*, ed. Roger A. Johnson, Philadelphia, 1977; *Encounter with Erikson: Historical Interpretation and Religious Biography*, ed. Donald Capps, Walter H. Capps, M. Gerald Bradford, Missoula, 1977; *Childhood and Selfhood: Essays on Tradition, Religion, and Modernity in the Psychology of Erik H. Erikson*, ed. Peter Homans, Lewisburg and London, 1978.

[18] Critiques of Erikson's use of historical evidence are provided by Roland Bainton, "Psychiatry and History: An Examination of Erikson's *Young Man Luther*," *Religion in Life* 40 (1971), pp. 450-478; Lewis Spitz, "Psychohistory and History: The Case of Young Man Luther," in *Encounter with Erikson* (above, n. 17), pp. 33-65. A critical summary of psychological analyses of Luther is given by Eric W. Gritsch, *Martin—God's Court Jester: Luther in Retrospect*, Philadelphia, 1983, pp.

XIII

240

Luther's familial relationships as a resource for understanding his
life and thought. There are, however, good grounds for conceptua-
lizing the significance of Luther's familial legacy in a manner different from Erikson. For, despite Erikson's sensitivity to Luther's
historical context and the nuanced character of his analysis, it
remains the story of a pathological condition, an identity diffusion,
that was healed after a long delay.[20] In the first place, it is in-
trinsically unfair to focus on psychological and developmental defi-
ciencies without recognizing that they are rooted in relational struggles. In the second place, it is possible to apply Luther's familial
legacy to the development of his life and thought in a way that does
not require a pathological diagnosis. This possibility is explored
through the non-psychoanalytical, non-pathological model employed below.

By the time Luther dedicated his treatise on monastic vows to his
father, November 21, 1521, Luther had been an Augustinian monk
for sixteen of his thirty-eight years. During that period he had
developed a strong loyalty to the monastic life. Luther demonstrated that loyalty by the seriousness with which he attempted to
follow the Augustinian rule,[21] much as a child reveals loyalty to its

---

146-152. A different psychohistorical approach, which focuses on the historical
perception of Luther instead of on Luther as a patient, has been sketched by
Joachim Scharfenberg, "Martin Luther in psychohistorischer Sicht," in *Europa in
der krise der Neuzeit: Martin Luther: Wandel und Wirkung seines Bildes*, ed. Susanne
Heine, Vienna, 1986, pp. 113-128.
[19] This criticism has been expressed by Mark U. Edwards, Jr., "Erikson, Experimental Psychology, and Luther's Identity," in *Childhood and Selfhood* (above, n. 17),
pp. 89-112. Edwards argues that Erikson's psychoanalytically-based theory is
more inferential than theories of experimental psychology which can be more
helpful to the historian. I fail to see, however, how Edwards' application of the
theory of cognitive dissonance to Luther's attacks on his Protestant opponents (pp.
103-105) is less inferential than Erikson's application of developmental theory to
Luther's youth.
[20] *Young Man Luther*. p. 99. On the same page Erikson reveals the pathological
character of his diagnosis: "The story of the fit in the choir has prepared us for the
pathological dimension in the spiritual struggle to come. We shall enlarge on this
dimension in the direction of *desperate patienthood* and then in that of *fanatic leadership*;
and finally, discuss a theme which these two conditions have in common: *childhood
lost*." Cf. Erikson, p. 148: "It seems entirely probable that Martin's life at times
approached what today we might call a borderline psychotic state in a young man
with prolonged adolescence and reawaked infantile conflicts."
[21] See Scott H. Hendrix, *Luther and the Papacy: Stages in A Reformation Conflict*,
Philadelphia, 1981, pp. 7-8. See also Martin Brecht, *Martin Luther: His Road to
Reformation 1483-1521*, transl. James L. Schaaf, Philadelphia, 1985 (German ed.:

XIII

parents by trying faithfully to please them and to follow their rules. Several remarks by Luther himself confirm the testimony of others that he was a serious and scrupulous monk. Defending himself in 1533 against a charge by Cochlaeus that he had violated his monastic vows, Luther contended: "If ever a monk went to heaven through monkery, I intended to get there likewise."[22] And, after explaining to his father why God allowed him to experience the monastery and scholastic theology, Luther stated succinctly that as a monk he lived indeed not without sin but without fault.[23]

Luther's words also indicate that he was more loyal to the monastic life as such than to the specifically Augustinian form of that life or to Augustine himself. When he recalls Hans's anxiety about himself as a young man, Luther is reminded of a single phrase from a passage in the *Confessions* in which Augustine describes his father's joy at the possibility of progeny.[24] Luther fails to note, however, a striking similarity between the concern of Hans for him and the fear, as her son describes it, that Monica had for the young Augustine.[25] Surprisingly, in the letter to Hans, Luther does not specifically mention the Augustinian Order at all. In fact, although Luther

---

1981), pp. 63-70.

[22] *WA* 38, 143.25-29: "War ists, Ein frommer Münch bin ich gewest, Und so gestrenge meinen Orden gehalten, das ichs sagen thar: ist jhe ein Münch gen himel komen durch Müncherei, so wolt ich auch hinein komen sein. Das werden mir zeugen alle meine Klostergesellen, die mich gekennet haben. Denn ich hette mich (wo es lenger geweret hette), zu tod gemartert mit wachen, beten, lesen, und ander erbeit, etc." Later in this same work (*WA* 38, 146.36-37), Luther declares that now (1532) to be an apostate and runaway monk, as he has been labeled, is one of his proudest boasts before God and his conscience.

[23] *WA* 8, 574.29-30: "Igitur vixi monachus, non sine peccato quidem, sed sine crimine." Cf. *LW* 48, 333.

[24] *WA* 8, 573.20-24: "Metuebas tu paterno affectu imbecillitati meae, cum essem iam adulescens, secundum et vicesimum annum ingressus, hoc est, fervente (ut Augustini verbo utar) adolescentia indutus, quod multis exemplis didiceras hoc vitae genus infoeliciter quibusdam cecidisse." Cf. *LW* 48, 331. Cf. also Augustine, *Confessions* II, 3 (6) (*CChr, Series Latina* 27, Turnholt, 1981, p. 20.22-27): "Quin immo ubi me ille pater in balneis vidit pubescentem et inquieta indutum adulescentia, quasi iam ex hoc in nepotes gestiret, gaudens matri indicavit, gaudens vinulentia, in qua te iste mundus oblitus est creatorem suum et creaturam tuam pro te amavit, de vino invisibili perversae atque inclinatae in ima voluntatis suae." Courcelle notes ("Luther interprète," p. 250, n. 78) that the attitude of Luther's father appears to be directly opposite to that of Augustine's parents. More striking, however, is the contrast between the way in which Augustine blames his father for his worldly attitude and the manner in which Luther credits his father's paternal concern.

[25] *CChr* 27, 20.27-32: "Sed matris in pectore iam inchoaveras templum tuum et

had enormous respect for Augustine, in general he does not link that respect to his membership in the Order. In 1525, Duke George of Saxony appeals to Luther to return to the bosom of the church for the sake of his master Augustine, "to whose rule he has sworn a vow." But Luther does not deign this appeal worthy of a reply.[26] An earlier remark is even more telling. Defending his preference for Augustine over Jerome to Spalatin in 1516, Luther maintains that it is not based on belonging to the Augustinian Order, since Augustine did not impress him at all before he [Luther] began to read his books.[27]

Luther's rejection of monastic vows appears to have had no direct relationship either to Augustine or to the Order named after him. The loyalty to his vows as monastic was stronger than his loyalty to them as Augustinian vows. This observation is pregnant with consequences for assessing Luther's relationship to Augustinianism, however it is defined. It explains why Luther's praise of Augustine, though mostly positive, is not unqualified, and why it is so difficult to prove that Augustinianism as a theological tradition within the Order had a decisive impact on him. At the same time, the weakness of a distinctly Augustinian loyalty suggests that the historian look elsewhere for the roots of his new religious loyalty. More precisely, in addition to his thought, it suggests that we look to Luther's relationships and actions and concretely to the struggle that led to his renunciation of the monastic life.

Even though he sought conscientiously to follow the monastic rule, Luther was not able to dismiss his father's strong disapproval of his decision to enter the monastery. In his letter, Luther recounts the story of that disapproval and what lay behind it. Hans was

---

exordium sanctae habitationis tuae: nam ille adhuc catechumenus et hoc recens erat. Itaque illa exilivit pia trepidatione ac tremore et quamvis mihi nondum fideli, timuit tamen vias distortas, in quibus ambulant qui ponunt ad te tergum et non faciem."

[26] *WABr* 3, 650.180-185 (no. 956; December 28, 1525): "Die Cristlich kirch schleust nicht den schoss dem widerkomenden. Hat dich deyn find gefurt in ufgeblasene hoffart, wie do pfleget zu tun die kunst, sich an den hoffertigen Arryaner, deynen meister Augustinum, des regel du gelobet und geschworn hast, kere mit yhme wider, halt nach deyn treu und eyd und wirt mit ime eyn erwelt liecht der Cristenheit." *WABr* 4, 18.4-5 (no. 973; January 20, 1526).

[27] *WABr* 1, 70.17-24 (no. 27; October 19, 1516): "Non quod professionis meae studio ad b. Augustinum probandum trahar, qui apud me, antequam in libros eius incidissem, ne tantillum quidem favoris habuit, ..."

XIII

afraid that his son would succumb to the temptations of "hot adolescence," which the monastic life could not control.[28] In his mind, Hans had another, more beneficial plan for Martin, namely, to help him settle down in a prosperous marriage. Luther also reports how the direct words of his father lodged in his mind and remained there. First, in response to Luther's claim that he was forced to enter the monastery by "terrors from heaven" that scared him to death, Hans had remarked: "I hope that it was not an illusion or a trick." This statement, says Luther, "penetrated to the depths of my soul and stayed there, as if God had spoken by your lips, ... "[29] Second, when Luther reproached his father for his indignation, Hans retorted: "Have you not also heard that parents are to be obeyed?" Luther describes these words as such an apt and opportune reply that scarcely in his entire life had he heard a word from any man that struck him so powerfully and stayed with him so long.[30]

Hans's words must have echoed in Luther's ears during his entire monastic career, encountering resistance at first,[31] but then, as the monastic life increasingly disappointed Luther, receiving more and more credibility. The power which Hans's words continued to have over him illustrates the strong loyalty that tied Luther to his father even while he was a monk. As a result, Luther was caught in conflicting loyalties between his religious vow to the Order and to his father. This conflict was not pathological. All children remain loyal to their parents by virtue of their birth, and the process of becoming adults requires the redefining of these loyalties so that

---

[28] See above, n. 24.

[29] WA 8, 573.30-574.4: "Memini enim nimis praesente memoria, cum iam placatus mecum loquereris, et ego de coelo terroribus me vocatum assererem, neque enim libens et cupiens fiebam monachus, multo minus vero ventris gratia, sed terrore et agone mortis subditae circumvallatus vovi coactum et necessarium votum: 'Utinam (aiebas) non sit illusio et praestigium.' Id verbi, quasi deus per os tuum sonaret, penetravit et insedit in intimis meis, sed obfirmabam ego cor, quantum potui, adversus te et verbum tuum." Cf. LW 48, 332.

[30] WA 8, 574.4-8: "Addebas et aliud, cum tibi iam opprobrarem filiali fiducia indignationem, repente tu me reverberas et retundis tam opportune et apte, ut in tota vita mea ex homine vix audierim verbum, quod potentius in me sonuerit et heserit. 'Et non etiam (dicebas) audisti tu parentibus esse obediendum?' " Cf. LW 48, 332. Cf. also WATR 1, 294.8-14 (no. 623).

[31] WA 8, 574.8-10: "Verum ego securus in iustitia mea te velut hominem audivi et fortiter contempsi, nam ex animo id verbi contemnere non potui." Cf. LW 48, 332. Cf. also WA 8, 574.3-4.

adult children are able to make positive decisions for themselves even in the face of parental disapproval.[32] Furthermore, "religion is a typical area for deep devotion and fundamental loyalty ties."[33] The religious loyalty of an adult child can be an expression of the invisible loyalty that ties the child to its parents; or, when religious devotion is chosen against the religious background or preference of the parents, that choice can be the child's attempt to separate from the parents and to delineate itself from them.

Luther's decision to enter the monastery could well have served both functions for him. On the one hand, his decision, however suddenly it was carried out, was a product of the piety with which he, like many children of his age, had been imbued. The direct source of this piety for Martin was his mother Margarethe, better known as Hanna, and her relatives in Eisenach. According to Luther's closest colleague, Philipp Melanchthon, and Johannes Schneidewein, rector of Wittenberg University, Hanna was God-fearing, prayerful, and virtuous.[34] From her visits to Wittenberg both Melanchthon and Schneidewein knew Hanna Luder well, and Ian Siggins has argued that they were "reporting quite accurately a piety which was characteristic of her and her Eisenach circle, and which did not fail to leave a lasting impression on her son."[35] In addition, Luther himself reported on the religious devotion of the kinsfolk and the related families among whom he spent the height of his adolescence in Eisenach.[36] For Martin, then, to enter the monastery in response to a religious vow was above all to express loyalty to his mother and to her family whom he knew best in the context of religious devotion. Although Luther does not attribute his piety directly to his mother, he does repay her devotion with a long letter of religious comfort written to Hanna as she lay dying.[37] This

---

[32] This concept of loyalty and of its significance for the decisions of adult children has been developed in the mode of family therapy known as contextual therapy or relational ethics. An elaboration of the concept and the way it operates in the family justice system is discussed in two major works on contextual theory: Ivan Boszormenyi-Nagy and Geraldine M. Spark, *Invisible Loyalties: Reciprocity in Intergenerational Family Therapy*, New York, 1984 (lst ed.: 1973), pp. 37-99; Ivan Boszormenyi-Nagy and Barbara R. Krasner, *Between Give and Take: A Clinical Guide to Contextual Therapy*, New York, 1986, pp. 73-133.
[33] *Invisible Loyalties*, p. 50.
[34] Ian Siggins, *Luther and His Mother*, Philadelphia, 1981, p. 16.
[35] *Ibid.*, p. 51.
[36] *Ibid.*, pp. 51-52.

XIII

concrete contribution of Luther's mother to his development gives due credit to the parent who, as Siggins realizes, is effectively absent from the treatment of Erikson, who calls Luther's development "an almost exclusively masculine story."[38]

Luther's flight into the monastery, therefore, may have been a choice for his mother over his father. Hans Luther was certainly not devoid of piety[39] and apparently tried to reconcile himself after the fact to Luther's decision. After all, in 1507 Hans arrived at the celebration of Luther's first mass with twenty horsemen and gave the Augustinian monastery a handsome gift of twenty gulden for food.[40] Nevertheless, it was Hans and not Hanna (as far as we know) who was severely disappointed by Luther's choice and expressed his stern disapproval. And thus it was Hans whom Luther chose to address when he published his judgment of monastic vows. The Latin language of the letter, which shows that it was intended for the scholarly public and not just private reading, and the polemic that punctuates it, may obscure the personal courage that lies behind the letter. What many adult children are unable to do, however, Luther dares to attempt: both to reclaim his father against whom he had chosen and to redefine his loyalty to Hans in such a way that freed Luther to make momentous personal and religious decisions.

At the most obvious level, Luther asserts that in opposing his becoming a monk Hans Luther had been both right and wrong. He was right because Hans knew and said that God's commandment to

---

[37] WABr 6, 103-106 (no. 1820; May 20, 1531); cf. LW 50, 17-21. In this letter Luther expresses the innate loyalty to Hanna that justifies the adding of his voice to those of her other comforters (LW 50, 18): "Nevertheless, I shall do my part too, and, according to my duty, acknowledge myself to be your child, and you to be my mother, as our common God and creator has made us and bound [verpflichtet] us to each other with mutual ties, so that I shall in this way increase the number of your comforters." Cf. WABr 6, 103.9-13.

[38] Young Man Luther, p. 71; see Siggins, Luther and His Mother, p. 9. Erikson (p. 208) does speculate that in the Bible Luther "at last found a mother whom he could acknowledge."

[39] When asked on his deathbed whether he believed the religious assurances that his son had written to him, Hans responded that he would be a fool if he did not believe them; WATR 1, 89.26-29 (no. 204); cf. WATR 5, 242.26-243.1 (no. 5563). In the letter of consolation sent to his father before he died, Luther appeals to Hans's faith as a resource and comfort; WABr 5, 238-241 (no. 1529; February 15, 1530); cf. LW 49, 267-271.

[40] WATR 2, 133.32-34 (no. 1558); cf. LW 54, 156.

obey parents was to be regarded more highly than anything else. Hans was wrong, however, because he did not act on that belief and pull Martin out of the monastery. Hans would have done that if he had really believed what he said.[41] Out of his disappointing experience with the monastic life, therefore, Luther both acknowledged that his father had been right and blamed Hans for not acting like a responsible parent.

Both the acknowledging and the blaming could be read as a statement of Luther's new understanding of obedience to authority. At the end of his letter, Luther uses the concept of authority to explain his new relationship to his father. Hans's authority over Luther still remains "so far as the monastic life is concerned." But, since God, who has taken him out of the monastery, has an authority that is greater than his father's, the authority of parents must yield to that of God and Christ.[42] In other words, once Luther learned that monastic vows were not God's command (i.e., commanded in Scripture), he could reject them on the basis of a higher authority: not just the command to obey parents, but obedience to what Luther calls the authority of Christ and the ministry of the Word.[43]

Unquestionably, authority was a primary issue for Luther and not just around 1521 at the time of his break with the papacy and the monastic life. The issue of authority and obedience is also compatible with Erikson's thesis that Luther had to resolve the problem of his father's authority in order to solve his own identity crisis. At one point Erikson describes Luther's letter to Hans as a witness to the dichotomy between Luther's obedience to his natural father and to his Father in heaven—a dichotomy that anticipated Luther's dilemma of obedience to God versus obedience to other authorities.[44] What Erikson does not adequately explain, however, is how

[41] WA 8, 574.11-13: "Hic vide, an non et tu ignoraris, mandata dei praeferenda esse omnibus. Nonne si scisses, me adhuc tum fuisse in manu tua, plane e cucullo autoritate paterna extraxisses?" Cf. LW 48, 332.
[42] WA 8, 575.32-35: "Sed nunquam iterum tuo te iure et autoritate spolio? plane autoritas tibi in me manet integra, quod ad monachatum attinet, verum is iam nullus in me est, ut dixi. Caeterum is, qui me extraxit, ius habet in me maius iure tuo, ..." Cf. LW 48, 335.
[43] WA 8, 575.36-576.3: "In ministerio enim verbi me esse, quis potest dubitare? ... sed si pugnet parentum et Christi vocatio vel autoritas, Christi autoritas regnare sola debet." cf. LW 48, 335.
[44] Young Man Luther, p. 49. Erikson does comment positively on Luther's public

XIII

Luther awakened to the reality of choosing for himself and, specifically, how he seized the freedom to choose to be loyal to expectations higher than his father's. Luther's letter, however, gives important clues as to how this liberation occurred.

That liberation is effected through the credit that Luther is able to give to his father. Although Luther charges that his father did not really understand God's commandment to obey parents (because Hans did not extract him from the monastery), he credits Hans nevertheless for the good intentions that stood behind his statements. Luther recognizes that it was fatherly love which underlay Hans's fear of what would happen to Luther in the monastery and also underlay whatever other ambitions he harbored for his son.[45] Luther also bears witness to the innate loyalty that still (*adhuc!*) binds him to his father and acknowledges that divine authority is on Hans's side while on his side there is nothing but human presumption.[46] And even when Luther asserts that the Lord has done what his father could not do, namely, withdraw Luther from the monastery, he does not blame Hans for ignorance or weakness, but tenderly protects his father by proposing that God took control of the situation so that Hans would not be tempted to boast of having done the right thing.[47]

These statements are evidence that Luther began crediting his father before he made his thoughts known in this dedicatory letter. It would make sense that this new recognition of his father's stance began to take hold as Luther became disappointed with monastic life and began to wonder if his father had been right after all. But whenever Luther began to credit his father, he also began to rework his loyalty and to repay his indebtedness to Hans. All children grow up loyal to their parents and indebted to them for the care they have received. Children remain loyal and indebted even when they go

---

revelations in this letter (p. 50): "Perhaps only a man of such stature could be sufficiently sensitive to the personal conflicts that contributed to his theological decisions, and would have enough honesty to talk about them."

[45] *WA* 8, 573.20-21: "Metuebas tu paterno affectu imbecillitati meae, cum essem iam adulescens,..." *LW* 48, 331.

[46] *WA* 8, 574.32-34: "Quid igitur nun cogitas? An adhuc me extrahes? adhuc enim parens es, adhuc ego filius sum, et vota omnia nullius sunt momenti. A parte tua autoritas divina, a mea parte stat praesumptio humana." Cf. *LW* 48, 333.

[47] *WA* 8, 575.23-24: "Sed ad te revertar, parens mi, Et iterum dico: Nunquid me extrahes adhuc? At ne tu glorieris, praevenit te dominus et ipse me extraxit." Cf. *LW* 48, 334.

against the wishes of their parents. But if their action is a rebellion born of despair that is based on blaming the parents, that action is only a reaction that betrays the bondage of their indebtedness. The opposite of loyalty-bound indebtedness is entitlement, the earned freedom of adult children to act positively on their own behalf. Entitlement is earned not by blaming, but by crediting parents for their care and the contributions which they made to their children's lives. When children are able to credit their parents' care for them, no matter how limited it might have been, children begin to pay off their indebtedness and to earn their freedom.[48] In earning this entitlement, children remain loyal to their parents, but that loyalty now undergirds their freedom instead of undercutting it.

As Luther reworked the loyalty to his father, he also redefined more fully his religious loyalty. That process of redefinition had already begun prior to 1521, insofar as Luther had gradually, and under pressure, withdrawn obedience from the papal hierarchy. By the time of his letter to Hans, Luther had been excommunicated from the Roman Church and was convinced that the pope was the Antichrist; but he was still a monk and a professor of theology at the University of Wittenberg. His academic position, especially his doctorate in theology,[49] was, in his eyes, the anchor of his credibility and legitimacy as a teacher, preacher, and critic of the Roman hierarchy. But his identity as a monk and a member of the Augustinian Order was on shakier ground. By late 1521 monks had already begun to abandon the monasteries, including the cloister of the Augustinians in Wittenberg where Luther lived. This development prompted Luther, who was in seclusion at the Wartburg, to issue his judgment on monastic vows.[50] Luther's purpose was to enable

---

[48] *Between Give and Take*, p. 100: "The person who gives care earns merit or *entitlement* as a reward. Effectively earned entitlement results in personal liberation, i.e., in the individual's security to let life unfold." In a letter to Melanchthon Luther credits his father most explicitly after he hears of his father's death; *LW* 49, 319 (June 5, 1530): "This death has certainly thrown me into sadness, thinking not only [of the bonds] of nature, but also of the very kind love [my father had for me]; for through him my Creator has given me all that I am and have.... Since I am now too sad, I am writing no more; for it is right and God-pleasing for me, as a son, to mourn such a father, from whom the Father of mercies has brought me forth, and through whose sweat [the Creator] has fed and raised me to whatever I am [now]." Cf. *WABr* 5, 351.22-24, 33-36 (no. 1584).

[49] See Hendrix, *Luther and the Papacy*, pp. 11-12.

[50] *WABr* 2, 404.6-405.11 (no. 441; November 22, 1521): "Vaga & incerta relatione didici deposuisse apud nostros quosdam cucullum, quod ne forte non satis firma

those who wanted to give up the monastic life to do so with good consciences; but, as the dedicatory letter to Hans makes clear, he was also wrestling with his own loyalty to the monastic life.

Other people were more sure of Luther's identity than was Luther himself. As soon as Luther's cause against the papacy had come into public view, Luther was glorified by the humanists who wanted to make that cause their own and Luther their champion.[51] In 1521, there even appeared in Strasbourg a parody which retold the story of Luther's appearance at the Diet of Worms as the passion story of Christ.[52] Although he did not identify himself with Christ, the glorification of Luther by friends and admirers did encourage him to interpret his conflict with the papacy as the work of Christ.[53] While that glorification provided external legitimacy for his public stand, however, at the end of 1521 Luther was still seeking for himself that personal entitlement which, in addition to his doctorate, would fortify that stand and guide him in the uncertain months that lay ahead.

The letter to Hans is thus a stop-action photograph that catches Luther at a crucial point in the reworking of his religious loyalty. The process was well underway because Luther's loyalty to the papacy had already crumbled. The question of acting against one's vows, however, for Luther and other monks, brought the process to a head, because monastic vows were the form of religious loyalty that was directly tied to Luther's filial loyalty. Luther's struggle with indebtedness and entitlement thus becomes visible at this point; and it is no accident that Luther dedicated *De votis monasticis* to Hans. Nor is the letter, as the Weimar editor maintains, an "atoning personal confession,"[54] as if Luther were trying to make up

conscientia facerent, timui. Hic timor extorsit mihi eum libellum, ut & mei nominis, siqua est, autoritate vel apud pios & bonos levarentur & apud semetipsos magis animarentur."

[51] Helmar Junghans, "Initia gloriae Lutheri," in *Der junge Luther und die Humanisten*, Weimar, 1984, pp. 288-318; first published in *Unterwegs zur Einheit - Festschrift für Heinrich Stirnimann.* ed. Johannes Brantschen and Pietro Selvatico, Freiburg [Switzerland] and Vienna, 1980, pp. 292-324.

[52] For a complete study and texts of this work, see Johannes Schilling, *Passio Doctoris Martini Lutheri: Bibliographie, Texte und Untersuchungen*, Gütersloh, 1989.

[53] Junghans, "Initia gloriae Lutheri," in *Der junge Luther und die Humanisten*, p. 317.

[54] *WA* 8, 565: "Dadurch wird seine Schrift zum sühnenden Selbstbekenntnis ...."

either for his mistake of entering the monastery or for his disobedience to Hans. Luther's conscience is not liberated by confessing or apologizing, but by crediting his father and by redefining his religious loyalty.

As Luther expresses it, his religious loyalty is no longer to the false service of the monks but to the true service of God.[55] And on the basis of that loyalty Luther claims a new religious identity, which he describes as being a new creature of Christ that does not depend on whether he wears the monastic cowl or not: "Therefore I am still a monk and yet not a monk. I am a new creature, not of the pope but of Christ."[56] Luther also testifies to the new freedom that accompanies this loyalty, defining it typically as the liberation of conscience, but then qualifying it exuberantly as liberation without measure (*abundantissime*)![57] Freedom of conscience does not mean that Luther now has no loyalty tie whatsoever, but that he has chosen to be religiously loyal in a new way, namely to Christ and the service of God, which he also embraces as the ministry of the Word.[58]

Luther's newly realized freedom is not only liberation from the monastery to which he had fled, but the earned capacity to choose for himself a new religious loyalty and identity. This entitlement is the product of crediting the good intention of his father and of being snatched by God, as he experienced it, from the false service of monasticism. Why, then, does Luther still make a point of faulting his father for not pulling him out of the monastery? Why did Luther not just agree that his father had been right and, on that basis, justify his renunciation of monastic vows? Erikson explains Luther's criticism of his father as his "ambivalent wish to be right at all costs."[59] It was not ambivalent stubbornness that motivated Luther, however; his refusal only to admit that his father had been right

---

[55] *WA* 8, 575.35-36: "Caeterum is [Deus], qui me extraxit, ius habet in me maius iure tuo, a quo me vides positum iam non in fictitio illo monasticorum, sed vero cultu dei." Cf. *LW* 48, 335.
[56] *WA* 8, 575.28-29: "Itaque iam sum monachus et non monachus, nova creatura, non Papae, sed Christi." Cf. *LW* 48, 335.
[57] *WA* 8, 575.27-28: "Conscientia liberata est, id quod abundantissime est liberari." *LW* 48, 335.
[58] *WA* 8, 575.36-37: "In ministerio enim verbi me esse quis potest dubitare?" Cf. *WA* 8, 576.5.
[59] *Young Man Luther*, p. 49. Erikson adds (pp. 232-233) that for Luther "the father had been wrong because God alone could be right; and only Martin could have found this out—by becoming a monk."

XIII

after all was part of his struggle for genuine entitlement. Crediting one's parents does not mean agreeing completely with them or admitting that they were, or are, always right. It includes acknowledging their limitations alongside their contributions. Moreover, gaining entitlement does not require surrendering the differentiation that one has attained from parents; instead, that differentiation is transformed into a positive force that enhances rather than dilutes the validity of one's own decisions. If Luther had merely made confession to Hans that he had been right all along, then Luther would not have gained freedom or entitlement; he would have remained loyalty-bound to Hans and indebted to him for permission to leave the monastery.

Luther's insistence, therefore, that God did what Hans could not do and that God's authority is greater than the authority of parents demonstrates how Luther's new religious loyalty complemented the crediting of Hans to earn him entitlement. In Luther's mind, only with the help of his new religious loyalty to Christ and the ministry of the Word was he able to rework his filial loyalty so that it brought liberation. This is the meaning of his puzzling statement: "Therefore—so I am now absolutely persuaded—I could not have refused to obey you without endangering my conscience unless [Christ] had added the ministry of the Word to my monastic profession."[60] The ministry of the Word, the object of his new religious loyalty, gave Luther the inner authority or leverage, as it were, to renounce his monastic vows without dismissing or finally blaming his father. That inner authority, together with the act of crediting his father's care, earned Luther the entitlement that made him a new, free creature, who was no longer bound either to his vows or to his father.

The statement just quoted could be interpreted to mean that Luther had an authority problem which he solved only by legitimizing the disobedience to his father (and consequently to other earthly authorities) with obedience to a higher authority (i.e., to God). Luther does explain what happened to him in terms of authority,[61] but again not by blaming his father or by trying to

---

[60] *LW* 48, 335. Cf. *WA* 8, 576.4-6: "Itaque sub conscientiae meae periculo tibi non obedire non possem (ita sum modo persuasissimus), ubi ministerium verbi ultra monachatum non accessisset."

[61] See above, page , and notes 42 and 43.

appease him. In that case, he would have transferred a rebellious stance against his father to the papacy and to monastic vows in the name of divine obedience. Instead, once again he credits his father's ignorance (and his own) of what it truly meant to put the commandments of God beyond everything else: to obey the call and authority of Christ when it contradicts the wishes of parents.[62] Concretely, this meant what neither Hans nor Martin could have known in 1505, but what Luther had since learned, namely, what the true calling and service of God were not. For monks and priests to withdraw themselves from obedience to parents under the cover of piety and in the name of serving God was neither to obey God's commandment nor to enlist in God's service.[63] In 1521, therefore, Luther's appeal to divine authority and against monastic vows was not a product of rebellion against his father's authority but a choice for a new religious loyalty that emerged from his own experience and was empowered through crediting his father.

Luther's new religious loyalty, however, was not the endpoint of his quest for freedom. While his personal entitlement enabled him to choose for Christ and the ministry of the Word over the papacy and monastic vows, it was also limited by this same choice. Or, more correctly expressed, although he experienced his conscience as liberated, his struggle to be free was not over. The struggle continued because personal freedom is never complete and personal entitlement is never perfect. Even adult children who have gained freedom from their parents' expectations are tempted to make parents out of other people, ideas, or institutions. This process, called parentification, "always implies one person's dependent clinging to an unmatched partner,"[64] from whom one expects excessive care and to whom one cedes unearned authority. Religious commitment always involves a degree of parentification insofar as

---

[62] WA 8, 576.1-7: "Non quod parentum autoritatem hoc verbo evacuaverit, cum Apostolus toties inculcet, ut filii obediant parentibus, sed si pugnet parentum et Christi vocatio et autoritas, Christi autoritas regnare sola debet .... Hoc est, quod dixi, neque te neque me scivisse antea, Mandata dei omnibus praeferenda esse." Cf. LW 48, 335.

[63] WA 8, 576.7-13. Cf. LW 48, 335-336.

[64] Between Give and Take, p. 328. Cf. Invisible Loyalties, p. 151: "By definition, parentification implies the subjective distortion of a relationship as if one's partner or even children were his parent." For further discussion of the concept and of the deparentification that accompanies the increase of entitlement, see Between Give and Take, pp. 327-329, and Invisible Loyalties, pp. 151-166.

XIII

some dependence on God is sought and accepted. When Luther transfers his loyalty from monastic vows to Christ and to the ministry of the Word, he also parentifies the latter. In Luther's letter to Hans this parentification becomes most evident when he exclaims: "Who can doubt that I am in the ministry of the Word?"[65] Of course, anyone could doubt that and many people did, Luther's conviction notwithstanding. Even his declaration of liberty near the end of the letter reveals how Christ has replaced all other superiors: "Although he [Christ] has made me the servant of all men, I am, nevertheless, subject to no one except to him alone. He is himself (as they say) my immediate bishop, abbot, prior, lord, father and teacher; I know no other."[66]

Nevertheless, in Luther's case, the parentification of Christ served remarkably well to protect the degree of freedom and entitlement that he had attained by the end of 1521. This freedom was enhanced by Luther's redefinition of faith in Christ, which has the essential features of innate family loyalty. For medieval scholastic theology, faith was either belief in the articles "of faith" or a power of the soul that could be broken down into its functions. For Luther, however, faith is not a power; instead, faith *has* power, and that power binds the believer to Christ.[67] Or to use Luther's more expressive words: "True faith embraces with wide-open arms and rejoicing the Son of God given for it and says: 'My beloved is mine and I am his' [Song of Songs 2:16]."[68] The bond of loyalty that ties family members together through their biological relationship is

---

[65] *WA* 8, 575.36-37 (above, n. 58).
[66] *LW* 48, 336. Cf. *WA* 8, 576.14-18: "Mitto itaque hunc librum, in quo videas, quantis signis et virtutibus Christus me absolverit a voto monastico, et tanta libertate me donarit, ut, cum omnium servum fecerit, nulli tamen subditus sim nisi sibi soli. Ipse enim est meus immediatus (quod vocant) Episcopus, Abbas, Prior, dominus, pater et magister. Alium non novi amplius." Luther's words recall his famous theses from the treatise on Christian liberty (*WA* 7, 49.22-25): "Christianus homo omnium dominus est liberrimus, nulli subiectus. Christianus homo onmium servus est officiosissimus, omnibus subiectus." Cf. *LW* 31, 344.
[67] This lucid analysis is made by Gerhard Ebeling, "Fides occidit rationem: Ein Aspekt der theologia crucis in Luthers Auslegung von Gal 3,6," in *Lutherstudien III*, Tübingen, 1985, pp. 181-222, here 183-186.
[68] *WA* 39 I, 46.3-4. Cf. *WA* 40 I, 285.5-286.2: "Sed fides facit ex te et Christo quasi unam personam, ut non segregeris a Christo, imo inherescas, quasi dicas te Christum, et econtra: ego sum ille peccator, quia inheret mihi et econtra, convincti per fidem in unam 'carnem, os' [Eph. 5:30,31: Vulg.] multo arctiore vinculo quam masculus et femina. Ergo illa fides non otiosa...."

much deeper than the psychological feeling of loyalty.[69] Unlike the feeling of loyalty that can wax or wane depending on circumstances, the bond of loyalty, rooted in trust, possesses the power of tying family members together in spite of the most serious estrangement. For Luther, the same inherent power belongs to the bond of faith that ties together Christ and believers; they are "bound together through faith into one flesh and bone by a much tighter bond than male and female."[70]

Although this loyalty bond of faith ties believers to Christ as to a parent, it deters believers from basing their faith on their internal power or feeling or on their own actions. Instead it keeps believers directed outward toward their relationship with Christ and forces them to rely for nurture on the address which comes from outside themselves, namely, the promise or Word of Christ. This, says Luther, is why "our theology" is certain, "because it snatches us from ourselves and places us outside ourselves (*extra nos*), so that we do not rely on our own powers, conscience, feelings, person, or works, but we rely on that which is outside ourselves, i.e., on the promise and truth of God which cannot deceive."[71] The central place which the *extra nos* holds in Luther's theology[72] is a result of his new understanding of faith as loyalty that binds the believer to Christ alone.

Because this relational, outwardly directed quality of faith parentified Christ and the Word, it prevented Luther from granting parental authority to religious experience, institutions, leaders, or agendas. The parentification of Christ alone and the nature of faith as ultimate loyalty to Christ alone gave to Luther and to the movement that continued to identify with him distinct characteristics that have been noted by historians. That distinctiveness

---

[69] *Between Give and Take*, p. 15.
[70] See above, n. 68.
[71] *WA* 40 III, 589.25-28: "Atque haec est ratio, cur nostra Theologia certa sit: Quia rapit nos a nobis et ponit nos extra nos, ut non nitamur viribus, conscientia, sensu, persona, operibus nostris, sed eo nitamur, quod est extra nos, Hoc est, promissione et veritate Dei, quae fallere non potest." Already in Luther's early lectures on Hebrews (1517-1518), faith in Christ has that non-psychological, relational quality which directs it outward toward the Word; see Kenneth Hagen, *A Theology of Testament in the Young Luther: The Lectures on Hebrews*, Leiden, 1974, pp. 73-76.
[72] See Karl-Heinz zur Mühlen, *Nos extra nos: Theologie zwischen Mystik und Scholastik*, Tübingen, 1972.

XIII

resulted from Luther's refusal, in the name of Christ, to attribute absolute legitimacy or authority to his own person, to his theology, or to a specific program of reform.

In regard to his person, Luther was convinced that God was working through him to accomplish the divine purpose, and he was occasionally willing to claim epithets, such as the German prophet,[73] that others were using for him. In spite of that, however, Luther asked his followers not to use his name to identify the work of Christ. At the same time that he wrote the dedicatory letter to Hans, he also issued an admonition against insurrection in which he urged his followers to name themselves Christian and not Lutheran: "I ask that you not mention my name but call yourselves Christian and not Lutheran. What is Luther? The teaching is not mine. I have not been crucified for anyone.... I am and will not be anyone's master. I possess in common with the community the only common teaching of Christ, who alone is our master."[74] At the moment Luther was trying to forestall religious unrest which might degenerate into a party struggle and discredit what he understood to be God's work. But these words also convey the stance that Luther would attempt to maintain as the reform movement took its course: neither he nor his theology should replace Christ as its leader and norm.

For Luther, the appropriation of faith was a lifelong struggle that was not voided by the learning of a correct theological system. Doctrine as teaching was important, and Luther was certainly convinced, to the consternation of his opponents, that he understood and taught the heart of Scripture. Nevertheless, he frequently doubted that his own faith was adequate and regarded it as continually under attack by the devil.[75] These doubts and attacks were not abolished by the theological tracts and confessional statements that issued from his pen. In fact, Luther has puzzled scholars because he did not produce a comprehensive statement of his theology along

---

[73] LW 47, 29; cf. WA 30 III, 290.28-34. Cf. also WA 7, 313.17-29.

[74] WA 8, 685.4-7,14-15; cf. LW 45, 70-71.

[75] For the emphatic elaboration of this point, see Heiko A. Oberman, Luther: Mensch zwischen Gott und Teufel, Berlin, 1981, pp. 326-337, esp. p. 335. Oberman cites a revealing personal statement from a letter that Luther wrote in 1527 to Melanchthon during one of his Anfechtungen: WABr 4, 226.8-13 (no. 1126; August 2, 1527). The constant struggle of faith with sin is not cancelled by the stance of the believer before God as simul iustus et peccator; see Jared Wicks, SJ, "Living and Praying as Simul Iustus et Peccator: A Chapter in Luther's Spiritual Teaching," Gregorianum 70 (1989), pp. 521-548.

the lines of Calvin's *Institutes*. On this point, Luther's reluctance is explained not only by the fact that he was a lecturer on Biblical theology and an *ad hoc* writer, but also by his realization that doctrine can be parentified in such a way that it no longer supports faith but supplants it. Luther's catechisms are the most appropriate statements of his theology, not because they were popular, or because they could be used for indoctrination, but because they were intended as supports for struggling believers in the worship and life of religious communities.

In regard to his work, Luther understood himself not as a reformer but as a forerunner of God's reformation.[76] As such, he refused to outline a program of reform, but made decisions on concrete questions of religious change as those questions arose. Almost three months before his letter to Hans, Luther expressed this attitude toward reform in a letter to Melanchthon concerning the changes proposed by Karlstadt in Wittenberg. At the end of the letter Luther addresses famous words to Melanchthon: "God does not save people who are only fictitious sinners. Be a sinner and sin boldly, but believe and rejoice in Christ even more boldly, for he is victorious over sin, death, and the world."[77] In context, these words are not only a theological protest against religious moralizing, but also a justification for making bold changes even when one fears that the changes might be mistakes. His refusal to develop a detailed reform program did not prevent Luther from making decisions. Luther successfully avoided parentifying religious institutions, although, as new Protestant structures emerged, he was perhaps too ready to allow princes and city councils to function religiously *in loco parentis*. Even so, Luther's insistence that God would take care of whatever reforming needed to be done is strikingly reminiscent of the way in which earned entitlement transforms indebtedness into the personal liberation that has the security to let life unfold.[78]

This entitlement and personal freedom gave to Luther's faith

---

[76] Heiko A. Oberman, "Martin Luther: Vorläufer der Reformation," in *Verifikationen. Festschrift für Gerhard Ebeling zum 70. Geburtstag*, ed. Eberhard Jüngel, Johannes Wallmann, Wilfrid Werbeck, Tübingen, 1982, pp. 91-119.
[77] *LW* 48, 282; cf. *WABr* 2, 372.83-85 (no. 424; August 1, 1521): "Deus non facit salvos ficte peccatores. Esto peccator et pecca fortiter, sed fortius fide et gaude in christo, qui victor est peccati, mortis et mundi."
[78] See above, n. 48.

XIII

that quality of foolhardiness which, according to Oberman, enabled Luther to bear the burdens of being a reformer.[79] To seek the roots of that foolhardiness in the interplay of filial and religious loyalties does not discredit the validity of Luther's faith or the strength that it gave him. Because psychohistorical diagnoses of Luther have been pathological in character, any suggestion that ruminations of the psyche accounted for Luther's religious insights and actions remains suspect. Historians who disagree about Luther's Augustinian heritage agree too easily, it seems, on this point.[80] The interaction of filial and religious loyalties, however, is not an intrapsychic process, but an interhuman dynamic that is not pathological in character. The reworking of filial loyalty is a task that in one way or another occupies all adult children. When that reworking also involves the redirecting of religious loyalty, it can inspire a new quality of faith that refuses to parentify old structures and beliefs or prematurely to yield authority to new ones. Luther identified that new quality as faith's folly, i.e. in Christian terms, the constant struggle to trust in Christ alone against the constant temptation to put that trust elsewhere. It is true that the Wittenberg reformation cannot be separated from the person of Luther; neither, therefore, can it be separated from the rebalancing of loyalties that enabled Luther in 1521 to say to his father that he was no longer a monk but a new creature of Christ.

---

[79] *Luther: Mensch zwischen Gott und Teufel*, p. 326. The characterization of Luther as a fool and court jester and of faith as foolhardiness is Luther's own. See, e.g., his dedication of *An den christlichen Adel* to Nikolaus von Amsdorf; *WA* 6, 404.23-405.3. Cf. *LW* 44, 123-124, esp. 124: "Moreover, since I am not only a fool, but also a sworn doctor of Holy Scripture, I am glad for the opportunity to fulfill my doctor's oath, even in the guise of a fool."

[80] Even Oberman declares that the Wittenberg reformation, while it cannot be separated from the person of Luther, cannot be said to derive from the processing of psychic burdens (*Luther: Mensch zwischen Gott und Teufel*. p. 326). Cf. Steinmetz, *Luther and Staupitz*, p. 143: "It was not the unresolved problems with his father—however serious those problems might be—but unresolved problems with his image of God which drove Luther to despair."

XIII

258

ZUSAMMENFASSUNG

Auf unterschiedlicher Weise hat man versucht, Luthers Verhältnis zu Augustin und dem Augustinismus zu interpretieren und mit seiner reformatorischen Entdeckung und Tätigkeit in Beziehung zu bringen. Hier geht es darum, aufgrund von Luthers Kloster- und Familienerfahrungen zu erklären, wie er sich von den Mönchsgelübden seines Ordens freimachen konnte. Es wird zum Teil von Begriffen und Einsichten aus der Familientherapie Gebrauch gemacht. Zum Beispiel, an dem Widmungsbrief an seinen Vater, den Luther seinem *De votis monasticis iudicium* (1521) vorausschickte, wird gezeigt, wie Luthers Anerkennung der Liebe und der guten Vorsätze seines Vaters ihm die Berechtigung zur Ablehnung der Gelübden und zur neuen Identität als Diener des Wortes schaffte. Der Glaube an Christus allein, der als eine neue Loyalität zu Christus mit dieser Berechtigung verbunden war, hat Luther auch daran verhindert, seiner Person oder seiner Reform oder seiner Theologie uneingeschränkte Autorität zu schenken. Von einer psychopathologischen Erklärung von Luthers Entwicklung, wie Erik Erikson vorgelegt hat, wird Abstand genommen.

XIV

Luther's Contribution to the Disunity of the Reformation

I want to address the theme of the unity of the Reformation by raising anew an old question: How did Luther contribute to the division that occurred within the early evangelical movement? Why did Luther break so uncompromisingly with Karlstadt and then later with Zwingli and with the others whom he labeled *Schwärmer?* Although this subject has frequently been studied, one scholar has claimed that "even more recent research has not been able to answer fully the question of why Luther and his followers disapproved of Karlstadt so categorically."[1]

My questions do not necessarily presuppose a common denominator between Luther and his followers that would allow historians to speak of the early Reformation as a unified movement. Early Reformation unity is an elusive phenomenon. Even though he became enormously popular by 1519, there exists neither a consensus as to why people liked Luther nor agreement that the majority of his followers shared his religious convictions.[2] According to Urbanus Rhegius, writing pseudonymously in 1521, many people, learned and unlearned, misunderstood Luther's views, and some of the common people followed him only because they thought he was against the priests.[3] Nevertheless, in spite of a variety of motives behind it, there did exist a

---

1. Sigrid Looss: "Radical Views of the Early Andreas Karlstadt (1520–1525)," in *Radical Tendencies in the Reformation: Divergent Perspectives,* ed. Hans J. Hillerbrand (Kirksville, MO, 1988), 43–53, here 43. - *Abbreviations: WA: D. Martin Luthers Werke. Kritische Gesamtausgabe* [Schriften] (Weimar, 1883–). *WABr: Martin Luthers Werke. Briefwechsel* (Weimar, 1930–). *LW: Luther's Works. American Edition,* 55 vols. (St. Louis and Philadelphia, 1955–1986).

2. Bernd Moeller: "Das Berühmtwerden Luthers," *Zeitschrift für historische Forschung* 15 (1988): 65–92. For pertinent questions about Luther's audiences, see Hans-Christoph Rublack: "Reformation and Society," in *Martin Luther and the Modern Mind: Freedom, Conscience, Toleration, Rights,* ed. Manfred Hoffmann (New York and Toronto, 1985), 237–278.

3. *Anzaygung das die Romisch Bull / und nit Doctor Mart. Luthers leeer / mercklichen schaden in gewissin mancher menschen gebracht hab / durch Henricum Phoeniceum von Roschach* (s.l. 1522), Aiᵛ.

Originally published in *Archiv für Reformationsgeschichte,* Special volume, The Reformation in Germany and Europe: Interpretations and Issues, ed. H.R. Guggisberg, G.G. Krodel and H. Füglister (Gütersloh, 1993), pp. 48–63, used by permission.

cohesive appreciation of Luther, such as that which resounded early in the chorus of humanists[4] and later in the sermons of evangelical preachers.[5]

At the end of this essay I will set forth my own proposal of how best to understand Luther's appeal and its consequences. Mainly, however, I want to explore the disunity of the Reformation as it was manifested among Luther and his Wittenberg followers. Why did the unity that *seemed* to prevail in Wittenberg until 1522[6] prove so difficult to maintain after Luther's return from the Wartburg? Luther made little attempt to reach a compromise with Karlstadt on the issues over which they disagreed: the interpretation of Scripture and the pace of reform. Although Luther gave clear reasons for his return to Wittenberg in defiance of Elector Frederick's wishes, he did not explain so readily why he exerted no effort to uphold an inclusive movement that would utilize Karlstadt's zeal and contributions. How could Luther, without much regret, allow his colleague and promoter to be so alienated from the evangelical movement?

Some answers are readily available. Karlstadt and Luther disagreed on the pace of reform in Wittenberg because they disagreed on how Scripture, as divine authority (*ius divinum*), should be applied to the mass, to images, and to monastic vows. For Luther, freedom based on the gospel should not be made into a new law, while for Karlstadt Scripture provided obligatory directions for removing stumbling blocks to faith.[7] Beginning with the reform measures which he implemented against the Elector's will, Karlstadt made his own situation untenable through radical personal and pastoral decisions. Meanwhile, Luther reasserted his claim to leadership of the reform in Wit-

---

4. Moeller, "Das Berühmtwerden Luthers," 77–80; Helmar Junghans: "Initiae gloriae Lutheri," in *Unterwegs zur Einheit. Festschrift für Heinrich Stirnimann,* ed. Johannes Brantschen and Pietro Selvatico (Freiburg and Vienna, 1980), 292–324.

5. Bernd Moeller: "Was wurde in der Frühzeit der Reformation in den deutschen Städten gepredigt?" *ARG* 75 (1984), 176–193.

6. In late 1520 Luther had to assure Lazarus Spengler that Karlstadt and Melanchthon did not disagree with one another although "sometimes at the university one says something in a way that is different from the other"; see *WABr* 12, 486. 8–12 (November 17, 1520).

7. See especially Ulrich Bubenheimer: "Scandalum et ius divinum: Theologische und rechtstheologische Probleme der ersten reformatorischen Innovationen in Wittenberg 1521/22," *Zeitschrift der Savigny-Stiftung für Rechtsgeschichte* 90 (kan. Abt.59) (1973), 263–342, esp.326–331; see also Bubenheimer: "Karlstadt, Andreas Rudolff Bodenstein von," *Theologische Realenzyklopädie* 17 (Berlin and New York, 1988), 649–658, esp.651.

tenberg in a manner that discounted Karlstadt's authority.[8] After dismissing the excuse of the Wittenbergers that Karlstadt, Gabriel (Zwilling) or Michael (the archangel) had preached to them how to behave, Luther continued: "That is no good. Everyone must take a stand for themselves and be prepared to do battle with the devil. You have to establish your foundation on a strong, clear saying of Scripture on which you can stand. If you do not have such [a foundation], then you will not be able to survive; the devil will blow you away like a dried-up leaf."[9]

Luther based his claim to authority over Karlstadt on the necessity of combatting the devil with a clear text from Scripture. Soon he would dismiss other evangelical opponents as driven by the same devil which had intruded into his flock in Wittenberg.[10] But how did Luther become so certain that his opponents were enemies motivated by the devil and why was he so sure that *his* choice of texts with which to thwart Satan was superior to the choices of his adversaries?[11] Historians have sought to answer these questions by pointing both to the intellectual sources and to the existential necessity of Luther's certainty. Mark Edwards has proposed that a metaphysical worldview derived from Augustine allowed Luther to stamp his opponents

---

8. In the so-called Invocavit sermons of 1522: *Acht Sermone D. M. Luthers,* in *Martin Luther Studienausgabe* 2 (Berlin, 1982), 539.7-10: "Es ist nicht genu(o)g / das du sprechen woltest / der vnd der hat es gethan / Ich hab dem gemeynen häuffen gefolget. Als vnns hatt der Probst Doctor Carlestatt / Gabriel oder Michael gepredigt / Neyn."

9. *Martin Luther Studienausgabe* (n. 8 above) 2, 539.10-14: "Neyn. Ein yetlicher mu(o)ss vor sich steen / und geru(o)st sein / mit dem theüffel zu(o) streytten / du mu(o)st dich gründen / auff eynen starcken klaren sprüch der schriefft da du besteen magst / wen(n) du den nit hast / so ist es nit müglich das du bestan kanst / der teüffel reyst dich hin weck wie ein dürre blat."

10. E. g. Zwingli. See *WA* 23, 83.11-21, esp. 83.21: "Ein teil mus des teufels und Gotts feind sein, Da ist kein Mittel." Cf. *WA* 23, 69.23-28: "Er [der Teufel] wirds aber dabey nicht lassen bleiben, sondern fehet am geringsten an mit den sacramenten, wie wol er bereit ynn dem selbigen stuck die schrifft schier ynn zehen löcher und ausflucht zurissen hat. Das ich nie schendlicher ketzerey gelesen habe, die ym anfahen unter sich selbs so viel köpffe, so viel rotten und uneynickeit habe, ob sie gleich ynn der heubtsache, Christum zu verfolgen, eintrechtig sind." See also note 36 below.

11. Writing against Zwingli, Luther also trusted that a clear, blunt text from Scripture would stop Satan: *WA* 23, 73.25-29: "Aber 'allein Gots wort bleibt ewiglich' [I Peter 1, 25], Die yrthum gehen ymer neben yhm auff und widder unter, Der halben ist mir kein sorge, das diese schwermerey solt lange stehen, Sie ist gar zu grob und frech und ficht nicht widder tunckel odder gewisse schrifft, sondern widder helle dürre schrifft, wie wir hören werden."

as false brethren spurred by Satan.[12] Heiko Oberman has argued that Luther's realization of his own spiritual impotence forced him to rely on the alien Word as the most powerful deterrent to the devil's wiles.[13] While they do help to explain Luther's sense of certainty, these proposals fail to account for the obstinate stands and aggressive stances which Luther assumed against his evangelical foes. Some motive more powerful and urgent bolstered Luther's refusal to credit his rivals or to strike compromises with them.

In a different frame of reference Oberman comes nearer to an identification of that motive. Speculating about how Luther would fare in a modern university, Oberman imagines that a psychiatric analysis of Luther would rob him of a chance at teaching because it would culminate in a diagnosis of *Paranoia reformatorica*.[14] For Oberman, this "Reformation madness" included the folly of faith, that trust which Luther placed in God to the point of foolhardiness, eschewing programs of reform and alliances with other reformers. To name even playfully, however, that foolhardiness paranoia, gives the false impression that Luther's obstinacy and hostility resulted from a psychic disorder. Although Oberman directly denies this conclusion, it would be easy for psychiatrists to dip one level deeper into Luther's psyche and diagnose his self-certainty and his demonic dismissal of others as delusional paranoia. Nevertheless, by focusing on Luther's personal complexity to explain the uniqueness of the man and his deeds, Oberman has taken seriously a dimension of Luther that other historians have too readily banished to the realm of psychohistory.

The motivation behind Luther's dismissal of his rivals and his designation of them as tools of Satan is explained at its most profound level by an analysis of his personal and relational development. Such an examination does run the risk of being labeled psychohistory. What I have in mind, however, is not an analysis of Luther's psyche, but the study of two elements that converged to form the religious identity of the mature Luther: 1. his assumption of the religious role of an evangelist that included his identification with the apostle Paul; and 2. Luther's relational history with his parents that shaped the ways in which Luther would relate to his evangelical

---

12. Mark U. Edwards, Jr.: *Luther and the False Brethren* (Stanford, 1975), 112–126. See also Edwards: "Suermerus: Luther's Own Fanatics," in *Seven-Headed Luther*, ed. Peter Newman Brooks (Oxford, 1983), 123–146, esp. 131–135.
13. Heiko A. Oberman: *Luther: Man between God and the Devil*, trans. Eileen Walliser-Schwarzbart (New Haven & London, 1989), 121, 226–227.
14. Oberman, *Luther: Man between God and the Devil*, 314–315.

opponents. Neither of these elements should be regarded as pathological. The focus on pathology, especially by investigators trained in psychoanalysis, has, in my opinion, discredited for most historians the insights that psychology or family therapy can contribute to history. In place of a pathological analysis, I want to offer a non-pathological interpretation of Luther's self-understanding and relational development as a means of defining more specifically his contribution to the disunity of the Protestant movement.

Thanks to recent research, Luther's self-understanding and assumption of religious roles is easier to map than his relational history. Luther presented himself as a servant of the Word, a proclaimer of the gospel that would liberate and support consciences against the devil's attacks in the last days.[15] As a model for his ministry Luther took the apostle Paul. This model was suggested to him already in 1519 by his college friend Crotus Rubeanus, who compared Luther's sudden decision to enter the monastery to Paul's conversion on the road to Damascus.[16] From early depictions of Luther we also know that Crotus was not the only one to believe that Luther's actions were divinely inspired.[17] Luther compared his ministry to that of Paul for the first time openly in 1521 and 1522 during his exile at the Wartburg. In his letters he not only employed the Pauline salutation, "grace and peace," as Zwingli also did, but he declared that he would henceforth call himself both a servant and an evangelist. Writing to Elector Frederick on his return to Wittenberg, Luther announced in the language of Paul's letter to the Galatians that he did not have the gospel from a human source, but straight from heaven through the Lord Jesus Christ.[18]

---

15. Heiko Oberman: "Martin Luther: Vorläufer der Reformation," in *Verifikationen. Festschrift für Gerhard Ebeling zum 70. Geburtstag*, ed. Eberhard Jüngel, Johannes Wallmann, Wilfrid Werbeck (Tübingen, 1982), 91-119; cf. Oberman, *Luther: Man between God and the Devil*, 302.
16. *WABr* 1, 543.105-109 (October 16, 1519): "Perge, ut coepisti, relinque exemplum posteris; nam ista facis non sine numine divum; ad haec respexit divina providentia, quando te redeuntem a parentibus coeleste fulmen veluti alterum Paulum ante oppidum Effurdianum in terram prostravit atque intra Augustiniana septa compulit e nostro consortio tristissimo tuo discessu."
17. See R. W. Scribner: "Incombustible Luther: The Image of the Reformer in Early Modern Germany," *Past & Present* 110 (1986), 38-68, esp. 47.
18. *WABr* 2, 455.38-43 (March 5, 1522). Luther's growing identification with Paul in these years has been carefully traced by Timothy Wengert, "Changes in Luther's Self-Understanding Reflected in His Early Correspondence" (unpublished paper, 1990). Wengert documents how the Pauline apostolic stance against false brethren,

Luther's stay at the Wartburg proved to be a turning point in his self-understanding. No longer was he just a doctor of Scripture who was defending his interpretation of the gospel. Now he had become an evangelist and apostle in his own right, who had received the gospel directly from heaven and who, like Paul, was obliged to defend evangelical freedom against those who would reimpose the law. Luther's adoption of a Pauline stance and Pauline language at the Wartburg is not surprising. His translation of the New Testament required an intense involvement with the Pauline corpus; and the parallels between those who wanted to force reforms in Wittenberg and the "Judaizers" in the Pauline congregations could scarcely have escaped his notice. Nor is it surprising that, having already identified the Antichrist at work in the papacy, Luther now saw Satan at work behind the disturbances in Wittenberg. Still, what explains the fact that Luther not only saw similarities between his situation and that of Paul, but felt himself entitled to act with indisputable apostolic authority? Something must have happened to Luther in order to produce this sense of authority and responsibility that Karlstadt and, later, many others could not accept.

In fact, at the Wartburg Luther did mark a critical moment in his relational history as well as in the development of his religious role. On November 21, 1521, Luther wrote a preface to his treatise on monastic vows in the form of a letter to his father.[19] This letter reveals that Luther's exercise of apostolic authority was preceded, or at least accompanied, by a reworking of the relationship to his father. Moreover, Luther connects this reworking to a transfer of loyalty from the pope and monastic vows to Christ and the ministry of the Word. For Luther this transfer of loyalty culminates in a new personal and religious identity: he is now a "monk and not a monk, a new creature, not of the pope, but of Christ."[20] These words contain the

---

which Edwards found so prevalent in the second lectures on Galatians, was assumed by Luther already at the Wartburg.

19. *WA* 8, 573–576. The letter is noted in Luther's correspondence in *WABr* 2, 404. I have previously discussed the import of this letter for understanding how Luther made the break with monasticism and the papacy and how he interpreted his new role in what came to be called the Reformation; see Scott Hendrix: "Luther's Loyalties and the Augustinian Order," in *Augustine, the Harvest, and Theology (1300–1650): Essays Dedicated to Heiko Augustinus Oberman in Honor of His Sixtieth Birthday*, ed. Kenneth Hagen (Leiden, 1990), 236–258. In this essay I carry that analysis one step further by applying it specifically to Luther's conflicts with his evangelical opponents.

20. *WA* 8, 575.28–29: "Itaque iam sum monachus et non monachus, nova creatura, non Papae, sed Christi."

seeds of Luther's amazing sense of freedom as an evangelical leader and of his intolerance of rivals to that leadership.

According to one theory of relational dynamics, the transformation of loyalty and the new identity which Luther describes were made possible primarily through the act of crediting his parents.[21] This crediting acknowledges the good intentions of parents and the limitations from which parents suffer as they raise their children. Because of the care they have received, children are loyal to parents and indebted to them. In order to make choices of their own, present themselves in new ways, and establish loyalty to spouses and friends, adult children need to discharge the indebtedness to their parents. They accomplish this task by crediting their parents and in turn earning the freedom or entitlement to shape their own lives. If instead they blame their parents for their mistakes and limitations, adult children are likely to bind themselves inordinately to new authorities and both grant to them excessive power and devote to them inappropriate loyalty.

Luther's letter to Hans from the Wartburg recounts how Luther both blamed and credited his father and testifies that the latter won out over the former. Initially, Luther scorned his father for disapproving of his decision to embark on a monastic life.[22] Later, from the perspective of 1521, Luther still does not fully exonerate his father. If Hans had really believed the commandment that children should obey their parents before all else, he should have extracted Luther from the cloister.[23] At the same time, Luther acknowledges that he too was ignorant of the commandment; otherwise, he would never have become a monk as long as his father remained against it. Luther then discloses that the disobedience to his father was not an assertion of freedom but a rebellion that landed him in a new kind of bondage, namely, the bondage of a vow made in accordance with "the doctrines of

---

21. The elements of this theory, such as loyalty, entitlement, and indebtedness, and their operation in the family justice system are discussed in two major works: Ivan Boszormenyi-Nagy and Geraldine M. Spark: *Invisible Loyalties: Reciprocity in Intergenerational Family Therapy* (New York, 1984 [1st ed.: 1973]), 37–99; Ivan Boszormenyi-Nagy and Barbara R. Krasner: *Between Give and Take: A Clinical Guide to Contextual Therapy* (New York, 1986), 73–133.

22. *WA* 8, 574.8-9: "Verum ego securus in iustitia mea te velut hominem audivi et fortiter contempsi, ..."

23. *WA* 8, 574.11-13: "Hic vide, an non et tu ignoraris, mandata dei praeferenda esse omnibus. Nonne si scisses, me adhuc tum fuisse in manu tua, plane e cucullo autoritate paterna extraxisses?"

54

men and the superstitions of hypocrites."[24] Luther became a creature of the pope and a slave to monastic vows in part because his blame of Hans prevented him from avoiding a new kind of bondage.

Luther's acknowledgement of his father's good intentions, however, dominates the letter from the Wartburg. Martin recognizes that paternal love motivated Hans' concern for his future and for what might happen to Luther in the monastery.[25] He also recognizes Hans' limitations and asserts protectively that the Lord took care of what his father could not manage, namely, withdrawing Luther from the monastery.[26] Later, Luther would credit both his parents for their good intentions in raising him, and at the same time of their deaths he would recall gratefully the contributions which they made to his life.[27]

This strong crediting of his parents and, in 1521, especially of his father earned for Luther the freedom to transfer his religious loyalty from the "false service of the monks" to "the true service of God."[28] And on the basis of that loyalty Luther identified himself as a new creature of Christ.[29] Luther also testified to the quality of that new freedom itself, defining it in reminiscence of Worms as liberation of conscience and calling it exuberantly liberation without measure [*abundantissime*]!"[30] Freedom of conscience does not mean that Luther now had no loyalty tie whatsoever, but that he chose to be religiously loyal in a new way – immediately to Christ and to the service of God, which he also embraced as the ministry of the Word.[31]

---

24. *WA* 8, 574.13-19: "Sed nec ego si scivissem, te ignorante et invito id tentassem, etiam si multis mortibus pereundum fuisset. Neque enim meum votum valebat hunc floccum, quo me subtrahebam parentis autoritati et voluntati divinitus mandatae, imo impium erat, et ex deo non esse probabat non modi id, quod peccabat in tuam autoritatem, sed etiam quod spontaneum et voluntarium non erat. Deinde in doctrinas hominum et superstitionem hypocritarum fiebat, quas deus non praecepit."
25. *WA* 8, 573.20-21: "Metuebas tu paterno affectu imbecillitati meae, cum essem iam adulescens, ..."
26. *WA* 8, 575.23-24: "Sed ad te revertar, parens mi, Et iterum dico: Nunquid me extrahes adhuc? At ne tu glorieris, praevenit te dominus et ipse me extraxit."
27. For his mother, see *WABr* 6,103-106 (May 20, 1531). For his father, see *WABr* 5, 351.22-24, 33-36 (June 5, 1530).
28. *WA* 8, 575.35-36 "Caeterum is [Deus], qui me extraxit, ius habet in me maius iure tuo, a quo me vides positum iam non in fictitio illo monasticorum, sed vero cultu dei."
29. See note 20 above.
30. *WA* 8, 575.27-28: "Conscientia liberata est, id quod abundantissime est liberari."
31. *WA* 8, 575.36-37: "In ministerio enim verbi me esse quis potest dubitare?"

XIV

Luther's new religious loyalty, however, also contained a limitation. While his personal entitlement enabled him to choose for Christ and for the ministry of the Word, his freedom was limited by this same choice. Even adult children who have gained freedom from their parents' expectations are tempted to make parents out of other people, ideas, or institutions. This process is called parentification.[32] When Luther transferred his loyalty from monastic vows and the pope to Christ and the ministry of the Word, he parentified both Christ and that Word. In his letter to Hans, Luther expressed this parentification in the form of absolute certainty about his vocation: "Who can doubt," he exclaims, "that I am in the ministry of the Word?"[33] Of course, anyone could doubt that and many people did, Luther's conviction notwithstanding. In fact, the declaration of liberty near the end of his letter demonstrated how, for Luther, Christ had replaced all other superiors, religious and parental. To his father Luther said: "I send you this book, therefore, that you may see with what signs and powers Christ absolved me from the monastic vow and endowed me with such liberty that, although he [Christ] has made me the servant of all, I am, nevertheless, subject to no one except to him alone. He is himself (as they say) my immediate bishop, abbot, prior, lord, father and teacher; I know no other."[34]

This exclusive subjection of himself to Christ had a substantial impact on Luther's relationship to his evangelical opponents. The parentification of Christ, which he experienced as liberation from old loyalties, allowed Luther to regard himself as accountable to no one except to Christ. This conviction of being accountable to Christ alone had two important components. First, because he experienced his liberation as coming directly from Christ, he felt he had a proprietary claim to the evangelical movement. Luther voiced this

---

32. *Between Give and Take*, 328. Cf. *Invisible Loyalties*, 151: "By definition, parentification implies the subjective distortion of a relationship as if one's partner or even children were his parent." For further discussion of the concept and of the deparentification that accompanies the increase of entitlement, see *Between Give and Take*, 327–329, and *Invisible Loyalties*, 151–166.
33. See above, note 31.
34. *LW* 48, 336. Cf. *WA* 8, 576.14–18: "Mitto itaque hunc librum, in quo videas, quantis signis et virtutibus Christus me absolverit a voto monastico, et tanta libertate me donarit, ut, cum omnium servum fecerit, nulli tamen subditus sim nisi sibi soli. Ipse enim est meus immediatus (quod vocant) Episcopus, Abbas, Prior, dominus, pater et magister. Alium non novi amplius." Luther's words recall his famous theses from the treatise on Christian liberty (*WA* 7, 49.22–25): "Christianus homo omnium dominus est liberrimus, nulli subiectus. Christianus homo omnium servus est officiosissimus, omnibus subiectus."

personal claim already in the letter to his father. Just after declaring that Christ was now his immediate superior, Luther stated directly to Hans: "Thus I hope that he [Christ] has taken from you one son in order that he may begin to help the sons of many others *through me* [emphasis mine]."[35] Luther's entitlement to his new identity as a creature – and, implied in his own words, a child – of Christ included a new sense of responsibility for others. This claim became stronger during his stay at the Wartburg as he watched the unrest in Wittenberg threaten the freedom of conscience that he had acquired. Finally, he felt compelled to return to Wittenberg to protect *his* flock which Satan had invaded and which he now regarded as his own children in Christ, entrusted to him by God.[36]

This proprietary claim to the movement went hand in hand with the second component of Luther's conviction that he was accountable to Christ alone. He became more and more convinced that his own interpretation of Scripture was superior to that of his opponents. In his early letters from the Wartburg, Luther debated the appropriateness of certain biblical texts for guiding the reform of the mass, images, and clerical vows. For the most part, however, he was expressing disappointment in the unconvincing exegesis offered by Karlstadt.[37] For Luther, the interpretation of Scripture proposed by the Wittenbergers had to be "brighter than the sun and all the stars" in order to make even a slight impression on their enemies.[38]

Apparently, Luther believed that his star would shine the brightest. By the end of his stay at the Wartburg, he no longer regarded his interpretations as debatable. When he admonished the Wittenbergers that each Christian had to take a stand on a clear text, it was tantamount to saying that the Wittenbergers had to stand on texts offered by Luther and not by Karlstadt or Zwilling. It was not permissible, said Luther, for the people to take action just because Karlstadt or Zwilling preached to them that it was right.[39] Why then should people listen when Luther preached that a different course of

---

35. *LW* 48,336. Cf. *WA* 8, 576.18–19.
36. *WABr* 2, 460.36–37, 43–44: "Die ander ist, dass zu Wittemberg, durch mein Abwesen, mir der Satan in meine Hürden gefallen ist, ... Sie ist je meine Hürden, mir von Gott befohlen, es sind meine Kinder in Christo."
37. E.g., *WABr* 2, 380.20–39 (August 15, 1521); *WABr* 2, 390.13–15 (September 9, 1521).
38. *WABr* 2, 374.20–23 (August 3, 1521): "Quod ideo dico, Quia vellem a vobis nihil prodire, quod obscuris & ambiguis scripturis nitatur, cum a nobis exigatur lux plusquam solis & omnium stellarum sit, neque sic vix videant."
39. See note 8 above.

action was right? Because Luther thought he was offering superior texts of Scripture that would withstand the assaults of the devil. And he thought his texts were superior because, like Paul himself, Luther believed that he had received the gospel directly from Christ and was accountable only to him. This stance of direct accountability to Christ and ownership of the evangelical movement placed Luther, in his own mind, on a level above those who held contrary interpretations of Scripture. After 1521 Luther was still willing to debate his opponents and to reply to their attacks, but his own interpretation of Scripture had become less arguable than the exposition of his opponents. In his letter to the princes of Saxony (1524), Luther claimed in opposition to Müntzer that "we who have and acknowledge the gospel ... have the right spirit" or at least the first fruits of the Spirit (Rom 8,23). "For", he continued, "we know what faith is, and love, and the cross ... Hence we can know and judge what doctrine is true or not true, and whether it is in accord with the faith or not."[40] In support of this claim, Luther alleged his ownership of the movement and declared what it had cost him to rescue the gospel. Müntzer and his followers, says Luther, "enjoy and use the fruits of *our* [emphasis mine] victory, such as marrying, and discarding the papal laws, though they have done no battle for it and risked no bloodshed to attain it. But I have had to attain it for them and, until now, at the risk of my body and my life."[41] Because he had risked everything for the sake of the gospel, Luther felt he deserved to be granted deference in deciding what that gospel allowed.

Luther's claim to be a Pauline evangelist, who was accountable to Christ alone and relied on the most powerful texts of Scripture, did not cow Luther's evangelical opponents into submission. Karlstadt, Müntzer, and Zwingli,

---

40. *WA* 15, 216.21-29: "Ich weys aber, das wyr, so das Euangelion haben und kennen, ob wyr gleych arme sünder sind, denn rechten geyst odder wie Paulus sagt 'Primitias spiritus' [Rm 8:23], das erstling des geysts, haben, ob wyr schon die fülle des geysts nicht haben. So ist ja keyn ander denn der selbige eynige geyst, der seyne gaben wunderlich austeylet. Wyr wissen yhe, was glaub und liebe und creutz ist, Und ist keyn höher ding auff erden zu wissen denn glaub und liebe. Daraus wyr ja auch wissen und urteylen künden, wilche lere recht odder unrecht, dem glauben gemes odder nicht sey. Wie wyr denn auch diesen lügen geyst kennen und urteylen, ..." Cf. *LW* 40,55.

41. *WA* 15, 215.24-28: "Denn sie hallten (Gott lob) uns doch fur erger feynde denn die papisten. Wie wol sie unsers siegs gebrauchen und geniessen, nemen weyber und lassen Bepstliche gesetz nach: da sie doch nicht erstritten haben, und hat yhr blut nicht drob ynn der fahr gestanden, Sondern ich habs must mit meynem leyb und leben, bisher dar gewagt, erlangen." Cf. *LW* 40,54.

however, all agreed on one thing: their chances of getting a fair hearing in Wittenberg or from Luther were slim. Karlstadt was forbidden to preach in Wittenberg, but Luther was not content to see this prohibition only as a political decision. Rather, Karlstadt deserved to be silenced because he, presumably unlike Luther, had usurped the authority of the gospel for his personal views. Karlstadt had ascended the pulpit by his own temerity, claimed Luther, without a call and against the will of God and men. Karlstadt did not come from God; thus he did not teach what was God's, and the fruit of his work showed whose word he spoke and whose glory he sought (namely, his own).[42]

Thomas Müntzer offered to defend himself before an unprejudiced assembly but not in a closed session before two or three examiners.[43] Luther made fun of his caution and attributed it to the fact that Müntzer had already suffered a bloody nose in Wittenberg.[44] Müntzer in turn claimed that he was merely following the example of Jesus, who had refused to repeat in private before the high priest Annas what he had already taught

---

42. *WABr* 2, 478.7-10 (March 19, 1522): "Certum est, ei interdicere suggestu, quod ipse temeritate propria, nulla vocatione, invitis Deo et hominibus conscendit. Ideo sicut ex Deo non venit, ita ex Deo non docuit, et fructus ipse probat, cuius verbum locutus sit et cuius gloriam quaesivit."

43. Thomas Müntzer: *Protestation oder Erbietung,* in *Schriften und Briefe: Kritische Gesamtausgabe,* ed. Günther Franz (Gütersloh, 1968), 239.27-240.7: "In diser entpietung und bedingung habe ich in einer summa gesagt von dem schaden der kirchen, welcher durch die unvorstandene tauffe und getichten glauben uns uberfallen hat. So ich im selbigen yrre, wil ich mich lassen fruntlich weisen fur einer ungefherlichen gemeine und nicht ane gnugsame getzeugen auff einem winckel, sondern am lichten tage. Durch mein vornemen wil ich der evangelischen prediger lere in ein besser wessen furen und unser hinderstellige, langsame Römischen brudere auch nicht verachten. Alleine thut mir mein urtel fur den gantzen werlt und auff keinem winckel. Dofur setze ich mein leib und leben ane allen hinterlistigen vorteydunck der menschen durch Jesum Cristum, den warhafftigen Gotisson, der euch alle ewig beware. Amen." Cf. *WA* 15, 213.30-33: "Denn also erbeut er sich ynn seyner schrifft, Er wölle offentlich fur eyner ungeferlichen gemeyne, aber nicht ym winckel fur zweyen odder dreyen stehen und antwortten, und leyb und seel auffs freyest erbotten haben etc."

44. *WA* 15, 213.34-214.5: "Lieber sage myr, Wer ist der mutige und trotzige heyliger geyst, der sich selbst so enge spennet und will nicht denn fur eyner ungeferlichen gemeyne stehen? Item er will nicht ym winckel fur zweyen odder dreyen antwort geben? Was ist das fur eyn geyst, der sich fur zweyen odder dreyen furchtet und eyn geferliche gemeyne nicht leyden kan? Ich wil dyrs sagen: Er reucht den braten, Er ist eyn mal odder zwey fur myr zu Wittemberg ynn meynem kloster auff die nasen geschlagen, drumb grawet yhm fur der suppen, ..."

XIV

openly to the world (John 18, 20). The Wittenbergers, whom Müntzer mocked as "unsere gelerten," feared the public. They wanted to be the only judges of faith with their "stolen Scripture," so that the common people would not become learned and equal to them.[45]

The opponent who offered the most perceptive comment on the difficulty of debating Luther was Zwingli. Behind Luther's apparent self-certainty he recognized Luther's hesitation to make himself accountable to the Christian community. Once upon a time, wrote Zwingli to Luther in 1527, you wanted to subject everything to the judgment of the church; but now, if the things that are written and told about you are true, you are doing everything you can to see that my view of the eucharist never reaches the churches.[46] Luther's hesitation was motivated in part by his belief that he was accountable only to Christ. But, in reference to Zwingli, Luther also revealed more of the dynamic that underlay his stance of superiority. Luther felt strongly that he deserved more credit for initiating the evangelical movement than he had received. After reporting to Michael Stifel that he had received a letter from Zwingli full of pride and temerity, Luther made this telling statement: "There is no crime or cruelty of which he does not accuse me, so much so that not even the papists, my enemies, slandered me as severely as those friends of ours. Without us and prior to us they were nothing and dared not even open their mouth. Now, boosted by our victory, they turn their full force upon us. *This is how people show thanks and give you credit for what you have earned.* Now I finally understand what it means for the world to be put under the evil one and Satan to be prince of the world [I John 5, 19;

---

45. *Ausgedrückte Entblössung des falschen Glaubens* (1524), in *Schriften und Briefe* (above, note 43), 269.32-270.24: "Den gefehrlichen winckel aber hab ich nicht anders geschewet, denn nach der sach foderung, wie auch Christus selber die naterzichtigen schrifftgelerten gemiden hat, Johan. 7 [John 7,11ff.], und wolt dem Hanne keyn ander rechenschafft seyner lere geben auffm winckel, denn das er in auff seine zuhörer, aufs gemeyn volck weyset, Johan. 18 [John 18,19ff.] ... Unsere gelerten wolten gern das gezeügnus des geysts Jesu auff die hohen schul bringen. Es wirt in gar weit feylen, nachdem sie nicht drumb gelert sind, das der gemeyn man in durch ire lere soll gleych werden, sondern sie wöllen alleyn den glauben urteylen mit irer gestolnen schrifft, so sie doch gantz und gar keynen glauben wider bey Got oder vor den menschen haben. Denn es sihet und greifft ein yeder, das sie nach ehren und güttern streben. Derhalben mustu, gemeyner man, selber gelert werden, auff das du nicht lenger verfüret werdest."

46. *WABr* 4, 185.15-17 (April 1, 1527): "Volebas olim omnia ecclesiae iudiciis deferre; nunc, si vera sunt, quae de te et scribuntur et narrantur, quibus potes autor es, ut ista de eucharistia sententia ad ecclesias non perveniat."

John 12, 31]. Up to now I thought these were only words, but now I see it in reality, and verily the devil rules the world [emphasis mine]."[47]

Luther's conviction that he was owed more appreciation and loyalty than he received was the main limitation on the entitlement and freedom that he had earned by crediting his parents. After fighting loyally for his new master Christ, Luther still felt that he had made so many sacrifices and taken such great risks that he deserved more credit from his potential allies. This sense of being owed points to a relational imbalance that persistently manifested itself in Luther's life even after he had positively resolved the relationship with his parents. Sometimes that imbalance led him to disregard the consequences of his action for others. This imbalance, I think, is what fueled Luther's disdain for his evangelical opponents and caused him to treat them in ways that seemed unfair and made them feel dismissed. Furthermore, as Luther's remarks to Stifel make clear, this sense of being owed proved conclusively to Luther that his opponents were driven by the devil.

A relational imbalance is not pathological, however, and it should not be seen as a sickness of the psyche; most people struggle throughout their life with a sense of being indebted to others or being owed by them. In Luther's case, the relational imbalance, combined with his parentification of Christ and the Word, led to actions that were experienced and decried as unjust. His evangelical opponents worried that the evangelical movement was sacrificing hardwon reforms, missing an opportunity to establish God's just order, and slipping back into papism. Luther saw it very differently. Convinced that the devil was doing all he could to destroy the gospel, Luther acted on his newly-earned loyalty to Christ and to the Word. As the only effective antidote to Satan, he took his stand on "clear texts," and to support his stand he appealed to his ownership of the movement and to his accountability to Christ alone.

Owing to these relational dynamics and their impact on Luther in the early 1520s, the evangelical movement was unable to form itself into a unified front. My judgement, however, needs to be hedged by three considerations. First, I have concentrated only on Luther's side in these conflicts. A more

---

47. *WABr* 4, 199.7-14 (ca. May 4, 1527): "Nihil est scelerum aut crudelitatis, cuius non reum me agat, adeo ut nec papistae sic me lacerent, hostes mei, ut illi amici nostri, qui sine nobis et ante nos nihil erant, ne hiscere quidem audebant, nunc nostra victoria inflati in nos vertunt impetum. Hoc est gratias agere, sic est mereri apud homines; summa, nunc demum intelligo, quid sit, mundum esse in maligno positum, et Satanam esse principem mundi. Hactenus putabam haec tantum esse verba, sed nunc video rem esse, et vere Diabolum in mundo regnare."

thorough study of the unity, or rather disunity, of the Reformation requires that the contributions of Karlstadt, Müntzer and Zwingli to that disunity also be assessed. There is truth to the assertion of Luther that he and the Swiss/South Germans were moved by different spirits.[48] But these spirits were not only theological in nature; they were also historical and relational. They were based on the personal histories and concrete circumstances which shaped the sense of accountability and indebtedness that each reformer acquired. Zwingli, for instance, felt accountable to the magistrates of Zurich in a way that Luther never considered himself accountable to any political authority. In his letter to Luther, Zwingli conceded that if his arguments were refuted and if his party was not willing to change its mind, nobody would hinder the magistrates from taking stronger measures against them.[49]

Second, Luther did not ignore the consequences of his actions for everyone. For the leaders of the opposition, yes, he had no hope of converting them to his side. But for the people, whom he continued to call the weak and the simple, he did feel responsible. His refusal to compromise for their sake would make it possible for them to be saved from Satan. Luther felt this responsibility, rightly or wrongly, for the followers of Zwingli, just as he had felt it for those who listened to Karlstadt in Wittenberg and for the common people who had believed Müntzer.[50] But although Luther felt responsible for their survival, he did not feel accountable to them or to their leaders in the sense of submitting his positions for their approval.

Finally, I would not say that Luther or his evangelical opponents destroyed an originally unified evangelical movement. Instead, I suggest that the process can better be described as a sequence of relational stages: indebtedness, parentification, disappointment, and entitlement. First, Luther's earliest followers, *gelerten* and *ungelerten*, were all indebted to Luther for various contributions which he made to their lives. These numbered, among others, new insights into the meaning of Scripture, release from salvation by religious ritual, freedom from clerical oppression, hope for social and political justice,

48. According to Andreas Osiander's report of the Marburg Colloquy in *Andreas Osiander d. A. Gesamtausgabe* 3 (Gütersloh, 1979): 437.10-14. Cf. *LW* 38,70-71.
49. *WABr* 4, 185.30-33: "Id autem, quum adhuc nemo sit uspiam, cui saltem libere licuerit de hac re disserere, convictus, si convicti essemus, iam nemo moraretur, si nollemus resipiscere, ut magistratus paulo durius in nos animadverteret."
50. *WA* 23, 75.21-24: "Ob ich nu auch keinen schwermer meister bekere, so sols doch daran nicht mangeln (ob Gott wil) das sich die warheit hell und dürre gnug will fur yhre augen stellen und etliche yhrer schuler abreissen odder yhe die einfeltigen und schwachen stercken und fur yhrem gifft bewaren."

the opportunity to marry, proof of superior Christian conduct, and an un-
leashing of the spirit. In return for these insights and the hopes they en-
gendered, those early followers also parentified Luther to some extent; they
ceded too much authority to him and depended too much on him to fulfill
their expectations.

Inevitably, therefore, some were disappointed when Luther either could
not or did not deliver what they wanted. Many blamed Luther for what they
did not get; but some leaders, like Zwingli, were able to credit Luther for
the contributions that he did make and claimed their own entitlement to
shape differently the reform which Luther had initiated. In the meantime,
by 1522 at the latest, Luther's own entitlement and mentality had merged
into the identity of an evangelist who was accountable to Christ alone, who
claimed ownership of the movement, and who felt that others owed him
more credit than they gave. Luther's sense of direct accountability to Christ
appealed to some followers like, for example, Lazarus Spengler. Already in
1519 he argued that everything which Luther taught was based *on mittel* on
the holy gospel, on the prophets, and on St. Paul.[51] For others, however,
Luther's sense of accountability to Christ alone and his demand for loyalty
meant that their texts and arguments were not respected and that they themselves were dismissed. A genuine dialogue could not ensue, and the initial,
amorphous support of Luther evolved into a multifaceted evangelical movement.

A fuller understanding of this process would require a broader study of
the relational histories of the participants and the integration of social, theological, and political factors into these histories. This essay is an initial
attempt to account for the multiformity of the Reformation by clarifying the
relational dynamics that shaped Luther's mentality and defined his contribution to the disunity of the Protestant movement.

---

51. Lazarus Spengler: *Schutzrede für Doktor Martin Luthers Lehre* (1519), in
Flugschriften der frühen Reformationsbewegung (1518-1524), ed. Adolf Laube, Annerose
Schneider, Sigrid Looss, 2 vols. (Vaduz, 1983), 1, 502.12-15: "Dann alles das der
selb Luther biss her gepredigt, geschriben und gelert, hat er allain auff das heylig
ewangelium, die sprüch der heyligen propheten und den heyligen Paulum on mittel
ergründet ..."

XV

Luther's Communities

With his book *The German Nation and Martin Luther*, A. G. Dickens offered to Reformation scholarship a work that accomplished exactly what Dickens himself said historical synthesis should involve: "writing books which form challenges to write better ones."[1] On the subject of Martin Luther and the German Reformation, historians have taken up that challenge with enthusiasm. Amplifying the by-no-means-novel approach of Dickens, they have concentrated on the setting in which Luther's ideas took shape and on the impact of his reforming activity, especially its impact on the urban populations of Germany. Social structures have taken their rightful place alongside personality and intellect in the gallery of historical forces that scholars seek to merge into a coherent and comprehensive picture of the Reformation.

One result of this inclusive method of studying Reformation history has been to render ambiguous the contribution of biography to that study. On the one hand, the story of the Reformation can no longer be told simply as the account of the lives of its most prominent leaders. On the other hand, leaders did exist for the Reformation as indeed they have for other historical movements, and their lives are an essential part of the story. How much influence should be attributed to their persons in reconstructing the story as a whole? Dickens's own solution to this dilemma was to portray Luther, like every hero of history in his opinion, as the product of social forces that swelled into the Reformation movement: "While Luther's own spirit lacked neither charisma nor intellect, it was the surge of forces within the nation . . . which elevated him to one of the rare titanic roles of western history."[2] However great Luther was as a person or as a scholar, it was society that made him a hero.

Such an approach seems to imply a radical disjuncture between biography and social history, but that is not necessarily the case. It was certainly not the case for Dickens himself, who, although he did not incorporate a biography of Luther into his book on the German nation, still paid considerable attention to the intellectual traditions that influenced Luther and to the theological character of his Reformation discovery. Biog-

XV

44

raphy need not be regarded as the refuge of the intellectual or psychohisto-
rians; instead, biographical studies can serve as case studies that disclose
the interaction of all those forces—social, political, and mental—which
produce historical movements of epochal character like the Reformation.
In the case of Martin Luther, some of that interaction can be discerned by
considering the various communities to which he belonged: a monastic
community, the university, the town of Wittenberg, the territory of Electoral Saxony, the German nation, and the church. A closer look at the
nature of these communities reveals how difficult it is to distinguish neatly
between social and intellectual forces. For example, as a member of the
monastic community, Luther belonged to concrete institutions, the Augustinian monasteries in Erfurt and Wittenberg, where specific regulations,
communal functions, and contact with individual brothers influenced his
daily life. Within these same walls, however, Luther simultaneously belonged to a larger, extramural, monastic community, the Augustinian Order in particular and the monastic culture in general. From the larger
monastic community Luther absorbed traditions that influenced both his
thinking and his piety; he responded to these intangible currents as well as
to his daily monastic environment. The same distinction applies to
Luther's other communities. He was exposed to a concrete form of that
community as well as to the intellectual currents that undergirded it and
circulated within it. The forces that elevated Luther to the rank of prominent reformer intersected and made their impact upon him as a member of
one or more of these specific communities.

1. The Monastery

Luther's sudden entry into the Augustinian monastery at Erfurt in July
1505 brought him into contact with the active core of religious intensity that
gripped the later Middle Ages. The monastic tradition had promoted the
cloistered life as the authentically religious life and it was widely regarded
as the most attainable form of Christian perfection. The demonstrable *con-
versio* of the monk epitomized the rejection of secular values that was
enjoined on the populace as a whole but not really expected of it. The
religiosity that laypersons and secular priests could demonstrate only
through the giving of alms, fasting, pilgrimages, and other good works
was surpassed by a total commitment to the religious life such as Luther
made.
Luther later described his own commitment to that life as involuntary,
claiming that he took the vow under duress while frightened by the threat
of sudden death.[3] Luther was certainly predisposed to use the religious
vow as an escape from his perilous situation; but did this predisposition
result primarily from the religious culture in which he grew up or was
Luther's vow merely the external expression of parentally induced emo-

tions? In his provocative study *Young Man Luther,* Erik Erikson argues forcefully for the latter by depicting Luther's decision to enter the monastery as a reaction against his father's desire that he study law. The religious vow was a convenient way of binding himself to a divinely willed course that not even his father could alter.[4] Most historians, to the contrary, have maintained that Luther's vow was more culturally than parentally induced. In the first place, the hard historical evidence for strong feelings of resentment against his father is lacking in Luther's case.[5] In the second place, the psychological explanation that Erikson offers minimizes the distinctiveness of Luther's epoch and reduces his experience to the level of an ahistorical Everyman.[6]

In the absence of evidence to the contrary, the religious culture of Luther's day offers the most convincing reason for his vow to enter the cloister. Still, it was the sensitive individual, Martin Luther, who made that vow and who then experienced the monastic life in the manner that laid the groundwork for his career as a reformer. Not everyone who entered the monastery found the religious life oppressive, but Luther did. He took his vocation as a monk with utmost seriousness, no matter how involuntarily he may have embarked upon it. Luther summed up the ambivalence of that experience in the following phrase: "I lived as a monk not, of course, without sin, but without fault."[7] Without fault, because of his zeal for piety and his strenuous adherence to monastic discipline, which was not only confirmed by friends like Philipp Melanchthon (d. 1560) but also conceded by critics like Johannes Cochläus (d. 1552).[8] As a monk Luther performed well under pressure. He did not perform without sin, however, because he could find no satisfaction and peace in his performance. He could not conquer his scrupulosity, and this failure, viewed through the lens of his Reformation theology and self-understanding, was his greatest sin.

Luther's scrupulosity was due as much to the formation of his personality, including the influence of his parents, as to the religiousness of his environment. On this point there is no need to pit culture against parental influence in assessing his development. The monastery, however, was the setting in which the traits of his personality and the traits of the culture interacted to produce his unsatisfying experience of medieval religion. In the monastery, a scrupulous and earnest personality encountered the most demanding challenge that medieval religion could offer, and the result was distress and disenchantment. Since the monastery was the stuctured religious setting that served as the catalyst for this conflict, the monastery and not his family was the primary community that contributed to Luther's development as a reformer of medieval religion. A scrupulous Luther in law school might also have led to disenchantment, but hardly to the Reformation.

How much difference did it make that the monastic order that Luther entered was the Order of Hermits of St. Augustine? Judged by Luther's own remarks, it made little difference; the specific order to which he belonged played a small role in Luther's assessment of his monastic career. Some specific features and personalities of the Augustinian Order did, however, have an important effect on Luther's development. The Augustinian houses in Erfurt and Wittenberg belonged to the reformed congregation of the order, which was governed by a new constitution prepared in 1504 by its vicar-general, Johannes von Staupitz (d. 1525). That constitution contained strict regulations that could have reinforced the scrupulosity of Luther and in this way spurred his religious development. By the same token, the houses contained brothers who sought to assuage the dissatisfaction and guilt that disturbed Luther. Among these was Staupitz himself, who consoled Luther with fresh insights into the nature of repentance.[9] And, according to Melanchthon, a senior member of the Erfurt community taught Luther that belief in the forgiveness of sins meant not forgiveness in general but pardon for his own sin.[10]

The Augustinians nurtured a strong appreciation of the study of theology in their order and harbored a theological tradition as well.[11] To what extent their theological school was really a distinct *via* of medieval theology is an issue still far from being settled. If a *via Gregorii* (named after the Augustinian doctor of theology Gregory of Rimini, d. 1358) did exist, as the statutes of Wittenberg University in 1508 indicate, scant evidence exists for determining its exact content or the nature of its influence on Luther.[12] Nevertheless, an acquaintance with Augustine's theology was passed down to Luther through his order. Both in Erfurt and in Wittenberg Luther had opportunity to read the works of theologians, like Gregory, who incorporated strongly Augustinian themes into their work. In preparing his lectures on the Psalms at Wittenberg between 1513 and 1515, he used the commentary of Jacobus Perez of Valencia (d. 1490) as an important resource. Luther could have learned directly from Staupitz more theology than the insights he received on the nature of repentance; but differences in the thought of both men seem to outweigh the similarities, especially at critical points such as their understanding of faith.[13] While late medieval Augustinianism hung heavy around the head of Luther during his years in the cloister, no single Augustinian current has as yet been isolated as the fresh breeze of an incipient Reformation theology.

From his years in the cloister Luther did gain an intimate knowledge of Scripture and stimulation to incorporate examination of the Bible into his study of theology. Luther himself remarked that he learned the Psalter by heart during those years, and Staupitz was credited with encouraging him to pay the closest attention to Scripture in his work.[14] Although Luther's hermeneutical method as a professor of biblical studies eventually differed from that of Staupitz,[15] the example of his Augustinian mentor helped make the biblical text the primary text of his teaching career. Not only his

XV

lifelong occupation with interpretation and translation of the biblical text, but also his advice on how to read and study the Bible reflect his monastic beginnings. The *oratio, meditatio,* and *tentatio* that Luther recommended as the access to Scripture in 1539 could have been used equally well by him in his cells at Erfurt and Wittenberg.[16]

Luther the reformer owed much to the monastic tradition, and he did not condemn it in toto. It was difficult for him to discard his monastic identity even after reforms were underway in Wittenberg. He finally stopped wearing the cowl in October 1524, but only after Erasmus had paid him the dubious compliment of not taking advantage himself of the freedom that he preached for others.[17] Monasteries were, affirmed Luther, originally instituted to foster Christian liberty, but that purpose had been undercut in the churches and cloisters of his day by the coercive use of religious ceremonies.[18] Hence his time in the monastery taught him on balance a negative lesson about medieval religion. Luther considered it a lesson worth learning and, typically, he saw the hand of God at work in his entry into the cloister. The Lord wanted him to experience, he said, the "wisdom of the schools" and the "holiness of the monasteries" so that no future opponent could boast that Luther was condemning what he had not known at firsthand. When, therefore, he began, his literary reckoning with monasticism in the treatise *Monastic Vows,* he dedicated it to his father in memory of his personal experience; but, more significantly, he declared his solidarity with all those who were being tormented in the iron furnace of Egypt and the raging fire of Babylon, that is, with all those who were suffering under the tyranny of conscience and sin.[19] Instead of removing him from the people, Luther's time in the monastery taught him all too well what people felt about the religion of their day. Many of these people became his followers.

2. The University

In addition to the holiness of the monasteries, said Luther, he had to learn at firsthand the wisdom of the schools. That side of his education began at the University at Erfurt in 1501 and continued there even after he entered the cloister. As a student he was associated primarily with the University of Erfurt, while as a teacher he spent over thirty-three years on the faculty of the University of Wittenberg. In terms of his occupation, the university succeeded the cloister as Luther's primary community.

Up to 1522, however, the monastery and the university were not so sharply distinguished in Luther's academic life. The impression he made in the Erfurt cloister led him to be selected to study theology in the first place. In Wittenberg, where both the Augustinian cloister and the university were established in the same year (1502), Luther was named *regens studii* of the monastery while simultaneously a member of the theological faculty.

XV

Luther learned and taught theology in both communities, and academic traditions flowed to him through both channels. Nevertheless, the wisdom of the schools was by definition the philosophy and theology taught in the universities, and in that setting it most directly affected Luther's career. Luther learned his scholastic theology well. His philosophy teachers at Erfurt, Jodocus Trutvetter and Bartholomew Arnoldi von Usingen, trained Luther in the *via moderna*. Luther was proud of his Ockhamist skills and on occasion wielded the razor handily himself.[20] His theological study, which did not cease when he began teaching in 1512, acquainted him also with the *via antiqua*, both through primary sources and secondarily through the works of Gabriel Biel (d. 1495), whose book on the canon of the Mass the young Luther considered outstanding. Melanchthon claimed that Luther knew large sections of the works of Biel and of Pierre d'Ailly (d. 1420) by heart.[21] Luther was well-versed and discriminating in his study of scholastic theology. In 1519 he gave trenchant expression to the results of that discrimination: "I know what scholastic theology did for me and how much I owe it! I am glad that I have escaped from it, and for this I thank Christ my Lord. They do not have to teach it to me, for I already know it. Nor do they have to bring it any closer to me for I do not want it!"[22]

Scholastic theology was the target of his first public attack in a set of theses prepared for debate at the university. Prior to this *Disputation Against Scholastic Theology*, which took place on September 4, 1517, Luther had been interpreting for his students the texts of biblical books such as the Psalms, Romans, and Galatians. While he used the terminology of scholastic theology as an aid to explanation, he also sought help in the commentaries of medieval exegetes, in the works of German mystics like John Tauler (d. 1361), and in the works of Augustine, especially the anti-Pelagian writings, which he did not use until his lectures on Romans in 1515–16. These works, in addition to the biblical language that he strove to elucidate, taught him a new form of theological discourse and led him to reject the scholastic *modus loquendi*.[23] He rejected the form of scholastic theology, however, because he discovered that its content, at least on matters of soteriology and revelation, did not conform to the content of the biblical books as Augustine and the mystical writers had helped him to understand it. In 1518 Luther summed up the content of what he had learned: "I teach that men should trust in nothing but Jesus Christ alone, not in prayers and merits or even in their own works."[24] The fresh comprehension of biblical terms like *righteousness*, *faith*, and *promise* did not fit into the scholastic framework, as Luther discovered most notably while wrestling with Romans 1:17. Although his "Reformation discovery" helped to resolve the tension in his religious life that the monastery had exacerbated, the new theological insight was first and foremost an academic discovery made in the context of his duties as a teacher at the university.

And the immediate consequence was not an attack on monasticism, but on the scholastic tradition in which he had been trained.

The influence of humanism on Luther's development should also be considered in direct relationship to his role as a professor of theology. Luther was never the center of a humanist sodality, but he was well aware of the movement, and its leaders cultivated contact with him. He had been exposed to humanist currents both at the University of Erfurt and through the Augustinian Order.[25] The University of Wittenberg already had a healthy department of humanities before Luther arrived, and Elector Frederick the Wise, founder of the university, remained committed to the humanities in university expansion programs thereafter. In the dedication of his second commentary on the Psalms to Frederick in 1519, Luther wrote: "Who is not aware that Prince Frederick supplies an example to all princes with his promotion of letters? Greek and Hebrew prosper gratifyingly at your Wittenberg; liberal arts are being taught more amply and skillfully than ever before. The pure theology of Christ is victorious; the opinions and questions of men mean practically nothing to teachers or to students."[26] Luther's own use of Greek and Hebrew in his lecture preparation, and his preference for the Bible and the Church Fathers over the scholastic theologians, corresponded to the curricular goals of other humanists and shaped the theological faculty of Wittenberg as well. In correspondence between 1517 and 1519 with friends who had humanist interests, Luther even signed his name in the manner of the humanists as "Eleutherius," a Greek play on words that meant "the free one."[27]

While the linguistic and patristic interests of humanists like Erasmus coincided with his own, their theology and hermeneutical method did not. As early as 1516 Luther criticized Erasmus's interpretation of Romans and divorced himself from Erasmus's preference for the literal sense employed by Jerome over the interpretation of Paul offered by Augustine in his anti-Pelagian writings.[28] When he responded to Erasmus's attack in *The Bondage of the Will* (1525), Luther was reacting to the same theological content that he had found objectionable in scholastic 'heology, particularly the doctrines of sin, grace, and merit. The debate between Luther and Erasmus in 1525 was not the colossal encounter of humanism versus the Reformation, but another chapter in Luther's attack on the wisdom of the schools. Luther's relationship with the older humanists was parallel to his relationship to the scholastics. While he rejected the content of their theology, he could utilize some of their tools. In both cases, however, Luther tailored those tools specifically to the academic setting where it was his job to teach theology. Anticipating that he would be judged brash for attacking Erasmus, Luther declared that he did so "for the sake of theology and of the salvation of the brothers."[29]

Some of Luther's colleagues at the university rallied to his theological cause, among them Nikolaus von Amsdorf, Andreas Rudolff-Bodenstein von Karlstadt, Melanchthon, and Justus Jonas. Karlstadt, the most enthusiastic devotee of Augustine in the group, and Melanchthon jumped actively into the literary arena so that one could speak of a "Wittenberg University theology"[30] in the earliest years of the Reformation. In 1518 Luther considered the reform of the study of theology the prerequisite for reform of the church.[31] He was wrong. In general, the theological faculties at other universities did not turn Protestant but remained bastions of scholastic theology and steadfast in their opposition to the Wittenberg theology. Not even in Erfurt was John Lang, prior of the Augustinian cloister and one of Luther's earliest pupils, able to convert Luther's former teachers.[32] This fact underscores the uniqueness and importance of Luther's theological *modus operandi* in the academic setting of Wittenberg. The German Reformation was not a case of spontaneous combustion that could have ignited anywhere.

Only in Wittenberg did a university serve as the motor of the Reformation, and it continued to do so after the movement had spread to cities and to the countryside. Many preachers who propagated the message were educated in the new theology at Wittenberg. Compared with 1516, the number of courses on biblical books had increased dramatically by the 1530s and 1540s;[33] among them were Luther's lengthy lectures on Galatians and Genesis and Melanchthon's lectures on Romans. In these lectures, and in disputations, which were reinstated as part of the academic routine, Luther's theology was refined and expanded. Strengthened by the offerings of Jonas, John Bugenhagen, and Caspar Cruciger, theological instruction made a vivid impact on the students of those decades.[34] Luther utilized members of the university community in the team that produced "his" translation of the Bible, and from the university Luther and his colleagues issued countless memoranda on practical matters of reform. The University of Wittenberg remained Luther's most important community and he was proud of it, as he showed in this remark from his later life: "In this school God revealed his word, and today this school and this city can stand up against all others both in doctrine and in life, even though we are clearly not perfect *in via.*"[35]

3. Wittenberg

As a member of the university faculty Luther remained a resident of the city of Wittenberg until his death. A striking symbol of the local changes to which the Reformation led was the conversion of the Augustinian cloister into the most famous Protestant parsonage by the gift of Elector John to Martin and his new wife, Katherine, in 1525. With just over two thousand inhabitants, Wittenberg may have looked small to a person who had lived in Eisenach (over four thousand) and Erfurt (sixteen thousand); but, in fact, Wittenberg was a medium-sized city that in population ranked among the top ten percent of the cities in sixteenth-century Germany.[36] Furthermore, Wittenberg was rich enough in institutions—the castle, the university, cloisters, and churches—to provide Luther with contacts with colleagues and with people of the town. Luther, of course, made the city famous just as he did the university. But more important, Wittenberg supplied Luther with an audience for his new theology and a testing ground for his reforms after the break with Rome occurred.

In addition to his brothers in the cloister and students at the university, the people in the town became a sizable segment of Luther's audience because of his frequent preaching. Luther's first preaching post was in the cloister and he preached at the Castle Church, especially on academic occasions and in later years when important visitors stopped over in Wittenberg. Luther also occupied the city preachership, which was financed by the city council and which called for him to preach in the City Church, where he had wider exposure to the people of the town.[37] When he began preaching against indulgences, private Masses, and religious fraternities, he had more than enough targets in Wittenberg itself. By 1519 visitors to Elector Frederick's relic collection could take advantage of almost two million years' worth of indulgences or benefit from one of the nine thousand Masses celebrated annually in the Castle Church.[38] Wittenberg was the prime example of a Reformation setting: a preacher in a publicly-financed pulpit who advocated Luther's theology and initiated reforms in the face of a thriving medieval piety.

Wittenberg fostered not only the spoken word but also the writings of Luther. After 1517 Luther began publishing tracts at an astonishing rate. By the time he was excommunicated in January 1521, as many as one-half million copies of his works may have been in circulation. Many of these were first published in Wittenberg, where by 1523 some six hundred editions of Luther's writings had been printed.[39] The town, which had no export business at all before 1500, became the most productive center of printing in Germany, not least of all due to its publication of Luther's German Bible in eighty-six editions between 1534 and 1626. In 1539 Luther tried to stop the Leipzig printer Nicholas Wolrab from reprinting the Bible because it would "take the bread out of the mouth of our printers."[40] Wolrab's own business of printing anti-Luther tracts had been hurt by the introduction of Protestantism into the Duchy of Saxony.

Through its listeners and its readers Wittenberg supplied the local popular audience to which Luther directed his reforming message. Once the conflict with Rome had flared, Luther took his case to the people as well as to the hierarchy. He defended the *Ninety-five Theses* in Latin for the theologians and he summed up his position in German sermons and treatises for the people. Indeed, he justified his protest against the indulgence practice by stressing the damaging effect it had on the people. They were being seduced by the lure of cheap forgiveness when they should be driven by a realistic assessment of their sin to repentance and trust in God. It was this advocacy of the people that remained the motivating force behind Luther's opposition to the papacy.[41] In refusing to retract his writings at the Diet of Worms in 1521, Luther appealed not just to his conscience held captive to the word of God, but to the consciences of the people as well. They had been tortured by the laws of the pope and the traditions of men, he said; and if he were to recant, he would be opening not just the windows but even the doors to more such godlessness.[42]

The primary purpose of the Reformation in Luther's eyes was to liberate the people from the burdensome and deceptive practices of the medieval church and to reeducate these same people to a new religious life based upon faith instead of upon religious performance. The message of liberation that resounded in Luther's most famous treatises like *The Freedom of A Christian* was clearly heard, while the call for a new devotion to one's neighbor, equally stressed in that treatise and in others, did not receive equal attention. The appeal to be lord of all was more popular than the call to be servant of all. For that reason, Luther wrote as many edifying works as he did polemical ones prior to 1522. These guides to the Christian life appeared as expositions of biblical books and of the Lord's Prayer, the Ten Commandments, and the Creed, and as sermons on the sacraments. Much of the material formed the basis for his catechisms of 1529, which were sparked by the religious ignorance and slackness he had discovered during the inspection of church conditions in Saxony. Even prior to the wide distribution of the catechisms, however, Luther had articulated the fresh view of Christian faith and life that made him the most popular religious writer in Germany.[43]

In addition to changing people's attitudes, the problem of changing religious practices and institutions had to be faced. This challenge emerged first in Wittenberg while Luther was still in hiding at the Wartburg. The changes that corresponded to the Wittenberg theology seemed obvious: clerical celibacy, monastic vows, and private Masses should be abolished; the public Mass should be celebrated in German; the people should receive both elements during Communion. The initiative was seized by Gabriel Zwilling in the Augustinian cloister and by Karlstadt in the university and in the community. Without waiting for approval from Elector Frederick, Karlstadt and Zwilling began making these changes and Karlstadt wrote a church order for the city that was passed by the city council. When disorder erupted in the City Church on February 6, 1522, and the council felt itself caught between the wishes of the elector and the demands of Karlstadt, Luther was recalled to Wittenberg to take charge of the reform.[44] The strategy articulated by Luther in his Invocavit Sermons of March 1522 was to make those changes which were absolutely necessary in order for people to hear the evangelical message but not to force any other changes on the unwilling. Hence the Mass was once again celebrated in Latin, but without those passages which implied that the Mass was a sacrifice. No one had to receive the wine as well as the bread in Communion. Eventually, Luther provided forms for both a Latin and a German Mass and the reception of both elements by the laity became the common practice. In contrast to Karlstadt, who deemphasized learning and rejected theology as an academic discipline, Luther supported the reopening of the city school of Wittenberg under John Bugenhagen and the reorganization of the university by Melanchthon.

In Wittenberg, Luther was able to demonstrate that his message could change religious practices and institutions without destroying them or the social order. Gradual implementation of reforms without the use of force was indeed possible. Reformation did not have to mean revolution. Luther utilized this argument for his cause against opponents like Duke George of Albertine Saxony who faulted this movement at just this point.[45] Perhaps the favorable outcome in Wittenberg made Luther too optimistic about changes in other cities. The only ecclesiastical institution to offer any real resistance was the All Saints' Chapter still cherished by Elector Frederick and dissolved only after his death in 1525. Plenty of Wittenberg students and teachers did lead the Reformation movement in other German cities, but they did not always find the social and ecclesiastical conditions so amenable to peaceful reform.

The initial success in Wittenberg may also have raised Luther's hopes for the qualitative impact of his movement to an unrealistic level. Luther expected people to change visibly as a result of becoming Protestant. When the people of Wittenberg and the surrounding towns did not commune more often or behave any better than previously, Luther was disappointed and occasionally took out that disappointment on Wittenberg itself. On a trip in July 1545 Luther wrote to his wife that he did not wish to return to Wittenberg and it would be best if they could "get away from this Sodom."[46] Luther frequently preached that doctrine meant more than morals, and for that reason Protestants could rightly claim they were better than the papists.[47] But Luther also hoped he had fathered a more serious and responsible populace. Luther's hopes, however, are less reliable criteria for judging the impact of his movement than the actual role that Wittenberg played as the cradle of his message and the proving ground for reform.

4. Electoral Saxony

The influence that Elector Frederick exercised during the disturbances at Wittenberg illustrated how important territorial authority was for the career of Luther and the German Reformation. Wittenberg was not a free imperial city; it was one residence of a territorial prince who was bent on consolidating his authority and reviving the prestige of his dynasty. Prior

XV

to 1517 the Wettin family of Saxony had lost ground to the house of Hohenzollern, which ruled the neighboring territory of Brandenburg. In 1513
Albrecht, the younger brother of Elector Joachim I of Brandenburg, succeeded the brother of Elector Frederick as Archbishop of Magdeburg and
administrator of the diocese of Halberstadt. One year later, when Albrecht
was also elected Archbishop of Mainz, the Hohenzollern family captured
its second electoral position within the empire. They also gained control
over the city of Erfurt, which lay in the middle of Ernestine lands.

This dynastic competition, which the papal legate Aleander called a
"deadly enmity," played a major role in Frederick's protection of Luther.[48]
Frederick was hardly disposed to surrender Luther because he had
criticized an indulgence promoted by Albrecht, which competed with
Frederick's own relic collection and accrued to the credit of the Hohenzollern. Frederick was strengthening his hand over against the emperor, and
his new university at Wittenberg was a symbol of the centralized control
that he had acquired over Ernestine Saxony. Luther both increased the
prestige of that university and provided Frederick with welcome leverage
in the delicate balancing of power between territory and empire. By the
same token, Frederick's own position as a candidate for emperor after the
death of Maximilian in 1519 gave him considerable freedom over against
Rome in handling the case of Luther. The appearance of Luther before the
Diet of Worms and his secure exile at the Wartburg demonstrated how
adroitly Frederick and his advisers managed Luther's case, even though
they did not win a favorable verdict for Luther. All in all, Luther owed
more to the fact that he lived in Saxony than he did to the person or to the
religious preference of Frederick.

Luther may have sensed that fact. Although he recognized how much he
was indebted to Frederick, he did not always obey him. On his way back to
Wittenberg from the Wartburg against the Elector's wishes, Luther assured
Frederick respectfully that he was going to Wittenberg under a far higher
protection than the Elector's and that he might be able to protect Frederick
more than Frederick could protect him.[49] That attitude was typical of
Luther; he was never a court theologian and always insisted on his independence and his right to comment on political matters. In 1542, for example, Luther defended his intervention in a feud between the two Saxonies
in a letter addressed to both Elector John Frederick and to Duke Maurice of
Albertine Saxony. In the first place, he said, 1 Timothy 2:1–2 commanded
preachers to look out for worldly rulers and to pray for peace on earth. In
the second place, the preacher and theologian must proclaim the word of
God in all situations, whether it be to comfort the sorrowful or to admonish
the stubborn.[50] Earlier, when Maurice's uncle, Duke George, forbade the
sale of Luther's German New Testament in Albertine Saxony, Luther used
a theory of two kingdoms to defend the integrity of the spiritual realm. The
boundary between the two kingdoms was just as real as the boundary
between the two Saxonies.[51] The theory of the two kingdoms was a two-

edged sword, however; it placed the temporal sphere as well as the spiritual realm under the rule of God and justified the political involvement of Christians, including, presumably, preachers. Luther himself commented freely on social and political issues as specific questions arose. He could have remained silent, but it was unlikely, given the fact that his own case was from the beginning a political matter and that his prince also exercised tight control over religious affairs.

Luther's personal involvement in territorial affairs reflected the various stages in his own reforming career and in the progress of the Reformation.[52] Elector Frederick never considered Luther an adviser and did not actively seek his counsel. For Frederick there was officially no new church to oversee, but only the unsettled case of Luther in which Luther himself never played an equal role. Between 1522 and 1525 Luther was involved primarily with the same concrete reforms of worship and Christian life at the local level as had surfaced during the Wittenberg movement. When Elector John took over in 1525, Luther's horizons widened. Unlike his brother, John was an ardent supporter of the new theology and the time called for active leadership in religious affairs. The aftermath of the Peasants' Revolt forced a closer look at religious and social conditions in Saxony itself, and the result was the organization of a territorial church structure. Protestant rulers like John, Philip of Hesse, and Ernest of Lüneburg were willing to take more aggressive action to bring about a resolution of the political status of imperial estates that followed Luther. Political stands were taken at the Diets of Speyer in 1526 and 1529, alliances were formed, and political Protestantism emerged as a force to be reckoned with in the empire. After Emperor Charles V failed to achieve religious reunion at the Diet of Augsburg in 1530, the question of resistance by the Protestant princes to the Emperor had to be faced. Luther was consulted on most of these matters and rendered judgments both political and theological in nature.[53] He might change his mind, as he did on the issue of resistance after the Diet of Augsburg in 1530; but during these crucial years Elector John usually followed Luther's advice, even though he might have to rule against his own chancellor and his son, John Frederick, who became Elector in 1532.[54]

Luther lived out his last years under the conditions of the Peace of Nuremberg (1532), which led to a political stalemate between the Smalcald League and the Empire. These last years mark the period of the older Luther.[55] It has received less attention from Luther scholars than the earlier years, not because Luther was less interesting but because the historical decisions made during these fourteen years seemed less obviously crucial than those made earlier and later. Luther's career was very much tied to the historical role of Saxony in the German Reformation, and that role, apart from Frederick's initial protection of Luther, was more pronounced between 1525 and 1532 and again after Luther's death. There were exceptions, of course, like the Diet of Smalcald in 1537, which was critical to

Protestant unity and perseverance. Here Luther was once again a key figure with his *Smalcald Articles*. As a rule, however, under John Frederick, Luther retreated from direct involvement in territorial politics in favor of Melanchthon.[56] Luther contributed polemical treatises on specific political encounters, especially in the 1540s, when tensions were again increasing, but most of his energy was spent on consolidating the Reformation in Saxony and in surrounding territories.[57]

The attitudes as well as the career of Luther were frequently shaped by the territory in which he spent all of his life after 1521. His firsthand acquaintance with other parts of Germany was slight, not to mention Europe as a whole. Although not isolated in Wittenberg, Luther often spoke in his letters of distant events in a categorical manner typical of one who was not in close touch with them. Rumors about the Turks, the pope, and the emperor, when relayed together, posed an ominous picture that fed Luther's long-held suspicion that the Last Days were at hand. His perception of the Peasants' Revolt might have been influenced by the relatively favorable situation of the peasants in Saxony.[58] In the beginning it may have appeared to Luther than their grievances could be settled without violence. After the unrest erupted, however, and Thomas Müntzer became identified in Luther's area with the cause of the peasants, the uprising assumed much more dangerous proportions in Luther's mind and led eventually to his harsh reaction. Even Luther's negative attitude toward the Jews expressed in his later life may have been related to the edict that Elector John Frederick promulgated in August 1536, forbidding Jews to do business in Electoral Saxony or to travel through his lands.[59]

As the predominantly territorial reformer of his later years, Luther remained in lockstep with the rhythm of the Reformation. In the 1530s territories joined forces to protect and intensify the reform initiated in the 1520s in city and territory alike. In northern Germany a significant expansion of Protestantism occurred around Luther's land in 1539. The conversion of Joachim II of Brandenburg was satisfying in view of the old rivalry between the Wettin family and the Hohenzollern, but the entry of Ducal Saxony into the Protestant camp was especially welcomed. On Pentecost Sunday, 1539, Luther preached in celebration of the occasion at St. Thomas Church in Leipzig. Three years later, when Luther intervened in the feud between the two Protestant Saxonies, he claimed that he was now respected by both sides as a servant of Christ and preacher of the Gospel.[60] Luther had become the reformer of both Saxonies.

5. Germany

"God favored much-celebrated Germany, the true Japhite (Genesis 10), with the imperial majesty, crown and sceptre at the end of the world and sent it a German prophet as well; therefore, Dr. Luther arose and, like a

German prophet, preached and wrote publicly against indulgences, and he taught the true nature of that blessed Christian repentance which makes one righteous in God's sight."⁶¹ In this encomium, Luther's first biographer, Johann Mathesius, applied a label to Luther that had been used earlier by Luther himself: the German prophet. It was not uncommon for Luther to be called a prophet; as early as 1518, in the preface to the first edition of Luther's writings published in Basel, Wolfgang Capito compared Luther with the prophet Daniel.⁶² "German prophet" was an ambiguous label, however. Luther's own use of the term was not without reservation. After identifying himself as the German prophet in the *Warning to His Dear German People* (1531), Luther added that he had to assume such presumptuous titles in order to humor the papists.⁶³ Just a half year earlier, while the Diet of Augsburg was still in session, Luther had written publicly that he was no prophet, but in the next breath he claimed that he had to speak out on behalf of miserable Germany, his dear fatherland.⁶⁴

There was good reason for the ambiguity. Luther was not the prophet of a militant German nationalism, as indeed Ulrich von Hutten and other German nobles like Franz von Sickingen had hoped. Luther shared their resentment of Roman control over German wealth and territory, but he did not share their dreams of a restored German glory or the rehabilitation of the knightly estate. Above all, he rejected the idea that blood might be spilled through his movement as it was in the revolt of the knights. When the failure of the Diet of Augsburg raised for Luther the possibility that Emperor Charles might go to war against the Protestant princes, he could bring himself only with great difficulty to counsel resistance to the emperor. Half seriously he called himself the German prophet because he was convinced that in this case his warning would promote the salvation of the German people and not his own glory.⁶⁵

Luther's identity with Germany was real, but it was tempered by the religious significance of his movement. In his early campaign against scholastic theology he let slip some enthusiasm for German theologians as the "best theologians" when he published the complete *German Theology,* an anonymous mystical work, in 1518.⁶⁶ His *Address to the Christian Nobility of the German Nation* two years later was, in Luther's words, more an appeal to the laity against the clergy than an appeal to Germans against Rome. The Saxon advisers who were behind the treatise knew that a responsive patriotic chord would be struck nonetheless. Even Duke George admitted that there was some truth in the treatise, although he agreed not to allow its publication in his territory.⁶⁷ The *Address* was Luther's most popular treatise to date, and he benefited from the resentment against Rome already bubbling in the empire more than he contributed to it.

The threats contained in the Edict of Worms made Luther's ultimate reception in Germany uncertain. By 1524, however, when it was clear he had survived and reform had proceeded apace in Electoral Saxony, he

XV

addressed an appeal to a different cadre of lay leadership in Germany on behalf of a specific reform proposal that he had mentioned in the address to the nobility: *To the Councilmen of All Cities in Germany That They Establish and Maintain Christian Schools.* Luther now identified his work openly with the land of Germany in a manner that revealed his emerging prophetic self-understanding. God had opened his mouth and commanded him to speak, said Luther, and it had become clear that God was standing beside him because his movement had expanded and grown strong in the face of opposition without Luther's own doing.[68] Confidence in divine direction was not new for Luther. During the initial years of the conflict with Rome he had frequently consoled himself with the thought that the whole affair was in God's hands. Luther wrote to Staupitz in 1519 that God was seizing and moving him and that he had no control over himself.[69] By 1524 Luther was convinced that God had not only vindicated his personal struggle but in addition had visited all of Germany with His word. Germany had never before heard so much of God's word as now, he exclaimed. Buy when the goods are at your door and gather in the harvest while the weather is good, he advised. Use God's gifts and word while they are available, for God's word is like a passing shower that does not return where it once has been. The Jews, Greece, and Rome had all had their chance, and the word would not tarry in Germany forever, either.[70]

Luther was now articulating a view of God's work in history that included a specific German dimension, and he was identifying himself with the coming of the word to Germany. As he put it, the Gospel had gone out from Wittenberg into Germany and to all parts of the world.[71] This interpretation of God's work in history and of his own place in it was a prominent part of his self-understanding as a reformer. That self-perception was aided by the fact that Luther lived in a climate where German self-consciousness was on the rise, but it was predominantly influenced by the success of a new religious movement in German territories that could be played off against an ecclesiastical hierarchy identified with Rome. Luther's original advocacy of the people of the church against the hierarchy, translated into the spatial terms of his spreading movement, became an advocacy of the German people against a Roman papacy, a Roman hierarchy and, if need be, against an emperor more loyal to Rome than to the Gospel and to his own German subjects.

In this sense Luther certainly fulfilled the function of a prophet, even of a German prophet: he interpreted history in terms of God's relationship to his own people. That interpretation was not limited to the contrast between Germany and Rome. The threat the Ottoman Turks posed to the empire in Luther's lifetime was explained by Luther as a sign of God's anger at the German people on account of their unbelief and ingratitude. The Turks became part of the team of forces which, in Luther's eschatological vision of history, opposed the Gospel and signaled that the Last Days were at hand. Nevertheless, Luther did not advocate a crusade against the Turks. Instead, he defended war against them on the ground that peace and order in the empire should be protected.[72] With this reasoning Luther sounded more like a modern theorist than a German prophet.

Whereas Luther hesitated to call himself a prophet without reservation, he unambiguously described himself as a faithful teacher of his fellow Germans.[73] That title reflected more accurately the purpose of his address to the city councilmen of Germany. Luther stressed the opportunity that had come to Germany through the shower of the word in order to convince the councilmen that they should establish "Christian schools," which would teach children languages and good literature for the good of both church and society. Luther eloquently defended the necessity of knowing biblical languages in order to interpret the word of God aright, even though he might have offended his own pastors by distinguishing between simple preachers who did not know these languages and true prophets of the word who could use them. Luther not only helped to shape the modern German language but also upheld the value of classical languages for German society as a whole. Still, he feared that the "foolish" Germans would not be willing to import a valuable commodity like languages, although they purchased all sorts of unnecessary wares from other lands.[74] The pamphlet literature of the sixteenth century described Luther as the educator and enlightener of the people and as the prophet of the Last Days.[75] Perhaps he should stand alongside Philipp Melanchthon as another *praeceptor Germaniae*.

Once Luther realized that his reform movement had spread to other territories, he was convinced that the interpretation of himself as the vehicle of God's work in Germany was true. Luther did not arrive at that self-understanding by himself but was drawn to it by humanists like John Lang, Christoph Scheurl, and Wolfgang Capito, who were impressed by his person and stimulated by his writings.[76] They were not impressed because Luther embodied any quintessential German traits of character. Even in the pamphlet literature Luther was seldom praised as a German, although it was maintained occasionally that Germany could now shake off the yoke of Rome if it would only take to heart the pure Gospel that Luther taught.[77] The Germany that received Luther and that he in turn regarded as the field of his work was the historical community, which responded to him in terms of the concrete circumstances of his age. It was not a spiritual Germany that could make out of Luther a metahistorical character of the German for all seasons.

6. The Church

While Luther's impact on Germany was limited to a geographical community, his relationship to the church involved him with the most exten-

XV

60

sive community in which he lived. In the first place, the church from which he emerged, the Roman Church, was more widespread than Germany alone, claiming for itself the ancient mark of catholicity. In the second place, the Protestant churches he helped to create were established on the premise that the true church was more extensive than the Roman Church. The true church was ecumenical in Luther's opinion; any institutional form of the church could claim legitimacy only by belonging to that universal community.

That universality already belonged to the view of the church that Luther formulated in his early lectures. True Christians were those who lived by faith in the promises of God. The church was not limited to any one ecclesiastical community but was present wherever people were able to hear the word of God.[78] Applied to the specific situation after 1518, this view asserted that the true church could exist beyond the Roman Church. History supplied examples of non-Roman Christian communities like the Eastern churches, and Luther utilized these examples in his arguments. On the same basis, the continuation of the church apart from the jurisdiction of the Roman bishops was possible after Luther's excommunication. His ecclesiology provided the underpinnings for an ongoing Protestant church structure as well as a bridge over his own break with the papacy. As adapted by other reformers, Luther's ecclesiology was the basic theoretical justification for the separation from Rome and the establishment of new Protestant religious structures.

At first Luther did not worry about what kind of structure might be best suited to his aims. He assured local parishes like Leisnig of their right to bypass the medieval patronage system and call a Protestant pastor.[79] The first concern was to see that local parishes were provided with Protestant preachers. The administration of emerging Protestantism was less important to him. The aftermath of the Peasants' War demonstrated the urgent need for instruction in basic Protestant belief and practice at the local level. Hence Luther agreed to ask Elector John for an official inspection of the parishes in Saxony. This visitation resulted in a territorial church structure in which control of church affairs was vested primarily in the prince and in agencies appointed by him. Historians have debated whether or not this development undermined Luther's original intention and contradicted his view of the church.[80] In the preface to his German Mass, Luther did voice, on behalf of those who earnestly desired to be Christian, the desire to assemble for their own worship and study.[81] Moreover, Luther seemed to be critical of the Elector's self-appointed role in the visitation and of new features of the Saxon church like the rite of ordination or the function of the consistory.[82] Did the territorial church gainsay the ideal of small congregations of devoted Christians and nullify Luther's chance of shaping the new church in Germany according to a more independent model?

Luther definitely did not prescribe a structure for Saxon Protestantism as

John Calvin did for the church in Geneva or Martin Bucer for Strassburg. In that sense he did not etch the face of German Protestantism. There is, however, little reason to believe that Luther was fundamentally displeased with the territorial church as he knew it. It did help to provide what Luther considered to be the most important element in an ecclesiastical organization: the educated pastor who could properly instruct his parish in Protestant doctrine and practice. Whether the territorial church conformed in every detail to his ideal, if indeed Luther cherished an ideal form, did not matter as long as the good pastor was supplied. Not the territorial church and certainly not the Lutheran Church, but the Protestant pastor was the visible legacy of Luther to the Reformation.[83] The pastor was critical because he was the vehicle through which the new theology and practice were transmitted to the people. The preacher was the key to the realization of Luther's reforming intention: to liberate and to reeducate the populace. To this extent Luther achieved a modicum of success. At least in his own territory the Protestant clergy were better educated and more responsible in performing their parish duties than the priests of the old church had been.[84]

Whether the new pastors, once they were in place, were able to reeducate the people is another question. The records of visitations in Protestant parishes in the second half of the sixteenth century indicate that Luther succeeded better as a liberator than as an educator. Many people did not learn the catechism, did not attend church regularly, did not treat pastors with respect, did not give up traditional beliefs, and did not behave any better than previously.[85] In other words, Reformation theology even when preached faithfully by good pastors did not necessarily root out popular religion or aversion to formal religion. If accurate, these results are not surprising, even if the records reflect the tendency of official inspectors to record what caused them dissatisfaction instead of what met their high ideals.

Luther was not very different from religious reformers of any age in this regard. In spite of his realistic appraisal of human nature, he still expected people to change both their behavior and their theology. In contrast to many reformers, however, he did not expect to create a perfect church or society. In fact, he regarded his movement as a prelude to the complete reformation of the church that God would effect at the imminent Last Days. The historical movement was more a holding action until the true Reformation should arrive.[86] People could change, but not necessarily become perfect in view of the fact that the end was approaching and evil was stronger than ever. This perspective on his work kept Luther from being naive about preempting God's own Reformation. He did reform the church by changing the worship, rituals, and structure of the medieval institution, but he did not expect to bring about a complete reform of the people in the church.

Martin Luther shaped all the communities to which he belonged and he was in turn shaped by them. It is tempting, but ultimately not very illuminating, to argue which community was the sine qua non for his development as a reformer. Without minimizing his own creative powers and the impact of his personality, one can still appreciate the uniqueness of the historical moment in which the person Luther and all those communities of which he was a part interacted to unleash the German Protestant Reformation. For this reason Luther's biography is not a restriction of perspective, but will remain an essential part of Reformation historiography.

NOTES

1. A. G. Dickens, *The German Nation and Martin Luther* (London: Edward Arnold, 1974), 210.
2. Ibid., 226.
3. *D. Martin Luthers Werke: Kritische Gesamtausgabe* (Weimar: Böhlau, 1883–) (cited as *WA*), 8:573.30–74.4. Cf. *Dokumente zu Luthers Entwicklung*, ed. Otto Scheel, 2d ed. (Tübingen: Mohr [Siebeck], 1929), 68 (no. 175).
4. Erik H. Erikson, *Young Man Luther: A Study in Psychoanalysis and History* (New York: Norton, 1962), 94–95.
5. See esp. Lewis W. Spitz, "Psychohistory and History: The Case of Young Man Luther," *Soundings* 56 (1973): 182–209; reprinted in *Psychohistory and Religion: The Case of Young Man Luther* (Philadelphia: Fortress, 1977), 57–87.
6. Steven Ozment stresses this point in *The Age of Reform 1250–1550: An Intellectual and Religious History of Late Medieval and Reformation Europe* (New Haven and London: Yale, 1980), 224–25. Erikson anticipated this criticism and rejected it, albeit ambiguously, in his discussion of Luther's vow: *Young Man Luther*, 94.
7. *WA*, 8:574.29–31.
8. Scheel, *Dokumente*, 198 (no. 532) and 201 (no. 533).
9. See Luther's letter to Staupitz, dated May 30, 1518: *WA*, 1:525.4–26.14. See also Heiko A. Oberman, " 'Tuus sum, salvum me fac': Augustinréveil zwischen Renaissance und Reformation," *Scientia augustiniana: Studien über Augustinus, den Augustinismus und den Augustinerorden. Festschrift Adolar Zumkeller*, ed. Cornelius Mayer and Willigis Eckermann (Würzburg: Augustinus, 1975), 349–94.
10. Scheel, *Dokumente*, 199 (no. 532).
11. See Adolar Zumkeller, "Die Augustinerschule des Mittelalters: Vertreter und philosophisch-theologische Lehre," *Analecta Augustiniana* 27 (1964): 167–262; idem, "Augustiner-Eremiten," *Theologische Realenzyklopädie* (cited as *TRE*), 4:728–39.
12. See H. A. Oberman, "Headwaters of the Reformation: Initia Lutheri—initia Reformationis," in *Luther and the Dawn of the Modern Era: Papers for the Fourth International Congress for Luther Research*, ed. H. A. Oberman (Leiden: E. J. Brill, 1974), 69–82. For a summary of the views of Luther's relationship to Augustine, see Ulrich Bubenheimer, "Augustin/ Augustinismus III: Augustinismus in der Reformationszeit," *TRE*, 4:718–21. While Oberman is convinced that late medieval Augustinianism was the *occasio proxima* of the new Wittenberg theology ("Headwaters," 82), Zumkeller categorically rejects any anticipation of Luther's theology by medieval Augustinian theologians: "Augustiner-Eremiten," *TRE* 4:731.
13. David C. Steinmetz, "Hermeneutic and Old Testament Interpretation in Staupitz and the Young Luther," *Archiv für Reformationsgeschichte* 70 (1979): 57; idem, "Religious Ecstasy in Staupitz and the Young Luther," *The Sixteenth Century Journal* 11 (1980): 35.
14. Scheel, *Dokumente*, 194 (no. 518); 204 (no. 536).

15. Steinmetz, "Hermeneutic and Old Testament Interpretation," 56–58. For an interpretation of the impact of monasticism on Luther's hermeneutic, see Darrell Reinke, "From Allegory to Metaphor: More Notes on Luther's Hermeneutical Shift," *Harvard Theological Review* 66 (1973): 386–95.

16. *WA*, 50:659.1–4.

17. Heinrich Bornkamm, *Martin Luther in der Mitte seines Lebens* (Göttingen: Vandenhoeck & Ruprecht, 1979), 230.

18. *WA*, 5:39.18–28.

19. *WA*, 8:574.26–29; 8:577.10–13.

20. H. A. Oberman, *Werden und Wertung der Reformation* (Tübingen: Mohr [Siebeck], 1977), 368–71, 425.

21. Scheel, *Dokumente*, 199 (no. 532).

22. *WA*, 5:22.18–21.

23. Leif Grane, *Modus loquendi theologicus: Luthers Kampf um die Erneuerung der Theologie (1515–1518)* (Leiden: E. J. Brill, 1975), 141–43. In 1531 Luther told his students it was still important for them to be acquainted with the scholastic *modus loquendi*: Scheel, *Dokumente*, 65 (no. 168).

24. *D. Martin Luthers Werke: Briefwechsel* (Weimar: Böhlau, 1930–) (cited as *WABr*), 1:160.10–11 (March 31, 1518).

25. Helmar Junghans, "Der Einfluss des Humanismus auf Luthers Entwicklung bis 1518," *Lutherjahrbuch* 37 (1970): 37–101; Oberman, "Headwaters," 69–70.

26. *WA*, 5:20.18–22. See Maria Grossmann, "Humanismus in Wittenberg 1486–1517," *Lutherjahrbuch* 39 (1972): 11–30; Heinz Scheible, "Gründung und Ausbau der Universität Wittenberg," in *Beiträge zu Problemen deutscher Universitätsgründungen der frühen Neuzeit*, ed. Peter Baumgart and Notker Hammerstein (Nendeln: KTO, 1978), 131–47.

27. Helmar Junghans, "Initia gloriae Lutheri," in *Unterwegs zur Einheit: Festschrift für Heinrich Stirnimann*, ed. Johannes Brantschen and Pietro Selvatico (Freiburg and Vienna: Herder, 1980), 313–17.

28. *WABr*, 1:70–71 (October 16, 1516).

29. *WABr*, 1:71.42–43.

30. Karl Bauer, *Die Wittenberger Universitätstheologie und die Anfänge der deutschen Reformation* (Tübingen: Mohr [Siebeck], 1928), 51.

31. *WABr*, 1:170.30–40 (May 9, 1518).

32. Oberman, *Werden und Wertung*, 332–34.

33. Scheible, "Gründung," 142–44.

34. See, for example, Simo Heininen, *Die finnischen Studenten in Wittenberg 1531–1552* (Helsinki: Luther-Agricola Society, 1980), 39–62.

35. *D. Martin Luthers Werke: Tischreden* (Weimar: Böhlau, 1912–) (cited as *WATR*), 4:674.9–11 (no. 5126).

36. Helmar Junghans, *Wittenberg als Lutherstadt* (Berlin: Union, 1979), 73–75.

37. Helmar Junghans, "Wittenberg und Luther—Luther und Wittenberg," *Freiburger Zeitschrift für Philosophie und Theologie* 25 (1978): 107.

38. Ibid., 111.

39. Bernd Moeller, *Deutschland im Zeitalter der Reformation* (Göttingen: Vandenhoeck & Ruprecht, 1977), 62, 193.

40. *WABr*, 8:491 (July 8, 1539).

41. A forceful statement of this advocacy is contained in Luther's *Warning to His Dear German People* (1531): *WA*, 30/3:308.23–16.38.

42. *WA*, 7:833.10–20.

43. Heinz Dannenbauer, *Luther als religiöser Volksschriftsteller 1517–1520: Ein Beitrag zu der Frage nach den Ursachen der Reformation* (Tübingen: Mohr [Siebeck], 1930), 6:30–42.

44. For sources and interpretation, see Nikolaus Müller, *Die Wittenberger Bewegung 1521 und .*

1522 (Leipzig: M. Heinsius Nachfolger, 1911); James S. Preus, *Carlstadt's Ordinationes and Luther's Liberty: A Study of the Wittenberg Movement 1521–1522* (Cambridge, Mass.: Harvard, 1974); Mark U. Edwards, Jr., *Luther and the False Brethren* (Stanford, Calif.: Stanford University Press, 1975), pp. 6–33.

45. Bornkamm, *Martin Luther*, 541–43.

46. *WABr*, 11:149.7–50.21.

47. For example, *WATR*, 1:294.19–95.5 (no. 624).

48. Paul Kalkoff, *Die Depeschen des Nuntius Aleander vom Wormser Reichstage 1521* (Halle: Verein für Reformationsgeschichte, 1886), 20. See the review of Wilhelm Borth, *Die Luthersache (Causa Lutheri) 1517–1524*, by Günter Mühlpfordt in *Deutsche Literaturzeitung für Kritik der internationalen Wissenschaft* 95 (1974): 897–906.

49. *WABr*, 2:455.75–78 (March 5, 1522).

50. *WABr*, 10:32.8–17 (April 7, 1542). See Eike Wolgast, *Die Wittenberger Theologie und die Politik der evangelischen Stände: Studien zu Luthers Gutachten in politischen Fragen* (Gütersloh: Gerd Mohn, 1977), 285–90.

51. *WA*, 11:263.13–21. See Bornkamm, *Martin Luther*, 108.

52. Wolgast, *Die Wittenberger Theologie*, 290–99.

53. Bornkamm, *Martin Luther*, 538–57.

54. Wolgast, *Die Wittenberger Theologie*, 295.

55. Bornkamm, *Martin Luther*, 9.

56. Wolgast, *Die Wittenberger Theologie*, 296–98.

57. Karl Trüdinger, *Luthers Briefe und Gutachten an weltliche Obrigkeiten zur Durchführung der Reformation* (Münster: Aschendorff, 1975), 142.

58. See Karlheinz Blaschke, *Sachsen im Zeitalter der Reformation* (Gütersloh: Gerd Mohn, 1970), 57–58, 65–67; Junghans, "Wittenberg und Luther—Luther und Wittenberg," 113.

59. See Luther's letter to the Jew Josel of Rosheim, who had appealed to Luther for help against the edict: *WABr*, 8:89–91 (June 11, 1537).

60. *WABr*, 10:33.23–25 (April 7, 1542).

61. In E. W. Zeeden, *Martin Luther und die Reformation im Urteil des deutschen Luthertums*, (Freiburg: Herder, 1952), 2:26.

62. Junghans, "Initia," 304–5.

63. *WA*, 30/3:290.28–30.

64. In an open letter to Archbishop Albrecht of Mainz: *WA*, 30/2:411.22; 412.20–23.

65. *WA*, 30/3:291.7–9.

66. *WA*, 1:379.7–12.

67. *WA*, 6:404.11–16. See *Akten und Briefe zur Kirchenpolitik Herzog Georgs von Sachsen*, ed. Felician Gess, vol. 1:1517–1524 (Leipzig: Teubner, 1905), 139.

68. *WA*, 15:27.12–20.

69. *WABr*, 1:344.8–9 (February 20, 1519).

70. *WA*, 15:31.33–32.14.

71. *WA*, 25:310.18–21. See Wolfgang Günter, "Die geschicntstheologischen Vorausset-zungen von Luthers Selbstverständnis," *Von Konstanz nach Trient: Festgabe für August Franzen*, ed. Remigius Bäumer (Munich, Paderborn, Vienna: Ferdinand Schöningh, 1972), 388–94.

72. Bornkamm, *Martin Luther*, 525–26.

73. In the *Warning*: *WA*, 30/3:290.28–32.

74. *WA*, 15:40.14–26; 15:36.9–20.

75. See Andrea Körsgen-Wiedeburg, "Das Bild Martin Luthers in den Flugschriften der frühen Reformationszeit," *Festgabe für Ernst Walter Zeeden*, ed. Horst Rabe et al. (Münster: Aschendorff, 1976), 157, 162–63.

76. Junghans, "Initia," 320–23.

77. Körsgen-Wiedeburg, "Das Bild Martin Luthers," 163–64.

78. See Luther's strong conjunction of the church with the word in an early sermon: *WA*, 1:

13.28–14.3. Compare the implications as drawn out by Luther in 1521: *WA*, 8:491.18–38; in 1539: *WA*, 47:774.15–75.5.

79. *WA*, 11: 411.13–30.

80. The earlier debate has been summarized by Hans-Walter Krumwiede, *Zur Entstehung des landesherrlichen Kirchenregiments in Kursachsen und Braunschweig-Wolfenbüttel* (Göttingen: Vandenhoeck & Ruprecht, 1967), 13–47. For more recent views see Irmgard Höss, "The Lutheran Church of the Reformation: Problems of its Formation and Organization in the Middle and North German Territories," *The Social History of the Reformation*, ed. Lawrence Buck and Jonathan Zophy (Columbus: Ohio State, 1972), 322; Krumwiede, "Reformatorische Theologie und die Selbstverwaltung der Kirchengemeinde," *Jahrbuch der Gesellschaft für niedersächsische Kirchengeschichte* 73 (1975): 211–29.

81. *WA*, 19:75.3–30.

82. The import of Luther's remarks in the introduction to the *Instruction for Visitors* (*WA*, 26:197.12–99.2) has been the subject of considerable debate. See also Trüdinger, *Luthers Briefe und Gutachten*, 82–85; I. Höss, *Georg Spalatin 1484–1545* (Weimar: Böhlaus Nachfolger, 1956), 373–74; Susan C. Karant-Nunn, *Luther's Pastors: The Reformation in the Ernestine Countryside* (Philadelphia: American Philosophical Society, 1979), 56–60, 73.

83. Martin Rade, "Der Sprung in Luthers Kirchenbegriff und die Entstehung der Landes-kirche," *Zeitschrift für Theologie und Kirche* 24 (1914): 259–60.

84. Karant-Nunn, *Luther's Pastors*, 19, 72.

85. See Gerald Strauss, *Luther's House of Learning: Indoctrination of the Young in the German Reformation* (Baltimore and London: Johns Hopkins, 1978), 307. Whether or not this means that the Reformation was a failure, as Strauss suggests, depends very much on the criteria for success and failure employed. Strauss's thesis and methodology are being debated at several points and his conclusions should not be uncritically accepted.

86. This perspective of Luther and the "reformation" is elaborated by Heiko A. Oberman, "Martin Luther: Vorläufer der Reformation," in *Verifikationen. Festschrift für Gerhard Ebeling zum 70. Geburtstag*, ed. Eberhard Jüngel, Johannes Wallmann, Wilfrid Werbeck (Tübingen: J. C. B. Mohr [Paul Siebeck] 1982), 91–119.

BIBLIOGRAPHICAL ESSAY

At the First International Congress for Luther Research in 1956, Heinrich Bornkamm warned scholars that they were in danger of losing sight of Luther the person because of their preoccupation with his theology. The same concern was voiced at the Fifth Congress in 1977. On the whole, however, Luther scholarship during the last twenty-five years has shown considerable interest in aspects of Luther besides his theology, and a more comprehensive picture of the man and his significance is emerging. This is due to several factors. First, more attention has been paid to the context in which Luther worked; second, new attempts have been made to assess Luther's impact on modern history; third, historical studies of phases of Luther's career, though not complete biographies, have laid the ground-work for a new, comprehensive, and critical biography of Luther. Add to these developments the continuing interest in Luther's theology, and Luther research has come far enough since 1956 to render the complaint of Bornkamm no longer necessary.

Historians have long recognized that Luther could not be isolated from his context; that was the presupposition of Karl Bauer's groundbreaking study: *Die Wittenberger Universitätstheologie und die Anfänge der deutschen Reformation* (Tübingen: Mohr, 1928). The same perspective has been adopted in such widely varying works as Ernest G. Schwiebert, *Luther and His Times: The Reformation from a New Perspective* (St. Louis, Mo.: Concordia, 1950), and A. G. Dickens, *The German Nation and Martin Luther* (London: Arnold, 1974). Luther's immediate context, the town of Wittenberg, has been closely examined by Helmar Junghans in his book *Wittenberg als Lutherstadt* (Berlin: Union, 1979). The relationship between Luther and his princes, the electors of Saxony, has been the subject of several works: Hermann Kunst, *Evangelischer Glaube und Politische Verantwortung* (Stuttgart: Evangelisches Verlagswerk, 1976), and Eike Wolgast, *Die Wittenberger Theologie und die Politik der evangelischen Stände* (Gütersloh: Mohn, 1977). On a larger scale, Luther's view of the constitution of the empire has been studied by Wolfgang Günter, *Martin Luthers Vorstellung von der Reichsverfassung* (Münster: Aschendorff, 1976). Günter determined that Luther changed his preference from a monarchical to an aristocratic model of imperial authority during the 1530s. This change corresponded to the course of the Reformation but was not determined solely by it. Günter's conclusion is typical of the results produced by all these studies: Luther both influenced and was influenced by the social and political structures in which he lived. The consideration of this reciprocal influence will make future interpretations of Luther more nuanced.

Taken in its broadest sense, context includes the intellectual as well as the political environment. Hence, the search continues for the antecedents of Luther's ideas and, in this connection, the old question of Luther's relationship to the Middle Ages and to modernity has again emerged. A new appreciation of the complexity of the question has led to answers that stress Luther's kinship with both periods. In his address to the Fourth Luther Congress ("Headwaters of the Reformation: *Initia Lutheri—Initia Reformationis,*" in *Luther and the Dawn of the Modern Era*, ed. H. A. Oberman [Leiden: Brill, 1974], 40–88), Heiko Oberman emphasized the medieval Augustinian context of Luther's beginnings while denying that this context provided a single answer to the question. Gerhard Ebeling, addressing the same congress, located Luther at a point that transcended both ages and enabled him to be critical of both ("Luther and the Beginning of the Modern Age," in ibid., 11–39). Luther's view of conscience put him in much the same position, according to the analysis of Michael Baylor, *Action and Person: Conscience in Late Scholasticism and the Young Luther* (Leiden: Brill, 1977). Although critical of ecclesiastical authority, Luther adhered to the scholastic idea of the authority of conscience; by tying the conscience to Scripture, however, Luther set the stage for the modern discussion of religious freedom, which depended on the relationship between conscience and religious faith. Works like these, which relate Luther to the larger historical context, manifest a distinct appreciation for the originality of his thought and preclude an easy explanation for that originality drawn from either age.

Although the social theory of Marxist historians has permitted them to overcome the medieval-modern dichotomy, it has locked them into an interpretation of Luther that allows little variation. Luther is associated with the "early bourgeois revolution," a concept that, though disputed, reflects Luther's role both in precipitating the social conflict of the sixteenth century and in preventing this conflict from becoming a thoroughgoing revolution. According to Gerhard Zschäbitz, *Martin Luther: Größe und Grenze* (Berlin: Deutscher Verlag der Wissenschaften, 1967), Luther created a religious ideology for the bourgeoisie as he revolted against the reactionary medieval church. A more intensive application of the theory of class conflict to Luther's early theology by Rosemarie Müller-Streisand, *Luthers Weg von der Reformation zur Restauration* (Halle: Niemeyer, 1964), also stresses Luther's submission to the ruling classes. In spite of this limitation, Luther's economic and social views have received some positive evaluation from Günter Fabiunke, *Martin Luther als Nationalökonom* (Berlin: Akademie, 1963).

The ecumenical character of modern Catholic Luther research was given its stamp by Jospeh Lortz in his book *Die Reformation in Deutschland,* 2 vols. (1939–1940; 4th ed. Freiburg: Herder, 1962). Lortz's regard for the catholicity of Luther's thought increased over the years, even though he continued to fault Luther for his subjectivism and maintained that Luther overcame a Catholicism that was no longer fully catholic. More of a parity between Luther and medieval theology has been discovered by other Catholic scholars, for example, by Otto Pesch in his book *Theologie der Rechtfertigung bei Martin Luther und Thomas von Aquin* (Mainz: Grünewald, 1967). Pesch distinguishes between the sapiential theology of Thomas and the existential theology of Luther and concludes that the different character of the theologies does not represent an antithesis that would justify anathemas. Catholic Luther scholars who have concentrated on the question of authority tend to draw a sharper line between Luther and the medieval period; a case in point is Remigius Bäumer, *Martin Luther und der Papst,* 2d ed. (Münster: Aschendorff, 1971). On the whole, however, the contemporary Catholic interpretation of Luther is quite positive, as exemplified by the appreciative works of Jared Wicks, *Man Yearning for Grace* (Washington: Corpus, 1968) and "Luther," in *Dictionnaire de Spiritualité* (9: cols. 1206–43).

That positive Catholic interpretation has spurred the quest for the distinctive nature and genesis of Luther's Reformation theology. Some scholars have followed Ernst Bizer (*Fides ex auditu,* 3d ed. [Neukirchen: Neukirchener Verlag, 1966]) in designating a new concept of the Word of God as the content, and 1518–1519 as the date, of Luther's Reformation discovery. In his book *Modus loquendi theologicus* (Leiden: Brill, 1975), Leif Grane offered a convincing rebuttal of Bizer's thesis without denying the importance of the initial conflict with Rome in drawing out the implications of Luther's theology for a reformation of the church. At stake is the relationship between that conflict and Luther's early theology in his development as a reformer. This question is still being examined at the level of methodology; see, for example, the essays by Heiko Oberman and Leif Grane in *Archiv für Reformationsgeschichte* 68 (1977): 56–111 and 302–15. A sampling of earlier essays on this subject is contained in *Der Durchbruch der reformatorischen Erkenntnis*, ed. Bernhard Lohse (Darmstadt: Wissenschaftliche Buchgesellschaft, 1968).

The stately figure of Karl Holl looms over that discussion as well as over many others. His essays on Luther, *Gesammelte Aufsätze zur Kirchengeschichte*, vol. 1: *Luther*, 7th ed. (Tübingen: Mohr, 1948), stressed the influence that Luther's religion and theology exercised on all aspects of his life. In spite of important contributions like those of Holl, however, the only comprehensive, critical biography of Luther remains the two-volume work by Julius Köstlin, *Martin Luther: sein Leben und seine Schriften*, first published in 1875, and revised under the same title by Gustav Kawerau, 5th ed. (Berlin: Duncker, 1903). Different phases of Luther's life have been studied since Köstlin. The young Luther was examined by Heinrich Boehmer in *Der junge Luther*, first published in 1925, 4th ed. (Leipzig: Koehler & Amelang, 1951), and Robert Fife published a thorough account of Luther's conflict with Rome up to 1521: *The Revolt of Martin Luther* (New York: Columbia University Press, 1957). Mark Edwards provided well-researched and well-written accounts of Luther's conflict with his Protestant opponents in *Luther and the False Brethren* (Stanford, Calif.: Stanford University Press, 1975). Fortunately, Heinrich Bornkamm helped to make his own earlier complaint obsolete by leaving far enough advanced for posthumous publication his study of Luther's middle years: *Martin Luther in der Mitte seines Lebens*, ed. Karin Bornkamm (Göttingen: Vandenhoeck & Ruprecht, 1979). And the older Luther, the man in his fifties and sixties, has received a colorful treatment from H. G. Haile, *Luther: An Experiment in Biography* (Garden City, N.Y.: Doubleday, 1980). Although not proposing different interpretations of Luther, these studies are dissimilar enough to justify the conclusion that no new and definitive interpretation of the whole Luther has yet emerged out of modern Luther research. The time is ripe for a new comprehensive biography, especially with the five-hundredth anniversary of his birth and the completion of the one hundred year-old Weimar edition of his works at hand.

XVI

Martin Luther und Albrecht von Mainz

Aspekte von Luthers reformatorischem Selbstbewußtsein*

Die Beziehungen zwischen Martin Luther und Albrecht von Mainz sind von besonderem Interesse, weil sie sich über die ganze reformatorische Tätigkeit Luthers und die ersten drei Jahrzehnte der Reformation erstrecken. Am 31. Oktober 1517 schickte Luther seine 95 Thesen der »Disputatio pro declaratione virtutis indulgentiarum« zusammen mit seinem »Tractatus de indulgentiis« und einem Brief an Albrecht, in dem er ihn aufforderte, seine »Instructio summaria« für die Ablaßprediger zurückzunehmen und den Pflichten eines Bischofs nachzukommen, dem Volk das Evangelium und die Liebe Christi predigen zu lassen.[1] Nachdem Albrecht die Thesen nach Rom weitergeleitet hatte, wurde das Verfahren gegen Luther eröffnet, das zur Trennung Luthers und seiner Anhänger von der römischen Kirche führte. Obwohl der Protestantismus nicht alle Gebiete übernahm, die zum Einflußbereich Albrechts gehört hatten, hat er trotz langem Widerstand von seiten Albrechts noch vor dem Tod Luthers in das an Kursachsen angrenzende Territorium des Erzstifts Magdeburg und in die beliebte Residenzstadt Albrechts, Halle an der Saale, soweit eindringen können, daß Albrecht 1541 nach dem Landtag zu Calbe das Erzbistum Magdeburg für immer verließ und sich nach Mainz zurückzog.[2] Als

---

* Anlaß zum Nachdenken über dieses Thema haben mir Professor Dr. Bernd Moeller und Professor Dr. Karl Stackmann gegeben, die mich während eines Forschungsjahres in Göttingen zur Teilnahme an ihrem Oberseminar »Luther als Gelegenheitsschriftsteller« einluden. Ihnen und allen Seminarteilnehmern möchte ich für die freundliche Aufnahme in ihren Kreis herzlich danken.

1 WA Br 1, 111, 37-42; 112, 53-60 (48); 12, 1-10 (4212 a). Über den jüngeren Albrecht und über diesen ersten Brief Luthers an ihn siehe Hans VOLZ: Erzbischof Albrecht von Mainz und Martin Luthers 95 Thesen. JHKV 13 (1962), 187-228.

2 Ob Albrecht den Ständen die freie Religionsausübung gegen die Übernahme seiner Schulden zugestanden hat, ist ungewiß; siehe Walter DELIUS: Kardinal Albrecht und die Wiedervereinigung der beiden Kirchen. ZKG 62 (1943/44), 187; DERS.: Die Reformationsgeschichte der Stadt Halle/Saale. B 1953, 66-69; Franz SCHRADER: Kardinal Albrecht von Brandenburg,

97

Luther 1517 den ersten Brief an Albrecht verfaßte, sprach er ihn als hochberühmten Kirchenfürsten an und nannte sich in ehrerbietigem Gegensatz dazu
»Abschaum der Menschheit«.[3] Ein Viertcljahrhundert später hat Luther über
die erneute Reliquienausstellung Albrechts in Mainz nur Spottzeilen geschrieben und Albrecht selbst als den »verdammten Kardinal« bezeichnet.[4]

Der öffentliche Umschwung in Luthers Stellung zu Albrecht symbolisiert
die durchgreifenden kirchengeschichtlichen Folgen von Luthers Bruch mit der
römischen Kirche und die von niemandem vorausgesehene Ausbreitung des
Protestantismus noch vor Luthers Tod. Wenn die Beziehungen zwischen dem
führenden Reformator und dem ranghöchsten Prälaten in Deutschland
genauer betrachtet werden, wird man sich wieder der wichtigen Rolle bewußt,
die führende Persönlichkeiten wie diese auf beiden Seiten im umwälzenden
historischen Prozeß gespielt haben. Eine unbedingte bittere Feindschaft hat
das Verhältnis der beiden zueinander gerade nicht andauernd belastet.
Albrecht soll gesagt haben, daß er nicht das Schlimmste über Luther dachte,
und er hat Luther sogar 20 Gulden zur Hochzeit geschenkt.[5] Nachdem die
ersten Auseinandersetzungen über den Ablaß vorbei waren, hat Luther zweimal öffentlich an Albrecht appelliert und sogar am Ende seines Lebens gegenüber dem Neffen Albrechts, Kurfürst Joachim II. von Brandenburg, behauptet
er habe oft gesagt und gepredigt, daß er dem Kardinal zu Mainz nicht gram
gewesen sei.[6] Wenn einer der beiden im richtigen Augenblick anders reagiert
hätte, hätte zumindest die deutsche Reformation einen anderen Lauf genommen. Der historische Prozeß wird sowohl von den Einstellungen und Entscheidungen einzelner als auch von den gesellschaftlichen Kräften vieler beeinflußt.

Erzbischof von Magdeburg, im Spannungsfeld zwischen alter und neuer Kirche. In: Vo
Konstanz nach Trient: Beiträge zur Geschichte der Kirche von den Reformkonzilien bis zu
Tridentinum = Festgabe für August Franzen / hrsg. von Remigius Bäumer. M; W 1972, 438
3 WA Br 1, 110, 7 (48).
4 WA 53, (402) 404f (Neue Zeitung vom Rhein, 1542); 51, 138, 10 (Predigt in Halle gehalten ar
26. Januar 1546).
5 AKTEN UND BRIEFE ZUR KIRCHENPOLITIK HERZOG GEORGS VON SACHSEN/ hrsg. von Felician Ge
Bd. 1. L 1905, 768, 1-3 (754). – Katharina soll das Hochzeitsgeschenk trotz der Ablehnur
Luthers und ohne sein Wissen entgegengenommen haben; siehe Heinrich BORNKAMM: Marti
Luther in der Mitte seines Lebens: das Jahrzehnt zwischen dem Wormser und dem Augsbu
ger Reichstag / aus dem Nachlaß hrsg. von Karin Bornkamm. GÖ 1979, 364.
6 WA Br 11, 50, 20f (4081), am 9. März 1545.

98

Die römisch-katholische Forschung bedauert das Fehlen einer neuen kriti-
schen Biographie von Albrecht und betont die dadurch entstandene Schwierig-
keit, ihn gerecht zu beurteilen.[7] Wie soll man z. b. die Haltung Albrechts am
Anfang der Reformation bewerten, die 1520 von dem Nuntius Hieronymus
Aleander so beschrieben worden ist: »Unter den Deutschen zeigt der vielver-
mögende Erzbischof von Mainz in seinen Worten sich völlig dem Papste, der
Kirche und Ew. Herrlichkeit ergeben, wie es seine Pflicht und sein Vorteil
erheischen; doch ist er so gutmütig und zaghaft und so nach altväterlichem
Brauch rücksichtsvoll gegen die übrigen Fürsten und Ritter Deutschlands, daß
ich ihn wirklich bisher wärmer gewünscht hätte, wie ich hoffe, daß er es in
Zukunft noch werden soll.«[8] Diese Beschreibung verrät sowohl den Eifer
Aleanders als auch die Unentschiedenheit Albrechts, aber nach Hans Wolter
lassen die meisten Quellen, die für eine neue Biographie vorliegen, »die
Kontouren des Menschen hinter den Umrissen des Politikers, des Verwal-
tungsreformers und auch des Kirchenfürsten« verschwinden.[9] Immerhin neigt
die neuere römisch-katholische Forschung dazu, die Stellungnahme Albrechts
für die alte Kirche als entschieden und konsequent zu beurteilen. Im Erzbistum Magdeburg hat sich der Kardinal nach Franz Schrader »von 1521 bis 1544
gegen die Einführung der Reformation ... gewehrt«.[10] In Mainz hat »die Wende
Albrechts von 1522/23 ... zu planmäßiger Abwehr und damit verbunden zu
einer erneuerten Seelsorge geführt«.[11]
Während seine Stellung zu Luther und zur Reformation wenigstens seine

---

7 Schrader: AaO, 420; Hans WOLTER: Kardinal Albrecht von Mainz und die Anfänge der
katholischen Reform. ThPh 51 (1976), 497. Die alte Biographie Jakob MAY: Der Kurfürst,
Cardinal und Erzbischof Albrecht II. von Mainz und Magdeburg. 2 Bde. M 1865, 1875, reicht
nicht mehr aus. Eine Zusammenfassung des Lebens von Albrecht und die dazugehörige
Literatur gibt Gustav Adolf BENRATH: Albrecht von Mainz (1490-1545). TRE 2 (1978), 184-
187.
8 DIE DEPESCHEN DES NUNTIUS ALEANDER VOM WORMSER REICHSTAGE 1521/ übers. und erl. von
Paul Kalkoff. 2., völlig umgearb. und erg. Aufl. Halle a. S. 1897, 30f (2), an Kardinal Giulio de
Medici [Mitte Dezember] 1520. Die Tatsache, daß Albrecht die von ihm gewünschte
Legatenwürde vom Papst nie erhielt, mag zu seiner zeitweiligen anscheinenden Gleichgültig-
keit geführt haben. Zu diesem und zu anderen Einflüssen auf Albrecht zur Zeit des Reichstages siehe Anton Philipp BRÜCK: Kardinal Albrecht von Brandenburg, Kurfürst und Erzbischof
von Mainz. In: Der Reichstag zu Worms von 1521: Reichspolitik und Luthersache/ ... hrsg.
von Fritz Reuter. Worms 1971, 257-270.
9 Wolter: AaO, 497.   10 Schrader: AaO, 443.   11 Wolter: AaO, 502.

99

Loyalität zur alten Kirche erhellt, läßt umgekehrt Luthers Stellung zu Albrecht bei verschiedenen Gelegenheiten jeweils wichtige Aspekte seines reformatorischen Selbstverständnisses hervortreten und dadurch besonders den späteren Reformator besser verstehen. Zu einer persönlichen Begegnung zwischen Luther und Albrecht ist es wohl nie gekommen, obwohl sie einander auf dem Reichstag zu Worms gesehen haben müssen. Statt auf seine Person Bezug zu nehmen, beruft sich Luther auf das jeweilige Amt Albrechts, das Luther gerade zweckmäßig erscheint. Es ist bemerkenswert, wie Luther dabei die verschiedenen Rollen Albrechts berücksichtigt und ausnutzt. Albrecht wird je nachdem als Priester, Bischof, Kirchenfürst, Deutscher Primas oder als Territorialfürst von Luther angesprochen. Aus Luthers Schriften erfährt man deshalb wenig über Albrecht den Menschen, aber gerade auch deswegen erweitert sich unsere Perspektive auf den Reformator.

In den Jahren von 1517 bis 1521 trat Luther mit seiner Kritik am Ablaßhandel hauptsächlich als Fürsprecher der Gläubigen auf. Es ging ihm darum, gegen die Irreführung der Gläubigen durch die Ablaßprediger und überhaupt durch die kirchliche Hierarchie zu protestieren und sich für die Freiheit der Gewissen einzusetzen. Aus diesem Selbstverständnis heraus schrieb er zum erstenmal an Albrecht am 31. Oktober 1517[12] und dann wieder am 1. Dezember 1521 von der Wartburg aus, nachdem Albrecht die an sein »Neues Stift« in Halle gebundene und mit großzügigen Ablässen ausgestattete Reliquiensammlung hatte ausstellen lassen. Nach Luther hat Albrecht »zu Halle wieder aufgericht den Abgott, der die armen, einfältigen Christen umb Geld und Seele bringet«.[1] Seit den 95 Thesen und immer wieder in seinen Schriften gegen Johann Tetzel, Silvester Mazzolini Prierias und Kardinal Jakob Cajetan de Vio hat dieser Beweggrund neben den theologischen Gründen für seinen Protest eine entscheidende Rolle gespielt. Das Eintreten für die Gläubigen war der Kern seines Verantwortungsbewußtseins als Lehrer der Heiligen Schrift und Pastor der Kirche.

Für Luther, den Lehrer der Kirche und Fürsprecher der Gläubigen, hat das Bischofsamt Albrechts die unmittelbarste Bedeutung gehabt. Zunächst gehörte Wittenberg zur Kirchenprovinz Magdeburg und dementsprechend be

---

12 WA Br 1, 111, 15-25 (48).
13 WA Br 2, 406, 25f (442).

zeichnete Luther sich als ein Exemplar aus Albrechts eigener Herde.[14] Aber an erster Stelle ging es Luther nicht darum, daß er an seinen eigenen Erzbischof und die rechtsmäßige kirchliche Instanz appellierte, sondern daß Albrecht als Erzbischof seine Pflicht gegenüber allen Gläubigen in seinen Gebieten vernachläßigt hatte. Deshalb bat ihn Luther, »das arme Volk unverführet und unberaubet« zu lassen und sich als »einen Bischoff, nicht einen Wolf« zu erzeigen.[15] Wenn Albrecht den Abgott zu Halle nicht abtäte, dann würde Luther Albrecht wie den Papst öffentlich antasten und der Welt den Unterschied zwischen einem Bischof und einem Wolf anzeigen.[16] Dieses Ultimatum läßt erkennen, wie Albrecht ausdrücklich als Mitglied der kirchlichen Hierarchie das Ziel von Luthers Angriff war. Als Georg Spalatin und Kurfürst Friedrich kurz vorher Luthers erneutes Vorgehen gegen Albrecht zu verhindern suchten, fragte Luther rhetorisch, ob er vor dem Geschöpf weichen sollte, wenn er dem Schöpfer Albrechts, eben dem Papst, schon Widerstand geleistet hatte. Keineswegs, beantwortete Luther seine eigene Frage, sondern für die Herde Christi muß mit allen Kräften diesem gewaltigen Wolf widerstanden werden, damit anderen ein Beispiel gegeben wird.[17] Im Lichte des neuen Ablaßangebots in Halle wird Erzbischof Albrecht für Luther zu einem Symbol der treulosen habgierigen Hierarchie, gegen die er gekämpft hatte und noch zu kämpfen bereit ist. Albrecht soll wissen, daß Luther das tun will, was christliche Liebe fordert, »nicht angesehen auch die höllischen Pforten, schweige denn Ungelehrte, Päpste, Cardinäl und Bischoffe«.[18]

In den Jahren von 1521 bis 1525 hat sich der Schwerpunkt von Luthers

14 WA Br 1, 112, 63f (48); 2, 29, 62f (248), an Albrecht am 4. Februar 1520; siehe Volz: AaO, 220, Anm. 128.

15 WA Br 2, 407, 40-42 (442).   16 WA Br 2, 407, 66-72 (442).

17 WA Br 2, 402, 4-12 (438), an Spalatin am 11. November 1521.

18 WA Br 2, 406, 31 – 407, 34 (442). Am 21. Dezember 1521 hat Albrecht von Halle aus mit einem sehr demütigen Brief Luther geantwortet (2, 420f [448]). Aber wegen der Taktik Wolfgang Capitos hat Luther den Brief Albrechts nicht ernstgenommen und »Capitos wohlgemeinten Regiekünsten den schlichten Unterschied von Glauben und Liebe« entgegengesetzt (Bornkamm: AaO, 49f); siehe den bekannten Brief an Capito (WA Br 2, 428-435 [451]). Über diese Auseinandersetzung und die verlorene Schrift, die Luther in der Tat gegen Albrecht gerichtet hat, siehe Gottfried G. KRODEL: »Wider den Abgott zu Halle«: Luthers Auseinandersetzung mit Albrecht von Mainz im Herbst 1521, ... LuJ 33 (1966), 9-87; LUTHER'S WORKS. Bd. 48: Letters. Bd. 1/ hrsg. und übers. von Gottfried G. Krodel. Phil 1963, 344-350.

reformatorischer Tätigkeit verlagert. Allmählich sah Luther seine Hauptauf-
gabe weniger in der Befreiung der Gläubigen von der Herrschaft des Papstes als
in der Ausbreitung und der Ordnung der evangelischen Bewegung. Schon vor
der Wartburg aus hat Luther Philipp Melanchthon ermahnt, daß es in Witten
berg ausreichende Lehrer und Prediger gab: »Wollt Ihr, daß das Reich Gottes
nur unter Euch verkündigt wird? Sollte das Evangelium nicht auch anderen
verkündigt werden? Wird Euer Antiochia keinen Silas oder Paulus oder Barna
bas für das Werk des Geistes freigeben?«[19] Danach befaßte sich Luther mit der
praktischen Fragen, die mit der Neuordnung der Gemeinde zunächst in
Wittenberg und dann anderswo zusammenhingen. Es handelte sich um Fragen
der Strategie, wie in der Auseinandersetzung mit Andreas Bodenstein aus
Karlstadt, und um die theologische Begründung von Streitpunkten wie Prie
sterzölibat, Laienkelch und Gestaltung des Gottesdienstes. Dazu kam, daß
Luther sein eigenes Leben neu verstehen und ordnen mußte. Der Übergang
vom Mönch zum verheirateten Geistlichen war für ihn nicht leicht, obwohl e
mehr Kontinuität als die meisten in Anspruch nehmen konnte, indem e
dieselbe Stelle an der Universität innehaben und in demselben Gebäud
wohnen bleiben durfte.[20]

Über die Priesterehe hatte Luther sich schon Gedanken gemacht, bevor e
sich endlich entschloß, selber zu heiraten. Er hat 1523 in seiner Auslegun
»Das 7. Kapitel S. Pauli zu den Korinthern« den geistlichen Stand mit der
Ehestand verglichen und ist zu dem Schluß gelangt, »das der ehestand goll
und der geistliche stand dreck ist, darumb das ihener zum glauben, disser abe
zum unglauben forderlich ist«.[21] Schon in dem Brief vom 1. Dezember 1521 ha
Luther Albrecht von Mainz ausdrücklich gebeten, er soll »die Priester mi
Frieden lassen, die sich, Unkeuschheit zu meiden, in den ehelichen Stan
begeben haben oder wollen, nicht sie berauben, das ihnen Gott geben hat«.
Dabei spielte Luther auf die eigene notorische Lebensweise Albrechts an.
Deshalb mag es 1525 Luther nicht allzusehr überrascht haben, als der Mansfe
der und Magdeburger Rat und Verwandte Luthers, Johann Rühel, ihm vo

19 WA Br 2, 359, 112-115 (418), Luther an Melanchthon am 13. Juli 1521.
20 Siehe dazu Bornkamm: AaO, 226-236.
21 WA 12, 108, 5-8.   22 WA Br 2, 408, 78-81 (442).
23 WA Br 2, 408, 93 (442). Gegen Beschuldigungen der Unzucht hat sich Albrecht gegenüb
  Herzog Georg von Sachsen in einem Brief vom 8. Dezember 1526 verteidigt. Felician Ges
  Herzog Georg, Kurfürst Joachim I. und Kardinal Albrecht. ZKG 13 (1892), 121.

schlug, Albrecht schriftlich zum Heiraten zu ermahnen.[24] Jedenfalls antwortete Luther, daß er zu schreiben nicht abgeneigt sei.[25] Der Zeitpunkt schien für einen solchen Schritt günstig. Obwohl Albrecht vorher in Halle und Magdeburg gegen die Anhänger Luthers vorgegangen war, bewogen ihn jetzt die Bauernunruhen des Jahres 1525 in beiden Städten nachgiebig zu sein.[26] Es gab auch schon Gerüchte, daß Albrecht heiraten und nach dem Beispiel seines gleichnamigen Vetters, Herzog Albrechts von Preußen, sein Territorium in eine weltliche Herrschaft verwandeln würde.[27] Luther hatte eben dem Herzog zur Säkularisation des Ordenstaates folgendermaßen gratuliert:»Das E.f.g. Gott der allmechtige zu solchem stand gnediglich vnd wunderlich geholffen hat, byn ich hoch erfrewet vnd wundsche furder, das der selbige barmhertzige Gott solch angefangenn güete an E.f.g. volfure zu seligem ende, auch des gantzen landes nutz vnd frumm, Amen.«[28] Auch wenn er kaum Erfolg erwartete, und das ist nicht einmal sicher, dachte Luther wohl, daß ein Brief an Albrecht von Mainz der Ausbreitung der evangelischen Bewegung und der Aufwertung des Ehestandes nun nicht schaden würde. Am 1. Juni schickte Luther eine Abschrift des Briefes an Rühel unter dem Vorbehalt, daß er nicht gedruckt würde, bevor man sicher wüßte, daß der Brief Albrecht gefallen hatte.[29] Erst 1526 erschien der Brief als »Sendschreiben an den Erzbischof Albrecht von Mainz und Magdeburg, sich in den ehelichen Stand zu begeben«.

Gleich am Anfang des Schreibens sagt Luther, daß er sich früher wegen anderer Leute an Albrecht gewandt habe, aber nun schreibe er wegen ihm selbst.[30] Aus den Gründen, die Luther für die Verwandlung von dessen Erzstift anführt, ergibt sich aber, daß er auch in diesem Fall andere im Auge hatte. Wie Albrecht war Luther auch an einem Ende der Bauernunruhen interessiert und er hat dieses gemeinsame Anliegen ausgenutzt, um Albrecht als hohem Geistlichen einen Schritt einzureden, der einen wichtigen Sieg der evangelischen Sache bedeutet hätte. Nach Luther gibt es soviel Aufruhr, weil Gottes Zorn über den geistlichen Stand erregt worden und das Volk so aufgeklärt ist,

24 WA Br 3, 505, 44 – 506, 47 (873), Johann Rühel an Luther am 21. Mai 1525.
25 WA Br 3, 508, 37f (874), am 23. Mai 1525.
26 Schrader: AaO, 425f.   27 WA 18, 403.
28 WA Br 3, 513, 5-8 (876), am 26. Mai 1525.
29 WA Br 3, 522, 3-9 (883).
30 WA 18, 408, 4-11.

103

daß dieser Stand ihm zum Ekel geworden ist. Wenn aber Albrecht umkehren und den geistlichen Stand ablegen würde, den er bisher nur zu verstärken geholfen habe, würde sein Volk ihm neuen Respekt zollen und ihm sich ordentlich fügen.[31]

Natürlich versäumte Luther die Gelegenheit nicht, Albrecht von Mainz das Beispiel des Herzogs von Preußen vorzuhalten. Er beruft sich auch auf die hohe Stellung des Erzbischofs unter den deutschen Fürsten und auf den großen Einfluß, den seine Heirat auf andere Bischöfe haben würde.[32] In beiden Zusammenhängen aber erwähnt Luther den tragenden Grund seines Schreibens: Albrecht würde große Ehre zukommen wie eben dem Herzog von Preußen geschehen ist, weil dem Evangelium Raum gegeben würde.[33] Der ganze Aufruhr des gemeinen Mannes wäre nach Luthers Überzeugung sogar nicht entstanden, »..., hettet jr Bischôff unnd Fürsten bey zeyt selbs darzû gethan unnd dem Euangelion rhaum geben, und was offenlich greuel ist, angefangen zû endern, ...«.[34] Also ist Luther weniger an Albrecht selbst als an der Ausbreitung des Evangeliums interessiert. Albrecht ist der höchste Kirchenfürst im Reich, dessen Übertritt ins evangelische Lager einen noch größeren Sieg als die Säkularisation Preußens bedeuten würde. Ihm gegenüber tritt Luther hauptsächlich als Stratege der neuen Bewegung auf, dem über die Befreiung von einzelnen Seelen hinaus die Befreiung von Gebieten vorschwebt.

Allerdings spricht Luther gleichzeitig seine ehrliche Meinung über der Ehestand aus. Wenn schon nicht um Deutschlands willen, so sollte Albrech doch heiraten, weil er ein Mann sei. Nach Gn 2 soll ein Mann ein Weib haben und kein Mann, es sei denn, daß Gott Wunder tue und aus ihm einen Enge mache, soll ohne Weib im Tode gefunden werden.[35] Man wird schwerlich de Vermutung entgehen, daß Luther sich hier mehr selbst als Albrecht anspricht In dem Brief, mit dem er das Schreiben übersendet, versichert er Rühel, daß e bereit sei, Albrecht »zum Exempel vorherzutraben, nachdem ich doch sons im Sinne bin, ehe ich aus diesem Leben scheide, mich in dem Ehestand finden zu lassen, welchen ich von Gott gefodert achte«.[36] In der Tat heiratet Luther zehn Tage später; aber auf das Schreiben hat Albrecht keine Antwor gegeben, und dem Beispiel Luthers ist er nicht gefolgt. Mit der endgültige

---

31 WA 18, 409, 1-3. 15-20; 409, 35 – 410, 1. 32 WA 18, 410, 5-20.
33 WA 18, 410, 8f. 13-15. 34 WA 18, 409, 6-8.
35 WA 18, 410, 21-37. 36 WA Br 3, 522, 13-18 (883).

Niederlage der Bauern hatte der äußere Druck auf Albrecht nachgelassen, und er ist gegen die Protestanten in Halle noch härter vorgegangen.

Albrecht hat seine Aufgabe als romtreuer Bischof nicht nur in stärkeren Maßnahmen gegen Evangelische gesehen, sondern er hat sich auch um die Klerusreform im eigenen Lager bemüht. Angeregt von Besprechungen auf dem Reichstag zu Speyer 1526, wollte er eine Reformation der Geistlichkeit veranlassen. Danach sollten Erzbischöfe und Bischöfe an erster Selle darauf achtgeben, daß die Pfarrämter in ihren Gebieten mit gelehrten, frommen und edlichen Leuten besetzt werden und diese Pfarrer dem Volk das Evangelium lauter und klar predigen.[37] Trotz dieser Reformbemühungen wurde das Verhältnis Luthers zu Albrecht getrübt, und zwar durch die Ermordung des hallischen Stiftspredigers Georg Winkler. Dieser hatte nach evangelischer Weise Sakramente gereicht und Gottesdienste gefeiert, was vor allem bedeutete, daß er das Abendmahl unter beiderlei Gestalt ausgeteilt hatte. Deswegen wurde er im Mai 1527 von Albrecht nach Aschaffenburg vorgeladen. Nach dem Verhör soll er auf der Heimreise meuchlerisch umgebracht worden sein.[38] Rühel bat Luther anscheinend darum, Albrecht nicht wegen Mitschuld an der Ermordung anzugreifen, da Luther am 26. August 1527 Rühel versicherte, daß er schon bei einer geplanten Trostschrift an die Hallenser gedacht hatte, Albrecht zu verschonen. Nichtsdestoweniger fügte Luther hinzu, wenn das Verbrechen nicht untersucht und aufgeklärt würde, wie könnte »ein menschlich Herz entweder die Pfaffen oder den Bischof rein achten, weil [solange] sie stille dazu schweigen?« Er würde so schonend wie möglich verfahren, schrieb Luther, sofern er sich nicht durch Heucheln mitschuldig mache.[39]

Sicherlich dachte Luther dann auch an Albrecht, als er die Schrift verfaßte, die spätestens Mitte November als »Tröstung an die Christen zu Halle über

---

37 Siehe den Brief von Albrecht an Bischof Adolf von Merseburg vom 22. September 1522 bei Schrader: AaO, 427-429. Die Reformen waren nicht nur für Merseburg bestimmt; siehe Wolter: AaO, 504-507. Dieser Ruf nach Reform von seiten Albrechts trifft sich mit einem Anliegen Luthers insofern, als Albrecht als Hauptgrund für eine Reform die scharfe Kritik des weltlichen an dem geistlichen Stand anführt.

38 Siehe den Bericht Luthers WA 23, 411, 17 – 413, 2. Nach Delius: Kardinal Albrecht ..., 180, mag Albrecht gegen Winkler im Rahmen seiner Reformbestrebungen vorgegangen sein.

39 WA Br 4, 238, 1 – 239, 13 (1136). Aus Luthers erster Bemerkung über die Ermordung läßt sich schließen, daß er das Gerücht von Albrechts Schuld schon gehört hatte (4, 207, 7 – 208, 10 [1110], Luther an Spalatin am 31. Mai 1527).

105

Herr Georgen, ihres Predigers Tod« erschien. An sein Versprechen, Albrecht zu verschonen, hat er sich gehalten, allerdings auf Kosten des Mainzer Domkapitels, dem er die Schuld zuschob. Es seien die Kapitel, die mehr Macht und Gewalt als die Bischöfe in ihren Stiftern hätten, sagt Luther. Und da die Ermordung Winklers vom Kapitel nicht fleißig untersucht werde, gebe es Grund, Verdacht zu hegen, obwohl er das Kapitel nicht mit Gewißheit beschuldigen könne.[40] Albrecht wird in diesem Fall von Luther als Kreatur des Mainzer Domkapitels behandelt, was hinsichtlich der starken Dombehörden und der häufigen Abwesenheit Albrechts historisch nicht so ungenau sein dürfte.[41]

Trotz der Ungewißheit, die über die Schuld noch herrschte, glaubte Luther den wahren Mörder identifizieren zu können: »... der Satan hatts gewislich gethan, ...«[42] Wenn die Domherren zu Mainz schuldig sind, dann sind sie nur Werkzeuge ihres Gottes, des Teufels, der am liebsten alle wahren Prediger Christi ermorden möchte.[43] Und das soll den Hallensern ein Trost sein, daß man auf diese Weise den Mörder doch wissen und den Mord verstehen kann. Dieses Leben ist immerhin »eine mord gruben dem teuffel vnterworffen, ...«.[44] Für Winkler ist es sogar besser, daß er zu der Zeit dem Teufel schon entkommen ist, als er Gott noch treu und gehorsam und noch nicht in Irrtum gefallen war. Denn sein Tod ist gewiß ein Zeichen dafür, daß »ein gros ungluck fur

---

40 WA 23, 407, 15-20; 409, 12-21.
41 Wolter: AaO, 502 f. Es mag von Sachsen aus politische Gründe für die Schonung Albrechts gegeben haben. In der für die Evangelischen unsicheren politischen Lage war Albrecht noch eine Schlüsselfigur. Ein Hinweis darauf ist vielleicht die Aufforderung Melanchthons im Mai 1527 an Albrecht, ein Nationalkonzil zu berufen: MELANCHTHONS BRIEFWECHSEL. Bd. 1 Regesten 1-1109 (1514-1530)/ bearb. von Heinz Scheible. S-Bad Cannstatt 1977, 247 f (551 vgl. CR 1, 874-879 (451); SUPPLEMENTA MELANCHTHONIANA. Abt. 6: Melanchthons Briefwechsel. Bd. 1 (1510-1528)/ hrsg. von Otto Clemen. L 1926, 366 f (558). Melanchthon war aber auch mit Albrecht durch das gemeinsame humanistische Interesse verbunden. So hat er ihm 153 seinen Römerbriefkommentar gewidmet, wobei er auf Albrechts Rolle bei den Nürnberger Friedensverhandlungen anspielte. Für die Widmung hat Melanchthon einen mit 30 Goldgulden gefüllten Pokal erhalten. Siehe MELANCHTHONS BRIEFWECHSEL. Bd. 2: Regesten 1110-2333 (1531-1539)/ bearb. von Heinz Scheible. S-Bad Cannstatt 1978, 79 (1276); CR 2, 611-613 (1076); Volz: AaO, 227, Anm. 157. Noch 1527 hat der Wittenberger Lukas Cranach d. Ä. eine von mehreren Bildern von Albrecht gemalt, und zwar von Albrecht als dem Kirchenvater Hieronymus (Helmar JUNGHANS: Wittenberg als Lutherstadt. B 1979, 140 und Abb. 63).
42 WA 23, 409, 12.   43 WA 23, 405, 24-27; 407, 28-31.
44 WA 23, 403, 33 – 405, 13, bes. 404, 1 f.

handen ist«, aus dem Gott die Seinen zuvor herausgerissen hat. Wir sollen
deshalb Gott dafür danken und nicht zürnen oder Rache wünschen.[45]
So deutet Luther den Tod Winklers und stellt ihn in einen eschatologischen
Zusammenhang hinein, wie er es immer häufiger in der späteren Zeit tut.
Diese Deutungsfunktion ist ein wichtiger Aspekt seiner reformatorischen
Tätigkeit und sollte nicht auf die Ebene einer privaten theologischen oder
eschatologischen Ansicht herabgedrückt werden. Luther hat schon früh seine
eigene Auseinandersetzung mit dem Papsttum ähnlich verstanden. Als die
reformatorische Bewegung wächst und die anderen Prediger mit den Behörden
zusammenstoßen, müssen ihre Siege und Niederlagen auch ähnlich erklärt
und die Gemeinden getröstet werden. Luther übt hier gleichsam die Funktion
eines evangelischen Bischofs aus, der vor dem Ausbau einer Kirchenorganisa-
tion die neuen Gemeinden und ihre Pfarrer tröstet, ermahnt und stärkt. Bei
Luther ist die theologische Deutung des Lebens ein wichtiger Bestandteil der
Verantwortung dieses Amtes. Im Fall von Georg Winkler tritt er als theologischer Berater und Deuter der Geschichte gegen die Werkzeuge des Teufels auf,
hinter denen Albrecht kaum in Erscheinung tritt.
Albrecht kam aber schließlich doch nicht so leicht davon. Als Luther im
April 1528 erfuhr, daß jener in Halle die Austeilung des Abendmahls in
beiderlei Gestalt ernsthaft verboten hatte, ermahnte er »die Christen zu
Halle«, diesem Gebot zu widerstehen.[46] Albrecht wird nun als »Euer Tyrann«
bezeichnet, der zu heucheln aufgehört hat.[47] Da es jetzt sicher war, daß
Albrecht »wider das klare Wort und Einsetzung Christi« handelte,[48] schonte
ihn Luther überhaupt nicht mehr. Trotzdem ging es Luther nicht vorrangig um
einen Angriff auf Albrecht, sondern um die Sache selbst und um die Stärkung
der Evangelischen in Halle, worum es ihm auch schon in der Trostschrift
gegangen war, in der er gleichfalls die Frage der Austeilung des Abendmahls in
beiderlei Gestalt ausführlich behandelt hat.[49]
Auf dem Reichstag zu Augsburg 1530 hat sich Albrecht den Evangelischen
gegenüber friedfertig verhalten.[50] Diese Erfahrung hat Melanchthon wohl ver-

---

45 WA 23, 423, 23-35; 425, 1-3; 427, 1-6; 429, 7-11. 30-33, bes. 427, 3f.
46 WA Br 4, 444f (1255), Luther an die Christen zu Halle am 26. April 1528; vgl. REFORMATOREN-
    BRIEFE: Luther-Zwingli-Calvin/... hrsg. von Günter Gloede. B; NK 1973, 98-100 (46).
47 WA Br 4, 444, 2f (1255).   48 WA Br 4, 444, 6f (1255).
49 WA 23, 413, 2 – 423, 5.
50 WA 30 II, 391f. Albrecht soll diese friedfertige Haltung bei der Eröffnungsmesse gezeigt

107

anlaßt, ihm am 3. Juni einen Brief zu schreiben, in dem er Albrecht bat, da
Seine zu tun, um einen Krieg zu vermeiden.[51] Im selben Brief behauptet
Melanchthon, daß Luther auch sehr friedliebend sei,[52] und er berichtete Luthe
später, daß unter den Fürsten nur Albrecht von Mainz und Herzog Heinric
von Braunschweig für die gefährliche Lage der Evangelischen Verständni
hatten.[53] Luther hat dann am 6. Juli an Nikolaus Hausmann geschrieben, da
der Kardinal von Mainz sehr friedfertig sein solle.[54] Wahrscheinlich in de
Woche darauf verfaßte er den »Brief an den Kardinal Erzbischof zu Mainz« un
sandte ihn zur Veröffentlichung an Wenzeslaus Linck in Nürnberg. Erst nac
der Drucklegung sollte der Brief an Rühel in Augsburg zur Übergabe a
Albrecht geschickt werden.[55]

Obwohl Luther am Anfang die Tatsache beteuert, daß der Brief veröffen
licht werden mußte, geht aus ihm hervor, daß er nicht nur für Albrecht selb‹
bestimmt war. Zwar beruft sich Luther auf Albrecht als »den vornehmste
und höchsten Fürsten in Deutschland«, der mehr als sonst jemand zur Bewa‹

haben: »Der bischof von Meintz hat das ampt in derselbigen messe gehalten und c
keiserliche cantorei die musica gehapt. Nach dem credo hat der pontificius Orator, c
welsche ertzbischof Papinella eine lateinische oration zum könige Ferdinando unter d‹
messe gehapt fur die key. Mat. und allen churfursten und fursten, ist eine geschwinde orati‹
gewesen, sehr giftig wider den turcken und die lutherischen. Wiewol er D. Luther nic
genant. Und unter anderm hat er gesagt. Wo S. Peter mit seinen schlusseln nicht w‹
angesehen werden, so muste S. Paul mit dem schwerdt drein schlagen. Aber der cardinal v
Meintz, der domals das ampt gehalten hat, sol selbst über solcher heftiger rede unwil
gewest sein« (Briefe und Acten zu der Geschichte des Religionsgespräches zu Marbu‹
1529 und des Reichstages zu Augsburg 1530/ hrsg. von Friedrich Wilhelm Schirrmach‹
Gotha 1876, 74).

51 Melanchthons Werke in Auswahl/ unter Mitarbeit von Peter F. Barton ... hrsg. von Rob
Stupperich. [Studienausgabe]. Bd. 7 II: Ausgewählte Briefe 1527-1530/ hrsg. von Hans V‹
GÜ 1975, 163-167, bes. 164, 21-23 (158) ≙ Melanchthons Briefwechsel 1, 388 (921).

52 Melanchthons Werke in Auswahl 7 II, 167, 59f (158).

53 WA Br 5, 371, 17f (1591), Melanchthon an Luther am 19. Juni 1530 ≙ Melanchthons Werke
Auswahl 7 II, 174, 20–22 (162) ≙ Melanchthons Briefwechsel 1, 393, (934); WA Br 5, 423,
(1616), Melanchthon an Luther am 30. Juni 1530 ≙ Melanchthons Werke in Auswahl 7
192, 11f (173) ≙ Melanchthons Briefwechsel 1, 398 (948); WA Br 5, 389, 91f (1590), Jus
Jonas an Luther am 18. Juni 1530.

54 WA Br 5, 440, 17 (1625).

55 WA 30 II, 392; WA Br 5, 467f (1640), Luther an Wenzeslaus Linck am 13. Juli 1530; WA B.
468f (1641), Luther an Rühel am 13. Juli 1530.

rung des Friedens tun könnte.[56] Aber es ist klar, daß Luther nicht nur den
Frieden sucht, sondern sich auch öffentlich rechtfertigen und entschuldigen
möchte, falls es zum Krieg kommt. Denn die Evangelischen hätten den Vorteil
bei Gott und die Ehre »bei aller Welt«, daß sie ihre Lehre frei und öffentlich
bekannt, Frieden gesucht und angeboten hätten.[57] Dabei spricht Luther seine
Zustimmung zum Augsburger Bekenntnis aus. Während Melanchthon aber
bestimmte Voraussetzungen zu einer Einigung mit den Altkirchlichen vorge-
schlagen hatte, hegt Luther keine Hoffnung auf ein Verständnis. Er möchte
nur durch Albrecht erwirken, daß die Evangelischen mit ihrer Lehre in Ruhe
gelassen werden.[58]

In diesem Brief tritt Luther zunächst als öffentlicher Verteidiger der evangelischen Sache auf. Albrecht wird dagegen nicht als altkirchlicher Führer
angesprochen oder gar als Vermittler zwischen den Parteien, da Luther von
einer Vermittlung keinen Erfolg erwartet. Als höchster Fürst in Deutschland
aber, der auch Frieden wünschen sollte, könnte Albrecht die anderen deutschen Stände davon überzeugen, die evangelischen Stände in Ruhe zu lassen.
Als öffentlicher Verteidiger der Evangelischen beruft sich Luther auch stärker
als bisher auf die Sorge aller Beteiligten um Deutschland und auf ihr deutsches
Bewußtsein. Ein Konfessionskrieg würde den Deutschen nur schaden und den
Papst zum Lachen bringen.[59] Luther leugnet, daß er ein Prophet ist, aber er
muß um des armen Deutschlands willen den Albrecht auf die teuflische
Heimtücke des Papstes aufmerksam machen, wie er es »seinem lieben Vater-
land« schuldig ist.[60] Eigentlich spricht Luther schon als ein »deutscher Prophet«, welchen Titel er dann 1531 nur ungern anerkennt.[61] Der Brief ist
einschließlich der Auslegung von Ps 2 ein ausgesprochenes politisches Zeug-

56 WA 30 II, 398, 19-22.
57 WA 30 II, 401, 21-25. »Alle Welt« schließt auch die Nachkommen ein, um die der ältere
Luther oft Sorge ausgedrückt hat.
58 WA 30 II, 398, 27 – 399, 16; 399, 17 – 401, 20.
59 WA 30 II, 411, 11-18.
60 WA 30 II, 411, 22 – 412, 15; 412, 20-23. In dem Brief an Rühel beruft sich Luther auch auf die
»Deutschen«: »Auch bitte ich E. A. (wie ich mich versehe, daß Ihr das fleißig tut), bei
S.K.F.G. mit treuem Vermahnen anzuhalten, daß S.K.F.G. den verzweifelten Walen nicht
traue noch gläube. Denn Ihr wisset zum Teil, was sie für Leute sind, wie sie uns Deutschen
bisher gemeint und noch meinen [gesinnt waren und noch sind]. Wir sind mit ihnen geplagt,
Gott helfe und behüte uns vor ihnen, Amen« (WA Br 5, 469, 11-16 [1641]).
61 WA 30 III, 290, 28-30 (Warnung an seine lieben Deutschen, 1531).

XVI

109

nis, in dem der »deutsche Prophet« sich an den deutschen Primas wendet, jetzt
nicht mehr wegen der Ausbreitung, sondern wegen der Wahrheit und des
Weiterbestehens der evangelischen Bewegung.

In seiner Ankündigung des Briefes an Albrecht bat Luther Rühel darum,
Albrecht seine »herzliche gute Meinung« anzuzeigen, wie Rühel das wohl zu
tun wüßte. Diese Bitte weist weniger auf Luthers echte Hochachtung vor
Albrecht als vielmehr auf die Höflichkeit hin, mit der Luther über Rühel wie
früher Albrechts Wohlwollen zu erwirken hoffte.[62] Bald aber wurde Luthers
Höflichkeit auf die Probe gestellt. Im April 1531 ging Albrecht gegen die
Hallischen Ratsmitglieder vor, die sich weigerten, an dem Abendmahl nach
alter Art unter einerlei Gestalt teilzunehmen. Luther plante dann eine öffentliche Schrift gegen Albrecht, wurde aber vom kursächsischen Hof gebeten,
davon abzusehen.[63] Am 8. Mai 1531 schrieb er an den Altkanzler Gregor Brück,
daß er Albrecht jetzt verschonen würde. Er wunderte sich aber, wie »der gute
Mann« Rühel dem »losen und falschen Mann« Albrecht weiterhin glauben
könnte, da er wüßte, daß nichts Gutes dahinter stehe.[64] 1534 hat Luther dann
gegenüber Rühel seiner Enttäuschung und Erbitterung Ausdruck gegeben.
Albrecht habe nun aufgehört zu heucheln und künftig könne der Teufel ihm
glauben. Rühel habe Luther »oft mit ihm betrogen« und Luthers Zorn ge-
dämpft, aber jetzt nicht mehr.[65] Luther hatte sich schon einmal ähnlich über

62 WA Br 5, 469, 8-11 (1641). – Hermann KUNST: Evangelischer Glaube und politische Verant
wortung: Martin Luther als politischer Berater seiner Landesherren und seine Teilnahme an
den Fragen des öffentlichen Lebens. 2. Aufl. S 1979, 337, ist geneigt, darin eine echte Meinung
Luthers über Albrecht zu sehen.

63 WA 30 III, 400f (Notizen zu einem offenen Brief an die Christen in Halle gegen Erzbischof
Albrecht von Mainz, 1531).

64 WA Br 6, 91, 12-16 (1814). Luther hatte schon eine abfällige Bemerkung über Albrecht
gemacht in »Wider den Meuchler zu Dresden«, 1531 (WA 30 III, 265, 24-26). Trotz der Kritik
an Rühel bat Luther ihn zur Patenschaft für sein in Kürze zu erwartendes Kind (Martin
geboren am 9. November 1531); siehe Kunst: AaO, 337f; WA Br 6, 220f (1880), Luther an
Rühel am 30. Oktober 1531.

65 WA Br 7, 15, 5-7. 9-13 (2085), Luther an Rühel am 25. Januar 1534. Zu dieser Zeit spricht man
von einer entscheidenden Änderung von Luthers Haltung gegenüber Albrecht; siehe z.B
Kunst: AaO, 337; Albrecht WOLTERS: Luther und der Cardinal Albrecht von Mainz. Deutsch
evang. Blätter 2 (1877), 717. Aber es handelt sich eher darum, daß sich Luthers private
Meinung jetzt mit seiner öffentlichen Stellungnahme völlig deckt. Auch Kunst: AaO, 330
weist darauf hin, wie sich Luther privat gegenüber Joachim I. von Brandenburg milder als in
der Öffentlichkeit ausgedrückt hat.

Albrechts Heucheln geäußert, aber trotz seiner Kritik an Albrecht in Briefen bisher keine öffentliche Schrift gegen Albrecht gerichtet. Die politischen Interessen Kursachsens hatten es nicht erlaubt, weil jede Herausforderung der altgläubigen Gegner den Frieden gefährdet hätte. Man wird an die unentschiedene politische Lage im Reich erinnert, in der Luther seine späteren Jahre verbrachte.[66] Es ist dann doch ein Umstand eingetreten, der Luther zum öffentlichen Angriff auf Albrecht bewegte. Im Juli 1535 ließ Albrecht seinen Kämmerer in Halle, Hans Schönitz, wegen angeblicher Unterschlagung hinrichten. Wahrscheinlich wollte Albrecht sich der Forderung der Magdeburger Stände nach Rechenschaft über die Verwendung von Steuergeldern entziehen. Obwohl Schönitz sein zuvor erpreßtes Geständnis widerrief und obwohl seine Familie sich bereit erklärte, die angeblich vermißten Summen zu ersetzen, wurde das Urteil vollstreckt. Mit den Rechnungsbüchern seines Bruders floh Anton Schönitz aus Halle, wie auch Ludwig Rabe, der als Finanzbeamter auch bei Albrecht gedient hatte und der nun nach Wittenberg kam.[67]

Als Albrecht einen drohenden Brief an Rabe in Wittenberg sandte, antwortete Luther mit einem heftigen Angriff auf den »hellischen Kardinal«. Er erwartete nicht, daß er damit »etwas Nutzes« schaffen würde, aber er mußte seinem Gewissen genugtun.[68] Luther kündigte dann im folgenden Jahr eine öffentliche Verteidigung von Hans Schönitz an,[69] wovon sämtliche brandenburgischen Fürsten ihn abzuhalten versuchten. Sie haben sogar über den sächsischen Kurfürsten Druck auf Luther ausgeübt. Trotz der gespannten politischen Lage aber, in der eine solche Schrift der evangelischen Sache mehr schaden als helfen würde,[70] veröffentlichte Luther das Werk. Ein letzter

66 Der politische Hintergrund von Luthers polemischen Äußerungen in den späteren Jahren wird von Mark EDWARDS betont in einem bisher unveröffentlichten Werk: »Luther's last battles: polemics and politics 1531-1546«, bes. Kap. 7.
67 Diese Geschichte faßt Kunst: AaO, 338-342, zusammen; vgl. WA 50, 387-393; Julius KÖSTLIN: Martin Luther: sein Leben und seine Schriften. 5. neubearb. Aufl./ fortges. von Gustav Kawerau. Bd. 2. B 1903, 417-423.
68 WA Br 7, 216-219, bes. 216, 1-5; 217, 40; 219, 92-95 (2215), Luther an Albrecht am 31. Juli 1535.
69 WA Br 7, 370, 56f (2297), Luther an Albrecht am 12.(?) Februar 1536.
70 So urteilt Kunst: AaO, 343. Luthers Angriff auf Albrecht dürfte in der Tat Joachim II. von Brandenburg daran gehindert haben, den Rat Luthers bei der Einführung der Reformation in

III

Anstoß dazu mag das Flugblatt gewesen sein, in dem Simon Lemnius in Epigrammen überschwengliches Lob auf Albrecht gespendet hatte. Nachdem das Blatt in Wittenberg bekannt wurde, ließ Luther sich am 16. Juni 1538 von der Kanzel über Lemnius aus und nannte dabei Albrecht einen »Scheißbischof« und einen »falschen verlogenen Mann«.[71]

Die langgefürchtete Schrift »Wider den Bischof zu Magdeburg Albrecht Kardinal« ist endlich 1539 erschienen. Darin trat Luther als der Anwalt von Hans Schönitz auf, der ohne Verhör ungerecht verurteilt worden war. Aber Luther ging es nicht nur um Gerechtigkeit für Hans Schönitz oder um das Amt des Anwalts, das er diesem zuliebe ausübte.[72] Es ging ihm auch um das Propheten- und Predigeramt, das er jetzt auszuüben gewohnt war. Der Prophet und der Prediger hatten die Pflicht, die Fürsten der Welt zur Rechenschaft über ihre Taten zu ziehen. Sowohl im Brief an den Altkanzler Brück als auch in der Schrift gegen Albrecht betonte Luther, daß das Haus Hohenzollern nicht das Ziel seines Angriffs sei, aber er könne nichts dafür, wenn aus einem löblichen Geschlecht ein ungeratenes Kind und ein verlorener Sohn gekommen sei.[73] Die Fürsten dürften die Prediger nicht beschuldigen, das ganze Geschlecht getadelt zu haben, wenn sie ein Familienmitglied ermahnt hätten.[74] Die Könige von Judäa waren der edelste Stamm im ganzen Menschengeschlecht, aber es bedeutete nicht, daß die Propheten den ganzen Stamm geschmäht hatten, als Jesaja Ahaz oder andere Propheten viele Könige straften.[75] Zusammengefaßt heißt der für Luther wesentliche Punkt: »..., konige vnd fursten sind unter

Brandenburg einzuholen; vgl. Paul STEINMÜLLER: Einführung der Reformation in die Kurmark Brandenburg durch Joachim II. Halle 1903, 57-59.

71 Siehe WA 50, 392; Köstlin: AaO 2, 421-423; WA 50, 351, 7-15 (Erklärung gegen Simon Lemnius, 16. Juni 1538).

72 Kunst: AaO, 338, behauptet, daß sich die Auseinandersetzung auf dem Gebiet der Ethik abspielt. Nach H[arry] G. HAILE: Luther: an experiment in biography. NY 1980, 183, ist das Hauptanliegen Luthers Gleichheit vor dem Gesetz. Ähnlich urteilte über diese Schrift Köstlin: AaO 2, 423: »Es spricht darin ein verletztes Rechtsgefühl, das durch keine Rücksichten mehr sich binden läßt.« In einer Predigt über J 3, 20f am 28. September 1538 führte Luther Albrecht als ein Beispiel der Ungerechtigkeit unter den Gegnern an: »Der Bischof von Meintz ist kleger und Richter und henget immer frei hinweg seines gefallens, wer ehr nur will« (WA 47, 127, 8-10 – Auslegung des dritten und vierten Kapitels Johannis in Predigten, 1538-1540).

73 WA 50, 396, 20-22; WA Br 7, 611, 21-37, bes. 30f (3115), Luther an Brück am 10. Dezember 1536.   74 WA 50, 397, 22-25.   75 WA Br 7, 611, 27-29 (3115).

Gott, der wil sie erstlich mit gnaden gestrafft haben, wenn sie bose schelcke sind. Solch gnedige strafe mussen die propheten mit worten thun, aber gar weidlich druber leiden.«[76]

Es läßt sich fragen, ob es in dieser Schrift zu einer entscheidenden Konfrontation zwischen Luther und Albrecht gekommen ist.[77] Eine erste wahrhaft öffentliche Auseinandersetzung war es auf jeden Fall. Albrecht wurde wieder in einer bestimmten Rolle von Luther angesprochen, und zwar als Fürst, der sich über das Recht erhoben hatte. Sein kirchliches Amt ließ Luther aber nicht unangetastet. Wenn schlechte Leute die Rechte und das Leben anderer verletzen, nennt man sie Mörder und Räuber. Wenn ein Kardinal der römischen Kirche es aber tut, heißt er ein guter, frommer Fürst.[78] Gegen diese fürstliche und kirchliche Würde trat Luther als Anwalt des Opfers und als Prophet des Herrn auf.

Die bisher besprochenen Schriften Luthers lassen erkennen, wie der spätere Reformator von verschiedenen Standpunkten aus eine bedeutende Figur wie Albrecht von Mainz in genauso verschiedenen Beziehungen ansprechen konnte. Mit seiner letzten Schrift gegen Albrecht aber kehrt Luther zum ursprünglichen reformatorischen Anliegen zurück. Nachdem sich Albrecht 1541 von Halle nach Mainz und Aschaffenburg zurückgezogen hatte, kündigte er an, daß er seine mitgenommene Reliquiensammlung jährlich in Mainz ausstellen würde. Luther verfaßte daraufhin eine Spottschrift, die er in Halle anonym von Hans Frischmut drucken ließ.[79] Darin sagte Luther, daß die Rheinländer den entblößten Knochen zu neuen Kleidern helfen sollten, da die Kleider, die sie zu Halle trugen, gerissen sind, und sie hätten erfrieren müssen, wenn sie länger dort geblieben wären. Neue Partikel seien hinzugekommen, wie ein schönes Stück vom linken Horn Mosi, drei Flammen vom Busch Mosi auf dem Berg Sinai usw. Und sogar Albrecht selber solle dem Heiligtum im Testament ein Quentchen von seinem treuen frommen Herzen und ein ganzes Lot von seiner wahrhaftigen Zunge vermacht haben.[80] Schließlich soll ein

---

76 WA Br 7, 611, 37-40 (3115).   77 So Kunst: AaO, 338.   78 WA 50, 401, 14-24.

79 Wegen der Verhaftung Frischmuts hat sich Luther bald als Verfasser bekannt (WA 53, 402; WA Br 10, 172-176 [3807], Luther an Jonas am 6. November 1542).

80 WA 53, 404, 10-13. 14-20; 405, 8-10. Eine Beschreibung von Albrechts Reliquiensammlung, auf die Luther sowohl 1521 als auch hier anspielt, bietet DAS HALLESCHE HEILTUM. MAN. ASCHAFFENB. 14/ hrsg. von Philipp Maria Halm und Rudolf Berliner. B 1931; Albrecht WOLTERS: Der Abgott zu Halle 1521-1542. Bonn 1877, 32-35.

113

päpstlicher Ablaß die Vergebung aller Sünden gegen einen Gulden versprochen haben.[81]

Mit diesen satirischen Zeilen schrieb Luther direkt gegen Albrecht und auch noch einmal gegen die Irrcführung der Gläubigen durch die Reliquien und durch den Ablaß. Diesmal aber schrieb er nicht als einer, der streng und ernsthaft die Gläubigen vor dieser Täuschung zu schützen versuchte, sondern als einer, der ausreichend zuversichtlich und frei war, die Ausstellung zu verspotten. Er forderte Albrecht nicht einmal auf, den Abgott zu Mainz abzuschaffen, sondern begnügte sich damit, die ganze Sache und Albrecht selbst lächerlich zu machen. Mit ähnlicher Zuversicht und Ironie hat sich nun der spätere Luther über Albrecht auch sonst geäußert. 1545 heißt es, er habe es nicht gern gesehen, daß Albrecht »also eilet vnd rennet zür Helle zu, als hette er sorge, Er mocht sie verseumen. So er doch zeitlich gnug hinein komen kan, wenn er schon langsam fus fur fus hinein trachtet«.[82]

Luther hat trotzdem nicht aufgehört, das Volk daran zu erinnern, was für eine Gefahr das ganze Ablaßgeschäft gewesen war. In einer drei Wochen vor seinem Tod in Halle gehaltenen Predigt berief sich Luther auf das Heiligtum, das der »verdammte Kardinal« dort aufgerichtet hatte: »Aber dis alles ist darumb gethan und angericht, uns also umb zu füren und zu teuschen, Das sie uns dadurch das lebendige, rechte und ware Heilthumb, das liebe wort Gottes nemen und das verfinsterten, Zu dem, das sie auch unser Gelt dadurch an sich brachten.«[83] In diesen Worten drückt sich wieder das reformatorische Uranliegen Luthers aus.

Schon 1877 hat Albrecht Wolters das Verhältnis Luthers zu Albrecht so zusammengefaßt: »Hat der lange Kampf Albrecht mehr und mehr zu der Partei herübergedrängt, die ihn nur als Bundesgenossen ohne jede Bedingung gebrauchen konnte, so hat er Luthern dazu gedient ihr gegenüber seine Stellung

81 WA 53, 405, 11-15.
82 WA Br 11, 50, 23 – 51, 3 (4081), Luther an Kurfürst Joachim II. von Brandenburg am 9. März 1545; vgl. WA 54, 390, 1-3; 391, 17-19 (An Kurfürsten zu Sachsen und Landgrafen zu Hessen von dem gefangenen Herzog zu Braunschweig, 1545). Albrecht erscheint auch als der bartlose Kardinal in zwei von den Papstspottbildern von 1545. Hartman GRISAR; Franz HEEGE: Luthers Kampfbilder. Bd. 4: »Die Abbildungen des Papsttums« und andere Kampfbilder in Flugblät tern 1538-1545. FR 1923, 23. 33; vgl. WA 54, 351.
83 WA 51, 138, 10-19 (Predigt in Halle gehalten am 26. Januar 1546).

immer fester zu nehmen und immer rücksichtsloser zu vertheidigen.«[84] Während diese Ansicht die Kontinuität in Luthers Haltung zum Ausdruck bringt, sollte man betonen, daß Albrecht in seinen verschiedenen Rollen Luther auch dazu gedient hat, geschickt und gezielt die Sache der evangelischen Bewegung an die Öffentlichkeit zu bringen. Dabei machte Luther Gebrauch von neuen Dimensionen seiner Führung als Reformator in den Jahren nach 1525: als Stratege und Förderer der evangelischen Bewegung, als theologischer und eschatologischer Deuter des reformatorischen Geschehens, als »deutscher Prophet«, als Anwalt der »Kleinen« und Prophet des Herrn gegen die großen Fürsten, immer noch als Lehrer und Pastor, der die Irreführung der Gläubigen als Gefahr stets in Erinnerung ruft. Dank Albrecht hat Luther nicht nur eine festere Stellung eingenommen, sondern auch sein reformatorisches Selbstverständnis allmählich weiter entfaltet.

84 Wolters: Luther und der Cardinal Albrecht von Mainz, 731 f.

XVII

Luther's Impact on the Sixteenth Century

CONFERENCES AND EXHIBITIONS that were held in connection with the five hundredth anniversary of Martin Luther's birth devoted more attention to the influence of the German reformer on his own century.[1] One aspect of that influence that has not been exhausted by recent research is the impact which the reformer had on religious attitudes and practice of people who became Protestant in sixteenth-century Germany. The incentive to clarify this impact has been given most forcefully by Gerald Strauss in his book *Luther's House of Learning: Indoctrination of the Young in the German Reformation.*[2] Strauss's study has two foci: first, an analysis of the pedagogical methods and goals of Luther and his colleagues; and, second, an evaluation of the results of their educational program as gleaned from the reports of inspectors of German parishes from the second half of the sixteenth century. Strauss concludes bluntly that the reformers failed to achieve their educational goals: "If it was . . . (the) central purpose (of Protestantism) to make people—all people—think, feel, and act as Christians, to imbue them with a Christian mind-set, motivational drive, and way of life, it failed."[3]

As far as Luther himself is concerned, Strauss has examined the impact of his message on popular mentality and behavior and found it

---

[1]Both the plenary sessions and the seminars at the Sixth International Congress for Luther Research, which met in Erfurt in August, 1983, focused attention on Luther's work in its sixteenth-century setting, although topics like "Luther and Culture," "Luther and Society," and "Luther and the Church" naturally exceeded the bounds of one century. The papers from the congress will appear in *Lutherjahrbuch* 52 (1985). The elaborate exhibition at the Germanisches Nationalmuseum in Nuremberg, "Martin Luther und die Reformation in Deutschland," touched almost every dimension of German history, especially in the first half of the sixteenth century. Its catalogue is a comprehensive and valuable collection of studies on the German Reformation: *Martin Luther und die Reformation in Deutschland* (Frankfurt: Insel Verlag, 1983). In celebrating the anniversary Luther's relationship to other centuries was not ignored. Already in 1982 the Verein für Reformationsgeschichte held a conference on Luther and the modern era. Its papers are contained in *Luther in der Neuzeit*, ed. Bernd Moeller (Schriften des Vereins für Reformationsgeschichte 192; Gütersloh: Mohn, 1983).

[2]Gerald Strauss, *Luther's House of Learning: Indoctrination of the Young in the German Reformation* (Baltimore: Johns Hopkins University Press, 1978).

[3]*Ibid.*, p. 307.

4

wanting. This grade of failure notwithstanding, Luther would have applauded Strauss's intention. Strauss does not waste time analyzing the effects of Luther's work on those strata of the sixteenth century where it would have mattered less to the reformer, e.g., on the political face of Europe, or on the structure of ecclesiastical institutions, or on intellectual disciplines such as literature, philosophy, or even theology. Luther's influence at these levels is a legitimate subject of inquiry, to be sure. And Strauss admits that pedagogy might not be the best vantage point for judging the achievement of Protestantism: "If it was the objective of the Reformation to complete the breaking up of the medieval church, it succeeded. If its goal was to rationalize ecclesiastical administration and coordinate it with the goals of the early modern state, it definitely succeeded. If it sought to channel the religious energies of an intellectual elite, it was in large part successful."[4] But Strauss is right in assessing the work of Luther and his colleagues at the point that mattered most to them: the liberation of people from false piety and the rehabilitation of these same people to adopt new religious attitudes and practices. Strauss has graded Luther where Luther himself would have chosen to be tested.

Strauss's conclusion is significant for another reason as well. At the level of popular mentality it calls into question the significance of the Reformation as an epoch in Western civilization. Beneath the intellectual ferment and ecclesiastical upheaval of sixteenth-century Europe the attitudes and behavior of the populace may have changed very little except where coercion was employed.[5] If the conclusion of Strauss can be validated for areas of Germany other than those which he studied, the traditional significance of the Reformation as judged by its popular impact might have to be reassessed. Historians have already risen to the challenge. James Kittelson has examined visitation reports from the rural parishes surrounding Strasbourg and concluded that the results contradict the findings of Strauss at every point. In particular, the catechetical instruction of the reformers, which Strauss found to be unfruitful, was according to Kittelson "an unquestionable success" around Strasbourg.[6] Kittelson admits that attendance at catechetical instruction and memorization do not prove that young people became thereby "true Christians." But he concludes that by the late sixteenth century "the Reformation received little resistance and

[4] Ibid.
[5] This implication of Strauss' conclusions is discussed vigorously by James M. Kittelson, "Successes and Failures in the German Reformation: The Report from Strasbourg," Archiv für Reformationsgeschichte 73 (1982): 153–175; esp. pp. 153–154.
[6] Ibid., p. 164.

much approbation from the vast majority in the villages under the authority of Strasbourg."[7]
More such studies of the impact of the Reformation need to be done, but the case of Strasbourg bids us be cautious in accepting the conclusions of Strauss. A cursory look at the results of a visitation in a very different part of Germany, the county of Oldenburg in 1609,[8] also advises against uncritical acceptance of Strauss's conclusions. The results do not portray an unblemished picture of ecclesiastical conditions and behavior, but such is hardly to be expected from official inspectors whose purpose it was to locate problems in the churches of the Grafschaft. Among the numerous questions used to ferret out problems, several bear directly on the thesis of Strauss. For example, the visitors inquired whether the pastor was diligently inculcating the catechism and at what times.[9] In most of the parishes responses indicated that the catechism was being read in church or taught in the school. Although parishioners were not always willing to attend church on weekdays to hear sermons on the catechism, some pastors based their Sunday sermons on it and had children recite the text in church. And sometimes the inspectors thought catechetical instruction was taking effect; reporting from Stolhamme they affirmed that the pastor was diligently teaching the catechism, "as indeed we can tell from the young people themselves."[10]
In the eyes of these same inspectors, however, catechetical instruction did not seem always to have had a lasting effect on the moral conduct of adults in the county. Plenty of notorious sinners were identified in answer to questions like: "Which grave sins are most common in the parish?" or "Are there any known adulterers, outright whoremongers, sorcerers, crystal ball gazers, blasphemers, imprecators, and the like among your parishioners?"[11] Answers to these questions varied widely. In Stolhamme the visitors found little that was objectionable. The principal problem was neglect of the Lord's Supper, and no adulterers could be identified. Only one woman, who had practiced soothsaying, was found worthy of mention, and she had repented of

[7]*Ibid.*, pp. 165, 163.
[8]"Articuli der oldenburgischen kirchenvisitation, gestellet an. 609," in *Die evangelischen Kirchenordnungen des XVI. Jahrhunderts*, ed. Emil Sehling, VII/II/2/1: Stift Hildesheim, Stadt Hildesheim, Grafschaft Oldenburg und Herrschaft Jever, ed. Anneliese Sprengler-Ruppenthal (Tübingen: Mohr (Siebeck), 1980): 1175–1195. Representative answers from the various parishes are summarized in the footnotes.
[9]*Ibid.*, p. 1177: "10. Ob er auch dem Catechismum Lutheri mit fleiß treibe und zu welcher zeit."
[10]*Ibid.*, p. 1177, n. 14: "Affirmant, wie wir dan solches in der tat an der jugend gespüret."
[11]*Ibid.*, p. 1181.

6

her past sins and promised to improve.[12] Stolhamme was not typical, however. Most parishes produced evidence of drunkenness and fornication, and several pastors, not surprisingly, complained of poor church attendance. In the parish of Abbehaus the inspectors admonished the pastor that poor attendance was his own fault because he did not adequately prepare his sermons.[13] Bardenfleth produced an especially long list of transgressions. Among other things it noted that one woman, who operated a house of ill repute near the church, refused to heed any warnings.[14]

From reports of such notorious behavior the historian might conclude that moral conduct and church attendance had, if anything, deteriorated since the introduction of the Reformation. One has to remember, however, that the questions were formulated in such a way as to elicit the special mention of immoral behavior, superstition, and laxity. The survey did not contain questions like: "How many persons of outstanding moral character are in your parish?" or "How many people receive the Lord's Supper on a regular basis?" In matters of conduct and performance of religious duties the visitors meant to discover what was wrong in the parish and not what was right. Whether or not the grade of failure for Protestants in the county of Oldenburg is justified depends in part on the weight which one assigns to such reports. How representative are they for the behavior and piety of the parishioners as a whole, and how does this conduct compare to that of the pre-Reformation period if indeed conduct for that period can be measured?

The evaluation of such evidence depends even more on which standard of religious activity and morality one establishes for success in the first place. At this point the first part of Strauss's study needs closer scrutiny, namely, the analysis of Protestant pedagogical goals and methods. His selection of this aspect of the reformers' work is appropriate, but his conclusions presuppose that reformers such as Luther expected to transform people into models of identifiably Christian motivation and behavior. "The whole object of their pedagogy," writes Strauss, was to "forge a motivational link between inner purposes and outward actions."[15] Luther would certainly not deny that he wanted to create such a link. In treatises like *The Freedom of A Christian* he described the link ideally as the spontaneous flow of faith into love for God and service to the neighbor: "See, therefore, how love and desire for God

[12]*Ibid.*, p. 1181, n. 41.
[13]*Ibid.*, p. 1181, n. 38.
[14]*Ibid.*, p. 1181, n. 41.
[15]Strauss, *Luther's House of Learning*, p. 237.

flow out of faith and how out of love flows a spontaneous, willing, joyful life that serves the neighbor for no reward whatsoever."[16] When he explained the Ten Commandments in the catechisms, Luther not only specified what they prohibited but also suggested the kind of piety and behavior which obedience to the commandments encouraged. Luther strengthened the connection between faith and practice when he asserted that adherence to the first commandment, to love God above all else, would lead inevitably to the fulfillment of all the commandments.[17] And one of his most frequently used metaphors, taken from the sayings of Jesus, argued against the *habitus*-concept of medieval theology by reversing the link between inner purpose and outward action. Good works did not make the person good, but a person, made good through faith, produced good works, just as naturally as a good tree produced good fruit.[18]

Nevertheless, one should ask whether Luther, like any other religious leader who advocates certain behavior in accord with beliefs, truly expected people to live up to the ideal pictures which he painted in his treatises and in his catechisms. Luther and his colleagues did expect the practice of piety and charity to improve once the false piety of the church of his day was abolished. When people learned to distinguish between spurious works of medieval piety, such as the religious rituals through which they hoped to acquire merit, and the genuine good works of civil responsibility and charity toward the neighbor for which faith liberated them,[19] then indeed one should be able to detect some change in the shape of piety and perhaps even behavior. The best one could hope for, however, was sporadic and localized improvement; one should not expect a widespread transformation of church and society. There are few Christians on earth, said Luther in 1523, when he

---

[16]*Von der Freiheit eines Christenmenschen 1520; WA (D. Martin Luthers Werke* [Weimar: Böhlau, 1883-]) 7, 36.3-4: "Sih also fleusset auß dem glauben die lieb und lust zu gott, und auß der lieb ein frey, willig, frolich lebenn dem nehsten zu dienen umbsonst."
[17]*Der große Katechismus deutsch* [1529] in *Die Bekenntnisschriften der evangelisch-lutherischen Kirche* (6th ed.; Göttingen: Vandenhoeck & Ruprecht, 1967), p. 572.8-14 (§48): "Das sei gnug vom ersten Gepot, welches wir mit Worten haben müssen ausstreichen, weil daran allermeist die Macht liegt, darümb, daß (wie vor gesagt) wo das Herz wohl mit Gott dran ist und dies Gepot gehalten wird, so gehen die andern alle hernach." Cf. *WA* 30/I: 139.8-12.
[18]E.g., in a popular treatise, see the extended discussion in *Von der Freiheit eines Christenmenschen 1520; WA* 7: 32.4-34.
[19]This distinction is crucial for understanding Luther's affirmation of good works as the spontaneous fruits of faith. It is drawn clearly also in *Von der Freiheit eines Christenmenschen 1520; WA* 7: 37.16-38.5.
[20]*Von weltlicher Obrigkeit 1523; WA* 11: 259.17-24.
[21]*Deutsche Messe 1526; WA* 19: 75.3-15.

8

was explaining the words in the Sermon on the Mount about not resisting evil.[20] And in 1526, as he prepared the German mass for ordinary laypeople, Luther regretted the fact that not enough people were
available who wanted to be Christians in earnest to form a small, more
informal congregation.[21]

The low expectations that accompanied Luther's high ideals derived partly from his sense of the reality of sin and evil and partly from
his interpretation of history and the place of the Reformation in it. On
the first point, Luther's conviction of the power of sin helped him both
to new insights into justification and to realistic expectations about
the behavior of even those people who appreciated the liberty which
his theology offered. For Luther, the Christian life was not freedom
from sin but constant struggle with sin and evil, or in Luther's unholy
trinity, with sin, death and the devil. The real hazards of this struggle
are depicted openly in the *Large Catechism*, which, together with the
Small Catechism, was intended to be used for instruction in Protestant
parishes. In the exposition of the Lord's Prayer Luther portrays
prayer as a weapon for use in daily combat with the devil, who is fighting to prevent faith from taking root and producing the fruits of charity. Even for justified and forgiven believers sin is a threat and can trip
them up at any time. At the sixth petition, "And lead us not into temptation," Luther begins:

> We have now heard enough about the trouble and effort required
> to retain and persevere in all the gifts for which we pray. This,
> however, is not accomplished without failures and stumbling.
> Moreover, although we have acquired forgiveness and a good con-
> science, and have been wholly absolved, yet such is life that one
> stands today and falls tomorrow. Therefore, even though at pres-
> ent we are upright and stand before God with a good conscience,
> we must pray again that he will not allow us to fall and yield to
> trials and temptations.[22]

In spite of ideal portraits of the Christian life that one finds in Luther's
treatises, Luther did not expect his own reforming work to transform
the majority into true Christians.

The production of perfect Christians was not the purpose of the
Reformation in Luther's eyes. That purpose can better be described as
preparation than as transformation or improvement. Heiko Oberman
has helped us to understand that Luther regarded reformation as

---

[22]*Bekenntnisschriften*, pp. 685.42-686.4 (§100). Cf. *WA* 30/I: 208.15-25. English
translation is by Robert H. Fischer in *The Book of Concord*, ed. Theodore G. Tappert
(Philadelphia: Fortress, 1959), p. 433.

God's work which would be accomplished at the Last Day. Luther was a prophet or, in Oberman's words, a "forerunner" of the Reformation, who viewed his own day as the time of tribulation and intense struggle with the devil that preceded the final reformation.[23] The purpose of preaching, teaching, and reshaping parish life was to help Christians survive the last furious onslaught of the devil. One might expect some improvement in conduct and especially in church attendance as people became more convinced of a crisis and sought help, but one could not expect a transformation before the end.

Oberman argues that Philipp Melanchthon and other reformers with humanist backgrounds robbed Luther's admonitions of their eschatological urgency and refined them into appeals for moral improvement and religious education.[24] If this were accepted, Luther could be exempted from a grade of failure such as Strauss has given to the Reformation while Luther's colleagues and successors would be left to take the blame because they, unlike Luther, expected the Reformation to be more of a transformation. This judgment can perhaps be supported for some sixteenth-century humanists, but Protestant church orders, at least Lutheran orders, advise against driving this wedge too broadly between Luther and his supporters. In the church order written by Urbanus Rhegius (1489-1541), the Lutheran superintendent of the duchy of Lüneburg, for the city of Hannover in 1536,[25] the perspective of the Reformation does not differ markedly from that of Luther. For Rhegius, the true church was always being persecuted but never so severely as "in this last age," when the prophecy of 2 Timothy 3:1-7 was being fulfilled. Christians, even bishops under the pope, were donning a false holiness and paying more attention to ceremonies than to faith and love.[26] Reformation was not a long-term plan for improvement but a last-ditch introduction of changes that became necessary because imperial diets were unwilling to enact reforms. "We have put off reformation as long as we could," writes Rhegius, "hoping that, at so many diets, consensus could be reached on how we should rightly teach and live; but our hope was in vain! If we were to wait on

---

[23]Heiko A. Oberman, "Martin Luther: Vorläufer der Reformation," in *Verifikationen. Festschrift für Gerhard Ebeling zum 70. Geburtstag,* ed. E. Jüngel, J. Wallmann, W. Werbeck (Tübingen: Mohr [Siebeck], 1982), pp. 91-119.

[24]*Ibid.,* pp. 115-117.

[25]*Die evangelischen Kirchenordnungen des XVI. Jahrhunderts,* ed. Emil Sehling, VI/I/2: Die Fürstentümer Calenberg-Göttingen und Grubenhagen mit den Städten Göttingen, Northeim, Hannover, . . . (Tübingen: Mohr [Siebeck], 1957): 944-1017.

[26]*Ibid.,* p. 961.

the decision and reformation of the bishops, we would have to stay sunk in error until the Last Day. No!"[27]

Reformers did promote new attitudes, especially faith in the gospel, but, more concretely, reformation meant the abolition of old ceremonies and forms of piety, namely, the masses, brotherhoods, and types of religious service that, in the eyes of the reformers, burdened and blinded people. Rhegius expressed the urgency which many reformers felt. The Last Day was at hand, and pastors could wait no longer to liberate people from the false piety which the devil was using to lead people astray. This urgency was not felt by the first generation of reformers alone. In 1573 the church order written for Oldenburg complained that Satan was still roaming around, anxious to obscure the gospel and to undermine the sacraments, and "would not cease to demonstrate his power, guile and poison in this last age of the world."[28]

Both Luther's theological pessimism about human nature and his conviction that faith was under frantic attack by the devil in the last times prior to God's reformation kept his expectations of piety and conduct modest. What did Luther then intend the effect of his theology and reform to be? We gain a different perspective of his intention if we look at a different kind of text—not the treatise in which Luther portrays the ideal Christian, but a letter of consolation in which he offers advice about faith and piety in a concrete situation. Bartholomäus von Starhemberg was an Austrian nobleman whose wife, Magdalena, died in 1524. Luther was requested by a third party, Vinzenz Wernstdorffer, to write to Starhemberg in order to counteract the typical piety of the day in connection with his wife's death. Luther reports that Wernstdorffer described "how you are making every effort to help her soul with many religious services and good works, especially private masses and vigils."[29]

Luther attacks this problem on two levels. First, he asks Starhemberg to adopt a different attitude toward the death of his wife and of God's role in it. This attitude is faith, and it amounts to the simple acceptance of God's will in this situation. Luther argues that Magdalena was a gift of God to Starhemberg and that, even while married to him,

[27]*Ibid.*, p. 999: "Wir haben mit der reformation lang verzogen in der hoffnung, man würde auf so viel reichstagen eindrechtiglich beschliessen, wie man recht leren und leben sol. Aber unser hoffnung ist vergeblich. Wenn wir auf der bischoff beschlus und reformation warten söllen, so müssen wir im irthum bis an jüngsten tag bleiben. Nein."
[28]Sehling, ed., *Kirchenordnungen*, VII/II/2/1: 986.
[29]*Sendbrief an Bartholomäus v. Starhemberg 1524; WA* 18: 5.22-25.

she still belonged to God, who has now taken back his own possession. Therefore,

> although it hurts us when God takes his own away from us, our heart should find greater consolation in God's most gracious will than in all his gifts. After all, God himself is immeasurably better than his gifts. It is much better to hold on to his will than to the best wife in the world, even though we cannot embrace his will as well as we can the wife. Faith can embrace that will, however.[30]

By modern standards this advice would not be judged effective grief counseling, at least not by most theologians. And Luther himself bewails the fact that most people could not make this faith their own: "Oh, how blessed and rich we all would be if we were able to conduct such a trade with God! We could if only we understood it. God encounters us daily with it; we, however, cannot grasp it."[31]

Luther moves to a second level, however, that is more realistic. This level has to do with the practice of piety. Bluntly, Luther requests Starhemberg to "do away with the masses, vigils, and daily prayers for the soul of your wife." As far as prayer is concerned, Luther advises it is sufficient to pray earnestly once or twice for her. When we pray over and over again for the same thing, says Luther, it is a sign we do not believe that God will answer prayer. Besides, notes Luther, there are always plenty of other things for which to pray.[32] Just as bluntly Luther advises Starhemberg to abolish the vigils and the private masses for the dead. The vigils are useless mumblings which make fun of God and provoke God to anger because they are not earnest prayers. The mass is a sacrament for the living, not a sacrifice for the dead as the priests and monks have promoted it for the sake of their bellies. They have no command from God for their vigils or

[30]*Ibid.; WA* 18: 6.8–15: "Dann sy war sein, Ee er sy gab, sy war sein, da er sy geben het, sy ist auch noch sein, nachdem er sy genommen hat, wie wir alle sein. Darumb ob es uns wol wee thut, das er das seyne von uns annimpt, soll doch das hertz sich höher trösten seines aller besten willen dann aller seyner gaben, dann wie gar unnmeßlich ist got besser dann alle seyne gaben? Also ist ye auch hye sein will besser zuhalten dann das aller böst weyb, wyewol man das nitt also füllen kan wie diß, der glaub fült es aber."
[31]*Ibid.; WA* 18: 6.18–20.
[32]*Ibid.; WA* 18: 6.21–7.1: "Auffs ander, genediger herr, Ist mein Byt, E. G. welle ablassen von Messen vigilien und täglichem gepet für jr seelen. Es ist gnug, wann E. G. ein mal oder zwir mit ernst für sy pittet, . . . sunst wa man solch gepet ymmer umb ain sach an treybtt, ist es ain zaychenn, das wir got nit glauben unnd also mit unglawbygem gepet nur meer ertzürnen, . . . Man soll ymmer zu bitten, ist war, aber im glauwben unnd ymmer gewyß sein, das man erhört sey, sunst ist das gepet verloren; so ist auch ymmer anders und anders verhanden zupeten."

masses, and a Christian should do nothing unless God has commanded it.[33]

Two years later Starhemberg had a Protestant preacher called to his estates, and his own son became a leader of the Protestant movement in Austria. But that is not the sole measure of the impact of Luther's letter. It was printed as a pamphlet and distributed because, as the editor points out, "although it reproaches serious abuses with only a few words, it still speaks clearly enough so that laypersons can easily understand it." "Devoted Christians," he says, "should be deprived of nothing however small which promotes the Word of God and teaches them to be wise."[34]

The pamphlet was published, then, as Protestant propaganda with a pedagogical purpose. It was intended to incite people to the same kind of faith and action that was requested of Starhemberg. As expressed in the letter, however, Luther's expectations are still modest when compared to a call for complete transformation. He did not expect people to adopt the stance of faith easily in such a situation. It would be better if we could accept adversity as the will of God, but Luther was under no illusion that people would or could gratefully take his advice. To the extent that one was able to act in faith, the only actions linked with this new attitude are the abolition of improper religious practices: excessive praying and masses for the dead. Except for the admonition that what praying one does should be done in earnest, the criterion for what is Christian is stated in terms of what one should avoid and not in terms of what one should do. "A Christian should do nothing unless God has commanded it." There is no admonition to frequent communion or, for that matter, to good moral conduct.

Admittedly, this minimal advice about conduct may be owing to the specific circumstances of Starhemberg's situation, but the letter was deemed worthy of publication and circulation as a pedagogical device.[35] Although one can supplement this negative counsel with posi-

[33]*Ibid.; WA* 18: 7.1-13: "Sonderlich aber Byt ich E. G., wellet die vigilien und selmessen nachlassen, dann das ist zumal ain unchristlich ding, daz got hochlich erzürnt; ... dartzu weil got die messz nicht für die todten sonder zum sacrament für die lebendigen hat eingesetzt. ... da well sich E. G. vor hüten und sich nit tailhafftig machen dises greülichen jrtumbs, welchen die pfaffen und münch umb jres bauch willen haben auffbracht. Dann ein christen soll nichs thun, er wisse dann, das es got also gepoten hab."

[34]*Ibid.; WA* 18: 6.13-15.

[35]I disagree with the judgment of the Weimar editors (*WA* 18: 2) that the letter does not contain any new, vigorous, or specifically Reformation ideas, but was appreciated for the purely religious sentiment and the warm religious inwardness which it expressed. Quite to the contrary, the direct opposition of faith to religious sentiment in the grief situation, the absolute trust in God's will in face of adversity, and the abolition of religious ritual (the good works of piety) in favor of faith (i.e., faith versus works) comprise the most vigorous Protestant advice that Luther could give.

tive recommendations from the catechisms, texts such as Luther's explanation of the sixth petition and the letter to Starhemberg lead one to judge cautiously what Luther expected of his readers and hearers. With this caution in mind, several conclusions about Luther's impact on religious mentality and conduct suggest themselves.

First, Luther did not expect to have as much impact on his own century as some historians expect him to have had. In spite of his descriptions of ideal Christian faith and behavior, Luther could express quite modest expectations of people who became Protestant. Religious reformers, like other reformers, tend to be idealists; and historians should distinguish between the theological ideals and the real expectations about how these ideals might be attained, especially when the reformers reveal a scepticism of their own.

Second, historians should also distinguish between abolishing harmful religious practices (false piety in the eyes of the reformers) and cultivating new, helpful practices. There were not many new practices for Protestants to cultivate although Luther certainly thought the abolition of private masses, vigils, and works of penance had cleared the way for appropriate public worship and instruction. He did encourage going to church, learning the catechism, and devoting oneself to secular duties now that the burden of religiosity had been lifted. These activities have a better chance of being measured than the strength of one's faith or the moral quality of one's conduct. But preachers' complaints about poor church attendance, neglect of the sacrament, or inattentiveness at catechetical instruction are not necessarily reliable evidence for assessing the impact of the Reformation. Seldom have preachers not complained about such things.

A better way to assess the impact of Luther on sixteenth-century Germany is to say that he abolished old practices in many territories and thus provided a space in which the new could be cultivated. Then we should not be surprised to find great diversity in the way the new piety developed. The ability of pastors to preach and of teachers to communicate would affect the extent of lay involvement in the parishes. And if people were spending more time on their daily responsibilities than on religious activities, this redistribution of energy accorded quite well with Protestant concepts of Christian freedom. A judgment about whether faith was producing fruits could better have been made by inquiring about acts of charity and contributions to the common chest than by searching for cases of immoral conduct. Local conditions, therefore, and the expectations which pastors and visitors harbored influenced the way results of visitations were received and recorded. Neither these conditions nor the expectations of the clergy necessarily would have matched Luther's own expectations.

14

Third, in assessing the results, categories of success and failure are not very helpful. They depend too much on accepting as criteria ideal statements by the reformers, or they assume that the reformers themselves understood such statements to be realizable educational goals for everyone. The same difficulty adheres to adjectives like meaningful and lasting in Strauss's own challenge to historians: ". . . the burden of proof ought now at last to be placed where it belongs: upon those who claim, or imply, or tacitly assume that the Reformation in Germany aroused a widespread, meaningful, and lasting response to its message. . . . Later in the century one finds mostly apathy."[36] Should "meaningful" and "lasting" be defined by the idealism of the reformers, or by what people themselves found meaningful? Perhaps the abolition of medieval religious observances was enough for them. Perhaps less religious activity produced more religious meaning and was the lasting concomitant of their faith. People who seemed apathetic to the inspectors may have understood the Protestant message of freedom from religious burdens better than the new preachers who preferred to see religious zeal and activity.

If one begins with the ideal of the complete transformation of popular attitudes and behavior, then failure is the only conclusion. If one begins with what Luther did—abolishing old forms and creating a theological basis for a new, secular piety—then something other than success or failure is a likely conclusion. For example, one might conclude that a lasting, in some cases meaningful, and widespread but not uniform response was typical of the German Reformation. This response entailed not only the mentality of the people, who found the admonitions to replace religious works with faith quite attractive, but also the fruits of that faith which, though imperfect, still directed their attention more toward secular duties than to the excessive piety of their parents. The burden of proof does not rest on anyone to argue that such changes involved either success or failure. The task for historians is rather to analyze what these changes in religious practice and attitudes meant for the institutions of church and society in the sixteenth century.

---

[36]Strauss, *Luther's House of Learning*, pp. 307–308.

INDEX

4   INDEX

GENERAL THEOLOGICAL SEMINARY,
NEW YORK

DATE DUE

MAY 2 2 1998		
MAY 1 9 2004		
		Printed in USA

HIGHSMITH #45230